Spellbound

Spellbound

The Fairy Tale and the Victorians

Molly Clark Hillard

THE OHIO STATE UNIVERSITY PRESS
COLUMBUS

Copyright © 2014 by The Ohio State University.
All rights reserved.

Library of Congress Cataloging-in-Publication Data
Hillard, Molly Clark, 1971–
 Spellbound : the fairy tale and the Victorians / Molly Clark Hillard.
    pages cm
 Includes bibliographical references and index.
 ISBN-13: 978-0-8142-1245-5 (cloth : alk. paper)
 ISBN-10: 0-8142-1245-X (cloth : alk. paper)
 ISBN-13: 978-0-8142-9348-5 (cd-rom)
 ISBN-10: 0-8142-9348-4 (cd-rom)
  1. Fairy tales—Great Britain—History and criticism. 2. English literature—19th century—History and criticism. I. Title.
 PR878.F27H55 2014
 398.20941—dc23
                        2013033411

Cover design by Laurence J. Nozik
Text design by Juliet Williams
Type set in Adobe Garamon Pro

∞ The paper used in this publication meets the minimum requirements of the American National Standard for Information Sciences—Permanence of Paper for Printed Library Materials. ANSI Z39.48–1992.

9 8 7 6 5 4 3 2 1

CONTENTS

List of Illustrations — vii

Acknowledgments — ix

Introduction: Nostalgia, Literacy, and the Fairy Tale — 1

Part 1. Matter

1. The Novelist and the Collector — 23
2. *Pickwick Papers* and the End of Miscellany — 38
3. The Natural History of Thornfield — 50
4. Antiquity, Novelty, and *The Key to All Mythologies* — 61

Part 2. Spell

5. Sleeping Beauty and Victorian Temporality — 77
6. Keats on Sleep and Beauty — 82
7. "A Perfect Form in Perfect Rest": Tennyson's "Day Dream" — 92
8. Burne-Jones and the Poetic Frame — 108

Part 3. Produce

9 Fairy Footsteps and Goblin Economies   131

10 The Great Exhibition: Fairy Palace, Goblin Market   138

11 Rossetti's Homeopathy   154

Part 4. Paraphrase

12 Little Red Riding Hood Arrives in London   173

13 Little Red Riding Hood's Progress   179

14 Little Red Riding Hood and Other Waterside Characters   197

Conclusion: Andrew Lang, Collaboration, and Fairy Tale Methodologies   217

Notes   225

Bibliography   253

Index   266

ILLUSTRATIONS

Figure 1	Edward Coley Burne-Jones's *The Prince Enters the Briar Wood*	114
Figure 2	Burne-Jones's *The Sleeping Beauty*	115
Figure 3	Burne-Jones's *The Briar Wood*	116
Figure 4	Burne-Jones's *The Council Chamber* 1872–92	117
Figure 5	Burne-Jones's *The Council Chamber* 1855–90	118
Figure 6	Burne-Jones's *The Rose Bower*	120
Figure 7	George Cruikshank's "The Dispersion of the Works of all Nations from the Great Exhibition of 1851"	143
Figure 8	John Tenniel's illustration for [Anonymous,] "The Cinderella of 1851"	145
Figure 9	Richard Doyle's illustration for [Anonymous,] "The Exhibition Plague"	146
Figure 10	Doyle's detail of *An overland journey to the Great Exhibition*	147
Figure 11	Richard Doyle's detail of *The Fairy Tree*	149
Figure 12	William Morris's *Fruit*	153

ACKNOWLEDGMENTS

This book would have been not spellbound but moribund without the help of many kind people, whom I gratefully acknowledge. My editor at The Ohio State University Press, Sandy Crooms, is an advocate who is a perfect mix of enthusiasm and patience. I appreciate her belief in the book and her work on my behalf.

Various institutions have sustained the project along its path. The University of Southern Mississippi and Seattle University supported my research in various ways and at various stages. A grant from the National Endowment for the Humanities enabled me to host "Fairy Tale Economies," an international conference that enriched this project in important ways. I have been enormously fortunate to be part of two vibrant research consortia: the Dickens Project and the Group for International Fairy Tale Studies, through which I have made lasting colleagues and friends. Portions of Chapter 7 originally appeared in *Narrative* 17:3 (2009). Portions of Chapter 14 originally appeared in *Studies in English Literature* 49:4 (2009). My thanks to The Ohio State University Press and Johns Hopkins University Press for permission to publish here.

Gratitude is due, too, to my various collaborators, editors, and mentors; Nathan Hensley, Matthew Kaiser, and Jennifer Schacker not only generously read and critiqued portions of this project at various stages, but also created opportunities for me to share the work at crucial moments in its development. I would not be the writer, teacher, and academic I am without the many gifts of teachers and mentors, notably Anne Fleischmann, Reginia Gagnier, Toni Littlestone, Esther Mackintosh, Robert Patton, Catherine Robson, David Simpson, and the late, great Alan Dundes.

I am indebted to my friends at USM and the University of Puget Sound, especially Kate Cochran, Tiffany Aldrich MacBain, Mita Mahato, and Eric Tribunella, for countless acts of buoyancy, wit slinging, and fine dining. To Miriam Agrell and Yali Bair, and to my communities in California, Maryland, Mississippi, Washington, and the United Kingdom, I owe more than can be acknowledged in words.

I thank my parents, Sandra and Terrell Hillard, for a lifetime of enthusiastic support. Finally, to my husband, Jacob Clark Blickenstaff—who has been by (and on) my side not only through this book's completion, but also through graduate school, adventures in foreign lands, several cross-country moves, and the arrival of our very own hobgoblins, Lucy and Henry—I lovingly and humbly dedicate this book.

INTRODUCTION

Nostalgia, Literacy, and the Fairy Tale

"Wild and Childish": The Fairy Tale and the Nation

This book examines the relationship between fairy tales and Victorian culture, and concludes that the Victorians were "spellbound." By this I mean that novelists, poets, and playwrights were self-avowedly enchanted by the fairy tale, but also that literary genres were bound to the fairy tale, dependent upon its forms and figures. The literary artists who adored fairy tales also feared that they exude an originative power that pervades and precludes authored work. In part to dispel the fairy tale's potency, Victorians treated the form as a nostalgic refuge from an industrial age, a quaint remnant of the pre-literacy of childhood and peasantry. *Spellbound* argues by contrast that fairy stories, rather than producing a narrative space outside of progressive modernity, significantly contributed to the language and images of industrial, material England.

Early in the nineteenth century, Sir Walter Scott proposed a study "on the origin of popular fiction, and the transmission of popular tales from age to age," which he hoped would explain why "such fictions, however wild and childish," continue to "possess such charms for the populace."[1] Scott epitomizes the nineteenth-century response to the fairy tale. On one hand, reception of the tale can be measured by its very proliferation across the century, and its rising consumption as family entertainment. A well-rounded Victorian library would be rich in collections of fairy tales and fairy legends from Arabic, Italian, French, and German traditions, as well as from Britain itself. The fairy tale and legend were also widely adopted into other literary genres: the poetry, fiction, and drama of both popular and elite media. On the other hand, Victorians were profoundly ambivalent about the fairy tale, tending simultaneously to pronounce it an expired form, and to obsessively rehearse its themes and characters. Scott, for instance, however admiring of "popular tales," sweeps them to the puerile margins of culture.

Then too, Scott's phrase, "wild and childish," indicates the nineteenth-century discourses into which the fairy tale was incorporated. Carolyn Steedman has noted the ways in which "growing up" was echoed across the century in small and large scale—that the ontogeny of the human body was thought to recapitulate the phylogeny of history and even biology:

> "The investigation of the forms of human culture (in what is now known as Anthropology) implied a material progression in human lives, which increased in symbolic importance during the course of the century, whereby that which was traversed (the course of an individual life; the growth through childhood to maturity; the development of a people or a nation) was, in the end, left behind and abandoned."[2]

Folk narrative was ingrained in Britain's sense of itself as an industrial nation, its longing to view London and Edinburgh as civilized centers surrounded by "wild and childish" rural regions and Celtic borders. Anna Eliza Bray's early ethnography *Traditions, Legends, Superstitions, and Sketches of Devonshire on the Borders of the Tamar and the Tavy* (1838) originated as a series of letters from Bray in Devon to Robert Southey in London; reporting from England's "marginally civilized" Cornish outskirts, Bray designed to "gather up whatever of tradition and manners can be saved from oblivion."[3] Thomas Keightley, the fairy legend collector, felt that fairy belief lived on in the Celtic borderlands but was "extinct" in England.[4] Though Keightley was writing in 1828, well before the popularization of Charles Darwin and even Charles Lyell, his progressivism depends upon the scientific language of geological treatises. Like a volcano or a dinosaur, inexorable forces of progress would doom the fairy tale.

This rhetoric should feel familiar: for seven hundred years of literary history we have mourned fairy stories as dearly beloved remains, lost en route to modernity. Chaucer's Wife of Bath, for example, blamed the advent of

Christianity and the enlargement of villages into towns for the loss of England's "fayeryes":

> But now kan no man se none elves mo,
> For now the grete charitee and prayeres
> Of lymytours and othere hooly freres,
> That serchen every lond and every streem,
> As thicke as motes in the sonne-beem.
> Blessing halles, chambres, kitchenes, boures
> Citees, burghes, castels, hye toures,
> Thropes, bernes, shipnes, dayeryes—
> This maketh that there ben no fayeryes.[5]

But consider that Brontë's Jane Eyre dates this fairy exile some four hundred years later: "The men in green all forsook England a hundred years ago . . . and not even in Hay Lane, or the fields about it, could you find a trace of them. I don't think either summer or harvest, or winter moon, will ever shine on their revels more."[6] Despite its eternally incipient demise, the fairy tale is alive and well in Chaucer as in Brontë. And yet, readers and authors call fairy tales immaterial: which is to say ineffable and intangible, but for that reason insubstantial and impertinent.

In *Imagined Communities*, Benedict Anderson suggests that a nation defines its modernity in part through an invented antiquity.[7] And, as part of this process, nations and groups passing through periods of rapid change collect folk narrative with greater urgency, believing that it will disappear forever in the face of newer knowledge. Indeed, early synonyms for tales—antiquities, fragments, remains, relics—suggest that which is left clinging to modernity as it thrusts onward and upward. To write down lore is to claim it for posterity, yet the very act of writing differentiates the literary artist from the teller of tales. To Samuel Taylor Coleridge, for instance, the paradoxical duty of modernity was "[t]o preserve the stores, to guard the treasures, of past civilization, and thus to bind the present with the past; to perfect and add to the same; and thus to connect the present with the future."[8] Associating folk narrative with a vanishing Old England simultaneously "binds" it to and separates it from the literary artist. As Jennifer Schacker has argued in *National Dreams: The Remaking of Fairy Tales in Nineteenth-Century England,* bourgeois subjectivity turns upon the oral tradition made literary, and the fairy tale industry of the nineteenth century depended upon a perceived distance between reader and fairy tale subject.[9] One pair of Victorian folklorists echoed Coleridge in describing their project as "treasuring up records of olden times."[10] Robert Patten has identified in Dickens a comparison between telling fantastic stories and "telling" (or counting) coins.[11] Studying the fairy tale was analogous to hording buried treasure, to "telling" and removing coins from circulation.

The extinct fairy was necessary to England's sense of itself as an evolving nation and empire, but also to its literary mastery. In Book V of *The Prelude* (1850), Wordsworth praises fairy tales, but declines to draw upon them:

> It might have well beseemed me to repeat
> Some simply fashioned tale, to tell again
> In slender accents of sweet Verse some tale
> That did bewitch me then and soothes me now.[12]

Wordsworth evidently concludes that "to tell again . . . some tale" is too "slender" a task for his *Prelude*. To him and other Romantics, outgrowing the fairy tale symbolized both a fully civilized nation and mature artistry. Victorian authors ratified and deepened this model, developing a narrative of loss with its origins in the Romantic child. Charles Dickens, for instance, frequently reverted to an evolutionary model of fairy tales. In "A Christmas Tree," an 1850 *Household Words* article, the narrator casts a nostalgic eye along a tree, its branches decorated with the gifts of successive childhood Christmases. In true arboreal fashion, as he mounts the tree, he progresses in intellectual and artistic endeavor: from an alphabet, to books of fairy tales, to pantomimes, to novels, to histories on the highest branches.[13] In *The Old Curiosity Shop*, the ideal girl and the ideal fairy converge, offering a sanctified, departed England. Nell, that "slight and fairy-like . . . creature," journeying to her death in a rural past "with small fairy footstep," prompts the novel's closing words: "so do things pass away, like a tale that is told"[14] (and not, Dickens hopes, like a novel that is published). As Vladimir Propp would later propose: "Folklore is the womb of literature. . . . Folklore is the prehistory of literature. . . . Literature, which is born of folklore, soon abandons the mother that reared it."[15] Like Propp, his Victorian predecessors figure fairy tales as simultaneously timeless and belated.

"Obscure Dread and Intense Desire": Victorian Ambivalence and the Fairy Tale

Nineteenth-century authors, then, reflected with sweet melancholy on tales as the remnants of a "wild and childish" past. The irony is that the fairy tale proliferated in every genre of Victorian literature, not whole and unchanged, but retailored to suit every author's particular purpose. In practice, the fairy tale was not the unearthed remains of a childish, primitive, or feminized culture, but an endlessly renewable resource. Valuing the fairy tale as a coin out of circulation was, paradoxically, what insured its currency.

Moreover, fairy tales frequently occasioned a more than nostalgic *frisson* in the readerly body. Contrasting sharply to his "soothing" memory of childhood tales in *Prelude*'s Book V, Wordsworth relates that upon seeing a corpse in the water of Esthwaite, he had "no vulgar fear" of it, since he had been "habituated": his "inner eye had seen / Such sights before among the shining streams / Of fairyland" (453–55). Similarly, Coleridge confesses to reading fairy tales with "a strange mixture of obscure dread and intense desire." He details his affective response to a particular tale: "it made so deep an impression upon me (I had read it in the evening while my mother was mending stockings), that I was haunted by specters, whenever I was in the dark . . . my father found out the effect which these books had produced and burnt them."[16] Here Coleridge reveals the fairy tale in all its continuing power to terrify, and (cocking an eyebrow at his mother's stockings) titillate. But Coleridge does not merely identify his personal reflex to the fairy tale's visceral themes; he describes the tale's broader impact upon philosophies of history, imagination, and artistic influence.

The same Victorian authors who mourned the fairies' passing imagined a middle-class identity located in the fairy tale. Jane Eyre, for instance, looks into the mirror and sees a fairy: "[T]he strange little figure there gazing at me, with a white face and arms specking the gloom, and glittering eyes of fear moving where all else was still, had the effect of a real spirit: I thought it like one of the tiny phantoms, half fairy, half imp, Bessie's evening stories represented as coming out of lone, ferny dells in moors, and appearing before the eyes of belated travellers" (21–22). Dickens likewise locates the fairy both outside and within himself when he remembers that his nurse's tales caused his "first personal experience of a shudder and cold beads on the forehead"; he suspects all fairy tales to be "responsible for most of the dark corners we are forced to go back to, against our wills."[17] Later in the century, Victorians understood fairy tales to represent England's political landscape. A reviewer of Edward Burne-Jones's last *Briar Rose* series contemplated the paintings with admiration and horror: "it is a sleep grown menacing as death . . . it is a presage and a prelude to the years yet to come, with their burdens of conscience, and their wages of winter and death."[18] All in all, these passages show that fairy tales not only resist obsolescence, but also exert a progressive, even apocalyptic energy.

What produces this "strange mixture" of horror and titillation is not only the brutal and erotic content of the tales, but meditations upon the form itself. Victorians found their literary genres to be in a state of flux and perturbation. The formation of the novel, and subsequent movements in narrative poetry and narrative painting, the perceived recession of poetry and drama's primacy, the growth of mass literacy, and the burgeoning of the media and popular press: all of these factors contributed to the way in which Victorian genres cross-pollinated. However initially skeptical, readers eventually pledged fierce allegiance to literary "hybrids" like Barrett's *Aurora Leigh*, Browning's Dramatic Monologues, the Moxon Tennyson, and even novel "autobiographies" such as *Jane Eyre*. Many enjoyed the publication boom that permitted writing to become a viable occupation, as well as the formal experimentation that enabled the variety and scope of literary magazines, serial fiction, and media publications. At the same time, with authorship increasingly tied to middle-class identity and income, the Victorian period saw a corresponding magnification of the figure, realm, and personality of the literary artist as a marketable commodity. The ownership and averred "uniqueness" of the author's literary produce, as well as the literary work's distinction from its source materials and artistic lineage, became a matter of anxious concern.

The sweaty, guilty terror of Coleridge or Dickens reflects the author's ambiguous relationship to the fairy tale: do the "dark corners" come from within, from a working-class woman's imagination, or from no discernable authority at all? And just what is a novel, a poem, or a play with a fairy tale at its heart? *Spellbound* reveals that, no matter how reluctantly or subtly, Victorians granted fairy tales what Mikhail Bakhtin called dialogic and discursive power. (Ironically, though, in his theory of the "dialogic imagination," Bakhtin was speaking of literature other than fairy tales, and did not grant fairy tales discursive authority.)[19] Fairy tales occupied, but also determined, conversations about how narrative is shaped, and by whom.

Part and Chapter Outline

In the pages that follow, I contend that, though widespread Victorian rhetorical strategy attempted to render the fairy tale an insubstantial pageant faded, in practice the form was integral to literature and culture's progressive ideologies. Each of four sections explores a distinct Victorian media production, in order to build a picture of the interdisciplinary and interpenetrated nature of genre formation in the nineteenth century. Part 1 considers the novel's uneasy collusion with Victorian collection, parts 2 and 3 examine poetic form and composition in relationship to visual and material culture, and part 4 discusses the dispersion of the popular theatrical into both poetry and the novel. These sections come together to demonstrate just how often the fairy tale supplied the medium through which this generic cross-pollination was generated and sustained. Wherever genres collided, there the fairy tale was to uncomfortably remind authors and readers of the dialogic force of its narrative. And just as the fairy tale offered a synecdoche for the interdisciplinary and communal nature of literary genres, it also provided a language through which authors and artists came to understand, represent, and contribute to social and political issues of the day. Each section treats a central discourse of the Victorian period—models of time, anxieties of industrial and imperial progress, and perceptions of labor—and each shows how the images, figures, plots, and language of fairy tales saturated that particular discourse. Far from remaining a nostalgic, marginalized, or immaterial form, then, the fairy tale proved itself again and again to be fundamental to Victorian intellectual culture.

PART 1: MATTER

I open this section with a contextual chapter, "The Novelist and the Collector." The nineteenth-century fairy tale and legend collection evolved as the consolidation of and negotiation between the closely related studies of antiquarianism, natural history, and folklore. These publications were immensely popular—indeed, the genre rivaled the novel in sales and prominence. Perhaps because of this rivalry, fiction of the nineteenth century more or less unkindly parodied the antiquarian. In one sense, to satirize the collector is to attack the genre: from Samuel Pickwick in Dickens's *Pickwick Papers* and Edward Casaubon in Eliot's *Middlemarch*, to the unnamed antiquary in Hardy's "Tryst at an Ancient Earthworks," the collector is reduced to his collection as dry, arcane, and laughably fragmented. This antagonism sought to deflect the close relationship between Victorian folklore study (which purports to record the nation's cultural formation) and the novel (which charts the formative years of a hero who tacitly embodies the nation). Indeed, the oldest definition of "novel" likens the work of the novelist and the antiquarian: "any of a number of tales or stories making up a larger work; a fable." The novel, in other words, is indebted to the collector of fables, the teller of tales. It is my contention that fairy tales *matter*, which is to say that they count, circulate, occupy space, take up time, produce, and reproduce. And this means that novelists were ever aware that their works operated as conduits for voices not their own. Through its antiquarian characters, novels express the mingled dread and desire that uncontained narratives might well up, break out, and matter forth. The chapters that complete this section examine Dickens's *Pickwick Papers*, Brontë's *Jane Eyre*, and Eliot's *Middlemarch*. Diverse as these novels are (representing the novel from early to mature production, picaresque to realist form, and male versus female authorship), they demonstrate novelists striving to define the very genre in relationship to an antiquarian's recording of history. If there is a concerted attack upon the antiquarian in the novel, it is part of a much larger semantic and taxonomic conflict: who was compiling the novel, what was it to encompass, what was its value in use and exchange? In "*Pickwick Papers* and the End of Miscellany," I show how Dickens's picaresque *Pickwick Papers* both anxiously and exuberantly reflects the antiquarian collection. Dickens attempts to "evolve" from miscellany to "novelty," but he ultimately concedes to a dependence upon the tale to build the novel. In "The Natural History of Thornfield," I consider *Jane Eyre* as a novel indebted to and in part modeled upon the natural history, a hybrid form that, like Brontë's work, mingles scientific inquiry, human nature, and gothic curiosities in the service of self-discovery and self-possession. In "Antiquity, Novelty, and *The Key to All Mythologies*," I suggest that Eliot's *Middlemarch*, albeit a historical and realist novel, is also at its roots a folkloric project, as full of "mythical fragments" as Casaubon's "Key to All Mythologies."[20]

PART 2: SPELL

This section demonstrates that the tale became a Victorian narrative of time, progress, and poetic composition. I begin with "Sleeping Beauty and Victorian Temporality," a brief history of "Sleeping Beauty" through the nineteenth century. In three short chapters ("Keats on Sleep and Beauty"; "'A Perfect Form in Perfect Rest': Tennyson's 'Day Dream'"; and "Burne-Jones and the Poetic Frame"), I put into dialogue three texts that reflect upon the tale: John Keats's poem "Eve of St. Agnes," Alfred Tennyson's poem "The Day Dream" (a reply not only to the fairy tale but to Keats's version of it), and Edward Burne-Jones's *Briar Rose* paintings (a series self-avowedly modeled upon these earlier poems). In nineteenth-century retellings, the tale is often reduced to two identifying features: the princess's hundred-year sleep and the prince's arrival. This particularly Victorian focus upon sleep and resurrection reflects preoccupations with emerging models of time. The tale genders the movement of time itself in the Kristevan sense, the princess rapt in cyclic slumber, the galvanic prince returning the narrative to linearity. And in the nineteenth century, the story of a dormant castle penetrated by a questing prince becomes a metanarrative of the feminized fairy tale resurrected as a helpmeet to masculine "high" art. Yet the tale, it seems, could not be so easily subordinated into the role of literary handmaiden. Each of these artists worked upon the "Sleeping Beauty" subject lingeringly, fretfully, over many years and many versions begun, laid to rest, taken up again, and bequeathed to other artists. To resurrect the tale is to "spell" the previous artist (that is, relieve him of duty), but ultimately to be spelled *by the tale*, since artists are mortal and tales are lasting.

PART 3: PRODUCE

This section explores fairies in representations of industry, including the Great Exhibition of 1851 and Christina Rossetti's "Goblin Market." I introduce this section with "Fairy Footsteps and Goblin Economies," a history of the fairy in Britain. We are accustomed to thinking of the fairy legend as a form utterly removed from material reality, and of fairies themselves swathed in gauzy ethereality. Yet a closer look at the fairy legend, so widely familiar in mid-century England, shows a narrative form steeped in the quotidian—in matters of money, sex, race, and class. The next chapter, "The Great Exhibition: Fairy Palace, Goblin Market" attends to literature surrounding the event of the Exhibition. One of the best-loved metaphors for the Great Exhibition was "fairy palace," and it may seem strange that fairies, associated with England's vanishing rural past, would inhabit a palace erected to modernity. However, the Great Exhibition self-avowedly captured a moment between past and future, yoking the spectacle of the monarchy with the "magic" of industrial and scientific progress. My study reveals that the fairy legend, given to matters of production and exchange, resonated with the Exhibition's rhetorical aims. Crucial to this investigation is Christina Rossetti's "Goblin Market," a text not hitherto identified as a critique of the Exhibition. The produce of Rossetti's poem, its fairies, consumption, contamination, and forced fruit, all appeared first in imaginative depictions of the exhibition hall: a fairy spectacle that to some critics concealed a goblin market within. The chapter "Rossetti's Homeopathy" begins by demonstrating this resonance. Fairies in the Great Exhibition labor in the service of mass-production (both of the Exhibition itself and of the illustrated literature turned out to describe it). "Goblin Market" tries to wrest the fairy story away from the "iterated jingle,"[21] from produce created with no discernable antecedents. It attempts to reinscribe the artisan craft of female storytelling, with no male intercessor to value or invalidate the production.

PART 4: PARAPHRASE

This section shows how "Little Red Riding Hood" came to tell the story of defiled urban girlhood. The first chapter, "Little Red Riding Hood Arrives in London," outlines the history of the tale, noting its transformation into a cautionary story for girls; I show how the tale's themes of pursuit, shameful knowledge, and violent ends offered Victorians a fairy analogue for the familiar narrative of seduced working-class maidens. In nineteenth-century revisions, Little Red Riding Hood journeys on foot, not to grandmother's house, but into London. In nineteenth-century revisions, the *riding* hood becomes a garment above the station of a girl compelled by economic circumstances to walk. The next chapter, "Little Red Riding Hood's Progress," explores the fraught relationship between urban childhood and the popular theater's fairy theatricals. "Little Red Riding Hood" was a favorite subject of nineteenth-century fairy dramas. I argue that "Little Red Riding Hood," a tale that plays between dressing up (trying on other identities) and dressing "up" (masquerading in garments of a higher class) offered productive narrative connections between childhood, theater, and commerce. The final chapter, "Little Red Riding Hood and Other Waterside Characters," reflects upon Dickens's life-long fascination with actresses, working-class girls, and fairy tales. Beginning with Dickens's recollection of Little Red Riding Hood as his ruined "first love," I investigate Dickens's speculation upon the literary value of tales. In his last novel, *Our Mutual Friend*, "Little Red Riding Hood" becomes, in Dickens's own words, a "paraphrase."[22] The novel's masquerades and performances, dressings up and down, wolfish seductions, and journeys through urban forests are shadowed by a ghostly pantomime of Dickens's lost "first love," who becomes a way to speak about various forms of labor, hunger, and desire.

All in all, these chapters work together to challenge any received idea that the fairy tale was a quaint or quiescent form, and instead reveal it to be adaptive, volatile, and eruptive. For Jennifer Schacker, writing on the Victorian pantomime, Mother Bunch becomes an important guise for this transgressive force:

> Mother Bunch is . . . both the transmitter and embodiment of fairy-tale magic. This is the case in an 1822 *London Magazine* review of the season's pantomimes. Here the readership is instructed to "cherish Mother Bunch, Mother Goose, and all those old enchanting mothers, who suckled us with fairy milk" (134). . . . Although Mother Bunch is not connected to potential transgression via ink, she is . . . associated nevertheless with a number of other densely symbolic fluids that threaten (or promise) to obfuscate boundaries, that intoxicate, impregnate, and nourish, that defy efforts to contain them (14–15).

Like Schacker, I am curious about how fairy tales were seen by the Victorians to transgress generic boundaries and to soak into literary culture. In *Spellbound*, I argue that Victorians imagined fairy tales simultaneously (and paradoxically) as procreative and as infectious. These metaphors—the fairy tale as engenderer of literary material and as circulator of disease—reveal Victorian preoccupations with authorial agency and debt, and with the production and circulation of written matter. Those authors who saw the fairy tale as an infection that infiltrates and co-opts an otherwise healthy Victorian literary body feared that they lacked sufficient defensive mechanisms to wield authorial power over their narratives. On the other hand, those authors who imagined the fairy tale as a generative, seminal force fretted that literary authors produced nothing new, but instead circulated narratives already created and codified, the written word (in Catherine Gallagher's terms) "multiplying unnaturally in the mere process of exchange."[23] Ultimately, both metaphors call into question the cult of the author, and indeed the very paradigm of single-author production, which drove so much of Victorian literary discourse.

Spellbound's four part titles—"Matter," "Spell," "Produce," and "Paraphrase"—aim to acknowledge and to some extent describe the cultural disturbance the fairy tale caused. Individually, each word appears in and is significant to the literature I discuss in that section. Together, these words suggest the processes of conduction and conveyance. A dilation upon each word in each section reveals that Victorian literary artists render fairy tale circulation within other genres as, variously, the mattering of infection, the pulsing of blood, the pressing of fruit juices, and the coursing of Thames water. This linguistic play reinforces Schacker's suggestion that Victorians routinely depicted the fairy tale as a variety of "densely symbolic fluids that threaten (or promise) to obfuscate boundaries."

The Fairy Tale: History, Definitions, and Uses

I have thus far used the terms *fairy tale, fairy story,* and *folk narrative* interchangeably. It is necessary to explain this choice, both for the literary critic who may know nothing of the terms, and for the fairy tale scholar and folklorist, to whom my elision will seem peculiar, if not irresponsible. However, it is a reasoned choice, and one that I hope will clarify *Spellbound*'s intervention into the field of fairy tale scholarship. The modern definition of folklore is

> the traditional art, literature, knowledge, and practice that is disseminated largely through oral communication and behavioral example. Every group with a sense of its own identity shares, as a central part of that identity, folk traditions—the things that people traditionally *believe* (planting practices, family traditions, and other elements of worldview), *do* (dance, make music, sew clothing), *know* (how to build an irrigation dam, how to nurse an ailment, how to prepare barbecue), *make* (architecture, art, craft), and *say* (personal experience stories, riddles, song lyrics).[24]

I would add to this definition that no form of folklore is static: all folklore alters across space and time to adapt to the exigencies of its users, and a single item of folklore will exist in (sometimes multiple) versions and variants.

Twentieth-century folklorists organized this capacious discipline into a complete taxonomy. The exhaustive work of such interdisciplinary scholars as Anti Aarne and Stith Thompson, Franz Boas, Claude Levi-Strauss and Vladimir Propp in the first half of the century, and Jan Harold Brunvand, Linda Dégh, Richard Dorson, Alan Dundes in the second half was instrumental in situating folklore as a discipline within the social sciences. According to this classification system, the stories that people transmit orally are placed into the broadest category of "narrative folklore" (or folk narrative), and usually further divided into myths, legends, and folk tales. Myths are sacred creation narratives—stories that explain global and cosmological origins. They take place outside of time, or in a "time before time." They are believed to be true by the teller and his or her audience. Legends are stories of personal, local, or historical significance. Like myths, they are stories believed to be true by both teller and hearer,[25] but differ in that they take place in a historical past that is at least approximately, if not absolutely, identifiable. They are usually highly local in concern; that is, they are meant to account for the (often uncanny or supernatural) experiences of relatives, neighbors, or heroes living in geographical proximity. They are, ultimately, narratives that circulate in a given society, and that (often metaphorically) reflect cultural anxieties and tensions. Folk tales, unlike legends and myths, are narratives that teller and audience understand to be fictional. They deal in largely human concerns, but like myths, they take place in an abstract, historically unverifiable time and place ("once upon a time"). Legends and folk tales often treat magical happenings, but legends are nevertheless seen to be straightforward accounts of concrete events. Legends are variable in structure (though with a finite number of motif sequences), while folk tales conform to a stricter structural pattern.[26]

According to the definition of scholars like Brunvand and Dorson, stories about *fairies* (the creatures, sometimes small, sometimes human-sized, that live underground or in mounds, or otherwise on the edges of British culture and consciousness) are *legends;* that is, they treat magical happenings, but take place in real time, and are believed to be true.[27] Classic folklore scholarship[28] of the twentieth century contends that fairy *tales,* by contrast, belong in the subcategory of folk tales.[29] According to this theory, fairy tales are a group of specifically European folk tales (such as "Sleeping Beauty," "Cinderella," "Bluebeard," "Rumpelstiltskin," "Beauty and the Beast," or "Little Red Riding Hood"),[30] some of which feature fairy characters who intercede, with aid or impediments, in human affairs. These scholars maintain that fairy characters were added to these tales in the seventeenth century through literary intervention, or oral modification, or both. Certainly, in the print history of those stories we now call "fairy tales" eighteenth- and nineteenth-century versions feature fairy godmothers and fairy antagonists, while fifteenth-, sixteenth-, and seventeenth-century versions (which are demonstrably antecedents of the same tale) are devoid of fairies.

However, there is, at this present time, a significant debate in fairy tale scholarship as to whether fairy tales should be categorized as folklore at all. This debate arises from contention over oral and literary designations. The theory of the fairy tale's origin is contested by scholars like Ruth Bottigheimer and Elizabeth Harries, who argue that fairy tales are not a subcategory of folktale, but are a purely literary form.[31] Such critics contend that, while surely indebted to both the folk tale and the fairy legend, fairy tales originate solely through authored texts. Any seeming effects of orality, they feel, are studied textual effects. Literary fairy tale adherents usually consider theirs to be a feminist argument: the creators of fairy tales, they insist, were not old wives or mother geese, but authors. Because they were often female authors, the "folklorizing" of fairy tales, these scholars feel, constitutes an erasure of authorial power, and an imposition of anonymity upon the female literary artist.

Spellbound cannot hope to settle this dispute. The question of origins is eternally vexed in folklore study, and I am not convinced that it can be unequivocally resolved. For this reason, I am more interested in the rhetorical uses to which Victorians put the fairy tale form. Whatever their "true" origins, Victorians firmly believed the folk tale, fairy tale, and fairy legend to be oral and therefore unauthored forms. Though Victorian authors themselves most often came by their knowledge of the fairy tale through books and other print materials, they routinely figured fairy tales as transmitted through a marginally civilized female body. We can find evidence of this in the now-apocryphal nurses of Coleridge, Dickens, and the Brontës; we can trace it in Andrew Lang's Color Fairy Books, where he pictures fairy tales first told by "naked savage women to naked savage children"[32]; and we can locate it in the oft-invoked figures of Mother Goose and Mother Bunch.[33] Ultimately, I am less concerned with navigating or adjudicating the "truth" of these origins theories than I am with understanding the Victorian reception of and contribution to these theories.

Though contemporary academics distinguish between folk tale, fairy tale, and fairy legend, Victorian authors made little distinction among these categories. Even those very scholars who codified distinctions between the tale and the legend in the nineteenth century purposely obscured those differences if it suited their purposes for publication or for rhetoric to do so. This was true even very late in the century; Andrew Lang, a founding member of the Folk-Lore Society, and a keen participant in emerging taxonomies of folklore, designed his eleven Color Fairy Books to indiscriminately blend folk tales, fairy tales, and legends. Because my purpose is to recapture the milieu in which Victorians wrote about these narratives, *Spellbound* attends to folk tale, fairy tale, and fairy legend texts as promiscuously as Victorians did themselves.[34]

Of course, the irony here is that the forms of fairy lore were so persistently and pervasively imagined as oral, when their rich print history in fact reveals the genre to be integral to the Victorian development of the book and of print media more broadly. Though fairy tales and legends took passage to England in many ways, it is through print history of the eighteenth and nineteenth centuries that we can most easily trace the reception of the tale. The most abiding, oft read, and oft repeated of tale cycles came from Arabic, Italian, French, and German traditions, as well as from Britain itself. The *Thousand and One Arabian Nights* is a tale tradition spanning six centuries of manuscript forms. Antoine Galland's *Les Mille et Une Nuits: Contes Arabes* (1704–1717) began the tales' European circulation. English translations of Galland began as early as 1706. Edward Lane's version, *The Thousand and One Nights*, the first to depart from Galland's translation, was published serially from 1838 to 1840. Other important English editions include those by John Payne (1882–84) and Sir Richard Burton (1885–86). From the Italian tradition came the tales of Giovanni Francesco Straparola, *Le Piacevoli Notti* (1550), and those of Giambattista Basile, *Il Pentamerone* (1634–36). Basile's work was translated into English in 1848 and Straparola's in 1894, but Basile's tales, at least, circulated in England in Italian and French editions throughout the nineteenth century. The seventeenth-century French *salon* culture introduced the French fairy tale to England. Madame d'Aulnoy, the grande dame of the *conteuses*, produced *Contes de Fées* in 1697. Indeed, it is this volume that popularized the term *fairy tale* in English after 1699, when *Contes des Fées* was first translated as *Tales of the Fairies* (1699).[35] The tales of Charles Perrault, *Histoires ou Contes du Temps Passé* (1697), was first translated into English by Robert Samber as *Histories, or Tales of Past Times: With Morals* (1729). A few decades later, the work of the Brothers Grimm, *Kinder- und Hausmärchen* (1812) and *Deutche Sagen* (1815), brought the German tale into prominence. The second edition of *Kinder- und Hausmärchen* was second only to the Bible in sales across Europe. It was first translated into English by Edgar Taylor in 1823, and throughout the century remained a staple of English reading.

The British fairy legend began its print history as material in medieval demonologies, sorcery manuals, and trial records.[36] Later literary movements such as the French, Celtic, and British lay cycles, the popularization of antiquarian pursuits, the court pageantry of Elizabeth, Spenser's *Faerie Queene* and Shakespeare's fairy plays made the fairy legend collection a ubiquitous item on eighteenth- and nineteenth-century bookshelves. Written by both Celtic and English authors, they include such titles as John Brand's *Observations on the Popular Antiquities of Great Britain* (1777), Thomas Crofton Croker's *Legends and Traditions of the South of Ireland* (1825), Thomas Keightley's *Fairy Mythology* (1828), Joseph Ritson's *Fairy Tales* (1831), Anna Eliza Bray's *Traditions, Legends and Sketches of Devonshire on the Borders of the Tamar and Tavy* (1838) and *A Peep at the Pixies* (1854), and Jeremiah Curtin's *Tales of the Fairies and of the Ghost World, Collected from Oral Tradition in South-West Munster* (1895).[37]

During the nineteenth century, these works enjoyed multiple reprintings, retranslations, and retellings (both in their entirety and as selections of tales) in two related literary markets: children's books (such as school books, toy books, and Christmas books), and "cheap" publications (such as blue books, chapbooks, and penny dreadfuls). The print history of legends and fairy tales served both to carve out a space for the British tale and legend, and to give Victorians a sense of participation in a pan-European tradition, one from which poets, novelists, and playwrights adopted and manipulated source materials.

And yet, in spite of important work that makes folk narrative a framework for considering national identities, I aim to move away from the question of whether folk tales accurately encode national character, and indeed from questions of veracity and fidelity entirely. Many studies of the English fairy tale and of folkloric material more generally have charged that England has no folklore of its own. Such works, perhaps most notably those of Elizabeth Harries, Susan Stewart, and Katie Trumpener, have contended that England, its colonial practices operating in print as on land, merely appropriated the European fairy tale and the French and Celtic fairy legend and ballad traditions, stripping these genres of any "genuine" folkloric value and leaving meaningless shells of what was originally a socially and politically contextualized form, upon which England could inscribe its own (spurious) agendas.[38] As deservedly acclaimed as they are, these works have not acknowledged important facts about the English fairy tale tradition. First, all nations and peoples have folklore, and therefore to say that an empowered, colonial nation does not is to suggest that folklore is a condition only of subalternity. The Victorian English considered that they *did* have folklore, as books (such as those by Alfred Nutt) on the English fairy tale and the English fairy legend attest. Secondly, while all nations *have* folklore, no nation *owns* folklore. The Italians derived much of their fairy tale material from the *Arabian Nights* traditions, while Perrault adapted freely from Basile, and the Grimms appropriated Perrault's plotlines and motifs. It is difficult and often impossible to find a tale's "real" national origin, or to reconcile whether a tale is "originally" oral or literary. All folklore, oral, material, and literary, is learned, appropriated, and adapted to fit geographical and temporal needs. In other words, the question of "validity" in Victorian England's use of the fairy tale and legend seems to me to be a false one: these narratives are undoubtedly recontextualized, but so is all folklore, everywhere, and in every time. Jennifer Schacker is at the forefront of "challenging accepted 'truths' regarding the history of the fairy tale in England," and acknowledges that "I myself have contributed to the solidification of part of this now conventional narrative"[39] that England had no "genuine" folklore. Whereas in *National Dreams,* Schacker argued that "in translation [fairy tale] texts had been progressively infantilized, stripped of subtext and innuendo," she announces that "[i]n my current research project, I am suggesting that this conventional narrative about the history of the fairy tale can be challenged, complicated, and enlivened."[40] I, too, aim to contribute to this challenge by examining the presence—and importance— of the fairy tale in various canonical genres. *Spellbound*'s larger purpose is to demonstrate that, while the act of appropriating a fairy narrative reshapes the narrative, it also materially alters and acts upon the literary or cultural medium into which it is adopted.

Spellbound's Fairy Godmothers and Fathers

Spellbound is not the first theoretical work to treat the fairy tale in the literary arena. It is therefore appropriate to briefly describe how my intervention is shaped by and differs from those classic and contemporary studies. Of course, Sigmund Freud is responsible for teaching us all—in *Dreams and Folk Tales* and *The Interpretation of Dreams*—to read tales as principally metaphorical texts. Indeed, fairy tale scholarship in the twentieth century was dominated by the psychoanalytic approach, most notably the works of Bruno Bettelheim, Alan Dundes, and Maria Tatar.[41] But I am specifically interested in the reception of the fairy tale before Freud's influence, and before its implicit meanings became codified into the single interpretation of psychic allegory. Though psychoanalytic theory certainly remains relevant, psychoanalytic approaches to the fairy tale tend to universalize meaning, without regard to periodicity or nationality. As important as these forerunners are, they do not explore the fairy tale's cultural, formal, or linguistic play, and this is an important distinction between their works and mine.

In the late twentieth and early twenty-first centuries, scholars have turned to historical and archival method as a way to respond to the universalizing tendencies of the psychoanalytic approach to fairy tales. Though ranging widely in subject, these works all consider cultural context, the specificities of economic, sexual, racial, and literary landscape, to be pertinent to the Victorian fairy tale. And while *Spellbound* is deeply indebted to this mode of inquiry, I also seek fresh territory. For instance, Jack Zipes and Jennifer Schacker interpret the historical and cultural significance of nineteenth-century fairy tale collections; though each part of *Spellbound* offers a short introduction acknowledging the publication and dissemination history of pertinent fairy narratives, I do not otherwise treat Victorian fairy tale collections as primary texts. Similarly, I do not, like Nina Auerbach and U. C. Knoepflmacher, examine Victorian children's fantastic literature written in the style of the fairy tale; instead, my interest lies in how fairy tales comingled with adult literature. I seek to demonstrate the fairy tale's integrality to the canonical poetry, fiction, and drama of the Victorian period, specifically to address and counter the persistent idea that the fairy tale is and was a subject only for children. *Spellbound* looks afresh at heavily trafficked texts like *Pickwick Papers, Middlemarch*, "Goblin Market," and *Our Mutual Friend;* it foregrounds the fairy tale's incursion into these works of literature in order to show how the form actually produces discourses within Victorian texts.

Carole Silver, Diane Purkiss, and Nicola Bown explore the figure of the fairy in literature and art; and Michael Kotzin, Harry Stone, and Caroline Sumpter treat fairy tales as they interact with single Victorian subjects, like the popular press or the novels of Dickens.[42] *Spellbound* owes much to these hybrid works of literature and culture, especially those of Silver, Bown, and Sumpter. But though *Spellbound* certainly engages in cultural study, it will not, ultimately, reinscribe those exhaustively researched archival projects. For one thing, this work has already been done, and done well—most notably by Silver and Purkiss. Because others have already established the ubiquity and vitality of fairy tales and legends in Victorian culture, I can simply take this proliferation as a starting point from which to launch an exploration of the fairy tale in specific literary contexts. Then too, these works of cultural study, however excellent and important to the field, primarily seek to impose an organizational structure upon their amassed data, rather than to bring extended analytical or theoretical focus to bear on any text or author.

In doing so, these scholars tend to preserve the notion that the Victorians sentimentalized fairies and the fairy tale as a nostalgic refuge from an industrial age. Nicola Bown, for instance, says she intends to create "a sympathetic study of one of the less admirable aspects of Victorian culture, the regressive longings and escapist fantasies that shaped its fascination with the supernatural" (9). I do not think that fairies are what fly in the face of change: I think that they *are* the face of change. *Spellbound* differs from these works in that I suggest that the Victorians regarded fairy tales on an entirely other register that centralized them, and made them vital to discourses of modernity.

Because the fantastic so saturates Victorian literature a few words are in order to explain exclusions and inclusions. This is, to begin with, a Victorian study, rather than a study in the long nineteenth century. While questions of childhood and loss, personal and cultural pasts, and artistic development inflected both the Romantic and Victorian perception of folk traditions, there were also crucial differences between the Victorian and Romantic uses of folklore. Though, as I have shown, authors in the Romantic period talked philosophically about the effects of reading and hearing fairy tales as children, the fairy tale's effects can be traced more concretely in the creative ideology than the content of Romantic poetry. It was not the tale but the ballad that lay at the heart of Romantic literary art, from the *Lyrical Ballads* of Wordsworth and Coleridge, to the neo-chivalric fiction of Scott. Keats is a notable exception to this general Romantic rule: his interest in fairies and fairy tales anticipates the Victorian fairy tale ardor. Because Keats is seminal to Tennyson's poetry, and because Keats bequeathed a legacy of Victorian preoccupation with sleep and beauty, his "Eve of St. Agnes" necessitates a brief prelude to the Victorian portions of the section.

In spite of its impact upon English literary history, I do not include extensive material about the Arthurian legend cycle, except insofar as "The Epic" and *Idylls of the King* is crucial to part 2. I do not enter into the Arthurian legends beyond this for two reasons: Firstly, because the literary artist who most famously and persistently adapted the Arthurian legends to his work was Tennyson, a considerable amount of criticism already exists. I am instead interested in Tennyson's more obscure poem "The Day Dream," for the way it sets out his early conception of the relationship between artistry and femininity, and for its lasting, subtle influence upon other Victorian artists. Secondly, Victorians thought of the Arthurian cycle as epic history, not folk narrative. Though to a folklorist, Arthurian legendry is a body of narrative folklore, its characters no more "historical" than *Briar Rose*, as I explain in part 2, Victorians conceived a crucial distinction between the forms.

While the first and final sections treat Dickens's reception of the fairy tale, this is not a book in the tradition of Michael Kotzin's *Dickens and the Fairy Tale* or Harry Stone's *Dickens and the Invisible World: Fairy Tales, Fantasy, and Novel-Making*, both of which identify and catalogue Dickens's various folk characters and plots.[43] Kotzin and Stone do important work to legitimize fairy tales as Dickens's source material; but these authors neither historicize the fairy tale, nor examine fairy tales' collective power as a genre, nor consider that each individual fairy tale has its own print history and discursive import. *Spellbound* seeks to deepen our perception, not only of Dickens's appropriation of fairy tales, but of Dickens's place in a larger cultural and literary phenomenology.

To sum up, then, *Spellbound* is neither so encyclopedic nor so narrowly defined as other works that have gone before it. I advocate a certain lawlessness in the wake of these important books, because fairy tales in the Victorian period are notable precisely for their resistance to order, for the way in which they evade neat taxonomies and generic stability. Folk narrative is sturdy enough to bear the weight of multiple agendas, conservative and liberal, male and female, popular and elite. Fairy tales do the nation in different voices. *Spellbound* shows that English authors depended upon the language and form of fairy tales to make sense of society, and art of that sense.

PART 1

Matter

CHAPTER 1

The Novelist and the Collector

Trysting Genres

Thomas Hardy's deceptively simple short story "Tryst at an Ancient Earthwork" (1893)[1] appears to record faithfully an event of local archeological excavation. The narrator meets his antiquarian friend in the dead of night atop Mai-Dun, an ancient motte-and-bailey fort in Dorset. Defying signs that forbid excavation, the antiquarian digs into the tumulus in order to "uncover, to search, to verify a theory or displace it, and to cover it up again. He means to take away nothing—not a grain of sand" (180). After excavating several Roman treasures, including a skeleton, a bottle, a sword fragment, and a small statue of Mercury, the antiquary appears to rebury the items. However, the narrator, whose "contribution to the labor is that of directing the light constantly upon the hole" (180) fancies that he sees his friend slip something into his pocket. This suspicion is borne out seven years later, when the statue is found among his friend's effects upon his death. The antiquary had indeed looted it from the site of excavation.

For me, this slim narrative serves as a fingerpost, pointing retrospectively into the nineteenth century and its many literary treatments of the antiquarian—later folklorist. At first reading, Hardy's story appears to critique not just the actions of the antiquary but also, by extension, the very nature of his investigative project. The nocturnal act of exhumation, which the antiquary justifies in the name of academic curiosity, the narrator describes in terms of both grave robbery and rape. "Mai-Dun" is modeled after a real hill fort, Maiden Castle in Dorset, and Hardy treats the antiquary rummaging around inside of a hitherto unexplored, or "maiden," fortress in explicitly sexual terms; every treasure brought from the earth "draws luxuriant groans of sensibility from the digger" (181), and when he inhumes the treasures once more, "each deposition seems to cost him a twinge" (183). Moreover, "this venerable scholar with letters after his name" (181) is unable to stop himself from thieving; we might conclude that the entire excavation, shadowed by dark lantern and signaled by a furtive hand in the pocket, is figured as a selfish and useless exhumation of the past. It is worth noting here that "rape" derives from "rapio," to capture or take; thus excavation and rape are etymologically analogous, too. The antiquary's discovery, hoarded to himself, its secret dying with him, is valuable only because "it proves all the world to be wrong in this great argument, and himself alone to be right!" (183) Even the physical appearance of this man is ridiculous and antiquated: "he is a man about 60, small in figure, with grey old-fashioned whiskers cut to the shape of a pair of crumb-brushes" (179). Finally, as if to underscore the antiquarian's obsolescence, the narrator tells the entire story without dialog, literally denying the antiquarian a voice.

The story's proportionally long exposition is devoted to the narrator climbing the hill to the fort, and here the narrator's descriptive writing has full voice: "At one's every step forward it rises higher against the south sky, with an *obtrusive personality* that compels the sense to regard it and consider. The eyes may bend in another direction, but never without the consciousness of its heavy, *high-shouldered* presence at its point of vantage . . . with the shifting of the clouds the *face* of the steeps vary in color and shade. . . . In this so-thought immutable spectacle all is change" (171, emphasis added). The narrator's personification of the hill foregrounds the fictionality of the piece in our hands, and thus appears to contrast the work of the antiquarian and that of the fiction writer. This opposition between antiquarian and fictional modes of interpretation is soon put into more playfully literary terms: "That the summit of the second line of defense has been gained is suddenly made known by a contrasting wind from a new quarter, coming over with the curve of a cascade. These *novel* gusts raise a sound from the whole camp or castle, playing upon it bodily, as upon a harp" (171). This hill, in other words, is being played by "novel gusts" as the author ascends it, penetrating the earthwork with words rather than a shovel.

And yet, for all its critique of folklorists as plunderers, Hardy's tale reveals his antiquarian thief and his narrator (who may or may not be Hardy himself) in uneasy collusion. In choosing the word "tryst" for his title, Hardy connotes a number of furtive liaisons that occur in the story; between past and present, certainly, but also between collector and author, and between antiquarian and narrative exploits. Perhaps most importantly, then, a "tryst" describes the very story Hardy himself designed: it is a sexualized encounter between archaic materials and their modern investigator. The first four sections of the story are dedicated to the narrator's penetration into the earthwork, and even before he encounters his friend, the fiction writer betrays a longing to reconstruct the past commensurate with that of the antiquarian: "The only semblance of heroic voices are [sheep and cows]; [n]ot a page, not a stone, has preserved their fame" (176). He imagines the fortress repopulated with the armies that built it: "Past and present have become so confusedly mingled under the associations of the spot that for a time it has escaped my memory that this mound was the place agreed on for the aforesaid appointment" (179). During the excavation, the narrator waivers between dismayed distance from the antiquarian and collusive "luxuriant groans" as he helps the antiquarian disrobe the hill: "It is strange indeed that by merely peeling off a wrapper of modern accumulations we have lowered ourselves into an ancient world" (182).

From one angle, Hardy's story might appear to suggest that the narrator, holding the light "constantly on the hole," illuminates the scurrilous nature of antiquarian desires; yet what it actually suggests is that this apparently critical literary observer is implicated in exhumations of his own. The narrative is constructed in present tense until the last few sentences of the story:

> Walking along quickly to restore warmth I muse upon my eccentric friend, and cannot help asking myself this question: Did he really replace the gilded image of the god Mercurius with the rest of the treasures? He seemed to do so; and yet I could not testify to the fact. Probably, however, he was as good as his word.
>
> It was thus I spoke to myself, and so the adventure ended. But one thing remains to be told, and that is concerned with seven years after. (183)

The immediacy of the first person present tense is given the lie at the end of the story, when we recognize that this narrative is, in fact, retrospective: "seven years" have passed since the events related here. Though the narrator observes the sign which reads "Caution: Any Person found removing Relics, Skeletons, Stones, Pottery, Tiles, or other Material from this Earthwork, or cutting up the Ground, will be Prosecuted as the law directs" (174), and though he admonishes his friend "we must re-bury them *all*" (179), this temporal remove indicates that the narrator himself is guilty of removing "other Material" from the site, material that comes in the form of the story itself: the narrator survives to publish this account of his friend's findings, presumably to gain financially from it. That Hardy's text plays with the forms of both fictional short story and antiquarian manuscript only further complicates this autoreferential gesture. Hardy insisted, for instance, that the story be published with photographs of Maiden Castle to mimic the verisimilitude of an ethnographic account. And in spite of, and in conflict with, those explicitly fictional, *novel* passages I have noted, there is no indication of a first-person narrative identity for the first five paragraphs of the story: the earliest descriptions of the hill fort could as easily be read as the work of a particularly fanciful antiquarian.

All in all, this short story, with its meditation upon theft, lucre, and retrospection, models a common way of thinking and debating about creativity in the nineteenth century: on the one hand it sets up a morally-charged opposition between the collector (as thief) and the literary artist (as creator), but on the other it recognizes that such an opposition cannot be sustained. Instead, literary authors and folklore collectors were revealed again and again to be mutually engaged in the same labor—that is, *both* creating *and* compiling national narratives. This essay begins with Hardy's fictional account of a "trysting" between literary artist and collector in order to exemplify both the interpenetrated nature of Victorian disciplines—where fiction-writing, folklore, and anthropology intertwine—and the ambivalence with which authors regarded such entanglements. Perhaps for Hardy the little statue of the mythical god Mercury is a sign that highlights the "trysting" of fiction writer and folklorist—after all, in the sixteenth and seventeenth centuries the "finger of Mercury" referred to a signpost. In legend, the messenger god Mercury is the protector of both traders and thieves, blurring the distinction between legitimate and illegitimate exchange. Indeed, he is sometimes depicted holding a purse, in allusion to his business functions. And "mercury" is a seventeenth-century term for a hawker of pamphlets and broadsheets. These meanings combine to make Mercury an apt figure for the fiction writer and collector alike, both traders in words in the Victorian literary marketplace.

Walter Benjamin's work on the *Arcades Project* (1927–1940)[2] will serve to demonstrate just how foundational the late-Victorian contretemps between authors and collectors would become for theorists and cultural critics, how instrumental for the eventual consolidation of the literary and social sciences as academic disciplines. Benjamin takes up the very questions that Hardy considers in "Tryst": does the collector engage in unique cultural labor? Is that labor useful or valuable? And what do the notions of "use" and "value" mean in the context of collection? According to Benjamin, the collector "makes his concern the transfiguration of things." He "dreams his way not only into a distant or bygone world but also into a better one— one in which . . . things are freed from the drudgery of being useful" (9). Under the auspices of this redemptive transfiguration, the act of collecting itself "is a form of practical memory" (205). Benjamin's analysis suggests that the collector holds a unique position in Victorian culture, for collecting means "that the object is detached from all its original functions to enter into the closest conceivable relation to things of the same kind" (205). Benjamin suggests that the collector integrates objects "into a new, expressly derived historical system" which "becomes an encyclopedia of all knowledge of the epoch, the landscape, the industry and the owner from which it comes." (204–5). Benjamin takes a more unequivocally positive view of collection than Hardy, a romanticism on the matter of lost fragments that makes sense in light of the *Arcades Project*, which is itself a massive, unfinished collection that attempts to unfold an "historical system": an "encyclopedia of all knowledge" or "landscape" of cited text. And yet, even Benjamin's approbation echoes the charges certain Victorian authors made about the nature of collection: that antiquarian compilations or collections of fairy tales are magical, irrational, detached from any original function, aesthetic rather than useful, and fundamentally retrospective.

Indeed, Benjamin's conclusions are shaped by nineteenth-century philosophies of collection, as well as by his extensive reading of nineteenth-century European novels, especially those of Charles Dickens. Benjamin's meditation upon collection both highlights and problematizes our entrenched ideas about Victorian authorship. This section reconsiders the role of collectors and collection in the Victorian novel. Focusing particularly on the collection of fantastic narratives, and its relationship both to the emerging novel form and to rising scientific discourse and academic discipline, I examine three important novels that span the nineteenth century—Charles Dickens's seminal *Pickwick Papers,* Charlotte Brontë's mid-century *Jane Eyre,* and George Eliot's post-Darwinian *Middlemarch.* These novels each apprehend collection, not as a wholly distinct cultural form, but as an alternate paradigm of authorship, one that necessarily embraces collaboration, and productively calls into question the very category of (single) authorship in the Victorian period. The collection both challenges and collides with the writing of fiction by constantly pointing to the novel's own collaborative nature and multivocal disruptions.

While the *Arcades Project* assembles quotations and "fragments" of text, rather than narratives or folk tales, Benjamin's understanding of "collection" certainly resonates with the compendia of fairy tales and legends so popular in the nineteenth century. The fairy tale and legend collection emerged as the consolidation of and negotiation between the closely related studies of antiquarianism, natural history, and folklore, all of which had significant foundations in material collection. These three fields waxed in popularity at different times in the century (antiquarianism in the early-, natural history in the middle-, and folklore in the late-Victorian periods), and each gave birth to disciplines in the sciences and social sciences (archeology, biology, and anthropology, respectively); nevertheless, these fields generated a publication history that shared considerable generic similarities, sufficient enough for twentieth-century folklorists to claim antiquarian and natural history works as the generic forebears to the folklore study. These works are characterized by a complex relationship between author (or editor) and informants (or subjects) that is situated in a conscious differentiation between periphery and center, and between orality and literacy. Their authors self-consciously explore the meaning of nation, and claim that they produce a national narrative, one actuated by the urgent need for preservation in the face of modernity. Finally, these works play between amateur and professional endeavor, with publication providing the line of demarcation.

Antiquarianism

Richard Dorson tells us that eighteenth and nineteenth-century antiquarians, whose characteristic local histories included both broad studies of regional material culture and local folk traditions, first established the popularity of the field that would eventually come to be called folklore.[3] The first formally-articulated design to chronicle English "miscellanies" was registered in the appointment of John Leland as King's Antiquary in 1533. From the first, antiquarian collection delighted in the remains of Roman material culture found on English soil, glorying in England's association with that advanced culture. However, scholars questing for tangible "remains" also searched for evidence of a uniquely English past. William Camden, for example, hoped that his 1586 *Brittania* would "restore Britain to its antiquities and its antiquities to Britain."[4] Antiquarian studies are miscellanies: they combine descriptions and illustrated reproductions of material artifact, but also descriptions of regional territory, parish records, local superstitions, legends (including ghost and fairy stories), and song. Early antiquarian works, however, were far from "popular": published only in Latin (if at all) they were meant for a select scholarly, and indeed, kingly, readership. When collections were written in English, they seem to have lain unpublished for centuries, as with country squire John Aubrey's *Miscellanies of British Antiquities* (1696). In 1718 the Society of Antiquities was founded; publications like Thomas Percy's *Reliques of Ancient English Poetry* (1765) and John Brand's *Popular Antiquities* in 1777 signaled a shift in antiquarian studies toward a wider audience, to the extent that Brand claimed in his preface: "The English antique has become a general and fashionable study, and the discoveries of the very respectable Society of Antiquities have rendered the recesses of Papal and Heathen antiquities easier of access."[5]

In actuality, however, Brand's work was more widely read in the early nineteenth than in the eighteenth century. This popularity was materially assisted by the printing societies of the 1830s, which published and disseminated antiquarian manuscripts. These groups, most famously the Camden Society and the Percy Society, recovered and brought to light unpublished works (like Aubrey's). Together with the burgeoning Royal Society, they transformed antiquarianism from a private, insular study to a fashionable hobby, one that combined the emerging middle-class pleasures of armchair research and regional tourism. James Paradis explains that "Antiquarianism . . . was an ambulatory, observational practice, most frequently carried out on a local, county scale, but often inspiring lengthy journeys to remote places . . . operating beyond the margins of memory, clusters of adepts exchanged correspondence and maintained communication with each other about old monuments, records and artifacts."[6] Antiquarian endeavor, then, could be practiced both at home and abroad, since its aims were to secure stories and artifacts from various peripheries, both far and near, into the English center. Paradis notes that "the river of artifactual and natural objects streaming in from the colonies to early nineteenth century England," including the Elgin Marbles and the Rosetta Stone, often passed through the Society Of Antiquaries in London.[7] And while Edward Said has argued that these appropriations "were decisive moments in the colonial interpretive control of the idea of the Orient," Paradis suggests that, "More broadly, such antiquarian projects provided a means of colonizing the past. Aestheticizing the past by celebrating its mystery and beauty opened its artifacts to new cultural uses and interpretations."[8] Whether producing an antiquarian record of the English Southwest or of Egypt, in other words, antiquarian practices sought to frame an interpretation of national identity that was consolidated through the practice of gathering up "fragments," "remains," or "relics" of a seemingly departed past, which, be it quaint or grand, barbaric or civilized, was removed from the collector and the reader by the very medium of print as well as the passage of time.

Antiquarian publications may have described and advocated antiquarian study as an amateur, leisured pursuit, but antiquarian writers themselves made successful livings through the sales of their books. It is important to reflect upon the antiquarian publication as the young Dickens would have experienced it—as a genre that reached its apex and began its decline concurrently with two other genres: the miscellany and the picaresque novel. The antiquarian study resonates with these literary forms: collective like the miscellany, and like the picaresque in its travel from rustic, rural, or barbarically exotic scenes to a civilizing center.

Natural History

As Philippa Levine has noted, "natural history [was] a common province of the antiquarian."[9] If the book of popular antiquities reached its apex in the first decades of the nineteenth century, the natural history grew out of that form, and for a long while remained closely connected to antiquarianism. While the scientific advances in geology, biology, and evolution in the mid-nineteenth century eventually separated natural from antiquarian study, natural histories published through the 1830s were eclectic studies. Many detailed the flora and fauna, the geology and geography, of a localized region; others were specialized in scope but broader in place, treating, for instance, all of Britain's birdlife.

The natural history of the eighteenth and nineteenth century (a staple of the Brontë libary) produced what Paradis calls "a stunning range of myth, lyrical landscape, folktale, legend [and] local color."[10] A maker of categories, it ironically resists categorizing within a single literary genre, mingling examinations of the geography and geology, but also the folklore and customs of a region. For example, Gilbert White's *The Natural History of Selborne* was first published as *The Natural History and Antiquities of Selbourne* (1789). White's stated purpose was to enlarge the boundaries of historical and topographical knowledge and to "[throw] some small light upon ancient customs and manners."[11] Both the prose and illustrated portions of Thomas Bewick's *History of British Birds* (1797 and 1804) combine ornithological science with the stuff of legends and tales.[12] In Hugh Miller's natural histories, his narrative gaze moves between antiquarian and geological fragments, and he concludes, "the antiquities piece on in natural sequence to the geology; and it seems but rational to indulge in the same sort of reasonings regarding them."[13]

Natural history's vivid description draws upon the literary traits of both the sublime and the Gothic. Its authors constructed for readers an almost supernaturally animated world. Mary Ellen Bellanca reminds us that, through natural histories, Victorian readers became "accustomed to seeing plants, and, especially, animals, represented with human characteristics, including self-awareness and speaking ability."[14] In addition to his fantastic vignettes, Bewick's narratives include legends and tales about birds, like the insatiable hunger of the heron and cormorant, the battle of the herons and rooks, and the two female eiderducks that shared a single nest.[15] Gilbert White records legends of bats coming down the chimney to eat bacon at the breakfast table, and of toads living to preternaturally advanced years in people's gardens. Anna Eliza Bray's *On the Borders of the Tamar and the Tavy* (1838) weaves fairy legends into her exploration of Cornwall's flora and fauna.

The natural history also highlights its own proto-ethnographic tendencies, calling attention to its author's perceptual organ that seeks to divine and master the names of things. The natural history of the nineteenth century created an explicitly autobiographical persona: the natural historian "is a self-conscious presence, a manager of spectacle and metaphor."[16] In these natural histories, the narrative "eye" that penetrated a local scientific and folkloric history was also the narrative "I" that simultaneously sought to reveal interior regions. Writing the natural history was an act intended to distinguish the natural historian from his subjects of investigation. There was by contrast, however, a tendency to conflate the author and his or her investigative material, to market the natural history as a discovered object, and its author as one who had drawn himself out of poverty or provincial obscurity through the written word. The natural history was often framed as letters from an avid amateur to a nationally recognized expert or literary giant. White's *Selborne,* for instance, began as a series of letters to naturalists Thomas Pennant and Daines Barington, and Bray's *Tamar and Tavy* originated as a series of letters from Bray to Robert Southey in London. These experts would usually preface the work, and their introductions stress the unimproved, remote, and isolated nature of both region and author; to bring hidden regions to light is also to polish human "diamonds in rough" for popular consumption. Natural historians became intermediaries between the urban and natural worlds; living in peripheral locations, but with connections to centralizing forces. On location to observe and gather up relics, these rural authors are yet perceived to be in need of an editorial hand to bring findings to light through publication in London or Edinburgh. Southey, for instance, congratulated Bray on transmitting her findings through him for the nation to see: "You have brought together . . . many things well worthy of preservation which must have otherwise been forgotten . . . and you have collected them just in time."[17] Passing natural history into the hands of an editor is represented as a modernizing process.

If the antiquary's labor most resembles the assorted and episodic miscellany and picaresque genres, the natural history reached maturity alongside the English bildungsroman, and shares narrative traits with it, perhaps most notably the successful economic and social development of a first person narrator, and the minute observations of an individual in particularized physical locations.

Folklore

When William John Thoms coined the term "folk-lore" in 1846 he called it a "good Saxon compound."[18] He proposed that the term replace "popular antiquities," thus advocating a Germanic rather than Latinate root to describe this national study. This "compound," I would suggest, also connotes a sort of cleansing: to scrub away the taint, in Camden's words, of "too curious a search after what is past"[19] for which antiquarians came under fire. Whereas antiquarians saw themselves as recorders and preservers of localized material and narrative, folklorists sought to determine how and why that folklore is transmitted within and between cultures. The founding of the Folklore Society in 1878, and the work of Lang, Thoms, Joseph Jacobs, Alfred Nutt, George Lawrence Gomme, and Marian Roalfe Cox up to and after that moment, all suggest the extent to which "folklore" had come to supplant "antiquarian" studies in learned circles in the late century.

This epistemological shift also marked the increasing specialization and disciplining of the field. The century saw the erosion of regional societies in the advent of professionalization.[20] Folklorists placed themselves within the burgeoning positivist framework, and allied themselves with scientists, like J. P. Lesley, who saw their practice as having abandoned amateur amusement for "serious toil" in the "hot and dusty light" of "the sun of science."[21]

Like the work in fields such as philology, anthropology, and comparative mythology, folklore practice in the second half of the nineteenth century was characterized by attempts (by sometimes bitterly feuding camps of scholars) to reconstruct interlocking histories of cultures and languages. Friedrich Max Müller's seminal essay, "Comparative Mythology" (1856) gave rise to the field of solar mythology, a philological study predicated upon what Müller called "the disease of language."[22] Müller, a classicist and Sanskrit scholar, believed India to be folklore's originator: the "cradle of the märchen," as Andrew Lang remarked.[23] Müller concluded that as Aryan peoples migrated from their cultural center, mistakes in words (through homonymy, for example) "distorted" the original meaning of mythology. Thus a pantheon of gods formed "accidentally" from what were originally words for sun and stars. What Müller saw as *linguistic* decay, later solar mythologists like George William Cox and James Frazer interpreted as *cultural* degeneration: the "disease of memory," not of language. What were originally myths describing cosmological processes "degenerated" with time, they thought, and turned into fairy tales and legends. Later scholars rejected philology in favor of ethnology in interpreting folklore. Edward Tylor's *Primitive Culture,* published in 1871, posited that peasants preserve folklore as "the tattered remnants of savage myths and animistic beliefs."[24]

Folklore came of age, appropriately, with the "loose, baggy monsters" of the mid-to-late Victorian period—the multiplot novels of authors such as Eliot, Trollope, and Dickens. Like these novelists, folklorists were fascinated with historical retrospection, and with linking stories together in an integrated, contiguous chain.

Fairy and Legend Collections

Throughout the nineteenth century, then, fairy tale and legend collections navigated the boundaries of fiction and the social sciences. These collections often presented the commercially viable face of the antiquarian or folkloric enterprise, where antiquarians and later folklorists who published for a scholarly market also produced fairy tale editions for the (literary) children's or Christmas book markets. For instance, antiquary Thomas Crofton Croker, a founder of the Percy and Camden societies, also wrote the fairy collection *Legends and Traditions of the South of Ireland* (1825). Joseph Ritson, an antiquarian of folk poetry, also wrote *Fairy Tales* (1831, actually a collection of fairy legends). Historian and classical antiquarian Thomas Keightley authored *The Fairy Mythology* (1828). Solicitor

Edgar Taylor, who was an amateur translator the New Testament, and of German poetry, translated into English the Grimms' *Kinder- und Hausmärchen* (1823). Natural historians commonly wrote separate volumes devoted entirely to fairy and animal lore. The Bewick brothers produced *Select Fables* (1776), *Fabliaux* (1796), and *The Fables of Aesop* (1818)[25]; Anna Eliza Bray, who wrote the natural history *The Borders of the Tamar and the Tavy* (1838) also wrote the fairy legend collection *A Peep at the Pixies* (1854). Folklorist Andrew Lang, author of critical studies like *Custom and Myth* (1884) and *Myth, Ritual, and Religion* (1887) was perhaps best known for his Colored Fairy Books, collections of fairy tales and legends. His fellow Folklore Society colleague Joseph Jacobs, who wrote monographs on Judaic folklore, was also the author of *English Fairy Tales* (1890), *Celtic Fairy Tales* (1892), and *Indian Fairy Tales* (1892). These are the collections that made the names, and sometimes the fortunes, of their editors, compilers, and translators. The for-profit nature of fairy-book publication shows that collections of the kind Benjamin both romanticizes and critiques might not be detached from commodity character or use value at all, as Benjamin hopes they will be, but rather aimed precisely at maximizing both.

Antiquity and Novelty

The nineteenth century marks the emergence not only of folklore as a discipline, but also of the recognizable figure of the antiquarian or folklore collector. Part of the folklorist's own creation narrative is the trajectory from amateur to professional, from armchair enthusiast to professional practitioner. This movement was grounded in concerted efforts to come to grips with folklore's greater discursive purpose. Was it nostalgic or progressive, a hobby or a science, a lucrative literary entertainment, or a cog in the rationalist, nationalist, and positivist movements? The same period of years mark the rise of the novel and novelist, a profession equally embedded in questions of identity. Novelists and folklorists register mutual antipathy, and resist acknowledging their entanglements and debts. The grand narrative relates that the novelist and the folklorist arose contemporaneously and battled over which form of authorship would achieve predominance as the national narrative. Folklorists (it was said) produced faithful collections from the mouths of the people, while novelists (most insisted) drew emplotted narratives from their own creative stores. Both fields disparaged any implication of crossover: the larger Victorian rhetoric was that literary artists misappropriated and distorted the fairy tale, while collectors faithfully transcribed it. Far into the twentieth century, folklorists disparaged or subordinated narrative folklore, and especially the fairy tale; the legitimization of the discipline depended upon a "disavowal of its intersection with popular discourses,"[26] and perhaps especially popular literary discourses. To this day, as my introduction suggests, battle lines are still drawn over the fairy tale, and whether it is a strictly oral form, or whether it has its roots, like the novel, in a popular print culture.

It is therefore useful to consider that, echoing many Victorian thinkers before him, Benjamin posited an essential distinction between collector and author, or what he terms the "allegorist." Where the collector "takes up the struggle against dispersion," Benjamin says, the allegorist depends upon it (211). The collector apprehends innate meaning by gathering items into proximity and relation, while the allegorist creates a diverse, seemingly disjointed "patchwork," out of which his authoring power (Benjamin calls it "his profundity") *makes* meaning (211). In this supposed distinction Benjamin recapitulates many Victorian prejudices about the opposition of (derivative) collectors and (profound) authors: the collector is cast as the conduit through which knowledge flows, infused with the magical (but involuntary) impetus toward "completion," while the allegorist is portrayed as the visionary forger of new connections. In each of the three chapters that follow, I show how novelists struggle to conceptualize collectors and authors in much the same way Benjamin would do a century later.

Recording versus creating, fragmentation versus cohesion, antiquity versus novelty—of course, such oppositions cannot bear close investigation. Benjamin himself could not or would not maintain this separation of roles, concluding that "in every collector hides an allegorist, and in every allegorist a collector" (211). Victorian folklore study, which self-avowedly recorded the nation's cultural formation, remained closely related to the novel, which charts "the formative years or spiritual education of one person," a hero who in the Victorian novel tacitly embodies the nation. The modern definition of novel, "a long fictional prose narrative, usually filling one or more volumes and typically representing character and action with some degree of realism and complexity," has inhered since the late seventeenth century. But the older definition of "novel," one that existed into the early twentieth century, erodes the difference between the work of a novelist and a folklorist: "any of a number of tales or stories making up a larger work; a short narrative of this type, a fable." The novel, in other words, is indebted to the collector of fables, the teller of tales. If there is a concerted attack upon the folklore collector in the novel, it is part of a much larger semantic and taxonomic conflict: who was compiling the novel, what was it to encompass, what was its value in use and exchange? Victorian novelists perhaps wished to alter the pejorative associations of the word and its variant, novelty, with uselessness, triviality, cheapness, and, more anciently and damningly, that "innovation in thought or belief" identified as "heresy."[27] But while Victorian novelists may have attempted to wrest the very definition away from the compilers of tales, time and again it is revealed that the two genres are mutually dependent, furtively trysting.

A perhaps predictable instantiation of this conflict can be found in the literary production of antiquarian and folklorist characters. "The antiquarian community," Levine notes, has "been by long tradition the legitimate prey of literary fun, if not derision"[28] in the eighteenth and early nineteenth centuries. In verse, Alexander Pope mocked the antiquarian Thomas Hearne in *The Dunciad*:

> But who is he, in closet close y-pent,
> Of sober face, with learned dust besprent?
> Right well mine eyes arede the myster wight,
> On parchment scraps y-fed, and Wormius hight,
> To future ages may thy dulness last,
> As thou preserv'st the dulness of the past![29]

And Robert Burns poked fun at his antiquarian friend Francis Grose, who had given up the shiny accoutrements of his military career for the detritus of antiquities:

> But now he's quat the spurtle-blade,
>   And dog-skin wallet,
> And taen the—Antiquarian trade,
>   I think they call it.
> He has a fouth o' auld nick-nackets:
> Rusty airn caps and jinglin jackets.[30]

In fiction, Sir Walter Scott created Jonathan Oldbuck, the titular character of *The Antiquary*, whom he treats with affection, but also with some amused contempt for the single-mindedness of his pursuit and the cluttered minutia of his collection.

Victorian fiction added to this long tradition of depicting the collector and his collection alike as dry, abstruse, belated, and laughably fragmented with the characters of Samuel Pickwick and Edward Casaubon. While there is no embodied collector figure in *Jane Eyre*, there is nevertheless a constantly-felt presence of a controlling, editorial hand. This hand may belong to the novel's purported author, Jane Eyre, or to Brontë's pseudonomous Currer Bell. Brontë's title page (*"Jane Eyre*, an Autobiography, Edited by Currer Bell) creates an intriguing parallel fiction in which Bell is the recipient and mediator of the manuscript sent by Jane from her rural seclusion at Ferndean. All three of these novels strive to deflect the similarities between antiquarian collection and novel making. Ultimately, though, these novelists recognize and, to some extent, accept, folk narrative's spellbinding effects.

As Jennifer Schacker has argued, "the very act of reading (fantastic) material marked a transformation of popular literary culture, asserting . . . cultural distance between English readers and the bearers of the narrative traditions about which they read."[31] Taking this into account, perhaps literary exploration of the folklorist marks the novelist's attempt to gain further distance from the collector, and therefore from his informants, the childish, girlish, or savage bearers of the fairy tale. Nevertheless, in the novels that I treat in this section, the fairy tale and its tellers are never far away. It is fascinating to realize that authors as various as Dickens, Brontë, and Eliot all come to the conclusion that to collect is not, ultimately, to contain or control. *Pickwick Papers*, *Jane Eyre*, and *Middlemarch* all experiment with ways in which the unmediated fantastic narrative might well up, break out, and matter forth.

CHAPTER 2

Pickwick Papers and the End of Miscellany

his chapter reexamines Charles Dickens's relationship to the oral source material that he brought into his work. Fairy tale material matters to Dickens, to his sense of novel making, to his pocketbook, to his popularity and populism. It *matters* also in the more troubling sense of purulence; Dickens frequently imagines folk narrative to infect and overwhelm his authored material. Therefore, for Dickens, the differences between telling, collecting, and authoring tales are often ambiguous, and nowhere more so than in his earliest novel, *The Pickwick Papers*.

Pickwick Papers is a difficult book to define and categorize. It was originally commissioned by Chapman and Hall as a series of sporting illustrations by the popular artist Robert Seymour. Dickens was hired (under the name of Boz) to write amusing copy for the engravings. To tie the illustrations together, Dickens conceived of the Pickwick Club, a band of roving antiquarian and folktale collectors, led by Samuel Pickwick. True to the spirit of miscellany, *Pickwick Papers*'s multiplot, fragmentary structure is interpolated with tales, legends, songs, valentines, and, after chapter 10, with Mr. Pickwick's servant Sam's now famous Wellerisms. This material, all written by Dickens, is nevertheless indebted to the form and content of legends, tales, and other folklore found in real antiquarian collections so popular at the time. When Seymour committed suicide in the middle of the serial publication, Dickens's role in the production altered radically: he demanded that he be no longer the ancillary to the illustrator, but the central figure, the author. In its completed state, the book remains a complex thing, interpenetrated by multiple genres.

However, we have historically smoothed over this rich conflict in order to erect a grand narrative of origin around the novel. Critics have suggested that *The Pickwick Papers* is the work in which miscellany collapses and the Victorian novel emerges triumphant.[1] Indeed, it is difficult to see beyond a denigrative reading of the antiquarian in a novel that so unrelentingly picks on Pickwick—where members of the club are robbed, mobbed, shot, swindled, beaten, impounded, sued, and besotted. Then, too, the book's opening pages make a genre shift seem inevitable. In Dickens's conceit, *The Posthumous Papers of the Pickwick Club* are brought to light through the editorial prowess of Boz. Searching "among the multifarious documents" that comprise the "Transactions of the Pickwick Club," he discovers minutes from May 12, 1827, in which the Club, after hearing Samuel Pickwick read his paper on the "Theory of Tittlebats," and sensible of the "benefits which must inevitably result from carrying the speculations of that learned man into the wider field," resolve that a new committee, "The Corresponding Society of the Pickwick Club" be formed. The members of this subcommittee, with Pickwick as chair, are "requested to forward, from time to time, authenticated accounts of their journeys and investigations . . . together with all tales and papers, to which the local scenery or associations may give rise, to the Pickwick Club, stationed in London."[2] From the outset, Dickens's Pickwick Club mimics the antiquarian clubs of the 1820s and '30s, reproducing the miscellaneous and peripatetic nature of antiquarian study, as well as the variety of editorial hands through which material passed. But also from the first, Boz's mocking narrative voice distinguishes itself from antiquarian editorship. Pickwick's essay on "Tittlebats," presumably baby talk for "sticklebacks," suggests the childish nature of antiquarian discovery, while antiquarian wanderings are figured as a form of bloated pleasure seeking, tied intimately to the body of Pickwick himself: "time and feeding had expanded that once romantic form" (17).

Pickwick's eleventh chapter is often cited as the point of departure from the "antiquity" of miscellany to the "novelty" of plot and character. In it, Pickwick finds a rock outside of a cottage reading

+
BILST
UM
PSHI
S. M.
ARK,

and concludes that he "had discovered a strange and curious inscription of unquestionable antiquity" (148). The events that follow constitute the apparent ridicule of antiquarian collection: Pickwick presents his findings to the Royal Antiquarian Society; he writes "a pamphlet, containing 96 pages of very small print, and 27 different readings of the inscription"; and as a result is "elected an honorary member of seventeen native and foreign societies, for making the discovery" (157). However, Pickwick's nemesis, Mr. Blotton, ultimately discovers that the cottager who sold Pickwick the stone carved it himself "to display letters intended to bear neither more nor less than the simple construction of 'Bill Stumps, his mark:' and that Mr. Stumps, being little in the habit of original composition, and more accustomed to be guided by the sounds of words than by the strict rules of orthography, had omitted the concluding 'L' of his Christian name" (157). This evidence notwithstanding, the seventeen learned societies indignantly maintain the stone's antiquity:

> several fresh pamphlets appeared; the foreign learned societies corresponded with the native learned societies, the native learned societies translated the pamphlets of the foreign learned societies into English, the foreign learned societies translated the pamphlets of the native learned societies into all sorts of languages: and thus commenced that celebrated scientific discussion so well known to all men, as the Pickwick controversy. (158)

In constructing this grand debate over a mark that reveals itself to be semi-literate signature rather than ancient hieroglyph, Dickens appears to cast antiquarian fervor as myopic gullibility, through which scholars foolishly cleave to a literally unreadable past.

Moreover, whereas antiquarians are figured as comically naïve, antiquarian miscellanies themselves are associated with tainted commerce. An instance of this occurs when the Club first falls in with Alfred Jingle, that knavish tour guide and hilariously truncated nemesis to Pickwick:

"Magnificent ruin," said Mr. Augustus Snodgrass, with all the poetic fervor that distinguished him, when they came in sight of the fine old castle.

"What a subject for an antiquarian," were the very words which fell from Mr. Pickwick's mouth. . . .

"Ah! Fine place," said the stranger, "glorious pile—frowning walls—tottering arches—dark nooks—crumbling staircases—old cathedral too—earthy smell—pilgrims feet worn away the old steps—little Saxon doors—confessionals like money-takers' boxes at theaters—queer customers those monks—Popes and Lord Treasurers, and all sorts of old fellows, with great red faces, and broken noses, turning up every day . . . fine place—old legends too—strange stories—capital." (29)

Jingle's summation of an antiquarian "subject" is riddled with economic language, from confessionals as money-takers' boxes to the monks as "customers" to the pairing of Popes and Lord Treasurers.[3] On one level, Jingle undermines the romance of castle and cathedral with a reminder that the medieval church was a commercial enterprise. But with his elision of "strange stories" and "capital," Jingle's speech—which is itself fragmented like an antiquarian volume—also voices the prevalent opinion that antiquarians capitalized upon the popular fondness for nostalgia.

Though *Pickwick Papers* also begins as a miscellany, Dickens's narrator slyly undermines the editorial and transcriptive function of the collector of antiquities:

We are merely endeavoring to discharge in an upright manner, the responsible duties of our editorial functions; and whatever ambition we might have felt under other circumstances, to lay claim to the authorship of these adventures, a regard for truth forbids us to do more, than claim the merit of their judicious arrangement, and impartial narration. The Pickwick papers are our New River Head; and we may be compared to the New River Company. The labors of others have raised for us a reservoir of important facts. We merely lay them on, and communicate them, in a clear and gentle stream, through the medium of these numbers, to a world thirsting for Pickwickian knowledge. (58)

It is a treacherous passage, and not only because its author purports to serve as "impartial" editor to a defunct antiquarian club. The New River Company was one of the suppliers of water to London in the early nineteenth century. Mark Wormald notes that cholera epidemics of the 1830s and '40s proved that no water company "supplied the fresh and healthy water they promised."[4] In Dickens's analogy, to "thirst" for antiquarian knowledge is to risk contamination at the hands of those who collect it and sell it for financial gain.

The tale oft told among critics is that after the stone is exposed as a fraudulent relic of antiquity, the fragmentary Jingle is exiled, replaced with Sam Weller, a raconteur working for and not against Pickwick, the interpolated material—tales, songs, legends, and confessions—scattered through the early chapters gradually falls away into the realism of the Fleet episode, and the Victorian realist novel emerges to dance upon the bones of miscellany. To be fair, critics thought they saw this transition in part because Dickens himself suggested he was making it. In the 1837 preface, Dickens is careful to explain that "the machinery of the club" was not his idea, that it "tended rather to his embarrassment," and that therefore "he gradually abandoned it" (6). The preface carefully constructs *Pickwick Papers*'s evolution. What was once edited by Boz is now introduced as "the author's object" (xi); what the dedication calls a "book" (5) the preface calls "a novel" (6). From now on, Dickens seems to insist, antiquarians shall transcribe miscellany, and novelists shall draw emplotted narratives from their own creative stores.

As I suggest in the introduction to this book, Dickens frequently reverts to an evolutionary model of fairy tales. For instance, about halfway through *Our Mutual Friend* the tenuous partnership between Mr. Venus, the collector and articulator of skeletons, and Mr. Wegg, the one-legged ballad salesman, hangs by a thread. The two have spent countless nights searching a dust heap for blackmail material. Perhaps not unlike the reader, Dickens intimates, Mr. Venus is weary of scooping and sifting a giant mass in search of valuable minutia. When he suggests disbanding, his pecuniary partner Wegg makes the following observation: "Rome, brother . . . a city which (it may not be generally known) originated in twins and a wolf and ended in Imperial marble: wasn't built in a day."[5] Here the ballad collector condenses Roman history to a trajectory from its folkloric beginnings to its defunct empire. It is a true Weggian turn, like Jingle at once comically amputated and wickedly apt. The legend of Romulus and Remus suckled by a wolf narrativizes a civilization nursed by tales and legends. The end of this civilization is marked by crumbled fragments of its art dispersed into the museums of new empires, or dug up by antiquarians from ancient earthworks. In a novel that fishes the fragments of legends, tales, proverbs, ballads, and nursery rhymes from the current of literary history and "pretty well papers the room" with them, or rearticulates them into skeletons, or retailors them into dolls' dresses or bequeaths them anew or in other ways shores them against our ruins, Wegg's Roman analogy reminds us of *Our Mutual Friend*'s self-proclaimed positioning within a cultural trajectory. But it also signals that Dickens, like many nineteenth-century authors, wished to view folk narrative as a developmental stage whereby artists lose their enchantment with fairy tales, a bereavement, but nevertheless necessary to artistic, and indeed national, progress.

Dickens publicly disavowed the social currency of the fairy tale—at least in the hands of other authors. In "Frauds on the Fairies" (1853), Dickens excoriates fairy tales altered and manipulated for political aims (most especially George Cruikshank's then-recent volume of temperance tales). Calling fairy narratives "the nurseries of fancy," he concludes: "The world is too much with us, early and late. Leave this precious old escape from it, alone."[6] In a letter to a friend, he proclaimed fairy tales as "beautiful little stories, which are so tenderly and humanly useful to us in these times when the world is too much with us, early and late."[7] In these nods to Wordsworth, Dickens signals a Romantic separation of past and present, serious and slender reading.

One might point out that, Alice-like, Dickens gave himself advice, but very seldom followed it, considering the extent to which he himself manipulated fairy tale plots to his own ends. In determining what constitutes "tender use," Dickens often meditated upon the problem of literary originality by discussing possible differences between theft and what we might call squatter's rights—the claim upon another's object that is not so much theft as productive repurposing. For instance, when dramatist William Thomas Moncrieff produced a theatrical version of *Nicholas Nickleby* (1838–1839) before Dickens had finished writing it, and an irate Dickens denounced the work, Moncrieff returned fire and accused Dickens of his own plagiarisms.[8] The next number of *Nickleby* involved the hero in debate with a dramatist, in which Nicholas admits "that Shakespeare derived some of his plots from old tales and legends in general circulation" but concludes: "whereas he brought within the magic circle of his genius, traditions peculiarly adapted for his purpose, and turned familiar things into constellations which should enlighten the world for ages, you drag within the magic circle of your dullness, subjects not at all adapted to the purposes of the stage, and debase the exalted."[9] In this interpretation, "old tales and legends" are "traditions peculiarly adapted" for appropriation because they are perceived to be both authorless and genreless. They belong to no one and are thus available to anyone. But Nicholas's assertion begs a question: if tales and legends are "peculiarly adapted" to fit into other genres, then just what *is* the fairy tale, and just what does it do to the genre it inhabits?

Critics have tended to decide that Dickens's folkloric plots are merely meant to elicit recollections of the childish imagination, as sentimental interruptions to his social commentary. To provide a single instance, Robert Alter, in his book dedicated to the mutual encroaching of fantasy and realism in Dickens's work, briefly notes the author's "fairy-tale perspective," but concludes, "I would prefer to give that notion a little more edge by suggesting that Dickens repeatedly exercises a faculty of *archaic vision* in which what meets the eye in the contemporary scene triggers certain primal fears and fantasies."[10] As these chapters will show, Dickens's fairy tale plots are plenty edgy. But Alter's paradox can be explained in his subsequent commentary: "the originality and fecundity of the metaphoric imagination constitute one of the chief reasons that [Dickens] is a law unto himself as a novelist, with no really convincing imitators. . . . Dickens's metaphors and similes are vividly original, often startling, and give the impression of being struck off in the white heat of improvisation."[11] Alter, like so many other critics, seeks to preserve Dickens's originality; to accept that the author deliberately, painstakingly, appropriated mature narratives long in existence threatens that idyll. To imagine him instead tapping into a primal fount of inchoate emotion, driven there by his own scorching vision, preserves the cult of literary genius. Alter's image reiterates the Romantic and Victorian burial of folklore in a necessarily receding past. In other words, we have been wont to read Dickens's use of folk narrative in spite of, not in terms of, his social politics.[12] By contrast, I contend that, belying his own irritable response to Cruikshank, fantastic narratives not only inhabit but supply the language of Dickens's social realism.

For, as frequently as Dickens miniaturizes these "beautiful little stories" and "bright little books,"[13] he just as often reveals a voltaic sense of the terrible and enduring power in folk narratives. Behind every claim staked by the "magic circle" of authorial genius, there lies a dreadful and titillating uncertainty of who or what wields narrative control when tales are appropriated into literature. For instance, in "Nurse's Stories" the Uncommercial Traveler remembers the "utterly impossible places and people, but none the less alarmingly real—that I found I had been introduced to by my nurse before I was six years old. . . . If we all knew our own minds . . . I suspect that we should find our nurses responsible for most of the dark corners we are forced to go back to, against our wills."[14] In this story, Dickens's own nurse, Mary Weller, is recollected as "a female bard—descended, possibly, from those terrible old Scalds who seemed to have existed for the express purpose of addling the brains of mankind when they begin to investigate languages" (93). This "bard"

> made a standing pretense which greatly assisted in forcing me back to a number of hideous places that I would by all means have avoided. This pretense was, that all her ghost stories had occurred to her own relations. Politeness toward a meritorious family, therefore forbad my doubting them, and they acquired an air of authentication that impaired my digestive powers for life. (93–94)

It is, therefore, not exactly the nurse herself who terrifies the boy who would become author, but rather the legacy bestowed on her as a tale teller whose purpose is to obscure the difference between reality and invention.

Significantly, Dickens describes his response to "the dark corners" as equal parts horror and erotic *frisson:* in the story of Captain Murderer, "an offshoot of the Bluebeard family" (89), who cuts off his brides' heads and bakes them into pies, the Captain's "horses were milk-white horses with one red spot on the back. . . . And the spot was young bride's blood. (To this terrific point I am indebted for my first personal experience of a shudder and cold beads on the forehead)" (89).[15] Likewise, at the climax of the tale of the shipwright who sells his soul to the devil and is plagued by rats ever after, "a special cascade of rats was rolling down my back, and the whole of my small listening person was overrun with them. At intervals ever since, I have been morbidly afraid of my own pocket, lest my exploring hand should find a specimen or two of those vermin in it" (92). This welling up of rats exemplifies folk narrative "mattering" in the darkest sense of the word. Dickens's sweaty, guilty terror arises in part from the ambiguous part he plays in the tale's creation: do the dark corners come from his exploring hand in his own pocket, from a working-class woman's imagination, or from no discernable authority at all? It is the "air of authentication that impaired [Dickens's] digestive powers for life," and no wonder: tales, those persistently oral things, trouble the certainty of consumer and consumed.

Dickens's oscillation between these two ideas of oral tradition, one serving only as touchwood and the other mattering deeply, exists in some measure in all of his novels. And I would argue that it is this tension, and not its resolution, that is announced in *Pickwick Papers.* In doing so, I join recent criticism recognizing that orality in *Pickwick Papers* is not a state to be gotten through, but a vital component in defining Dickens's oeuvre.[16] For instance, Robert Patten has recently argued that critics should not term the tales, legends, and manuscripts scattered throughout *Pickwick*

Papers "interpolated," which, Patten says, wrongly explains away *Pickwick*'s phantasmagoria as idiosyncratic. (I would also point out that "interpolation" carries the pejorative associations of adulteration, or inserting spurious matter into a genuine work.) Rather, Patten argues, these tales are "intercalated"; that is, interstratified, or interbedded, organically a part of *Pickwick Papers*.¹⁷ Indeed, in the oldest meaning of the word, to intercalate was to insert additional days in the calendar in order to bring the current reckoning of time into harmony with the natural solar year. *Pickwick Papers* introduced additions, in other words, perhaps not of irritant foreign matter, but of differences brought into harmony. Meredith McGill has noted that the most frequently excerpted portion of *Pickwick Papers* (in magazines, scrapbooks, anthologies, folklore collections, and periodical literature) was the imbedded material. Given the extraordinary commodification of *Pickwick Papers,* it is important that its most lucrative extractions emphasized (in McGill's terms) "the variety of genres that are held in a tense solution" in *Pickwick Papers*.¹⁸ Knowing this, one is hard-pressed to disentangle what "genuine" or "original" means in this context, and what can be deemed of most "value" in this novel.

As I suggested in the introduction to part 1, Dickens participates in the broader tendency of nineteenth-century novelists to displace onto the antiquarian and folklore collector uncomfortable perceptions about writing as an occupation: that it is at once solipsistic and self-dispersing, that it is by definition retrospective, that it is a form under the influence of other voices, that it is grounded in economic concerns. But though Dickens himself signaled that *Pickwick Papers* marked the end of collection and the beginning of creation, I find everywhere evidence of the commonality, the communality, of the novelist, the folklore collector, and the tale teller. One example can be found in the character of Sam Weller, mouthy servant and popular hero, the former bootblack whom Mr. Pickwick hired away from a London inn. The memorable scene in which Sam draws a popular audience and occasions bursts of disruptive laughter in a courtroom turns upon defiance of the written word:

> "What is your name, Sir?" enquired the Judge.
> "Sam Weller, my Lord," replied that gentleman.
> "Do you spell it with a 'V' or a 'W'?" enquired the Judge.
> "That depends upon the taste and fancy of the speller, my Lord," replied Sam, "I never had occasion to spell it more than once or twice in my life, but I spells it with a 'V.'" Here a voice in the gallery [Sam's father Tony] exclaimed aloud, "Quite right too, Samivel; quite right. Put it down a we, my Lord, put it down a we." (463)

In *Dickens and the Popular Radical Imagination*, Sally Ledger cites this scene as evidence that Sam's popularity depends upon his oral mediation.[19] In other words, Sam doesn't write the name Weller, he speaks it, but if he *were* to write it, he would put it down a "we." We for Weller links Sam's orality to the larger spirit of collectivity in the novel, and this fact makes the courtroom scene echo the Bil Stumps episode in unexpected ways. "Mr. Stumps, being little in the habit of original composition, and more accustomed to be guided by the sounds of words than by the strict rules of orthography, had omitted the concluding 'L' of his Christian name" (157). Alex Woloch has argued that, like Sam Weller's spelling, this is another moment when orality makes a triumphant mark in the text.[20] I agree, for if Bil stumps, Sam wells: both names signify upon the confounding and overwhelming power of the oral over the written. If this is so, then what at first appears to be a major blow to antiquarian collection (Mr. Blotton's inky blot on folklore) is in fact every bit the thrilling discovery Pickwick thinks he has made: "original composition" bows down before the "we" of antiquarian collectivity. If we look carefully, we see that Bil Stumps's mark at the top of the inscription is not a cross, but a plus. Put it down a "we."

The additivity of the novelist, the collector, and the tale teller is again expressed in an "intercalation" occurring soon after Pickwick hires Sam. Pickwick falls sick, and Sam nurses him through by telling him stories. When the other Pickwickians come to visit, "Mr. Pickwick, with sundry blushes, produced the following little tale, as having been 'edited' by himself, during his recent indisposition, from his notes of Mr. Weller's unsophisticated recital" (229). The story is "The Parish Clerk: a Tale of True Love," featuring protagonist Nathaniel Pipkin. Pickwick's blushes, the suspicious quotes around "edited," and the clerk (a writerly figure with a name that picks up the homophonic register of Samuel, Pickwick, and Dickens) all erode the boundaries of collector, author, and teller.

This slight incident points to other Pickwickian fungibles. In naming master and man Samuel, Dickens upsets the received hierarchies of collector and teller. This is especially significant because Sam Weller shares a last name with another storyteller, Dickens's nurse, Mary Weller, memorialized as "Mercy" in "Nurse's Stories." As J. Hillis Miller has pointed out, Wellerisms materialize in the space between oral and literary, legend and history, speech act and written word. They co-opt the tragic themes of mortality and desire and mingle them with the hilarity of the folkloric episodes.[21] Sam's Wellerisms are as full of sex and violence as Mary Weller's tales, as liable to threaten bodily harm to fair maidens and small boys. For instance: "Nothing so refreshing as sleep sir, as the servant-girl said afore she drank the egg-cupful o' laudanum" (213). "Now we look compact and comfortable, as the father said ven he cut off his little boy's head, to cure him o'squintin" (370). "I only assisted natur', ma'am; as the doctor said to the boy's mother, arter he bled him to death" (629). "I think he's the wictim of connubiality, as Blue Beard's domestic chaplain said, with a tear of pity, ven he buried him" (269). Through suicidal servant girls, to decapitated and exsanguinated schoolboys, to the recurrence of the "Blue Beard" tale, Dickens links the nurse to the "boots." In his fiction, both are subversive servant figures, infectants from whom folk matter, a substance as fundamental as breast milk or shoe blacking, oozes into the narrative.

Like Mary Weller, Sam Weller's character foregrounds the question of originality and authority. When one of Sam's more risqué Wellerisms ("That's what I call a self-evident proposition, as the dog's-meat man said, when the housemaid told him he warn't a gentleman" [293]) causes the offense of Pickwick's new gentleman acquaintance, Pickwick hastens to aver that Sam is "not exactly a friend": "The fact is, he is my servant, but I allow him to take a good many liberties; for, between ourselves, I flatter myself he is an original, and I am rather proud of him" (293). But Dickens knows that Sam is the very reverse of original: the Wellerism is an ancient proverbial form that Dickens has borrowed.[22] And Dickens also knows that whether or not the author allows it, the storyteller will "take . . . liberties" in the text. Mary and Sam Weller: two servants, then, both seemingly descended from the "terrible old Scalds" who addl[e] the brains of mankind" by forcing them to return to the "dark corners." As in "Nurse's Stories," Pickwick's servant is a subtly threatening, erotic force in the novel, the locus where stories come welling up: not exactly a friend, and merciless to middle-class discomfort, to cold beads on the forehead or personal shudders.

Whereas young Nicholas Nickleby knows, with utter confidence, the difference between plagiarism and communal composition, *Pickwick Papers* is less certain of demarcations between authors and the folk. Ultimately, the novel acknowledges, and occasionally even revels in the knowledge, that novels are heavily trafficked spaces. The narrator reflects, for instance, that

> there still remain some half dozen old inns, which have preserved their external features unchanged, and which have escaped alike the rage for public improvement, and the encroachments of private speculation. Great rambling, queer, old places they are, with galleries, and passages, and stair cases, wide enough and antiquated enough, to furnish materials for a hundred ghost stories, supposing we should ever be reduced to the lamentable necessity of inventing any, and that the world should exist long enough to exhaust the innumerable veracious legends connected with old London Bridge. (129)

Inns, like novels, are nodal points. They occupy a space between public improvement and private speculation. Both are places of commercial and gratis entertainment. They are situated at a crossroads between the written word and the oral tale, for stories come in, and the post goes out, and the two cross-pollinate within its walls. Their passages are antiquated, and haunted, but furnish forth new matter, too. In *Pickwick Papers,* this inn instigates the real, mutual debt between oral and literary, for it is where Pickwick collects Sam Weller.

Pickwick's parting speech underscores this mutuality, and therefore reads like a précis to the rest of Dickens's oeuvre:

> I shall never regret having devoted the greater part of two years to mixing with different varieties and shades of human character: frivolous as my pursuit of *novelty* may have appeared to many. Nearly the whole of my previous life having been devoted to business and the pursuit of wealth, numerous scenes of which I had no previous conception have dawned upon me—I hope to the enlargement of my mind. (749, emphasis added)

Pickwick's pursuit of novelty has been Dickens's too, and at the end of *this* novel (which so many have fixed as the beginning of *all* novels), his definition of novelty is achieved *through* phantasmagoric collection, not in spite of it. In fact, in the 1847 preface, Dickens acknowledges the thin line between tale and novel: "in the course of the last dozen years, I have seen various accounts of the origin of these Pickwick Papers; which have, at all events, possessed—for me—the charm of perfect novelty" (760). Perfect novelty: on one hand, a wry comment that the narrative of Pickwick's origins didn't originate with Dickens. More profoundly, though, the statement suggests that perfect novelty is a communal effort. Dickens's formal practice of "intercalation" may have ceased (trickling to a stop in *Pickwick Papers,* attempted and then quickly aborted in *Nicholas Nickleby* and *The Old Curiosity Shop*), but his use of folk narrative did not. If anything, as Dickens's career progressed, he became more dependent upon fairy material—the rat in the pocket, the welling forth of matter—not as a counterpoint to his realism, but as an inextricable part of it. The tensions between storytelling and novel composition persist throughout Dickens's oeuvre, as he uneasily ponders to what extent he is indebted to both the "bright little books" and the "dark corners" for his own authorial powers, in which he avers that "things pass away, like a tale that is told,"[23] yet tells those tales again and still again, unearthing and re-minting them as Victorian coin.

CHAPTER 3

The Natural History of Thornfield

Jane Eyre begins with a reading of Bewick's *Birds of Britain*, an act of curiosity—and a curious volume—that triggers passionate, recurring discourses upon women's imagination, authority, and self-determination. Banished from the Reed family circle, solitary Jane heads for the bookshelf. There she "possessed herself of a volume," a reflexive verb comparing self-possession to book selection.[1] "Shrined in double retirement" (that is, wrapped in the window seat curtain, and rapt in a book), she thrills to Bewick's descriptions of "solitary rocks and promontories," "death-white realms" and "forlorn regions of dreary space" (14). Part of Jane's enjoyment lies in her fledgling attempts to decipher this natural history.

And to be sure, Bewick's *Birds* is a weird book. Its vignettes, the small illustrations at the end of each chapter that Bewick called "tailpieces" and, sometimes, "tale pieces,"[2] have little or nothing to do with birds. Presumably, they offer scenes of country life, but they are the very reverse of picturesque. They depict graveyards, shipwrecks, public hangings, suicides, projectile vomiting, monkeys tending fires, monsters waylaying travelers, and goblin pursuit. "Each picture," as Jane says, "told a story, mysterious often to my undeveloped understanding and imperfect feelings, yet profoundly interesting" (15), though they are also, Jane acknowledges, "objects of terror." Like all natural histories, Bewick's *Birds* combines scientific and romantic narrative; in Bewick, romantic narrative is mainly presented as visual tableaux of Gothic grotesqueries. Both kinds of narrative—visual and written—create in Jane a thrill of simultaneous longing and repulsion; this exchange between natural and preternatural subjects, between written word and told story, will continue to draw and challenge Jane throughout the novel. Indeed, Jane arguably echoes this earliest of literary influences through her very artistic production—both her semiautobiographical drawing and painting, and her retrospective reimagining of herself as a narrator.

But just as Jane begins to master this reading material, enter cousin John, who insists that she call him Master Reed, proclaims her a "dependant" and a beggar, and flings her book at her head. In this bloody altercation for possession—of the written word, of privacy, of one's very self—the natural history emerges as a site of contention for female authority (as the very name Master Re[a]d suggests). *Jane Eyre* came of age in the age of natural history, a form that, like this novel, is equally devoted to discourses of self-making and narrative control. In this chapter I argue that Brontë draws upon and responds to the formal and authorial concerns of the natural history in the architecture of *Jane Eyre,* at least those aspects of the natural history that fuse scientific realism with fantastic narrative.

Charlotte Brontë had an abiding interest in natural history. To best friend Ellen Nussey she recommended the reading of Gilbert White, Bewick, and Oliver Goldsmith as a pleasure on par with the literature of Shakespeare and Sir Walter Scott.[3] As I suggested in Chapter 1, the English bildungsroman reached maturity alongside the natural history, and shares narrative traits with it, like the successful economic and social development of a first-person narrator, and the minute observations of an individual in particularized physical locations. However, simultaneously, Brontë could hardly have failed to notice that collectors and producers of natural histories portrayed their publications as not only an evolutionary but also a masculinizing endeavor. As Hardy's "Tryst" suggests, such studies often metaphorized their subjects as a female body. Antiquarian Charles Roach Smith asserted that, to the antiquary, "every relic which he picks up or secures, is pregnant with instruction."[4] Andrew Lang feminized the process of narration and transmission. Tales, he says, are ancient, first told by "naked savage women to naked savage children."[5] Barbara Gates notes that the study of natural history was imagined as a romance or grand passion: "Adoration . . . came to the beholder through the sense of sight." And though Gates argues that this "romance with nature cut across class and gender barriers,"[6] and while women certainly participated in antiquarian and natural historian endeavors, they were formally excluded from those institutions, since women could not join the Royal Societies.[7]

The natural history, then, presented a hybrid form, in that it blended scientific and romantic narrative, and also in that it was at least partially democratizing: both middle- and working-class writers could successfully author and publish natural history. But like all early ethnographic work, the natural history simultaneously discouraged female producers, and erected a hierarchy between subject and observer. Successful production of the genre depended upon the narrative opposition in which civilized male observer encounters queer, or quaint subjects, and, in describing them, feminizes, captures, and contains them. Brontë is writing into this formal and generic complexity with the very narratological apparatus of *Jane Eyre*.

On the one hand, Jane's "autobiographical" production often approximates that of the natural history: Jane's investigative eye (which we might also call her investigative "I") similarly seeks both intense connection to and objectifying distance from its natural and cultural subjects. In her insistence, with increasing intensity throughout the novel, "I was a lady" (179), and in her often bitter commentary upon the intellects of those approximating her own class, employment, or social situation (characters like Adele, Mrs. Fairfax, and Grace Poole), Jane, "poor, obscure, plain and little" (284), defines herself through writerly powers that elevate her from the regions and classes she describes.

To be sure, Jane resists being associated with the fantastic material she records. She shrinks away from the spoken word, narrative, and outburst, for she associates orality with ungovernable and eruptive desires. Beginning with the title page of the novel's first edition, *Jane Eyre* produces layers of mediation between an editor's hand and a young woman's mouth. Brontë's initial title page, which reads "*Jane Eyre*, an Autobiography, Edited by Currer Bell," creates an intriguing parallel fiction in which Bell is the recipient of the manuscript sent by Jane from her rural seclusion at Ferndean. As with the natural histories of White, Miller, or Bray, Jane sends her raw materials—that is, the manuscript of *Jane Eyre*—from a marginally civilized periphery to an authorizing center (London, perhaps, or Edinburgh) where they are subjected to a firm editorial hand. The words "*Jane Eyre*, an autobiography, edited by Currer Bell," suggests a masculine hand hovering over Jane's narrative, ordering and mediating its production. Taken one way, the title page lends the appearance of collusion between editor Bell and narrator Jane in ordering and categorizing Jane the character's oral eruptions.

In thus apprehending Brontë's Jane as facets of character, narrator and editor, I join critics like Robyn Warhol, James Buzard, and Carla Caplan, who account for Jane's torsions between feeling and thinking, and between speaking and writing, by arguing for a distinction in *Jane Eyre* between protagonist and narrator. Warhol explains this as the difference between the Jane who narrates and the Jane who acts.[8] For Kaplan, these distinctions are a problem of reading as much as writing, and she asks us to consider "how we might view and understand Jane's evolution into a writer who, like Brontë, must assess her narration to [a] very heterogeneous . . . public.[9] The novel, says Kaplan, early and often establishes Jane's love of narration.[10] We see this affinity in her fascination with Bewick, in her hunger for and terror of nurse Bessie's stories, and in her attaching herself to her storytelling school friend Mary Ann Wilson, who has "a turn for narrative" (91). Buzard, alive to the contest between oral and written narration in *Jane Eyre,* contends that understanding intersubjectivity in the novel "means actualizing, through the resources distinctive to narrative—chiefly the relationships between-discourse-and story-spaces, silent print and evoked voices—the powers distinctive to Englishness as a 'heterogeneous thing.'"[11] He notes that "[t]he general tendency in *Jane Eyre* is to move from the domain of voice to authorship and print, and then, jarringly, back through voice again."[12]

The novel, then, records Jane's oscillation between observer and subject, between detached recorder of her environment, and impassioned informant against that environment. Buzard ultimately decides that "Brontë makes Jane's writing an instrument for containing and even breaking off the flow of Jane the character's speech." Brontë's goal, Buzard says, is to "align the relationship between writing and speech with that between past powerlessness and present authority."[13] It is, finally, "Jane the narrator's regular practice to subject her earlier and now-self-quoted outbursts to the countervailing effort to frame and control them, to keep the indignant voice, however just its cause, from having uncontested sway."[14]

Indeed, Jane's embattled position with both Rochester and St. John Rivers is due in part to her refusal to speak, to become their oral informant. As Rochester seeks to divine Jane, he examines her artistic productions, the work of her hands, but is perplexed as to how to interpret them. He therefore attempts to coax her to commit herself verbally: "it would please me now to draw you out: to learn more of you—therefore speak" (151).

Moreover, the word *novel* is used twice as a description for Jane and her history. In Rochester's retrospective narrative of Jane's existence at Thornfield, he describes her *"novel* and piquant acquaintance" (353, emphasis added). When St. John Rivers recounts his own investigations into Jane's history, he tells her, "Before commencing, it is but fair to warn you that the story will sound somewhat hackneyed in your ears; but stale details often regain a degree of freshness when they pass through new lips. For the rest, whether trite or *novel*, it is short" (424, emphasis added). Brontë evidently differentiates between being a novelist and being novel material for the fascinated perusal of others. Jane strives for writerly mastery, to resist the attempts to make her novel through a man's narrativizing gaze.

When Jane verbally rebels, she is conscious of being "out of herself" and recalls, "I don't very well know what I did with my hands" (17). By contrast, the painting she learns at Lowood, symptomatic of the self-control she learns there too, she calls "all the work of my own hands" (87). To write, then, is to know what one's hands are doing.

However, like Warhol, and in contrast to Buzard, I ultimately believe that Brontë routinely undoes the binaries she herself establishes of Jane the speaker and Jane the writer. In locating moments of simultaneity, where the "narrator's consciousness remains in the realm of realism, and the character's departs for the precincts of Gothic romance,"[15] Warhol concludes that Jane the actor cannot be permanently contained by Jane the writer. I concur with Warhol in seeing compelling evidence of narratological effects, which, though "contributed by the narrating self, mirror the . . . state of mind of the experiencing self."[16]

There are, for example, two passages in the novel that exist in the present tense; these are commonly agreed to mark places where Jane the character and Jane the writer momentarily collide. These are moments when Jane the author calls attention to the work in her (and our) hands, for both are bits of narrative surrounding a purse. The first occurs in the drawing room at Thornfield, where a tortured Jane is made to sit with the affluent ladies and gentlemen of Rochester's house party: "I try to concentrate my attention on those netting-needles, on the meshes of the purse I am forming—I wish to think only of the work I have in my hands" (197). The second takes place two days after Jane flees Thornfield to escape the discovery of Bertha Mason: "I am alone. At this moment I discover that I forgot to take my parcel out of the pocket of the coach, where I had placed it for safety; there it remains, there it must remain; and now, I am absolutely destitute" (362). These handbags reflect a kind of self-support. The first, the linked purse Jane "is forming" is a genteel occupation that Jane exercises to retain self-control. The second, the purse Jane loses, contains her wages as a governess. As moments translated into the present tense, they conflate the labor (both artistic and salaried) of character Jane with that of author Jane, and thus signify upon the newly genteel and lucrative act of writing. However, because both events represent failures in self-mastery for Jane, a failure to maintain her composure and her wages respectively, they also underscore Brontë's awareness of the tenuous position that writing women held, especially when those women invited in fantastic narratives.

Engaging with fantastic narratives means accessing a vast, vivid body of oral source material located outside of the writer, and beyond his or her control. And though various critics have claimed that Jane Eyre allegorizes a particular folkloric source—for instance Bluebeard, Cinderella, or fairy legends[17]—in fact, Brontë's fantastic references are too numerous and varied to be able to claim just one as her primary source. Rather, I would suggest, *Jane Eyre* more closely resembles the natural history in its widespread collection and interpolation of the fantastic. Rochester's uncanny gypsy fortune-telling scene, Jane's dream signs, visitations from ghosts, moon goddesses, vampires, and fairies, Rochester's psychic scream that reaches Jane across England: as in the natural history, fantastic, Gothic, and preternatural narratives triangulate with scenes of nature and human nature in *Jane Eyre*.

The Red Room mirror reflects back to Jane an uncanny self: "the strange little figure there gazing at me, with a white face and arms specking the gloom, and glittering eyes of fear moving where all else was still, had the effect of a real spirit: I thought it like one of the tiny phantoms, half fairy, half imp, Bessie's evening stories represented" (21–22). Years later, Rochester also associates Jane with the fairy folk: at their first meeting, he asks her if she was waiting for her "people . . . the men in green" (139). He calls her paintings "elfish" (144) and herself "sprite," "elf," and "changeling" (307). But Jane avers that fairies "all forsook England a hundred years ago . . . " (139). And perhaps because of this, Jane's self-description as "fairy" is tinged with fear and loathing: to call her "fairy" is to dismiss her from modern, civilized England, and place her in a natural, even pastoral, but brutalized, setting. I would argue that Jane's terror in the Red Room is triggered in part by the "half fairy, half imp" she sees when she looks in the mirror. For it is only through this mirror image that the mysterious light on her wall becomes uncanny in the Freudian sense.

> At this moment a light gleamed on the wall. Was it, I asked myself, a ray from the moon penetrating some aperture in the blind? No; moonlight was still, and this stirred; while I gazed, it glided up to the ceiling and quivered . . . prepared as my mind was for horror, shaken as my nerves were by agitation, I thought the swift darting beam was a herald of some coming

> vision from another world. My heart beat thick, my head grew hot; a sound filled my ears, which I deemed the rushing of wings. (24)

Jane fears being haunted, not by something other, but by something sympathetic to herself—something too like the "uncongenial alien" (24) she sees in the mirror.

It is this same resonance with the preternatural that turns Rochester's gypsy disguise from a merely weird practical joke into a near-identity crisis for Jane.

> Where was I? Did I wake or sleep? Had I been dreaming? Did I dream still? The old woman's voice had changed: her accent, her gesture, and all were familiar to me as my own face in a glass—as the speech of my own tongue. I got up, but did not go. I looked; I stirred the fire, and I looked again: but she drew her bonnet and her bandage closer about her face, and again beckoned me to depart. The flame illuminated her hand stretched out: roused now, and on the alert for discoveries, I at once noticed that hand. It was no more the withered limb of eld than my own; it was a rounded supple member, with smooth fingers, symmetrically turned. (227)

This familiarity, I would argue, is not that of a woman recognizing her beloved's eyes, hands, and tongue. Rather, Rochester's guise as a (cultural stereotype of a) gypsy reflects Jane to herself—socially marginal, itinerate, hirable, but also able to harness uncanny forces to observe and judge.

These mirroring episodes famously crescendo in the moment that Jane first sees Bertha Mason.

> "She took my veil from its place; she held it up, gazed at it long, and then she threw it over her own head, and turned to the mirror. At that moment I saw the reflection of the visage and features quite distinctly in the dark oblong glass."
>
> "And how were they?"
>
> "Fearful and ghastly to me—oh, sir, I never saw a face like it! It was a discoloured face—it was a savage face. I wish I could forget the roll of the red eyes and the fearful blackened inflation of the lineaments!"
>
> "Ghosts are usually pale, Jane."
>
> "This, sir, was purple: the lips were swelled and dark; the brow furrowed: the black eyebrows widely raised over the bloodshot eyes. Shall I

tell you of what it reminded me? . . . Of the foul German spectre—the Vampyre." (317)

Of course, Jane first sees Bertha's face in the mirror in Jane's own wedding clothes; and while many critics have linked this moment to the Red Room, few have commented on the other connections here, in which fantastic figures intervene in scenes of psychological realism.

The fairy, the gypsy, the spectral vampire: all of these figures in one way or another appear in the mirror as aspects of Jane's seething interior; all of these moments in one way or another describe Jane's "secret soul" (166). On the one hand, these uncanny episodes point to the larger body of folk material surrounding the novel. Linking Jane to this tradition allies her to the figural vigor and narrative power embedded within the genre—the power to represent. On the other, as these examples reveal, Jane fears that her uncanny experiences identify her with the "savage" natural and preternatural subject, rather than with the natural historian's mastering gaze. Jane's attention to the play of firelight and moonlight upon eyes, hands, and mouths in these scenes reflects Brontë's novel as a contested space, a place where fantastic and realist—oral and written—narratives actively vie for control.

Mrs. Reed characterizes Jane's resistance as "breaking out all fire"—a confrontation that culminates in Jane crying out "in a savage, high voice." The Jane who acts exults in her outburst, while Jane the narrator emphasizes the wasting results of her rage: "A ridge of lighted heath, alive, glancing, devouring, would have been a meet emblem of my mind when I accused and menaced Mrs. Reed; the same ridge, black and blasted after the flames are dead, would have represented as meetly my subsequent condition, when half-an-hour's silence and reflection had shown me the madness of my conduct" (47). For Jane the writer, to *speak* is to be a blasted, savage, natural landscape. Attempting to control this overweening impulse, Jane once more approaches the bookshelf, and her choice is telling: "I would fain exercise some better faculty than that of fierce speaking; fain find nourishment for some less fiendish feeling . . . I took a book—some Arabian tales; I sat down and endeavoured to read. I could make no sense of the subject; my own thoughts swam always between me and the page" (47). Jane has opened the *Arabian Nights* tales; as I discussed in the introduction to this book, the work is composed of material collected from the "barbaric" peripheries to English soil during the height of the eighteenth-century antiquary and natural history craze. We might therefore expect to see the work have salutary effects upon Jane, since it is an exemplar of the oral contained by the literary. Nevertheless, the *Arabian Nights* proved untamable. The proliferation of translations and variants rendered impossible an "authoritative" text. And it is important to remember that its bawdy, violent, and grotesque content filled Samuel Taylor Coleridge "with a strange mixture of obscure dread and intense desire."[18] In fact, this volume cannot coax Jane into a less "fiendish," less fantastic, and more orderly frame of mind, and no wonder: her own interiority swims in the space between her eyes and the page. Because her reading of the tales follows the battle over *Bewick's Birds*, Jane's "savagery" is literally bookended by natural history and antiquarian reading.

Ultimately, Jane the character cannot or will not resist entanglement in the hybrid space between natural and fantastic narratives. Returning to Gateshead ten years after her exile, Jane claims to feel nothing but pity for her dying aunt. Nevertheless, in entering her chamber, she reflexively "looked into a certain corner near, half-expecting to see the slim outline of a once dreaded switch which used to lurk there, waiting to leap out imp-like and lace my quivering palm or shrinking neck" (259). Though she attempts to order and dispel all resonance between the "imp-like" switch and the "imp" that Jane sees in the Red Room mirror (both inflictors of violence that burst out of corners), when the bedridden Mrs. Reed spurns her, "I felt pain, and then I felt ire; and then I felt a determination to subdue her—to be her mistress in spite both of her nature and her will" (259). Jane's desire to master Mrs. Reed is rendered once more as an uncanny compulsion to verbally "accus[e] and menac[e]."[19]

All in all, *Jane Eyre*'s preternatural material signposts the moments when Jane's speakerly force overmasters her writerly conduct. Returning to the early moment in which Jane's cousin demands to be called "Master Reed," we might wonder whether Jane's "determination to subdue" reflects those places where oral power overmasters readerly power. If this is so, then I would suggest that we read Jane's periodic apostrophe "reader" as oppositional and othering, not the inclusive, intimate, and even affectionate address that we are used to considering it.

Perhaps *Jane Eyre*'s most compelling resonance with the natural history is its interest in Thornfield's cabinets. The "cabinet of curiosities" had existed since the seventeenth century as a display of specimens from antiquarian and natural history collections. This was either a case or an entire room devoted to containing and displaying artifacts. Beginning in the late eighteenth century, the word was also given to literary titles of antiquarian and natural history, collections of tales, and other, similar studies. For example, *Le Cabinet des Fées* (1785–1789) was the first large-scale fairy tale anthology, a title that acknowledges the extent to which natural history blended science with fantasy in regional investigation. Because the term applied both to collections of antiquities and to volumes of writing describing such collections, a "cabinet" is a repository of both material and literary curiosities.

Interestingly, Bertha Mason's room is described several times as a "cabinet" (237, 327, 348). At first glance, Brontë appears to use this word in the sense both of "a secret receptacle, treasure-chamber, or store-house" and "a den or hole of a beast."[20] Bertha inhabits, as Rochester says, "a secret inner cabinet," which is also "a wild beast's den" and "a goblin's cell" (348). And yet, this cabinet is oddly decorative: its "front, divided into twelve panels, bore, in grim design, the heads of the twelve apostles, each enclosed in its separate panel as in a frame" (237). Jane describes this paneled facade as Bertha's "pictorial cabinet" (327). Reading more closely, then, I would suggest that the shape of the cabinet, its wooden panels made up of partitioned frames, with "each picture [telling] a story" (as Jane said earlier of Bewick), represents both the material and literary natural history "cabinet."

Like the natural history's hybrid form, Thornfield is a secret storehouse for wild beasts and goblins (and hyenas, gypsies, brownies, witches, fairies, imps, and other creatures) that inhabit the novel. But if a cabinet binds and contains specimens for observation, Rochester's cabinet has a faulty lock: his curio routinely escapes and rampages through Thornfield, biting, shredding, and burning as it goes. Bertha Mason reflects the tension between Jane's drive to observe and record, and her utter intolerance of being the object of anyone's speculative gaze. Like Bertha, Jane is a character in whom "natural" and "unnatural" histories collide productively; the "imp," the "alien," the "heterogeneous thing" cannot remain still, and so must be tied down, lest her goblin form wander freely, making mischief.

Of course, a cabinet also retains the sense of "a small chamber or room; a private apartment, a boudoir." Bertha's "boudoir" is, ironically, replaced by a "cell"; indeed, Rochester incarcerates Bertha *because* of her "giant propensities" in the boudoir (345). Brontë seems to beg a comparison between the cabinet of curiosities and the transgressive female body. In fact, the Brontë sisters evidently shared this interest in weird beds as a manifestation of women striving to define themselves in face of social strictures. In *Wuthering Heights,* Lockwood passes a haunted night in Catherine Earnshaw's cabinet, a paneled "little closet," into which the young Catherine has scratched "Catherine Earnshaw . . . Catherine Heathcliff . . . Catherine Linton,"[21] variations that are both a meditation on her prospective marriage choices and a précis of the biological legacy that unfolds in the novel. Lockwood's attention moves from this writing to Catherine's small library of books, into which she has inserted a running "diary, scrawled in an unformed, childish hand" in "every morsel of blank that the printer had left."[22] By "spelling over"[23] these textual transgressions, Lockwood calls up Catherine's uncanny revenant, and unleashes the powerful retrospective narrative into the novel's framework. As in *Wuthering Heights*, Bertha's pictorial cabinet bodies forth the triangulated contestation for mastery. It reflects upon Jane's earliest action in the novel, to "possess herself of a volume." While the verb "possess" appears throughout the novel, on only two other occasions does Brontë use its reflexive form. Upon the revelation of his secret, Rochester "possess[es] himself of [Jane's] hand" with a "hot and strong grasp" (324). Bertha Mason, by contrast, "possess[es] herself of the keys" (348) to her cabinet. For Brontë, the reflexive verb signals an attempt to seize narrative control, and to curtail the manual conduct of others. Bertha Mason's refusal to remain in her repository echoes the way in which Jane resists the colonizing force not only of Rochester, but of her own narrativizing and editorializing hands.

Bertha's laugh, that "goblin ha! ha!" (225) signals the novel's uneasy dependence on the same dialogic structure that sustained the natural history. Her creepy giggle is "preternatural" (113); it is "syllabic in tone" and "terminate[s] in an odd murmur" (113). That which erupts into passages (of Thornfield and the novel), therefore, is the vigorous and irrepressible spoken word. But the laugh is also, conversely, "formal" (112); that is, it has form, it is structured and material. It is tempting to think of fantastic inclusions in natural histories as weird, inchoate interruptions to scientific form. As the nineteenth century wore on, folklore, antiquities, and uncanny narratives were often framed as that which made natural histories quaint, regressive, belated. But Brontë, I think, was alive to the materiality of fantastic narrative: her uncanny material has legs. It has teeth. It is in *Jane Eyre,* as in the natural history, the strain that resists both naturalizing and historicizing.

CHAPTER 4

Antiquity, Novelty, and *The Key to All Mythologies*

Academics who read George Eliot's *Middlemarch* (1871–72) often find the musty scholar Edward Casaubon—and his head-wagging, sing-songing, soup-chewing, mole-sprouting, Latin-spouting, and story-collecting propensities—a bit too close for comfort. Perhaps for this reason, critics cannot agree upon Casaubon's discipline. He has been variously defined as a historian, philologist, and philosopher (but not by historians, philologists, or philosophers). His vocation is clerical, but he neglects those duties in favor of his avocation as the permanently incipient author of *The Key to All Mythologies*, a work as difficult to define as its progenitor. Its grand theory, he tells his fiancée, Dorothea Brooke, is that "all the mythical systems or erratic mythical fragments in the world were corruptions of a tradition originally revealed. Having once mastered the true position and taken a firm footing there, the vast field of mythical constructions became intelligible, nay, luminous with the reflected light of correspondences."[1] His project, then, is to uncover the single, universal origin of all cultural tradition and to prove that the world degenerates from grand mythic narratives to fragmented fairy tales. Given this précis, one wonders why no critic has called Casaubon a folklorist; of all possibilities, this strikes closest. The term *folklore*, William John Thoms's "Anglo-Saxon compound," had been in use for twenty-five years, Max Müller's theory of comparative mythology had been established fifteen years before, and Edward Tylor's *Primitive Culture* was published in the same year as *Middlemarch*. The Folklore Society formed in 1878, seven years after *Middlemarch* arrived, but was anticipated for a decade before. So while *folklorist* would have been anachronistic in 1829, when the novel takes place, Casaubon's practices and intellectual squabbles precisely mirror those of the comparative folklorists contemporary to the novel's composition and publication.

The period between 1837 and 1871 (or between *Pickwick Papers* and *Middlemarch*) marked sweeping changes in the folklore field—its tentative emergence into the field of social science, and also its lingering affiliation with armchair scholarship, literary study, and the popular press. This chapter considers another Victorian folklore collector, created thirty-five years after Samuel Pickwick, but eliciting for Eliot some of the same anxieties and revelations as Pickwick did for Dickens. While much of *Middlemarch* appears to divide the epistemologies of novelists and antiquarians—new from old, active from reactive, serious from childish, authoring from grave robbery—ultimately Eliot recognizes folklore and folklore collection to be integral to the particular web that makes up the historical novel.

Nevertheless, as with the Pickwick Club, it is at first difficult to see beyond Eliot's derogation of her folklorist. Casaubon himself admits "I live too much with the dead. My mind is something like the ghost of an ancient, wandering about the world and trying mentally to reconstruct it as it used to be, in spite of ruin and confusing changes" (13). What others say of Casaubon is much less laudatory. Mr. Cadwallader the vicar protests, "I know no harm of Casaubon. I don't care about his Xisuthrus and Fee-fo-fum and the rest; but then he doesn't care about my fishing-tackle" (62). To which his wife responds, "Oh, he dreams footnotes, and they run away with all his brains. They say, when he was a little boy, he made an abstract of 'Hop o' my Thumb,' and he has been making abstracts ever since" (63). The anti-intellectual Cadwalladers reduce what Casaubon characterizes as a sweeping lifework to a hobby akin to fishing, and the principles of fairy tale analysis to a childish occupation producing virtual idiocy. The narrator, too, likens Casaubon's efforts to amass and rearticulate long-dead ideas to rummaging through catacombs: "in an exposure of other mythologists ill-considered parallels, [he] easily lost sight of any purpose which had prompted him to these labors. With his taper stuck before him, he forgot about the absence of windows, and in bitter manuscript remarks on other men's notations about the solar deities, he had become indifferent to the sunlight" (181). In contrast to her husband, Dorothea does not "want to deck herself with knowledge, wear it loose from the nerves and blood that fed her action" (77). Even more explicitly, the narrator compares the couple's epistemologies: "What was fresh to her mind was worn out to his, and such capacity of thought and feeling as had ever been stimulated in him by the general life of mankind had long shrunk to a sort of dried preparation, a lifeless embalmment of knowledge" (180). Eliot emphasizes that, like Dorothea, her narrator seeks to examine human lives: "I at least have so much to do in unraveling certain human lots, and seeing how they were woven and interwoven, that all the light I can command must be concentrated on this particular web" (128). The narrator does not only oppose the human lots of novels to the "lifeless embalmment" of antiquities, her lighted to Casaubon's darkened labor. More fundamentally, she rejects Casaubon's theory of a single originating tradition in favor of a model of interwoven histories.

On the other hand, Eliot does not reject the uses of enchantment. Near the novel's end, Mary Garth, Eliot's plain and plain-spoken heroine (hired as housekeeper and nurse to her wicked uncle Peter Featherstone), tells the story of Rumpelstiltskin to a rapt crowd of her fiancé's little siblings. In this context, the fairy tale is of clear domestic use value. In an odd double-bind, therefore, Casaubon's work is deemed at once too fanciful and too prosaic: too fanciful because it encompasses mythography, superstition, and fairy tale (subjects apparently divorced from current events like scientific discovery, voting reform, and the conditions of tenant farmers) and too prosaic because *The Key to All Mythologies* has no perceptible aesthetic value to give it purpose as a sweet subject for the kiddies. Casaubon's lifework, it would seem, is actually deathwork; all of the living (and the breathing, blooming, beating, flushing, and sobbing) belongs to Dorothea, and through her, to the narrative itself.

This apparent opposition suggests a battle not merely between scholarship and political activism, but also between folklore and novel making. Certainly, there is an established critical tradition linking Eliot's incarnation of the realist novel to positivist reasoning. Gillian Beer has demonstrated that if Dorothea embodies the novel's political progressivism, the physician and research scientist Lydgate represents Eliot's narratological practice, which she repeatedly figures as a microscope turned upon provincial life.[2] As a result, many critics have divided folkloric from scientific inquiry in Eliot's work, contending that Eliot seeks to discredit the fantastic as a viable representational mode. For Kathleen McCormack, Eliot's novels insist that a reading audience is polluted by romance and fantasy.[3] David Carroll accounts for the existence of the uncanny in *Middlemarch* by positing two distinct worlds of the novel: the world of external fact and the world of internal interests.[4] Carroll concludes that all fantastic references occur as a negative byproduct of the pursuit of purely internal interests. Thus folklore is associated with delusional selfishness. Sophia Andres claims that Casaubon's view of history is monologic (while Dorothea's is dialogic or multivalent), and that Casaubon reflects the larger monologism of comparative mythology and antiquarian study, which, Andres says, treats only great men and great deeds.[5]

Eliot does appear to bar folklore study from the positivist paradigm, connecting Lydgate, Dorothea, and writing itself through the opposition of the words "novelty" and "antiquity." Lydgate reflects upon "the novelty of . . . the introduction to Miss Brooke, whose youthful bloom, with her approaching marriage to that faded scholar, and her interest in matters socially useful, gave her the piquancy of an unusual combination" (83). Dorothea is *novel*—a new thing to Lydgate—by virtue of the "unusual combination" of both beauty wed to age, and beauty wed to activism. In introducing Lydgate, the narrator describes the provincial Middlemarch forced to submit to intellectual and economic change: "Municipal town and rural parish gradually made fresh threads of connection—gradually, as the old stocking gave way to the savings bank, and the worship of the solar guinea became extinct. . . . Settlers, too, came from distant counties, some with an alarming novelty of skill, others with an offensive advantage in cunning" (86). Lydgate is the settler with the alarming "novelty of skill" and is thus linked to Dorothea's own intellectual novelty. The Middlemarchers' "worship of the solar guinea" is likened to Casaubon's lifeless study of solar deities—both "extinct" belief systems. To be sure, Eliot at times leads us to believe that *Middlemarch* is a realist novel openly opposed to the romance. In describing Lydgate's determination to make not a woman but "the primitive tissue" his "fair unknown" (246), the narrator wonders, "is it due to an excess of poetry or of stupidity that we are never weary of . . . listening to the twanging of the old Troubadour strings?" (131). Lydgate himself echoes this perception that the romance, palpably based upon the stuff of legend and tale, is "stupid": "Oh, I read no literature now. . . . I read so much literature when I was a lad, that I suppose that it will last me all my life. I used to know Scott's poems by heart" (246). As elsewhere in Victorian literature, a *Middlemarch* character identifies folk material as childish stuff best put aside in maturity.

Of course, Lydgate's initiation to scientific discovery occurs not in a laboratory but in a library: "he took down a dusty row of volumes with gray-paper backs and dingy labels—the volumes of an old Cyclopaedia which he had never disturbed. It would at least be a novelty to disturb them. They were on the highest shelf, and he stood on a chair to get them down. . . . The page he opened on was under the head of Anatomy, and the first passage that drew his eyes was on the valves of the heart" (130). In other words, *novelty* is a new way of reading faded books, a new way of knowing in the face of faded scholars. It is only when Lydgate begins to have fairy tale desires for the imminently unsuitable Rosamond that his troubles begin: "Ideal happiness (of the kind known in the Arabian Nights, in which you are invited to step from the labour and discord of the street into a paradise where everything is given to you and nothing claimed) seemed to be an affair of a few weeks waiting, more or less" (319).

Novelty opposes not only the provincialism of Middlemarchers but also the antiquarianism of Casaubon, to whom his young cousin Will Ladislaw refers as "this elaborator of small explanations about as important as the surplus stock of false antiquities kept in a vendor's back chamber" (187). The novelty of discovery for the utility of mankind seems to be contrasted to the (dubious) exchange value of antiquities. It is therefore fitting that Casaubon and Dorothea's antagonism climaxes in a writerly battle: after implying that Cousin Will has paid Dorothea inappropriate attention, he dismisses her to amanuensis work: "Mr. Casaubon dipped his pen and made as if he would return to his writing, though his hand trembled so much that the words seemed to be written in an unknown character." Dorothea, by contrast, is authoritative: "She began to work at once, and her hand did not tremble; on the contrary, in writing out the quotations that had been given to her the day before, she felt she was forming her letters beautifully, and it seemed to her that she saw the construction of the Latin she was copying, and which she was beginning to understand, more clearly than usual" (258). Meanwhile, Casaubon, standing on a library ladder to reach a book down, has a heart attack. Where Lydgate reaches for a book and opens the doors— the valvae—to novelty of skill, the folklorist's identical gesture brings on cardiac arrest—blocked passages. Casaubon is struck down in part because Dorothea's novel powers are growing. The occluded battle between antiquarians and novelists is underscored when Dorothea's Uncle Arthur Brooke (possibly the most middling of marchers) recommends that Dorothea read novels to the folklorist to hasten his convalescence. Adding insult to injury, Mr. Brooke suggests that reading Smollett "'might be new to you.' 'As new as eating thistles,' would have been an answer to represent Mr. Casaubon's feelings" (261). One could conclude this reading by arguing that, because Casaubon dies with *The Key to All Mythologies* unfinished, the folklorist is quite literally vanquished by a novelist who invests herself with the authority to claim and restructure the national narrative.

The problem with this interpretation is that, while Eliot was composing *Middlemarch,* she was also sitting on the floor reading books of fairy tales. The *Middlemarch* notebooks demonstrate that a large proportion of her parallel reading and writing in 1871 and 1872 was devoted to folkloric materials. She read the mythology and *volksmärchen* studies of the Grimms and Max Müller, as well as older studies like Jacob Bryant's *A New System or Analysis of Ancient Mythology.*[6] In August of 1868 Eliot was reading Richard Verstegen's *A Restitution of Decayed Intelligence in Antiquities* (1634), a volume perhaps most famous for containing the first English version of the "Pied Piper of Hamelin."[7] In 1869 she was working on a poem taken from Boccaccio's *Decameron* ("How Lisa Loved the King").[8] Finally, as she completed *Middlemarch,* she was reading John Fiske's *Myths and Mythmakers* (1872), a work in comparative world folklore, which sets about defining myth, legend, and folktale, and which contains chapters on transmogrification, dowsing, cosmology, and ghosts. According to Fiske himself, Eliot "became so absorbed in it that she sat on the *floor* all the afternoon, till Lewes came in and routed her up!" (original emphasis).[9] In other words, the material that compelled Eliot, that lay at her feet and on her writing desk throughout her workday, was the very stuff of *The Key to All Mythologies.*

The most compelling critics of *Middlemarch* contend that Eliot seeks to dismantle the barricades between folk matter and material realism, and more broadly, between history and fiction. Sally Shuttleworth reminds us that Eliot embraced Ludwig Feuerbach's notion that "the creation of myth was a continual process, inseparable from the writing of history."[10] Michael Carignan, contravening Andres, argues that, whereas positivism sought to break from the past, *Middlemarch* urges rather that subjectivity and creativity be part of scientific endeavor, so that history, fiction, and science are not at odds.[11] Jessie Givner likewise denies any dichotomy between literature and history, between description and narration, or between passive figuration and active practice. Refuting Eagleton's theory that Eliot's web metaphor dehistoricizes, Givner notes that, since "webs" (i.e., woven textiles) were made in factories by 1871, Eliot consciously moved her metaphor from the drawing room to an industrial arena: textuality and figuration must, therefore, be inherently historical and material.[12] Givner's discovery that Eliot's most famous metaphor is not universal and abstract, but instead "particular" and historically contextualized, enables us to consider that all of her allusions are of equal material use to her as a historicizing medium. To this end, Brian Swann works against the received notion that producing realism means rejecting fable, legend, and myth. Similarly,

U. C. Knoepflmacher feels that Eliot constantly fuses fact and myth and argues that Eliot sees myth as the conduit between the past and the present/future.[13] Penny Boulmelha argues more fundamentally that Eliot does not participate in "classical realism" as defined by Roland Barthes, Colin McCabe, or Catherine Belsey (for whom classical realism signifies a political as much as a formal term, and to whom the endings of classical realism are unequivocal and truth-based). Rather, Boulmelha states, to have a *George Eliot* means we are always already outside of realism. Indeed, Boulmelha contends that Eliot's very practice of pausing to discuss the production of a text marks it as unreal.[14] Beer concludes that in *Middlemarch,* science and mythology are ultimately united because they similarly "perform humanist functions: they bind perceptions together and they enrich with meaning the recurrences of human experience; they allow at once for exploration and mystery; they include the recognition of latent or immanent worlds. . . . Although George Eliot early rejected the supernatural, she remained in two minds about the preternatural."[15] After all, in spite of *Middlemarch*'s insistence upon progress, this 1871 novel takes place in 1829, forty years in the past. That retrospection is one defining feature of the Victorian novel returns us to Casaubon, whose "mind is something like the ghost of an ancient, wandering about the world and trying mentally to construct it as it used to be" (13). It seems that, in spite of the novel's tendency to abase him, Casaubon's research resonates with the novelist's project, and indeed, with the spirit of the age.[16]

As others have noted, Eliot resembles Casaubon in her minute archival accuracy, and that she fretted about whether extensive research was a killing agent upon creative imagination. Henry James unkindly commented of *Romola,* "it is overladen with learning, it smells of the lamp,"[17] and Eliot appears to have feared that this might be true of her novels in general. A letter from Eliot to Harriet Beecher Stowe provides provocative testimony to this. Stowe asked Eliot of whom Casaubon was a portrait, and Eliot replied: "I fear that the Casaubon-tints are not quite foreign to my own mental complexion."[18] Eliot's mythologist reveals her anxieties about writing broadly conceived, but also (as her *Middlemarch* notebooks suggest) her relationship to folklore and folklore collection specifically. Neil Hertz, in arguing that handwriting, printing, and inking are "all clustered around the figure of Casaubon,"[19] and that Casaubon is made to seem like "a personification of the dead letter, the written word,"[20] points out that Eliot's personal letters playfully describe her own writing as hieroglyphic: "you will be ready to compare my scribbled sheet to the walls of an Egyptian tomb for mystery, and determine not to imitate certain wise antiquaries or antiquarian wiseacres . . . in deciphering information."[21] Hertz concludes that over the course of the novel Casaubon transforms from the materialization of writing to the embodiment of narcissism so that he may be safely separated from the writer, and banished from the novel. Like Hertz, critics Beer and LaCapra have similarly concluded that *Middlemarch*'s aim is to displace onto Casaubon uncomfortable perceptions about writing. Beer holds that the relationality between narrator and reader is the only thing that allays Eliot's fears about authorship, the "determinism and solipsism" in the act of writing fiction.[22] However, I would argue that Eliot's folklore collector is never entirely banished from the novel, and that, ultimately, it is folklore collection—or at least its communality, its sense of a historical continuum, and its perceptions of interconnectedness—that redeems Eliot's fears about the heresies of novel writing.

OFTEN in *Middlemarch*, Eliot's narrator binds antiquarian study together with other kinds of writing:

> Who shall tell what may be the effect of writing? . . . As the stone which has been kicked by generations of clowns may come by curious links of effect under the eyes of a scholar, through whose labors it may at last fix the date of invasion and unlock religions, so may a bit of ink and paper which has long been an innocent wrapping or stop-gap may at last be laid open under the one pair of eyes which have knowledge enough to turn it into the opening of a catastrophe. (376)

The similitive force here lies in the fact that both the antiquary and the author wield an uncanny and often catastrophic power of interpretation. And this suggests that Lydgate's search for the "primitive tissue" (what we would now call a cell) is not so very different from Casaubon's search for the "Key to All Mythologies," nor from Eliot's construction of her "particular web." Like bodies, novels are composed of primitive tissue—fairy tale matter—that divides and multiplies within the narrative. Similarly, most of *Middlemarch*'s folklore inclusions appear as brief analogies or metaphors. It is seeded then, like Casaubon's *Key*, with "erratic mythical fragments" that nevertheless unite into a "vast field." These interwoven metaphors return us to the older definition of novel: "any of a number of tales or stories making up a larger work." The *OED* exemplifies this definition by referencing the folk and fairy tale collections of Bocaccio and D'Aulnoy, two sources that Eliot read as she composed *Middlemarch*. It is no coincidence, then, that both Eliot and Lewes referred to *Middlemarch* in its early stages as "a series of tales."[23]

Daniel Tyler's radical suggestion that Dorothea completes, rather than abandons, *The Key to All Mythologies*, is especially persuasive in light of Eliot's self-identification as a writer of tales.[24] Several of Middlemarch's citizens may think that folklore lies forgotten in many a quaint and curious volume. But Eliot herself apprehended that transformation and emergence is at the heart of the fairy tale. Eliot's research notebooks for *Middlemarch* are fairly crawling with folkloric metamorphoses: swan maidens, lycanthropes, and pied pipers, and this reflects her understanding that integral to the transformation of the Victorian self was the malleability of the fairy tale tradition for modern purposes. Though Eliot never validates Casaubon's *approach* to *The Key to All Mythologies*, she also never rejects the comparative project. Rather, she suggests that Casaubon's flaw is perspectival. *Middlemarch* everywhere indicates that folklore is not, as Casaubon believes, degraded fragments of an ur-culture, but its own ductile tradition.

Indeed, *Middlemarch*'s narrator imbues her language with fairy analogy; this is most noticeable when she describes characters' interior spaces (especially through free indirect discourse). For instance, Will Ladislaw, the narrator implies, feels that he would know better how to behave if they were all characters in a legend: "She must have made some original romance for herself in this marriage. And if Mr. Casaubon had been a dragon who had carried her off to his lair with his talons simply and without legal forms, it would have been an unavoidable feat of heroism to release her and fall at her feet. But he was something more unmanageable than a dragon: he was a benefactor with collective society at his back" (191). And he heatedly reflects that "if (Casaubon) chose to grow grey crunching bones in a cavern, he had no business to be luring a girl into his companionship" (327). Will might compare Casaubon's research to a "stock of false antiquities," but he is unable either to denigrate Casaubon or exalt Dorothea without drawing upon the very narratives that Casaubon studies.

The same is true of Dorothea. Returning to Lowick after her honeymoon, and perceiving her surroundings, she realizes that "the stag in the tapestry looked more like a ghost in his ghostly blue-green world; the volumes of polite literature in the bookcase looked like immovable imitations of books" (248). In this beautifully implicit comparison between Dorothea's unused body and unused mind, "Her blooming, full-pulsed youth stood there in a moral imprisonment which made itself one with the chill, colourless, narrowed landscape, with the shrunken furniture, the never-read books, and the ghostly stag in the pale, fantastic world that seemed to be vanishing from the daylight . . . each remembered thing in the room was disenchanted, was deadened as an unlit transparency" (250). The touching irony here is that Dorothea's disenchantment is utterly enchanted—with ghostly stags, shrinking furniture, and imprisoned maidens. Eliot's description relies upon tropes of the gothic romance to describe this doomed marriage. Furthermore, upon learning that Casaubon expects her to complete *The Key to All Mythologies* after his death, she "pictured to herself the days, and months, and years which she must spend in sorting what might be called shattered mummies, and fragments of a tradition which was itself a mosaic wrought from crushed ruins—sorting them as food for a theory which was already withered in the birth like an elfin child" (436). Though rejecting antiquarian artifact and legendry, Dorothea cannot "picture" without calling forth mummies and elves—according to our narrator, she thinks in the language of folk study.

This imaginative dependence is especially concentrated through the novel's various wills: wills in *Middlemarch* produce legacies of all kinds, but especially imaginative ones. Wills are narratives, and narratives leave new generations deeply in your debt. This is first instantiated in the Garth/Vincy plot. Unlike Lydgate, Mary does still read Scott. As her uncle Featherstone lays dying, she is reading *Anne of Geierstein, or The Maiden of the Mist,* newly published in the retrospective timeline of the novel. When the town auctioneer Mr. Trumbull arrives, he discovers the book and reads the title "as if he were offering it for sale" (284). This very slight incident, oddly present in a deathbed scene, nevertheless directs us to connect the value of books with the last will and testament of Peter Featherstone: "In chuckling over the various vexations he could inflict by the rigid clutch of his dead hand, he inevitably mingled his consciousness with a livid stagnant presence, and so far as he was preoccupied with a future life, it was with one of gratification inside his coffin. Thus old Featherstone was imaginative, after his fashion" (293). For Featherstone, legacy is tantamount to imagination. Because this passage occurs only a few pages after the Scott title is figuratively auctioned, we might conclude that Eliot finds the reverse to be true as well: imagination is legacy. Scott claims folklore as his legacy, and Eliot acknowledges Scott as hers, notwithstanding her realist project. As with all legacy, to be deeply in the debt of other books is to be under the spell of a dead hand.

Eliot reiterates the connection between will, legacy, and imaginative dependency when Casaubon's will mandates Dorothea's disinheritance if she marries Ladislaw. Heading the chapter in which we learn that Casaubon's (legal) will forbids Dorothea to marry Casaubon's (nephew) Will, Eliot presents this epigraph:

ANTIQUITY, NOVELTY, *THE KEY TO ALL MYTHOLOGIES* 71

> A task too strong for wizard spells
> This squire had brought about;
> 'Tis easy dropping stones in wells,
> But who shall get them out? (440)

This is one of the many chapter epigraphs in *Middlemarch* that Eliot wrote herself. Edward Casaubon is evidently the "squire" named here, and in more than one sense: he is the principle landowner of Lowick parish with the authority to will property, and he is servant to his own errant *Key to All Mythologies*. Casaubon's act of "mortmain" sends the young people into each other's arms, and critics have complained that this is an "unrealistic" thread in this realist text. I agree, but would argue that it is not a symptom of poor writing. Rather, it is Casaubon who deploys the unreal plot, a "task too strong for wizard spells": through denying the marriage, he ensures it, and thus Ladislaw's fairy tale imagination has been activated in the text through Casaubon's dragonish act of holding Dorothea prisoner. Dorothea might resist completing the *Key*, protesting in a letter to her dead husband: "Do not you see now that I could not submit my soul to yours, by working hopelessly at what I have no belief in?" Nevertheless, the text immediately subverts her unbelief in the rhetorical power of folk narrative:

> But her soul thirsted to see [Will]. How could it be otherwise? If a princess in the days of enchantment had seen a four-footed creature from among those which live in herds come to her once and again with a human gaze which rested on her with choice and beseeching, what would she think of in her journeying, what would she look for when the herds had passed her? Surely for the gaze which had found her, and which she would know again. Life would be no better than candle-light tinsel and daylight rubbish if our spirits were not touched by what has been to issues of longing and constancy. (490)

For Dorothea as for Will, "longing and constancy" are expressible only through analogies "from the days of enchantment." Indeed, humans must be "touched by what has been" to make sense of material reality, for old tales wed with new narratives make meaning, make novelty. Whether Dorothea chooses Will Ladislaw or a will laid as law, she also chooses a life constructed through, and authorized by, folklore. In one way and another, Eliot's realist plot bends to the will of the folklorist.

Independently of any character's perspective, the narrator also directly represents characters and plots with metaphors from the folklore collection, and thus imposes fairy tale language not only through free indirect discourse (which, after all, could be perceived as ironic distancing, and might be explained away as characters' "stupidity" in thrilling to the troubadours' twanging). Will and Casaubon, for instance, are described in opposing terms as a sun god and god of the underworld: "The first impression on seeing Will was one of sunny brightness . . . the little ripple in his nose was a preparation for metamorphosis. When he turned his head quickly his hair seemed to shake out light, and some persons thought they saw decided genius in this coruscation. Mr. Casaubon, on the contrary, stood rayless" (191). Elsewhere, perhaps prompted by her reading of Verstegen, Eliot describes Ladislaw as the Pied Piper (421). As Carol Senf has pointed out, both Lydgate (605) and Bulstrode (141) are described as having a vampire's taste.[25] And Virginia Hyde found that a delightfully ironic Arthurian plot winds through the novel, with the Tory (read Norman) Arthur Brooke and the Whig (read Saxon) Alfred Garth the engineer presenting competing models of England built upon the names of pseudo-legendary kings.[26] As in *Pickwick Papers* and *Jane Eyre*, novels are spellbound things, depending upon echoes to make meaning. When Rosamond plays the piano, the narrator reflects that "a hidden soul seemed to be flowing forth from Rosamond's fingers; and so indeed it was, since souls live on in perpetual echoes, and to all fine expression there goes somewhere an originating activity, if it be only that of an interpreter" (146). In other words, Rosamond may well be a fraud ("only want[ing] to know what her audience liked" [146] and playing it for them without flaw, but also without personal passion), but then again, Eliot reflects, all artists are interpreters: an "originating activity" lies behind all artistic production. Though Eliot manifests anxiety about her originality and progressivism, and though *Middlemarch* suggests an occluded battle between folklorists and novelists, Eliot also acknowledges that folk narratives, and the people who collect them, are not ghosts of ancients, not shattered mummies, but rather historicized, materialized, present.

In this sense, perhaps the most telling—the most *material*—example of fairy tale matter within *Middlemarch* is Mary Garth's recitation of "Rumpelstiltskin." Eliot's most pointed attention to a folkloric intertext is given, not to a myth or a legend, but to a fairy tale. Eliot does not offer the story directly: rather, one of Mary's young audience members cries to her mother "[t]he little man stamped so hard on the floor he couldn't get his leg out again!" (587). A Victorian reader of fairy tale collections would recognize that Mary has told the Grimm version of the tale; Eliot, it seems, expects her readership to know it by heart. A miller brags to a king that his daughter can spin straw into gold. The king, intrigued but skeptical, imprisons the girl in a room to spin for him on pain of death. The girl, who can perform no such task, is understandably distressed. A little man appears, and offers to spin straw into gold in exchange for the girl's necklace. The next day the king, impressed but still doubtful, forces a repeat performance; the girl bargains with the dwarf to spin in exchange for her ring. The king once more commands her to spin, promising to marry her as a reward. The little man agrees to spin again in exchange for her first child. The girl marries the king, and bears a son. The dwarf arrives for the baby, but offers to break the bargain if the queen can guess his name in three days. The queen sends a messenger to scour the land, who, on the third day, overhears the little man boast that none could guess his name: Rumpelstiltskin. The queen guesses correctly, the enraged dwarf stamps his leg into the floor, and in trying to remove it, tears himself in two.[27]

There are certainly coincidences between the "Rumpelstiltskin" tale and the *Middlemarch* plots. The woman virtually imprisoned by and made to work for a man echoes Dorothea's marriage to Casaubon, as well as Mary's abusive employ with Mr. Featherstone. Alternatively, Rumpelstiltskin's defeat when a woman discovers his secret self resembles Casaubon's demise once Dorothea discovers that *The Key to All Mythologies* is a moribund project. However, I believe that the tale is more important to Eliot for its allegory of authorship. The fairy tale woman who is compelled to produce for a powerful and skeptical audience has an uncanny man working secretly for her gain—indeed, for her survival. One cannot help but syncopate it with the tale of Marian Evans, who, through George Eliot, spun her own form of gold. Neil Hertz calls the author's shifting signature—Mary Ann Evans, Marian Evans, Marian Lewes, George Eliot—"a space in which a certain play of transformation becomes plausible."[28] Transformation of one's self and one's materials is at the heart of "Rumpelstiltskin," and of *Middlemarch*, too. The primary motif of "Rumpelstiltskin" returns us to *Middlemarch*'s weaving metaphor: "I at least have so much to do in unraveling certain human lots, and seeing how they were woven and interwoven, that all the light I can command must be concentrated on this particular web." If the tale centers upon spinning the quotidian into the extraordinary, the real into the enchanted, Eliot takes up the thread of folk narrative and interweaves it with "human lots" into the "particular web" of *Middlemarch*, a text that refuses to unravel antiquity from novelty.

PART 2

Spell

CHAPTER 5

Sleeping Beauty and Victorian Temporality

Victorian reflections upon temporality often conjure up metaphors of an enchanted sleep that threatens progress. In *Past and Present* (1843), Thomas Carlyle distinguishes between "a virtual Industrial Aristocracy, as yet only half alive—spell-bound amid money-bags and ledgers; and an actual idle aristocracy seemingly near dead in somnolent delusions"[1] and implores his "Princes of Industry" to wake: "It is you who are already half-alive, whom I will welcome into life; whom I conjure in God's name to shake off your enchanted sleep and live wholly!"[2] In casting himself as author-prince, giving the kiss of life to the capitalists, Carlyle refers overtly to the narrative of "Sleeping Beauty" (also called "Briar Rose"), a fairy tale that not only inhabited but also shaped the diverse Victorian discourses of political economy, architecture, philosophy, and poetry. In *Stones of Venice* (1851–53), John Ruskin posits, "It is that strange disquietude of the gothic spirit that is its greatness, that restlessness of the dreaming mind . . . and it can neither rest in, nor from, its labour, but must pass on, sleeplessly, until its love of change shall be pacified forever in the change that must come alike on the them that wake and them that sleep."[3] Ruskin imagines a historical age as a mind that dreams but paradoxically must not sleep in order to enact change, and thus, like Carlyle, renders "sleep" as a narcotic "quietude" that must be shaken off. Still later in the century, the narrator of George Eliot's *Theophrastus Such,* though "determined . . . not to grumble at the age in which I happen to have been born" nevertheless confesses to "an inborn beguilement which carries my affection and regret continually into an imagined past." Here nostalgia casts a charm so powerful that it can make us "lose all sense of moral proportion unless [we] keep alive a stronger attachment to what is near."[4] These authors, then, identify progress as a wakeful, restless, moral, linear impetus. However, they conjure themselves into an imaginary past to make these very progressive arguments.

By contrast, Gerard Manley Hopkins's undated, unfinished sonnet "To His Watch" renders the forward motion of time itself as an unbreakable spell:

> Mortal my mate, bearing my rock-a-heart
> Warm beat with cold beat company, shall I
> Earlier or you fail at our force, and lie
> The ruins of, rifled, once a world of art?
> The telling time our task is; time's some part,
> Not all, but we were framed to fail and die—
> One spell and well that one. There, ah thereby
> Is comfort's carol of all or woe's worst smart.[5]

The title might at first suggest that a human speaker addresses his timepiece. However, though the poem compares the "warm beat" of the human heart with the "cold beat" of the clock, "mortal my mate bearing *my* rock-a-heart" (emphasis added) identifies the *timepiece* as the speaker, guardian over its human "watch." Time binds the machine to the machine who fashioned it; there is but "one spell," and this suggests both the brevity of mortal life and the community of all things governed by time. Finally, the verse's very fragmentation proleptically points to the poet's body and the poem: both spellbound, metered worlds of art.

Whether their authors believe that literature orders time or is ordered by it, these passages read time and social progress at least obliquely through the spells and slumbers of "Sleeping Beauty." "Temporal" means the condition of being temporary; it relates to material acquisition; it refers to structures situated in the temples (like the temporal artery); it describes our placement in time.[6] These chapters demonstrate that this fairy tale provided Victorian artists with a narrative of temporality in all senses of the word. Victorian renditions of "Sleeping Beauty" attempt to claim the tale in order to transfix it and bypass it for other, worthier subjects; simultaneously, however, the very act of retelling this story enables it to burst temporal boundaries (the barriers of time but also of individual heads), and evade authorial control. Mikhail Bakhtin explained "dialogism" as a conversation between mutually interacting texts. He stresses that texts exist in time and simultaneously inform and are informed by previous and future texts.[7] Therefore, to call fairy tales immaterial is, if not to reject them as narratives, at least to deny them (both as an entire genre and as individual fairy tales with publication histories) dialogic power. This study of "Sleeping Beauty" suggests that fairy tales cannot be denied discursive structure: they are subjects of reasoning (as distinguished from subjects of pure feeling or perception), and as such they occupied, but also determined, Victorian conversations about how narrative is shaped, and by whom.

Our most familiar renditions of the tale we now call "Sleeping Beauty" include the princess's hundred-year trance, the sleeping palace around her, and the prince who breaks the briar hedge and awakens the princess with a kiss. However, these elements of the narrative (title included) are eighteenth- and nineteenth-century revisions to significantly more violent precursors, dating from the fourteenth century. Early versions in Catalan, French, and Italian record the rape of a girl in a coma, rather than the heroic rescue of a spellbound princess.[8] The sleep itself does not afflict the castle, and takes up very little of the tale's exposition. Not a kiss, but giving birth to twins awakens her, not a hundred years but nine months later. Giambattista Basile's is the earliest such version that gained general English readership. It was translated into English in 1848, but editions in Italian, French, and German circulated in England prior to that date.[9] In Basile's "*Sole, Luna, e Talia,*" a girl catches a chip of flax under her nail and falls into a swoon or coma. Her grief-stricken parents close her up in the palace and depart. A king out hunting comes upon her:

> When the king beheld Talia, who seemed as one ensorcelled, he believed that she slept, and he called her, but she remained insensible, and crying aloud, he felt his blood course hotly through his veins in contemplation of so many charms; and he lifted her in his arms and carried her to a bed, whereon he gathered the first fruits of love, and leaving her upon the bed, returned to his own kingdom, where, in the pressing business of his realm, for a time thought no more of this incident.[10]

Nine months later, Talia gives birth to twins, one of whom sucks on her finger, draws out the flax chip, and wakes her mother. The king returns and takes this family back to his castle. However, the king is already married, and his jealous wife plans to slay Talia and the children and feed them to the king. The king discovers the plot, executes his wife instead, and marries Talia. Focus in this story is not with the (here unspecified) length of sleep, and certainly not with the churlish king, but with the girl and her trials.

The similarities between Charles Perrault's "*La Belle au Bois Dormant*" and "*Sole, Luna, e Talia*," demonstrate that Perrault knew Basile's work; but it was evidently Perrault who first lengthened the sleep to one hundred years, and made it the effect of fairy enchantment rather than an unexplained coma. To the tale's exposition he adds a sequence about the princess's birth, in which fairy godmothers are invited to a celebratory feast. One fairy is omitted by accident, and curses the child to prick her hand on a spindle and drop down dead. Another fairy commutes the sentence to a hundred years of "profound sleep," to be broken when "a king's son shall come to awaken her." Perrault also is the first to send the entire castle to sleep: whereas in Basile's tale, Talia's parents close up the castle and depart, in Perrault's version, the kind fairy puts the palace under a spell to keep the dormant princess company:

> She touched with her wand everybody . . . who was in the castle—governesses, maids of honor, ladies-in-waiting, gentlemen, officers, stewards, cooks, scullions, errand boys, guards, porters, pages, footmen. . . . The moment she had touched them they all fell asleep, to awaken only at the same moment as their mistress. Thus they would always be ready with their service whenever she should require it. The very spits before the fire, loaded with partridges and pheasants, subsided into slumber, and the fire as well. All was done in a moment, for the fairies do not take long over their work. . . . Proclamations were issued, forbidding any approach to [the castle], but these warnings were not needed, for within a quarter of an hour there grew up all round the park so vast a quantity of trees big and small, with interlacing brambles and thorns, that neither man nor beast could penetrate them. The tops alone of the castle towers could be seen, and these only from a distance.[11]

After a hundred years, the kingdom passes into other hands, and the king's son approaches the briar hedge, which parts to let him through. In this considerably chastened version, the prince dropping to his knees before the princess is sufficient to break the charm. The two are married, and the plot continues as in "Sun, Moon, and Talia," except that the princess's children are legitimate, and Perrault converts the king's jealous wife into the prince's mother (who, being half-ogre, wants to eat the children herself). The Grimms' "*Dornröschen*" resembles the first half of Perrault's tale, save for one significant detail: the Grimms' princess, through the very act of drifting off, causes the dormancy of the entire realm: "in the very moment when she felt the prick, she fell down upon the bed that stood there, and lay in a deep sleep. And this sleep extended over the whole palace" (120).[12]

By the early nineteenth century, then, the tale's motifs had shifted. With the princess's enchantment lengthened to a century, slumber in the tale became explicitly linked to temporality in its sense of the human placement in time; moreover, sleep became something specifically feminine and blamable, a somnolence that radiates outward from the princess to infect the kingdom around her. The "rude awakening" of rape had been effaced, and reinscribed as positive action: the prince fighting through the hedge to rescue the beauty from her own torpor. As these next chapters shall show, literary and visual artists in nineteenth-century England made the princess's hundred-year sleep and the prince's resurrective arrival the focal features of their appropriations. These interdependent alterations coincide with changes in the philosophies of heroism and cultural progress.

CHAPTER 6

Keats on Sleep and Beauty

John Keats is an originator of Victorian artistic interest in Briar Rose. But while critical discussion of "The Eve of St. Agnes" has thoroughly explored Keats's source material, few critics care to acknowledge "Sleeping Beauty" as one of those sources. Instead, Shakespeare (from *Romeo and Juliet* to *Titus Andronicus*), saints' legends, and old girlfriends all receive their tributary due in place of the fairy tale. And yet, the narrative similarities seem obvious: in both "The Eve of St. Agnes" and "Sleeping Beauty" a questing nobleman penetrates a defended castle to claim an ensorcelled sleeper. The word *rose,* repeated five times, and always in association with Madeline, also suggests Keats's mindfulness of the tale. The poem's title refers to the January 21 ritual in which maidens pray to St. Agnes to show them their future husbands in a dream. In the poem the hero, Porphyro, travels through a snowstorm to see his beloved, Madeline, the daughter of his father's enemy. He sneaks into the castle and, with the help of her maid, into Madeline's room (when he decides to hide there, the "thought came like a full-blown rose").[1] He watches Madeline enter (up the stairs "Madeline, St. Agnes' charmed maid/Rose" [192–93]), undress (the warm light of the room throws "rose-bloom" [220] upon her body), retire to bed, and sleep ("as though a rose should shut and be a bud again" [243]). Under the spell of St. Agnes' Eve, she dreams of Porphyro and calls his name. Hearing this, the now supernaturally aroused Porphyro deflowers her while she sleeps ("into her dream he melted, as the rose/Blendeth its odour with the violet" [320–21]). She awakes in despair to find herself violated; Porphyro promises to take her away and marry her. The poem ends as the two flee into the storm. Porphyro's triumphant rush to possess beauty leads one to suppose him an allegory for poetic power. Nevertheless, in the poem's (literally) climactic moment, all narrative empathy flows to the dreaming princess; raped by her lover, she is awakened into a literally and figuratively cold world. This is, as many critics have noted, a poem about effaced boundaries, both spatial and temporal[2]; Keats's blending of source materials—"Sleeping Beauty" with the legend of Saint Agnes and the rape of Philomel—is a vital factor of that elision, contributing to his affective, at times reluctantly empathetic, focus upon his sleeping beauty.

Though there is no indication that Keats owned a copy of Perrault's *Contes du Temps*,[3] the tales were, as I have noted, available in English translation as early as 1784. The *Contes* were so widely circulated that it would have been anomalous if Keats had not read them, either in English or in French.[4] The Grimm version *"Dornröschen,"* the first to call the princess Briar Rose, was not available in English translation until 1823. But by 1819, the year Keats wrote "Eve of St. Agnes," *Kinder- und Hausmärchen* was second only to the Bible in German sales, and again Keats had almost certainly at least heard of the tale of "Briar Rose." However, that Keats had read an *erotic* version of "Sleeping Beauty" is everywhere evident in "Eve of St. Agnes." *The Pentamerone* did not exist in English translation in Keats's life; nevertheless, Keats studied Italian during revision of "The Eve of St. Agnes," and, indeed, mentally linked the two activities: he wrote to John Taylor on September 5, 1819, "am now occupied in revising *St. Agnes' Eve* [*sic*] and studying Italian."[5] Basile does not appear in Keats's personal library, either, but friends' libraries may have led him to *The Pentamerone*.[6] Finally, Keats's Italian studies coincide with a significant manuscript change. The first version of Porphyro's encounter with Madeline reads:

> See while she speaks, his arms encroaching slow,
> Have zoned her, heart to heart—loud, loud the dark winds blow!
> For on the midnight came a tempest fell;
> More sooth, for that his quick rejoinder flows
> Into her burning ear—and still the spell

> Unbroken guards her in serene repose.
> With her wild dream he mingled, as a rose
> Marryeth its odour with a violet . . . [7]

While the final version reads:

> Beyond a mortal man impassioned far
> At these voluptuous accents, he arose
> Ethereal, flushed and like a throbbing star
> Seen mid the sapphire heaven's deep repose;
> Into her dream he melted, as the rose
> Blendeth its odour with the violet—
> Solution sweet . . . (316–22)

The revised lines work to clarify a sexual union that is sublimated in the manuscript version. Keats's friend Richard Woodhouse jocularly noted the change in a letter to a mutual friend:

> As the poem was orig[inall]y written, we innocent ones (ladies and myself) might very well have supposed that Porphyro, when acquainted with Madeline's love for him, and when "he arose, Ethereal, flush[ed]" &c &c (turn to it) set himself at once to persuade her to go off with him, and succeeded and went over the "Dartmoor Black" (now changed for some other place) to be married, in right honest chaste and sober wise. But, as it is now altered, as soon as M has confessed her love, P [instead] winds by degrees his arm round her, presses breast to breast, and acts all the acts of a bona fide husband, while she fancies she is only playing the part of a Wife in a dream. This alteration is of about three stanzas; and tho' there are no improper expressions but all is left to inference, and tho' profanely speaking, the Interest on the reader's imagination is greatly heightened, yet I do apprehend it will render the poem unfit for ladies, and indeed scarcely to be mentioned to them among the "things that are." He says he does not want ladies to read his poetry: that he writes for men—and that if in the former poem there was an opening for doubt what took place, it was his fault for not writing clearly and comprehensibly.[8]

Though we cannot verify whether Keats discovered an erotic version of "Sleeping Beauty" while in the process of revising "The Eve of St. Agnes," it is tempting to see in the alteration some of the same differences between the Perrault and Basile versions: the "spell/Unbroken" that "guards" the chaste beauty in "*La Belle au Bois Dormant*" cannot protect Talia in "*Sole, Luna e Talia*" from the aroused king. Indeed, there is a descriptive similarity between the male arousal implicit in Keats's lines ("Beyond a mortal man impassioned far / At these voluptuous accents, he arose / Ethereal, flushed and like a throbbing star") and Basile's ("crying aloud, [the king] felt his blood course hotly through his veins in contemplation of so many charms").

"The Eve of St. Agnes" is not a conventional frame-tale; it is, however, a poem about breaking through the frames that separate outside and inside, chill and warmth, sacred and secular, quick and dead. The poem begins with a description of the wintry landscape and the deserted chapel where a Beadsman prays amid chill funerary statues, and moves into the castle, into Madeline's room, and, ultimately, into Madeline. Keats sets both Porphyro and the reader to breeching these concentric barriers that conceal the sleeping form at the center.

In the "bitter chill" of the winter-encrusted frame, then, where "[t]he hare limp'd trembling through the frozen grass, / And silent was the flock in woolly fold" (3–4), we witness the near incapacitation of the man of God in an ironic trinity of Spenserian stanzas.

> Numb were the beadsman's fingers, while he told
> His rosary, and while his frosted breath
> Like pious incense from a censor old
> Seemed taking flight for heaven . . . (5–8)

The chapel, icy and bereft, is filled only with the storm and chill funerary statues, not with spiritual fervor.

> The sculptured dead on each side seem to freeze,
> Imprisoned in black, purgatorial rails;
> Knights, ladies, praying in dumb orat'ries,
> He passeth by; and his weak spirit fails
> To think how they may ache in icy hoods and mails. (14–18)

Within this frame, the Beadsman must serve "harsh penance on St. Agnes' Eve" (24), as his benefactor the Baron hired him to do. The reader, however, edges past this frame and penetrates the castle, which, in contrast to the chapel is filled with "Music's golden tongue" (21) "chambers . . . glowing to receive a thousand guests" (32–33), and an array of eroticized angels, "ever eager-eyed, / Star'd, where upon their heads the cornice rests, / With hair blown back, and wings put crosswise on their breasts" (34–36). The castle grows increasingly warmer with the introduction of Porphyro, who, with "heart on fire" (75) entertains ideas that periodically "flush his brow" and "ma(ke) purple riot" in "his pained heart" (137–38). The handmaid leads Porphyro and the narrative leads us "in close secrecy / Even to Madeline's chamber," where Madeline's mere presence warms the room; the "wintry moon," filtered through stained glass, leaves "warm gules" and "rose-bloom" on her breast and folded hands (217–20). Matching the sensual cornice angels, Madeline too, "seem'd a splendid angel," (223), who has "on her hair a glory like a saint" (222). The lovers' exhalations (Madeline pants [65; 295], moans [294; 303], weeps [302] and sighs [303]; Porphyro flushes [137; 318], breathes [249], and sings [289–93]) apparently contrast the Beadsman's "frosted breath" and gelid orations, and thus seemingly value erotic over religious devotion.

Both the Beadsman and Madeline pray; but Madeline's earthy prayers to St. Agnes carve a folkloric heart out of the cold, sacred frame of the poem. Madeline's servant is named Angela: no angel she, but rather a fairy tale witch, whom Porphyro looks upon "Like puzzled urchin on an aged crone / Who keepeth closed a wondrous riddle-book, / As spectacled she sits in chimney nook" (129–31). And though Porphyro hopes to "win . . . a peerless bride," he plans to enter the bonds of holy matrimony profanely, "while legioned fairies paced the coverlet / And pale enchantment held her sleepy-eyed" (167–69). Drawing upon "Sleeping Beauty" narratives, "The Eve of St. Agnes" separates beauty through enchantment, stills her, renders her available for observation, for exploration through and through.

In this sense, Keats initially allies his narrative attention to his questing prince, the "flushed" and "throbbing" Porphyro, whose name suggests the "purple riot" of his own heartbeats, the "violet" spurt of venous blood, and the "solution" of male potency.[9] His breaking and entering appears as a valorized action: carpe diem (or noctem) and gather ye Briar Roses while ye may. It would seem, at least at first blush, that Keats means to represent artistic breakthrough, the poet's thrust, past rigid religiosity and chill temporality, into a moment of sensual immortality.

The sexual politics of this poem have been discussed at length, most vigorously during the 1980s and early 1990s.[10] About the poem, Keats himself apparently said "that he sh[oul]d despise a man who would be such an eunuch in sentiment as to leave a [Girl] maid, with that Character about her, in such a situation: & should despise himself to write about it."[11] Keats's defense of the poem belies the actual complexity of his seduction scene; but so do these "sexuality debates," which rely on odd characterological interpretations of the poem, arguing, for instance, whether Porphyro is a hero or a villain, and whether Madeline is actually awake and therefore a "femme fatale" who participates in her own seduction. These questions are doomed, not only because they are unanswerable but also because they do not address the subtler poetics of "The Eve of St. Agnes." In the poem's crisis it is not upon Porphyro but upon Madeline that Keats dwells. Her first fully conscious words hardly match Porphyro's ecstasy:

> "No dream, alas! alas! and woe is mine!
> Porphyro will leave me here to fade and pine.—
> Cruel! What traitor could thee hither bring?
> I curse not, for my heart is lost in thine,
> Though thou forsakest a deceived thing;—
> A dove forlorn and lost with sick unpruned wing." (328–33)

This litany —"alas," "woe," "cruel," "traitor," "lost," "deceived," "forlorn," and "sick"—obviously (indeed, humorously) undercuts Porphyro's sensual triumph. An earlier manuscript version also stressed the disparity between Madeline's fantasy and her reality. The original stanza explains that the St. Agnes' Eve ritual promises Madeline a glimpse of her "future lord," who would woo her "all in the dream," yet allow her "to wake again / Warm in the virgin morn, no weeping Magdalen."[12] Keats preserved the sense, if not the lines: while the girl begins the poem "like a saint" and "like a splendid angel," she concludes it, after all, a weeping Ma(g)dalen. As in Basile's "*Sole, Luna e Talia,*" Madeline must commit herself into the hands of the man who has occasioned her rude awakening; both the Basile and Perrault versions of the tale stress that simply arriving at the beloved's home does not guarantee a happy ending.

As I have noted, "Sleeping Beauty" was not Keats's only source for the poem; when taken together, these narratives suggest that poetic vision lies with the spellbound girl. The most obvious of these is the legend of Saint Agnes for whom the superstition is named. Agnes, a thirteen-year-old Roman girl, refuses marriage to the son of a prefect. When the prefect sends her naked to a brothel to be defiled, God clothes and shields her. Agnes is ultimately martyred by having a sword thrust through her throat.[13] In setting his poem on St. Agnes' Eve, Keats seems to take full measure of the hagiographic irony of receiving marital predictions from the female saint who, for refusing earthly marriage, is threatened with rape and painfully martyred. Beverly Fields argues that Philomel, another silenced heroine, may be a source for "The Eve of St. Agnes." Keats owned a copy of *Titus Andronicus,* which both cites and echoes Ovid's rape of Philomel.[14] Over the disturbing exchange in which two male characters taunt the raped, tongueless, and handless Lavinia, Keats drew angry, heavy lines of eradication[15] as if committing violence to the book to blot out the sight of the playwright's brutality. Keats certainly underscores the rape of Philomel when Madeline prepares for bed, pained in her heart, "as though a tongueless nightingale should swell / Her throat in vain, and die, heart-stifled, in her dell" (205–6).[16] Saint Agnes, Philomel, Lavinia, and Basile's Sleeping Beauty: the poem is haunted with raped and voiceless heroines. If Keats's poem is the first nineteenth-century literary recasting of "Sleeping Beauty," by making Madeline a palimpsest of martyred women, *sub rosa* so to speak, he invests the fairy tale with unexpected pathos. In contributing to the critical history of "The Eve of St. Agnes," then, the task is not to discover whether Porphyro rapes Madeline (which has been answered in the affirmative), and certainly not to divine how Keats "feels" about this, but rather, to address the poetics of power in "The Eve of St. Agnes."

Keats's poetry frequently considers the dynamic between sleep and poetic vision. In "Ode to a Nightingale," Keats frets over the boundaries of sleep. The speaker longs "for a draft of vintage! that hath been / Cool'd a long age in the deep-delved earth, / Tasting of Flora"[17] so that he "might drink, and leave the world unseen, / and with thee [i.e., the nightingale] fade away into the forest dim" (19–20). This "tasting" of Flora resonates with Porphyro "blending" his "odor" with the rosy Madeline into a "solution sweet." The poet's pursuit of the nightingale, though, leads to wandering in "embalmed darkness," where the speaker falls "half in love with easeful Death," and calls "him soft names in many a mused rhyme" ("Nightingale," 52–53). Ultimately, the "faery lands" (70) recede, but leave the speaker questioning "do I wake or sleep?" (80). Dreamy abstraction, it seems, leads to confusion not only between waking and sleeping worlds, but between male and female genders. And in "Sonnet to Sleep," the poet is utterly in thrall to a sleep that wields a deathly power, that "soft embalmer of the still midnight"[18] which, if it chooses, can close the poet's eyes "in the midst of this thine hymn" (6), and which he calls upon to "seal the hushed casket of my soul" (14). In poems like "Sleep and Poetry" and "The Fall of Hyperion," Keats describes the "true" poet as the agent bringing dreams out of sleep and into words, an action that he renders as the breaking of a charm or enchantment:

> For Poesy alone can tell her dreams,
> With the fine spell of words alone can save

Imagination from the sable charm
And dumb enchantment.[19]

Poesy here is female but has a male interpreter, whose action resembles that of the prince carrying beauty from the castle, of Porphyro spiriting Madeline over the moors. But in this unfinished fragment, Keats identifies the developing poet, not with the prince, protector from "dumb enchantment," but with the sleeping princess. The speaker is summoned to the prophetess Moneta, who avers that "The poet and the dreamer are distinct, / Diverse, sheer opposites, antipodes" ("Hyperion," 198–200), and informs him that he has hitherto been a dreamer: "What benefit canst thou do, or all thy tribe, / To the great world? Thou art a dreaming thing" (167–68).

All written within six months of "The Eve of St. Agnes," these poems reveal Keats binding his poetic identity to a feminine sleeper. But they also demonstrate Keats's refusal to sustain an idyllic depiction of sleep as timeless dream space—instead, hints of mortality intrude upon and inexorably mingle with these dreamscapes, rendering them uncomfortably temporal. Movement inward in "The Eve of St. Agnes" reverses upon Madeline's awakening:

Into her dream he melted, as the rose
Blendeth its odour with the violet,
—Solution sweet: meantime the frost-wind blows
Like Love's alarum pattering the sharp sleet
Against the window-panes; St. Agnes' moon hath set. (320–24)

No sooner does Porphyro rape Madeline than the storm invades the castle: the actions are separated only by a colon. The narrative then follows the couple outward into the chill of the storm, in a literal dampening of the sensual pleasure which Porphyro, at least, has enjoyed. But, long before this chilly conclusion, uneasy connections between Madeline's room and the Beadsman's deathly chapel abound from the moment Porphyro sets foot there. When Porphyro enters the room it is "pale, latticed, chill, and silent as a tomb" (113). When Madeline herself enters, "out went the taper as she hurried in; / Its little smoke, in pallid moonshine, died" (199–200). Madeline herself later lies "in azure-lidded sleep" (262), like a corpse, or like the funerary monuments in the crypt outside. These are subtle moments, but they disrupt what at first seems a simple opposition between the secular and sacred spaces of the poem. And if the Beadsman does "harsh penance on St.

Agnes' Eve," so too does Madeline. Once Porphyro leads Madeline downstairs, they begin to fade: "They glide, like phantoms, into the wide hall; / Like phantoms, to the iron porch they glide" (361–62). All pronouns vanish, and the front door seems to open itself: "The key turns, and the door upon its hinges groans" (369). And there, upon the threshold, Keats leaves the reader clutching a ghost story.

> And they are gone—aye, ages long ago
> These lovers fled away into the storm.
> That night the Baron dreamed of many a woe,
> And all his warrior-guests, with shade and form
> Of witch and demon, and large coffin-worm,
> Were long be-nightmared. Angela the old
> Died palsey-twitched, with meagre face deform;
> The Beadsman, after thousand aves told,
> For aye unsought for, slept among his ashes cold. (370–78)

Though Keats has been at some pains to separate the blooming Madeline from the winter storm, the specters of Christianity, and the haggard priest, Porphyro's awakening thrusts her into that icy frame, pairing her with the doomed Beadsman, connecting her to the Baron's dreams of "coffin-worm." The poem ends in cold ashes; long since buried, the couple is converted into the beadsman's "sculptured dead."

"Porphyro" means "purple," but the name also evokes "porphyry," an Egyptian marble prized for sculpture by the Romans. Porphyro: suffused with life, then, or rigid, hard, and cold? He signifies both heartthrob and headstone, both erect phallus and rigor mortis; perhaps then, a figure for time itself, the force that claims all dreamers, poets and princesses alike. Even supposing that Keats wished to syncopate with the questing prince, claiming power over sleep through poesy, the ill young man saw himself instead as ensorcelled sleeper—dreamy, visionary, but also bound and helpless—penetrated through and through by time. Less than a year after Porphyro and Madeline vanished "over the Southern moors," Keats disappeared Southwards into Italy, and into death. And in this way, the Beadsman, too, becomes entangled with Keats' estimation of his poet self: a haunted figure, prematurely aged, dying alone. In the temporal frame sits the man compelled to count (Spenserian) beads.

The poem's preoccupation with time, literary composition, and a poet's longevity would lead new generations of young men to approach the "Sleeping Beauty" tale over the nineteenth century. "The man I count greater than them all—Wordsworth, Coleridge, Byron, Shelley, every one of 'em—is Keats, who died at 25—thousands of faults! . . . But he's wonderful!" said Tennyson to William Allingham.[20]

I will conclude this chapter by noting that Tennyson's early poetry separates Keats' "The Eve of St. Agnes" into contemplative components. It is not accidental that many of the titles of Tennyson's early work evoke "The Eve of St. Agnes": "Madeline," "St. Agnes' Eve," "Rosalind," and "The Sleeping Beauty" are especially obvious examples. As James Hood has argued, these poems strive to hold the subject still for intense observation, as is evidenced by images (often violent) of binding and restraint: "We'll bind you fast in silken cords, / And kiss away the bitter words / From off your rosy mouth"[21]; "If prayers will not hush thee, / Airy Lilian, / Like a rose-leaf I will crush thee, / Fairy Lilian."[22] Of course, these examples also overlay ladies with roses, suggesting that Tennyson had "Briar Rose" in mind. His fragment of 1830, "The Sleeping Beauty," reinforces a connection between Keats, stilled poetic subjects, and Briar Rose:

> The silk star-broider'd coverlid
>   Unto her limbs itself doth mould
> Languidly ever; and, amid
>   Her full black ringlets downward roll'd,
> Glows forth each softly-shadow'd arm
>   With bracelets of the diamond bright:
> Her constant beauty doth inform
>   Stillness with love, and day with light.[23]

In his earliest work, Tennyson puzzles through Keats's relationship to sleep and beauty; he looks to "The Eve of St. Agnes" to shape his own questions of temporality, and remodels it in a Victorian frame in "The Day Dream."

CHAPTER 7

"A Perfect Form in Perfect Rest"

Tennyson's "Day Dream"

"The Day Dream" is virtually absent from criticism, except in stray single sentences, the primary adjectives of which are words like "frivolous" and "juvenile."[1] But the poem is not juvenilia: it was composed over the same years as Tennyson's other sleeping figure poems, "The Kraken," "Tithonus," "The Epic," and the first book of *In Memoriam;* "Day Dream" alone of these has escaped significant critical attention. This very silence is an important feature of the poem, for it marks an erasure of the "The Day Dream" that Tennyson himself labored to ensure. The poet strove to outgrow and abandon the fairy tale, even within the very poem on the subject. Ultimately, however, "The Day Dream" reflects the opposing positions that I articulated in the introduction to this section: that to tell the tale of "Sleeping Beauty" is to claim it and then abandon it for other, "worthier" forms, but also that in the act of retelling, Tennyson cedes authorial power to the tale.

Tennyson's "The Sleeping Beauty," written in 1830, initiated the fairy tale subject that would come to occupy him for over a decade. It observes a princess rapt in enduring stasis—dreamless, motionless, and quite possibly breathless as well:

> She sleeps: her breathings are not heard
>   In palace chambers far apart.
> The fragrant tresses are not stirr'd
>   That lie upon her charmed heart.
> She sleeps: on either hand upswells
>   The gold-fringed pillow lightly prest:
> She sleeps, nor dreams, but ever dwells
>   A perfect form in perfect rest. ("The Sleeping Beauty," 17–24)

This fragment was not included in *Poems Chiefly Lyrical,* which may indicate Tennyson's own uncertainty of how to categorize his brief musing upon a spell. It seems to pledge allegiance to the lady poems, those early "erotic devotions," which scholars have suggested we see as deliberately "disembodied . . . types" that construct "a grammar of longing."[2] But it also bears resemblance to "The Kraken," Tennyson's poem of the same year, which meditates upon another fantastic, dreamless sleeper. It seems that "The Sleeping Beauty" was a sketch for a longer meditation on time and the nature of stasis and change.

Published in 1842, "Day Dream" grew around this fragment like the briar hedge around the princess. From 1834 to 1836, Tennyson added "The Sleeping Palace" as well as the sections treating the prince's "Arrival," "Revival," and "Departure" with beauty. In 1837–38 he wrote a Victorian frame, the "Prologue," "Moral," "Envoi," and "Epilogue," in which a speaker addresses his friend Flora, instructing and wooing her through the "Briar Rose" tale. This expansion coincided with such widely read works as Carlyle's *Sartor Resartus* (1832–33) and *On Heroes* (1840), and Macaulay's "Review of Southey's Colloquies" (1830)—all narratives of, and allegories for, national and historical progress. Given these textual models, it makes sense that Tennyson did not care to leave his 1830 beauty sleeping; in "The Day Dream" he figures her awakening as the rebirth of culture.

"The Day Dream" opens upon the Victorian Flora, who has just awakened—not from a charmed hundred-year sleep, but from a charming hourlong nap:

> O Lady Flora, let me speak:
>   A pleasant hour has passed away
> While, dreaming on your damask cheek,
>   The dewy sister-eyelids lay.
> As by the lattice you reclined,

> I went through many wayward moods
> To see you dreaming—and behind,
> A summer crisp with shining woods.
> And I, too, dreamed, until at last
> Across my fancy, brooding warm,
> The reflex of a legend past,
> And loosely settled into form. ("Prologue," 1–12)

In watching Flora sleep, "the reflex of a legend" passes across the speaker's "fancy." Tennyson uses "reflex" here in two senses: the physiological, "an involuntary action" and the linguistic, "a form corresponding to, or derived from, another comparable form."[3] Without volition of the speaker, then, Flora becomes a "reconstructed" Briar Rose.

This passage reveals how "Day Dream" participates in Tennyson's experiments with form, evident in his concurrent composition during this decade: "The Kraken," "The Day Dream," "Tithonus," "The Epic," and the first part of *In Memoriam*. Tennyson was contemplating the human relationship to time, but also questing after the form (both the poetic mode and the dormant figure) to best express the relationship. This struggle is most evident when comparing "The Epic" and "The Day Dream," two frame tales wrapped around resurrected stories of resurrection. "The Epic"'s reluctant poet figure provides the poem's crux by dismissing his own twelve-book Arthurian epic with "why should any man / Remodel models?"[4] His reading of the eleventh book, "Morte D'Arthur," salvaged from the fire where he threw it, and his friends' rapt response, answers the question:

> To me, methought, who waited with the crowd,
> There came a bark that, blowing forward, bore
> King Arthur, like a modern gentleman
> Of stateliest port; and all the people cried,
> "Arthur has come again: he cannot die." (343–47)

To "remodel models" is to resurrect narrative, to retailor old ideas with the new clothing of societal need. But the poet's labor is explicit: he and his friends call the work "his King Arthur" (28), "his epic" (28), "these twelve books of mine" (38), "his work" (331). There is no such assurance of authoritative control with "the reflex of a legend" that "loosely settles into form." When placed side by side, the "remodeled model" and the reflexive day dream beg a distinction between involuntary vision and imaginative labor.

"Day Dream"'s speaker begins the tale, not with its conventional exposition, but with the "Sleeping Palace":

> Here rests the sap within the leaf,
>   Here stays the blood along the veins.
> Faint shadows, vapours lightly curl'd,
>   Faint murmurs from the meadows come,
> Like hints and echoes of the world
>   To spirits folded in the womb. ("The Sleeping Palace," 3–8)

Importantly, this enchanted caesura is likened to a gestation that is cyclic and dreamy, much as the fairy tale passes across the speaker's brooding fancy. This passivity suggests a marked contrast to the labor described in remodeling models, and into this stillness Tennyson interjects:

> When will the hundred summers die,
>   And thought and time be born again,
> And newer knowledge, drawing nigh,
>   Bring truth that sways the souls of men?
> Here all things in their place remain,
>   As all were order'd, ages since.
> Come Care and Pleasure, Hope and Pain,
>   And bring the fated Fairy Prince. (49–56)

Thoughtless, timeless, and radiating lassitude, the princess occasions a pregnant pause in a world that cannot deliver itself of the enchantment. The prince who penetrates this feminine languor brings "care" and "pain" with him, but these are productive labor pains, corollary to "knowledge," "truth," "hope." This invocation of the prince immediately precedes the "Sleeping Beauty" section, which remains identical to the 1830 fragment. No longer a "perfect form" unto itself, the poem must, for the sake of the realm, be roused from "perfect rest."

As Clinton Machann has noted, "From the beginning of his career, Tennyson was sensitive to his own ambiguous social status as a male poet in the Romantic tradition, associated with the suspiciously feminized qualities of imaginative inwardness, emotive openness, isolation from the aggressive 'entrepreneurial manhood' valorized by bourgeois ideals."[5] Like Machann, John Hughes documents that "from the 1830s and 1840s onward, Tennyson was continually retreating from the insinuations of his critics . . . that his inspiration was lacking, as *Athaenium* put it, in 'the manly courage . . .' appropriate to a poet of the time."[6] As if to counteract this criticism, the prince of "The Day Dream" gazes soberly at "the bodies and the bones of those / That strove in other days to pass" ("The Arrival," 9–10), then "he breaks the hedge: he enters there" (18). This metaphor suggests a larger poetics of breaking and entering: no passive dreamer he. Tennyson appears to assert the connection between poet and prince that Keats could not—or refused to—sustain. Elsewhere Tennyson insisted that the "great sage poets, who are both great thinkers and great artists," must deliver both beauty and prophesy into the world.[7] Artistry, then, must not be a dreamy, introspective process, but a determined rush toward beauty and truth. Though Keats introduced this very subject, in this very language, in "The Fall of Hyperion," Tennyson adopts it here to resist Keats and other Romantic "dreamers." Linda Shires contextualizes this impetus within the widespread early Victorian turn from Romanticism and toward "the myth of a strong, paternal masculinity in England. . . . In part, the Victorians invent a patriarch to run the country on behalf of the young queen."[8]

"The Day Dream" offers two historicizing moments. The first is a synchronic literary history in which Victorians reject Romanticism, linking it (however reductively) to feminized self-absorption, to beauty without prophecy. In the section titled "Moral," the speaker coyly protests that there *is* no moral—other than aesthetic:

> Go, look in any glass and say,
>   What moral is in being fair.
> Oh to what uses shall we put
>   The wildweed-flower that simply blows?
> And is there any moral shut
>   Within the bosom of the rose? ("The Moral," 3–8)

However, the speaker immediately subverts this moral for "*L'Envoi*," a second historicizing moment in which he imagines the tale diachronically, an endlessly repeating pattern of sleep and resurrection:

> Well—were it not a pleasant thing
>   To fall asleep with all one's friends;
> To pass with all our social ties
>   To silence from the paths of men;
> And every hundred years to rise
>   And learn the world, and sleep again;

> To sleep through terms of mighty wars,
>   And wake on science grown to more,
> On secrets of the brain, the stars,
>   As wild as aught of fairy lore;
> And all else that the years will show,
>   The Poet-forms of stronger hours,
> The vast republics that may grow,
>   The Federations and the Powers;
> Titanic forces taking birth . . .
> So sleeping, so aroused from sleep
>   Thro' sunny decades new and strange,
> Or gay quinquenniads we would reap
>   The flower and quintessence of change. ("L'Envoi," 3–24)

The first moral abandoned for the second reflects the poem's own composition history, reaching across the decade from Romantic to Victorian literary production, from timeless fragment (a perfect form in perfect rest) to timely narrative (a fairy kingdom framed by a Victorian present). Yet this passage also proposes a model of cultural evolution as punctuated equilibrium, with "thought and time" periodically galvanized. In the moment of transformation, with priapic hyperbole "the charm was snap't / There rose a noise of striking clocks. . . . And sixty feet the fountain leapt" (1–2, 8) and like water breaking before a birth, "all the long-pent stream of life / Dash'd downward in a cataract" (15–16). Time accelerates as metaphors of climax, gestation, and delivery converge in a single moment. As if the prince were both proud father and doctor on house-call, he successfully delivers the kingdom of a curse.

Tennyson's fascination with the sciences is axiomatic, and if in "The Princess" and *In Memoriam* his "analogical thinking" rests upon evolutionary biology, geology, and physics, in "The Day Dream," it tends toward physiology, specifically the circulatory system.[9] As Kirstie Blair notes, "the rapid rise of physiological and medical explanations of bodily processes meant that the embodied heart assumed a vital role in culture and literature."[10] Tennyson himself received a copy of Percival Lord's *Popular Physiology* (1834) for Christmas in 1838, and Blair argues that this gift markedly influenced Tennyson's concurrent poetic composition.[11] Whereas Blair's *Victorian Poetry and the Culture of the Heart* explores the Victorian physiological heart as a somatic analog for the emotional register and metrics of Victorian poetry, I am more interested in the idea that the Victorian heartbeat becomes an epistemological device for investigating both personal and public temporality, that is, the intersection between individual development and social progress.

In *Sartor Resartus,* Carlyle describes punctuated progress as the "long-drawn Systole," periods of cultural advancement, the arterial spurt to all parts of the body (politic), "and long-drawn Diastole," periods of stagnation that Carlyle imagines as a passive pause before the next action (112).[12] Two decades later, James John Garth Wilkinson's *The Human Body and Its Connexion With Man: Illustrated by the Principal Organs* appears to have adopted and significantly extended Carlyle's physiological model.[13] Wilkinson's book studies the "principal organs" in turn: the brain, the lungs, the stomach, the heart, and the skin, often bewilderingly conflating physiological processes with the functioning of the British body politic. In the chapter on the heart (the longest in the book), Wilkinson both personifies and politicizes the circulatory system: "The heart, as the blood's executive power, gives corporeal substance to the frame, inasmuch as the body itself arises from the blood. The existence of the human machine depends upon the heart."[14] The heart is likewise "the agent" that "in successive moments forces life upon the arteries" (186) (which are compelled into "expansion or receptiveness") and thereby "perpetuate[s] the commonwealth" (187). Here the heart is the executive that determines the timely functioning of the machine, the ordering of the empire, and the linear narrative of life: at once shop owner, prime minister, and author.

At first, Carlyle and Wilkinson appear to differ slightly in their heart/culture analogies: in Carlyle's model, the heart is divided against itself, systole must constantly strive to dispel the passivity of diastole; for Wilkinson, the heart is a fully active agent, forcing both orderliness and progress upon the passively receiving arteries. Later in the chapter, however, Wilkinson reverts to a binarized model of the heart far more like Carlyle's when he differentiates between the "private or venous" and the "public or arterial sides of the heart" (234). The blood's cycle from the heart, to the lungs, and back into the heart is likened to the progress of an individual from family home, to school, to premarital passions, to marriage, to public (i.e., political) life, with service to the state being the apex and arrival of an individual man: "As it is with the child, so it is with the young blood—it has the capacity of going through human life, and of being and doing whatever lies in, or issues from, the heart" (236). This individual motion Wilkinson reproduces and amplifies into the progress of nations:

> The blood that it throws forth is scarlet with force . . . it is public feeling in all its forms, and we have already anticipated its name, and called it

the patriotic heart. Rule and empire throb forever here, founded in the purple of the blood. The body corporeal streams from the height of the left ventricle, as the body politic from the heart of dominion, which is the instinctive architect of the state. If vicegerency of functions establishes connections between life and organism, then the love of country or empire must sit on the throne of this ventricle, whose lordly stroke reaches the confines of the body, and seizes the central blood itself within a conqueror's grasp. (235)

Ultimately, both Carlyle and Wilkinson imagine within the circulatory system a simultaneously synchronic and diachronic temporality. Progress battles stagnation with every pulse; this pattern is extended into an ontegenetic, then historical and cultural model.

Both Carlyle and Wilkinson attempt to impose a linear, developmental, and productive pattern on a process that is essentially circular. Though Wilkinson says that the purpose of the heart is "to perpetuate life by incessant cycles of formation, destruction and reformation" (189), and elsewhere comments upon "the living wheel" of the human circulatory system (190), and though he insists that one can begin a description of the circulatory system at any point in the cycle, his entire analogy is constructed as a narrative of linear progress—like the motion of the factory line, or the impetus of a leader, blood is "forced," "driven, "discharged" (185) and "throw[n] forth" (236) by the heart. Though their metaphors are dependent upon the spatial nature of the heart's "chambers," both Carlyle and Wilkinson emphasize the departure of the blood from those chambers as reflective of a larger systemic progress. Both, in other words, seem anxious to temporalize the heart and to despatialize it insofar as possible. Following Julia Kristeva's logic in "Women's Time," I would go so far as to say that both authors appear to be attempting to gender the heartbeat (at least the systolic force of the heartbeat) masculine.[15]

Recent work on time shows how Victorian interest in linear temporality dovetailed with scientific and technological developments of the first half of the century: Charles Lyell's *Principles of Geology,* the second law of thermodynamics, Darwin's *Origin of Species,* the railroad and its clock, the factory and its assembly line, the relative affordability of the pocket watch and mantle clock.[16] It is not, as earlier critics suggested,[17] that these innovations *created* a *new* sense of time, or vice versa; rather, these scientific and industrial changes provided a new set of metaphors and analogs with which to imagine time, and to imagine its relationship to power structures. Circulatory analogies thus participate in the wider discourse of temporality taking place in these decades, with constructs of human history undergoing paradigmatic disruption, and with the new and uncomfortable understanding that history as "lived time" must be differentiated from and somehow reconciled to "deep time."[18] If the heartbeat is the fundamental unit of human time, it is undeniably cyclic, and therefore by Victorian terms worrisomely feminine; moreover, the heart was the historically feminized *space* of emotions. There seemed to be an urgency to make over that basic unit into a linear, and masculinized, temporal flow.

The writings of Carlyle and Wilkinson straddle Tennyson's production of "The Day Dream." As Blair says, Tennyson was writing into a heightened anxiety about relationships between the ticking of the clock, the motions of universe, and the rhythm of poetry.[19] Indebted to Carlyle's "long-drawn systole and long-drawn diastole," anticipating the analogical thinking of Wilkinson and Paget, Tennyson makes human physiology hermeneutic for temporality itself. Carlyle's systole and Tennyson's prince: both throbbing injections of life. Tennyson's "Sleeping Palace" "stays the blood along the veins"—a veritable "long-drawn diastole"—until the prince delivers the dormant princess into the world, just as "great thinkers" deliver civilizations into golden ages. This returns us to Carlyle's exhortation in *Past and Present* for the capitalist middle classes to be wakeful princes, and not sleeping princesses. And whereas *Sartor Resartus* undoubtedly influenced the "The Day Dream," it is likely that the "The Day Dream" gave *Past and Present* (published the following year) its "Sleeping Beauty" metaphor. Moreover, in all three of these cardiac analogies, neither the heart nor its societal analog moves in inexorable reflex, but rather, appears to beat in mindful, deliberate labor—a remodeled model. This emphasis upon the agentive heartbeat is underscored in the almost eerily regular meter of "The Day Dream," its iambs ticking away steadily like a heartbeat, until:

/ ˘ ˘ / ˘ / ˘ /
When will the hundred summers die. ("The Sleeping Palace," 49)

The approaching prince is signaled, perhaps, by the pounding of the metrical heart; the trochee in the first foot creates a systolic pump that reacts mimetically to the thrusting force of this Carlylian hero.

I may be lending Carlyle's figuration more erotic charge than is actually there, imagining in his biocultural simile another, subtler narrative in which the blood that has entered the private space of chamber then spurts out in an act of begetting both personal and national. If I overreach, it is due in part to the subsequent productions of both Wilkinson and Tennyson, who,

I think, remodeled Carlyle's brief image into more overt elisions between the heartbeat, male climax, and progress into civic duty:

> though at the top of the public impulses, it is the most secret of the chambers, and is not only the house, but the bed of the organ. . . . The grasp of the auricle, which consummates this life in the blood, drives it onwards, as before, into the next chamber, or left ventricle.[20] The signification of this fourth heart cannot be doubtful. It is the accumulated power of the passions. The blood that it throws forth is scarlet with force . . . it is public feeling in all its forms, and we have already anticipated its name, and called it the patriotic heart. (Wilkinson, 235)

In Wilkinson's admittedly confusing metaphor, the passage of the blood from the aortic valve into the left chamber and thence into the arteries is likened simultaneously to a private, erotic "consummation" and a propulsion into systemic action.

Here, too, Tennyson's "Day Dream" anticipates Wilkinson's analogy. I have already suggested the erotic register of Tennyson's "Day Dream" upon the princess's waking. It is also true, however, that Tennyson develops metaphors for "sleeping" and "waking" on every scale, and therefore the erotic pulse of the poem echoes in its descriptions of heartbeats and of global policy alike. Imagined organically, the palace's stilled heartbeat ("here stays the blood along the veins") is countered by the prince's own cardiac fitness ("his heart / Beats quick and quicker, till he find / The quiet chamber far apart" ["The Arrival," 26–28]; imagined reproductively, the princess's hymeneal "charm" is "snap't" by "a touch [and] a kiss" (followed promptly by the fountain's ejaculatory surge); imagined gestationally, the realm's eternally suspended pregnancy ("spirits folded in the womb") is delivered ("the long pent stream of life dash'd downward in a cataract"), a figurative parturition echoed in the speaker's proleptic vision of cultural evolution as "titanic forces taking birth." These metaphors enfold and encroach upon each other (where heart chamber suffused suggests climactic spurt suggests egg fertilized suggests waters broken) and by effacing the discursive boundaries between circulation, conception, gestation, and delivery, personal punctuation and historical progress are linked together through the narrative of the spellbound female aroused. In moving from "spirits folded in the womb" in "The Sleeping Palace" to the "titanic forces taking birth" in "*L'Envoi*," the poem enables the ontogeny of the human body to recapitulate the phylogeny of historical development. Vitally, the prince wages control over each of these personal and historical rhythms. "Thought and time" cannot "be born again" without the prince, and in the frame tale's cultural corollary "Titanic forces" are *taking* birth": no feminine force *gives* birth in this poem. Instead, diastole is likened to pregnancy, and pregnancy to diastole, and both are figured as destructive cyclicism. There is no female generative agency in this poem, but rather image after image of introspective feminized stagnancy, which the prince and the speaker redeem with "the noise of striking clocks." Neither heartbeat, nor conception, nor gestation, nor delivery can be completed without the prince. Like the chambers of the heart, like the chamber of the princess, the princess herself becomes the space to be filled with time.

Thus, in Victorian England, the "Sleeping Beauty" fairy tale unites discourses of corporeal and cultural temporality.[21] The "Sleeping Beauty" tale from its inception is part of a genre in which "fertility control" poses its own discursive question, but is also, importantly, a metaphor for narrative control.[22] In the nineteenth century, with expanded knowledge of physiological and geological processes, the tale swelled to include temporal power structures within in its interrogative boundaries.[23] Victorian remodelings of "Sleeping Beauty" demonstrate that most writers imagined a fundamentally narratological pattern of development. According to Kristeva, the trope of linear time is imagined as a "prospective unfolding," including within its terms departure, progression, and arrival.[24] In these terms, linear time occupies even the basic level of "language considered as the enunciation of sentences" and that "mastery of language is mastery of time."[25] Departure, progression, arrival: narrative, which shares these characteristics of "unfolding," might be conceived of as the "natural" mode of articulation of a normative "masculine time." To impose narrative on physiological and cultural processes imposes a comforting linearity on what must have seemed disturbingly cyclic.

I have traced the similarities in these circulatory, gestational, and temporal tropes existing in the national discourse, in philosophy, medicine, and literature alike. But the very permeability of these narratives between disciplines is itself a kind of circulatory system, and one that troubled the ameliorative rhetoric of literary history. As Catherine Gallagher has noted, writers since Aristotle have been "uncertain about whether writing most resembled the natural generativity of plants and animals or the unnatural generation of money, which, through usury, proliferates through mere circulation but brings nothing qualitatively new into being."[26] In this understanding of writing, where nothing and no one is original, but everything borrowed and returned with interest, poetic composition comes uncomfortably close to the reflex of a legend: that is, the supposed circulation of fairy tales and legends through nurses and other nameless storytellers. Young authors like Tennyson labored to efface this troubling cycle of debt.

Like all fairy tales, "Sleeping Beauty" is a narrative; but fairy tales, whether their print histories reflect a primarily male or female authorship, are stereotypically identified as a female cultural production, reflective not of temporalized narrative, but of ineffable space.[27] In "The Day Dream," Tennyson claims the "Sleeping Beauty" narrative in order to transfix and then bypass it. In *Poems*, Ricks includes a manuscript version of the first seven lines, in which the speaker reads Flora like a written text:

> I pored upon you as you dreamed
> > Beside the casement till there grew
> I know not what of strange: you seemed
> > No lady Flora that I knew
> But some perfection of the Mind
> > As minted in the golden moods
> > Of some great Artist. (48)

Tennyson may have altered the verse, but he retained the sentiment: when pored over by the poet, Flora becomes a carefully cultivated Briar Rose, and this separates the male literary author, firmly situated in the linear stream of history, from the female dreamer, the space of interpretation. Indeed, Sleeping Beauty fades into the background in subordination to the prince. If "newer knowledge" for men is soul-swaying, for women it is sexual education. Asleep, Beauty's torpor is complete; awake, she eagerly attaches herself to the Prince: "'I'd sleep another hundred years, / O love, for such another kiss / . . . O whither goest thou, tell me where?'" ("The Departure," 9–10, 26) Briar Rose's self-absorbed—indeed, all-absorbing—sleep ends in her absorption in another; "Beyond the night, across the day, / Thro' all the world she follow'd him" (31–32).

For Tennyson, "The Day Dream" is not an end unto itself, but another moment of arrest and contemplation before continuing on to epic—to the remodeled model. And this very fact has deterred critical commentary on "The Day Dream": its own terms deflect its import, for what is a daydream compared to an epic? In "Sleep and Poetry," Keats maps out a plan whereby he shall move from pastoral, which he terms the "realm . . . of Flora" (102), to epic, which he terms "the nobler life, / Where I many find the agonies, the strife of human hearts" (123–25). The name of Tennyson's frame heroine, Flora, is surely no accident. Keats did not live to complete his epic, but Tennyson did. "The reflex of a legend" "develops" into the ringingly triumphant

"Arthur has come again, he cannot die." In "The Day Dream" Tennyson both adopts Keats's developmental model, and passes by Keats tangled in the briars at his feet, one of "the bodies and the bones of those who strove in other days to pass." We don't write about "Day Dream" because Tennyson encourages us to see it as a phase he was going through. Though in the tale the prince incorporates the princess into the world, in the generic sense, Tennyson tries to conjure "Sleeping Beauty"—and with her his own associations with Romanticism and the suspicious femininity of his poetic production—into a dreamless sleep. The poem asks to be read as an immature, even girlish literary production, traversed after a decade, abandoned for two epics, each with a sleeping Arthur at its center.

The word *spell* supplies the heartbeat of this chapter. In its earliest usage (in *Beowulf*), and deriving from Old English spill or *spiel*, it means to utter, declare, relate, or tell a discourse, narrative, tale, or fable. The word originated, then, in the transmission of fabulous oral narrative. In the sixteenth century it becomes "a set of words, formula or verse supposed to possess magical powers; a fascinating or enthralling charm." In this same century, the word *spell*, deriving from a different root, the Old English *spala* (spare), begins to refer to time and labor: "a turn of work in order to relieve others." And as the word came to be associated with temporality, it altered from treating the spoken narrative to insisting upon the written word: "to enunciate or write letter by letter" from the sixteenth century, and by the nineteenth century "to turn out (literary work or writing) with some difficulty." The *OED* exemplifies this meaning with a quote by Sir Walter Scott, from a journal of 15 May 1829: "I have spelled out some work this day, though I have been rather knocked about."[28] How appropriate that this definition of "spell" should come to us from the man who fretted about his literary reconstruction of ballads in *Minstrelsy of the Scottish Border* in this famously ambiguous statement: "In many respects, if I improved the poetry, I spoiled the simplicity of the old song."[29] Spoil: a telling word; indivisible from its associations with ravaging and plunder, the sentence spells out literary victory. And it is not necessary to stoop to jokes about "Sleeping Booty" to point out that spoiling *is* tantamount to spelling: to write with difficulty means to strip the definition of "spell" away from its oral roots. Tennyson's speaker may "daydream" the tale in an idle hour, but Tennyson the poet resists reflexivity, framing the modern moral around the tale over a decade. This, Tennyson insists, is a stage en route to literature; it is not, in Wordsworth's terms "to tell again . . . some tale" but painstaking labor: spelling, word by word. But if it is necessary to ravage the tale to make the poem, the fairy tale's disruptive potential is implicit. Though Tennyson tries to put the tale to bed, he also seems to understand that the tale will burst its temporal and generic boundaries.

For what, after all, *is* "The Day Dream"? To what form or genre does it belong? Its originating fragment was not included in *Poems, Chiefly Lyrical,* nor is it considered one of the "lady poem" lyrics; the completed version is not counted among the "English Idyll" poems. "The Princess," not "The Day Dream," is generally cited as the first of Tennyson's "topical poems." Perhaps our critical neglect is part of a larger problem: what is a form that has a fairy tale at its heart? It may be helpful to reflect that Bakhtin's writing is currently enjoying its own resurrection with critics who understand "dialogism" not only as voices competing within a single form, but as disjunctive *genres* that cross-pollinate, inhabiting each other uncomfortably and productively. For us, for Tennyson, to allow the fairy tale to join the poem's dialogism means acknowledging that the fairy tale is a narrative genre, one that matters, one that can disrupt and threaten other forms by inhabiting them.

If we are at a loss to find a generic resting place for the poem, "The Day Dream" wants to know what it is, too. Indeed, it is a poem quite literally taken up with form; the word appears six times in the poem, with meanings at anxious variance: is this "a perfect form in perfect rest," or one of "the poet-forms of stronger hours," or something that is only "loosely settled into form," something that causes within the poet or the poem itself "many a wayward mood?" Dialogism abounds in the poem through its wayward forms, its weird temporalities.[30] There is, in the poem's transition from frame to tale, an immediate problem of time and space. The *frame* begins in the past tense ("A pleasant hour has passed away / While dreaming on your damask cheek the dewy sister eyelids lay"); the *tale* begins in the present tense ("Here rests the sap along the leaf, here stays the blood along the veins"). Then, too "here rests . . . here stays" is purposely dislocating: where is "here"? Moreover, the frame, though beginning in the past tense, moves to the present when Flora asks to have the fairy tale recited, while the tale remains in the present until the princess awakens, when it shifts to past tense. On the one hand, temporal difficulties would seem to be resolved by the end of the poem: the fairy tale is left in the past tense, the Victorian frame joins the present tense. On the other hand, these tense shifts are confusing, preventing any simple certainty of linear evolution from past to present, sleeping to waking: rather, the tenses move the poem in a suspiciously circular motion. Tennyson, as he so often did, deliberately tangles the frame and tale, making a "lattice," (or "casement," or "portal," he used these terms interchangeably) between the temporalities of Victorian present and imagined past, leaving us with the reflexive perception that fairy tales cast a spell we can't quite spell out.

Like Mikhail Bakhtin's work on conflict, Kristeva's work on gendered time is enjoying a revival, adopted not to replicate the oppositional categories of "male time" and "female time" that Kristeva critiques, but to recognize the extent to which these modes coexist and punctuate each other, the extent to which any author in any era, as Jago Morrison has argued, "negotiates an understanding of personal and social time by mediating between these feminine and masculine-identified modes" within himself or herself and his or her writing.[31] Many of the studies I have already cited in these pages understand Tennyson's poetry to negotiate precisely this mediation.[32] However, these critics also emphasize the anxiety with which Tennyson regarded the supposedly feminine qualities of his own compositional practices and productions. William Weaver has argued about "The Princess" that "Ida's negative response to [the lyric] 'Tears, Idle Tears' bespeaks her [. . .] refusal to see herself as anything but an epic figure" (131). Yet Ida's failure to establish a university for women and join the ranks of epic heroes illuminates the gender and genre problems of "The Day Dream." Why may not a princess be an epic subject?[33]

The twelve years that Tennyson devoted to work upon "Sleeping Beauty" is itself epic—epic in time committed and labor performed, if not in the actual poem's length or form or scope. And yet the same twelve years shows us Tennyson striving both to write the fairy tale and to "outgrow" the fairy tale—to differentiate the "loose form" of daydream from the "remodeled model" of *Arthurian* epic. Though the composition process was just as complex, just as layered for "The Day Dream" as for early work on *Idylls of the King* or *In Memoriam,* Tennyson seemingly felt that epic authorized itself as a vehicle for recording history, heroism, and mastery. The epic "celebrates in the form of a continuous narrative the achievements of one or more heroic personages of history or tradition."[34] To a folklorist, Arthurian legendry is, like fairy tales, a body of narrative folklore, its characters no more "personages of history" than Briar Rose. However, a long line of critics have insisted upon epic's power to create a linear (and thus masculinized) historical continuum between the epic subject and the epic poet: in Georg Wilhelm Friedrich Hegel's terms, "in spite of this separation in time a close connection must nevertheless still be left between the poet and his material. The poet must still be wholly absorbed in these old circumstances, ways of looking at things, and faith, and all he needs to do is to bring a poetic consciousness and artistic portrayal to his subject which is in fact the real basis of his actual life."[35] If by spelling Sleeping Beauty,

Tennyson is also trying to reject his critic's charges of girlish reflexivity, of himself "being all too dearly self-involved," then he appears to have decided that a formal solution, a turn to epic, was in order: epic narrative as antidote to fairy tale.[36] However, Tennyson's process for writing followed the same bodily metaphor that he constructs in the Sleeping Beauty tale of both gestation and heartbeat: periods of dormant, inward-looking rumination, followed by bursts of outward action. And while it is one thing to employ the tale as a diachronic trope for cultural evolution, or as a synchronic trope for gendered spaces and actions, to locate the model within his own body, within his own labor, is a considerably less comfortable proposal. To be both princess and prince is to destabilize the very principles of separate temporal spheres, and to challenge the primacy of linear narrative authority.

CHAPTER 8

Burne-Jones and the Poetic Frame

Tennyson's "Day Dream" is, as I have noted, a frame-narrative, purporting to hold the tale in the center of a Victorian binding. In the poem, the relationship between tale and frame is as important visually as aurally. The frame presents a pair of twenty-line stanzas, while the internal tale is divided into eight-line stanzas, ordered by Roman numerals. The form visually replicates Tennyson's stress upon narrative control, where short, carefully ordered stanzas offer glimpses of stilled vignettes, surrounded by an ornate Victorian frame. The visuality of this poem is important in light of Edward Burne-Jones's *Briar Rose* series, which would follow the poem more than forty years later, and which reflects the interpenetration of painting, poetry, and the fairy tale. Like "Eve of St. Agnes" and "The Day Dream," the *Briar Rose* series is a study in generic dialogism, in violated frames.

Helen Groth has investigated the interplay between poetry and visual imagery, and is especially helpful in illustrating how Victorian poetry is reflected in mid- and late-century visual art.[1] It is undoubtedly true that Keats's and Tennyson's poetry were among the most popular subjects for mid-to-late century visual artists, illustrators, painters, and photographers alike. Exhibiting not long after the publication of "The Day Dream," John

Everett Millais's "Mariana" (1851) may have been the earliest artistic interpretation of the poet's work. Henry Alexander Bowler's "The Doubt: Can These Dry Bones Live?" (1855) gives shape to the play of faith and doubt in *In Memoriam*. The Moxon edition of Tennyson's *Poems* (1857) included eighteen drawings by Millais, seven by William Holman Hunt, and five by Dante Gabriel Rossetti. While the book was not commercially successful (of the ten thousand copies printed, fewer than three thousand sold), and while Tennyson himself disliked the edition, established and incipient artists alike read and admired the book, and it proved seminal to later Victorian artistry. Some of the volume's illustrators, like Hunt, used their drawings as the bases for later, finished paintings.[2] As the parts of *Idylls of the King* advanced through publication, these, too, inspired later Victorian painters like William Morris and Burne-Jones. Keats's verse was also translated into Victorian painting: "*La Belle Dame Sans Merci*," "Isabella and the Pot of Basil," and "The Eve of St. Agnes" were some of the most frequently executed subjects, reproduced visually by artists such as Hunt, Arthur Hughes, and Millais. All in all, by the middle of the nineteenth century, the viewing public was used to seeing Keats's and Tennyson's work remodeled by the Pre-Raphaelites and their successors. Indeed, a May 3, 1890 *Punch* parody of the *Briar Rose* series hints that Burne-Jones's connection to Tennyson in particular was axiomatic. The cartoon, "The Legend of the Briar-Root,"[3] replaces Burne-Jones's enchanted sleepers with figures who have anesthetized themselves with tobacco smoke, a parody that plays upon growing medical claims that tobacco caused lethargy and even impotence.[4] Because Tennyson was a notorious tobacco addict, it is also surely a playful hint at Burne-Jones's debt to "The Day Dream."

Most importantly, Burne-Jones himself reported the influence of verse. Asked where he found his subjects, Burne-Jones answered, "I do not find them, I make them—or at least, I entirely remake them from vague impressions left by poems which I have forgotten."[5] These poems are surely "The Eve of St. Agnes" and "The Day Dream." The "impressions" left were not, in fact, so very "vague," not "forgotten" after all; for one thing, the sleeping faces of Keats and Tennyson appear in the series. For another, Burne-Jones, like Tennyson, labored on the *Briar Rose* series in tandem with another, similar subject: "The Sleep of Arthur in Avalon." I read *Briar Rose* as Burne-Jones's own "reflex of a legend."

When Edward Burne-Jones exhibited his *Briar Rose* series at Agnew's Gallery in 1890, his *Times* obituary would later remark, "Thousands . . . hastened to see, and passionately to admire, the painter's masterpiece."[6] Ultimately, though, the public regarded the four panels, not with unalloyed pleasure, but with a mixture of admiration and horror. Ellen Terry took one look and burst into tears.[7] Art critic Robert de la Sizeraine recalled his visit to the gallery as a journey to an enchanted space: "I found . . . a crowd of well-dressed women sitting in silence, a tiny pamphlet in their hands, and so immovable that it would have been easy to fancy that they had all been pricked by the fatal fairy spindle, and were sleeping beauties themselves."[8] But given his uneasy conclusion about the paintings, the "spell" they cast seems ominous: "What is the moral of the legend? . . . That the most righteous cause, the truest ideas, the most necessary reforms, cannot rise triumphant, however bravely we may fight for them. . . . The strongest and the wisest fail. They exhaust themselves with battling against the ignorance and meanness of their generation, which hem them in . . . like the branches of the briar-rose."[9]

Another reviewer found the paintings spectrally prophetic: "It is a sleep grown menacing as death . . . it is a presage and a prelude to the years yet to come, with their burdens of conscience, and their wages of winter and death."[10] This discomfiture is understandable: the panels depict a tangle of sleepers and rose brambles, in Burne-Jones's own words, "thick as a wrist and with long, horrible spikes. . . ."[11] Furthermore, the series offered these tableaux: *The Briar Wood* (in which the prince encounters his failed predecessors), *The Council Chamber* (featuring the slumbering king and his ministers), *The Garden Court* (with maidens suspended in various labors), and the *Rose Bower* (depicting the sleeping princess). Four lovely still lifes in all,[12] about which the artist said, "I want it to stop with the princess asleep and to tell no more, to leave all the afterwards to the invention and imagination of the people"—including, one must assume, the imaginary "afterward" in which there is no awakening. The series exudes a melancholy, if not threatening, sense of eternal stasis.

Like Keats and Tennyson, Burne-Jones retained a life-long interest in both medieval romance and the fairy tale. From his earliest paid work, drawings for Archibald MacLaren's *The Fairy Family*, to his last acclaimed paintings, his art found affinity with the Arthurian legends and the tales of Perrault and Grimm.[13] A member of the Folk-Lore Society, Burne-Jones attended the International Folklore Congress of 1891 in London. And like Keats and Tennyson as well, Burne-Jones worked upon the "Sleeping Beauty" subject lingeringly, fitfully, over many years and many versions begun, laid to rest, taken up again. He muses upon this dedication to "Briar Rose" in his 1883 cartoon: "The artist attempting to join the world of art with disastrous results."[14] In the drawing's five frames, Burne-Jones sits in front of a canvas, which bears a few sketchy briars in bloom; he rises to his feet, head thrown back in despair; seated again, he stares fixedly at the painting; he leaps into it; finally, he sits dejectedly on the floor on the other side of the canvas, in which an Edward-shaped hole gapes. In this self-caricature, Burne-Jones wryly acknowledges his obsessive work on the series.

Well might Burne-Jones have paused to reflect on the longevity of his attachment, given its three-decade span. In 1864, he designed nine decorative tiles for William Morris and Company titled *Sleeping Beauty*. The tiles make a grid of three lines of three pictures, representing nine scenes from the tale in narrative order, beginning with the princess's birth and ending with her marriage:

1	2	3
4	5	6
7	8	9

Turning to canvas, he created a first complete series in oil, this time with only three scenes—*The Briar Wood, The Council Chamber,* and *The Rose Bower*—and thus beginning, like Tennyson, in the middle of the tale. This series was finished in 1873[15]; in that same year Burne-Jones began on a larger series, adding a fourth scene, *The Garden Court*, but omitting *The Briar Wood*. This second series took over a decade to finish.[16] In 1885 he contracted the paintings to his dealer, Agnew, but became dissatisfied with the result and took them back. From 1885 to 1890 he painted a third series with the same four subjects as before. During this time he also created several studies in bodycolor and gouache, and some solo paintings of Sleeping Beauty in both oil and gouache.[17] In 1890 the third and final *Briar Rose* series was sold to financier Alexander Henderson, later first Lord Faringdon, for his newly purchased Oxfordshire estate, Buscot Park.[18] However, Burne-Jones made a period of public exhibition a condition of sale. In the end, it exhibited for over a year, first at Agnew's on Bond Street, and then at Toynbee Hall in Whitechapel.[19] The paintings were eventually placed in the Saloon at Buscot Park. Burne-Jones visited shortly afterwards (he was staying with Morris at nearby Kelmscott), and, displeased with the effect, undertook the reinstallation himself. He designed heavy, gilded frames for the main paintings, as well as a series of connective panels to create a continuous frieze around the room, save for the windowed Northeast wall. Morris had written quatrains for each painting in the series,[20] and these he inscribed directly onto the gilded frames in black lettering. For *The Briar Wood:*

> The fateful slumber floats and flows
> About the tangle of the rose.
> But lo the fated hand and heart
> To rend the slumberous curse apart.

For *The Council Chamber:*

> The threat of war, the hope of peace
> The Kingdom's peril and increase.
> Sleep on, and bide the latter day
> When fate shall take her chains away.

For *The Garden Court:*

> The maiden pleasance of the land
> Knoweth no stir of voice or hand,
> No cup the sleeping waters fill,
> The restless shuttle lieth still.

And for *The Rose Bower:*

> Here lies the hoarded love the key
> To all the treasure that shall be.
> Come, fated hand, the gift to take
> And smite the sleeping world awake.

The frieze remains in the Saloon of Buscot Park today. It is worth noting that, as the century advanced, the time artists spent with the tale increased, six months for Keats, a decade for Tennyson, and thirty years for Burne-Jones. Throughout these thirty years, Burne-Jones seems to tacitly understand that meditation on this subject was itself "reflexive" of historical and artistic evolution. His work deliberately manipulates not only the tale, but also Keats's and Tennyson's versions of it.

In Burne-Jones's decorative tiles, the prince arrives in the fifth scene, and thus occupies a position both literally and figuratively central. His primacy is underscored by the caption at the base of the tiles: "Of a certain Prince who delivered a King's daughter from a sleep of a hundred years, wherein she and all hers had been cast by enchantment." The title "Sleeping Beauty" or "Briar Rose" does not appear. The prince's starring role here accords with the "fated Fairy Prince" of Tennyson's 1842 poem.[21]

The central prince tile was the only composition that Burne-Jones retained when he turned to oil and canvas. His first series appears to give form to Keats's and Tennyson's attempts (and indeed, the attempt of the Victorian age) to make the prince a figure of artistic progress and potency. In the first *Briar Wood* painting, Burne-Jones has recreated Tennyson's hedge-breaker, Keats's throbbing Porphyro (fig. 1). His face and body are tensed for action, his shield is up, his bent knee and elbow suggests a man in motion. Though he stands to one side, he is unquestionably the focal point of the painting, with prostrate princes tangled in the briars all around. More important still is the curious fact that the models for the *Briar Wood* princes were artist Maria Zambaco (Burne-Jones's favorite model, with whom he was ending an affair), William Morris's wife, Jane (the regular model and lover of Dante Gabriel Rossetti), and Burne-Jones's own wife, Georgiana.[22] At the prince's feet, then, lies a little heap of artistic models and muses. These intimate connections stilled, transformed into inert artistic studies, the prince can neatly sidestep them on his way to the "perfect form," the masterpiece in the final panel. This early *Rose Bower* turns to Tennyson's 1830 "Sleeping Beauty" and Keats's Madeline as its subject (fig. 2). Its sleeping beauty is a buxom "Pre-Raphaelite stunner" in a transparent gown. Her long ringlets spread over her pillow, revealing her arched neck. Capturing beauty, that elusive artistic goal, is here rendered in erotic visual allegory: a still, exposed prize for poets and painters to claim.

Nearly twenty years later, the final series operated within a very different framework. Into these canvases, the mature Burne-Jones incorporated the subtler nuances and troublings of the Keats and Tennyson poems, but also the cultural changes of the intervening years. This last series becomes a subtle account of capitalism, empire, and fin de siècle decadence.

Unlike in the first series, the Buscot Park prince in *The Briar Wood* is a despondent fellow (fig. 3). His face is shadowed; in fact, he has been tucked far into the corner, the frame cutting off part of his helmet. This prince's body stance is relaxed, hip and head cocked resignedly, and his sword hangs limply. He does not appear to be moving forward; the impediments in the next panel clarify his inertia. In the 1873 iteration, the *Council Chamber* figures include the king, his ministers, and a musician, and the objects in the room are benign: a lute, a pipe, a few books and quills (fig. 4). In the Buscot Park *Council Chamber*, Burne-Jones shifted from a courtly to a martial setting, replacing the king's musician with an armed guard, and several mailed soldiers sprawled outside (fig. 5). The figure in the center of the room has his hand in a seemingly empty purse. The years between 1873 and 1890 brought the climax of England's empire, and

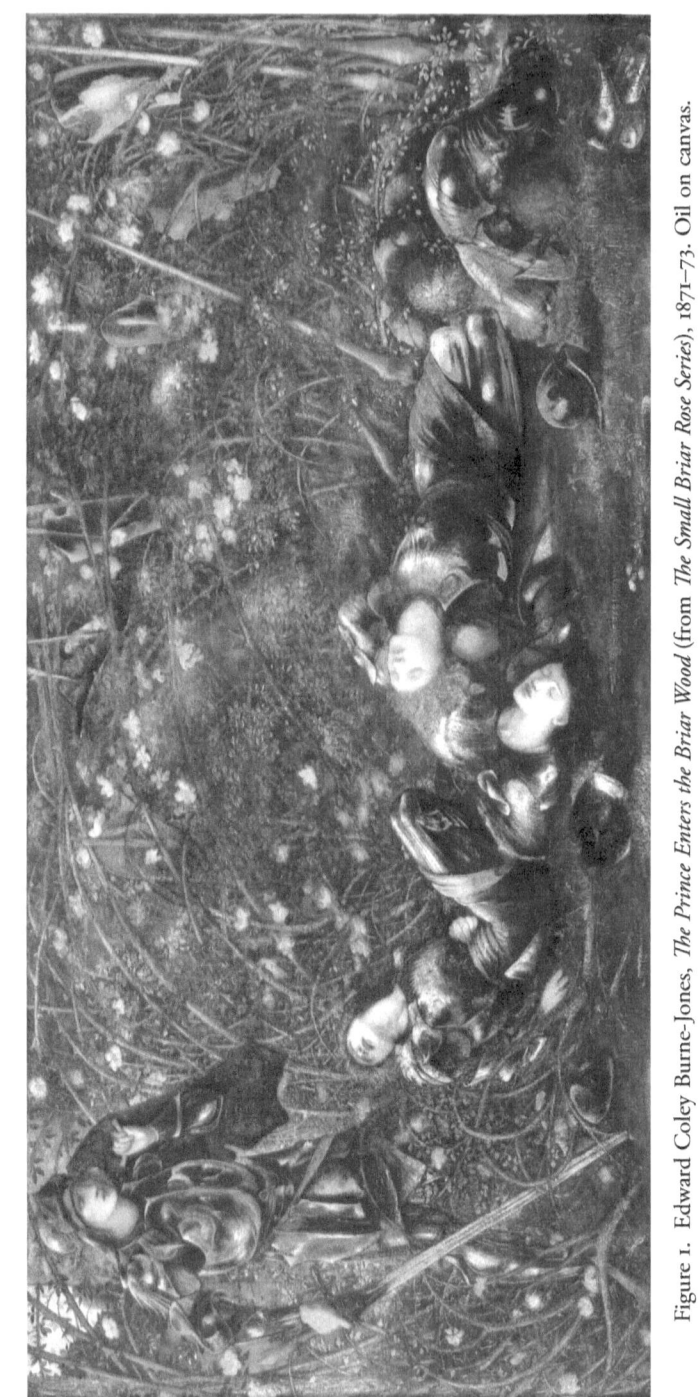

Figure 1. Edward Coley Burne-Jones, *The Prince Enters the Briar Wood* (from *The Small Briar Rose Series*), 1871–73. Oil on canvas. Museo de Arte de Ponce Collection, Puerto Rico. The Luis A. Ferré Foundation, Inc. 59.0112

Figure 2. Burne-Jones, *The Sleeping Beauty* (from *The Small Briar Rose Series*), 1871–73. Oil on canvas. Museo de Arte de Ponce Collection, Puerto Rico. The Luis A. Ferré Foundation, Inc. 59.0114

Figure 3. Burne-Jones, *The Briar Wood*. 1874–84. Oil on Canvas. The Faringdon Collection Trust, Buscot Park, Oxfordshire

Figure 4. Burne-Jones, *The Council Chamber*, 1872–92. Oil on canvas. Delaware Art Museum, Samuel and Mary R. Bancroft Memorial, 1935

Figure 5. Burne-Jones, *The Council Chamber*. 1885–90. Oil on canvas. The Faringdon Collection Trust, Buscot Park, Oxfordshire

Burne-Jones opposed the seemingly endless scramble for territory. In commenting upon the Boer War, he criticized British and Continental forces alike as "thieves" bent upon "grabbing every spare bit of land everywhere."[23] To him, the Zulu, Afghan, and Chinese wars were all conquests that would "make [nations] into insolent tyrants."[24] Morris's quatrain for this painting underscores Burne-Jones's representation of the financial and military toll upon England.

In the Buscot Park series, according to Kirsten Powell, the artist is no longer represented by the prince but by the king. She asserts that the king in the *Council Chamber*, aged and bent, barely able to support the weight of his preposterously large crown, resembles Burne-Jones, and argues that this demonstrates a sorrowful sense of his receding powers as an artist. It is certainly true that Burne-Jones's daughter Margaret modeled for Briar Rose in the final panel of the Buscot Park series, shortly before her marriage. And the princess in the *Rose Bower* has become considerably more childlike than in the first series (fig. 6). Her gown is now opaque, her hair demurely covers her neck, and a banner depicting the Virgin Mary hangs directly over her head, echoed by the blue sash that binds her girlish form in place. Perhaps, after thirty years of labor, the aging artist found that the beauties of the world were no longer lovers, but daughters. And yet, the painting plays against its own erotic nostalgia, for Burne-Jones transformed the setting of "The Rose Bower" from a bare room to one littered with icons of feminine vanity: caskets of jewels, a comb, a mirror. All in all, it is a troubling tableau: the limp prince on one side, the languid princess on the other, and a weighty political and material world between them. Like Tennyson's Flora, this Briar Rose exhibits the symptoms of being "all too dearly self-involved." But whereas Tennyson's Beauty is redeemed from her indolent introspection, charged "in the name of wife," Burne-Jones denies his story a conclusion. The lovers remain at opposite ends of the Saloon at Buscot Park, eternally separated by a tangle of sleepers and rose brambles—a continuous frieze (freeze) indeed. Burne-Jones imagines no reviving Carlylian flush of systole to end long-drawn diastole, no completed circulation in the sequencing of the paintings.

Nineteenth- and twentieth-century scholars alike read Burne-Jones's artwork as droopy, deathly, and defeated. Even at the height of his fame, critics complained about Burne-Jones's "morbid vision" and "unmanly types," and Henry James, who admired the artist's work, agreed that his figures were "lacking in 'manhood,'" and altogether "weak and weary."[25] Modern critics tend to echo the prevalent fin de siècle reception of Burne-Jones's late artwork. Even in modern critic Christopher Wood's terms, Burne-Jones's

Figure 6. Burne-Jones, *The Rose Bower*. 1886–90. Oil on canvas. The Faringdon Collection Trust, Buscot Park, Oxfordshire

art "is passive, brooding, introspective; if there are heroes in Burne-Jones's pictures, they are passive, hesitant, almost effeminate."[26] Wood's elision between a "brooding" Burne-Jones and his "effeminate" artwork treats introspection as a Romantic infection, thus recalling nineteenth-century criticism of Tennyson. On the one hand, Burne-Jones's comments about his own work appear to confirm the Romantic absorption of which he stands accused: for instance, he stated that he painted subjects from a variety of folkloric and historic pasts in order to evoke "a beautiful romantic dream of something that never was, never will be . . . in a land no one can define or remember, only desire."[27] This statement certainly resonates with the normative Victorian understanding of the fairy tale—a sign of England's lost innocence and imaginary perfection. And yet, the final *Briar Rose* series undermines its own idyllic qualities in every panel. We therefore should not conflate Burne-Jones's figures with Burne-Jones the artist, much less the man. Near the end of his life, he remarked to M. H. Spielman, "My politics are those of a thousand years hence—the politics of the millennium, and therefore of no account."[28] The comment is deceptively self-effacing; Burne-Jones describes himself as marginalized by modernity, yet vested with sufficient moral authority to claim accelerated evolution, passing beyond the current social and economic frame of Britain. I would resist the general consensus of art critics then and now that the *Briar Rose* paintings exemplify Burne-Jones's weary withdrawal into timelessness in the face of encroaching modernity, and argue instead for a *temporal* reading of the series, and that not in spite of, but because of its subjects.

Burne-Jones's relationship to the "aesthetic" movement (of which he was supposed to be the forerunner) was strained. He did not approve of this title, nor did he accept the "art for art's sake" label that came to be associated with him, especially as he was obliged to share the aesthetic crown with decadent artists, like Aubrey Beardsley, whom he despised, and Oscar Wilde, whom he ridiculed. Burne-Jones kept an uneasy eye upon the decadent movement, speaking of it as a "wickedness," which he seems to associate with male artists channeling a monstrously excessive femininity. In fact, he uncharitably and unreasonably saw Wilde's trial as just punishment for both personal and artistic excess.[29] Critics like Elizabeth Campbell and Patricia Murphy find this sort of reaction to exemplify a much larger social anxiety that "woman's time" was waxing at the end of the century, a fear that extends from artistry into polity.[30] This theory resonates with the Buscot Park *Briar Rose* series; the princess's petrifaction spreads outward from her into scenes of domestic labor and politics. And the mirror that lies face up on the *Rose Bower* floor suggests the trappings of decadent vanity, but it also suggests that the series was intended as a looking glass for the drawing room in which it hangs, a mirror image of its purchasers as torpid, feminized, and past tense. *The Council Chamber* appears to reflect the "Industrial Aristocracy" that Carlyle was so anxious to see awaken. However reliant on those very middle-class values of production and consumption for his livelihood, Burne-Jones was disgusted with the industrial project, and somberly points to a capitalist ruling power still "spell-bound amid money-bags and ledgers," not propelled forward by the wealth of the railroad industry. The man with "the politics of a thousand years hence" separates himself from the fin de siècle drawing room, characterizing it, like Tennyson before him, as a feminine space to be filled with time.

Like Tennyson, Burne-Jones was well aware that his work's masculinity (if not his own) was under fire. Upon first meeting him, Rossetti called Burne-Jones "one of the nicest young fellows in dreamland." And while Burne-Jones undoubtedly sought citizenship in that particular nation, he also attempted to police its borders. His self-caricature, "The artist attempting to join the world of art," illustrates his attention to the dangers of sleep. Powell has read this cartoon as evidence of Burne-Jones's literal desire to join the world of art. However, this interpretation (which makes Burne-Jones sound a little daft) doesn't attempt to interpret the "disastrous results" that attend the artist's plunge: that the artist destroys the picture by trying to join it. In a humorous nod to Tennyson's "Palace of Art," perhaps, in which immersion in the art world becomes immurement in a dead world, Burne-Jones emphasizes the importance of retaining narrative control. To break the form, to violate the frame, is to lose control, and to lose the art as well. As I have noted, the cartoon was drawn in 1883, as Burne-Jones was concluding his second series (and second decade with Sleeping Beauty) and as he was beginning *The Last Sleep of Arthur in Avalon*. The cartoon may have allowed Burne-Jones to imagine putting his obsession with *Briar Rose* to rest; in jumping through the painting and coming out the other side, he may be playing with the idea of distance from the tale, of "getting through" Sleeping Beauty so as to turn to Arthur. Burne-Jones gives every indication of apprehending the significance of Tennyson's sequencing. Like Tennyson, he follows Sleeping Beauty with Arthur, thus evidently supplanting the "timeless" fairy tale with epic history, and associating himself and his millennial politics with the once and future king. *Briar Rose* was certainly not Burne-Jones's only series, nor his only instance of painting multiple versions of a subject. Like Keats and Tennyson, the cyclic production of versions is Burne-Jones's uneasy métier: uneasy because it brings him, like others before him, uncomfortably close to the putative feminine origins of the fairy tale. Once again, then, Burne-Jones painstakingly absorbs the tale into a model of masculine linear progress, where labor upon Arthur serves as his own timely recovery from the reflex of a legend.

However, I do not mean to suggest that Burne-Jones was attempting to faithfully translate Tennyson's poetic project of "The Day Dream" to a visual medium. Instead, his reluctant avowal of intertextuality ("I do not find them, I make them—or at least, I entirely remake them from vague impressions left by poems which I have forgotten") plays between crediting and discrediting his poetic sources. As I have demonstrated in other chapters, this ambivalent remark is common to artists who adopt formal conceits across genres. In accounting for the afterlife of Victorian poetry in late nineteenth-century photography, Helen Groth emphasizes the commercial uses of nostalgia: "The conflation of poetry with an idealized notion of tradition was, in effect, the symbolic currency of all those in the business of selling poetry to a wider audience through popular forms. . . ."[31] According to Groth, late-century photography set about "capturing" poetry as if it were a dying form, thereby making a visible show of rendering poetry "eternal," and wrapping the older genre into the newer in a lucrative rhetorical gesture not unlike the literary "traversing" of the fairy tale. And while Groth's study treats photography alone, her thesis seems applicable to visual representations of Victorian poetry more broadly. For, in contrast to those critical readings that send Burne-Jones retreating into idyllic headspace, I find his peripheral comments upon his art (both verbal and visual) to be insistently temporal in subject, to plot a timeline that carefully places himself in reference to other artistic and social movements. In painting the Buscot Park *Briar Wood*, Burne-Jones did not again use his female models: the princes all have masculine faces. Still, there is a familiar face there. The prince in the center of the pile, with his face pointed downward, resembles, in facial features and posture (albeit inverted), the Severn sketch of Keats on his deathbed.[32] And while Powell has argued that the king in the *The Council Chamber* be seen as Burne-Jones himself, I wonder if in the tall, lean figure, aquiline nose, and impressive beard, Burne-Jones did not rather, or at least, did not *also* mean to portray Tennyson, who died in 1892, two years after the completion of the paintings. In this way, Burne-Jones appears to play visually with *form*. Fairy tales, poems, and poets—sleeping forms all, shaped by the painter who has survived to interpret their legacies.

And yet, the frames Burne-Jones built for his Buscot Park canvases suggest that even painting is not exempt from obsolescence. The gilt frames literally encroach on the artwork, partially decapitating the prince and thus obscuring the form. He may have meant to convey that gilded modernity, materialism itself, is the new "form" on which to train a wary eye. In any case, I would argue that the framing is where the clearest political subversion lies. In visiting the Saloon at Buscot Park, one is conscious of the installation as a series of *defaced* frames. The ornate frames that Burne-Jones added seem to be a concession to the taste of the Gilded Age. However, Morris's poems are painted directly upon the frames in unadorned, even austere black lettering. The verses themselves are simple, each pair of couplets neither florid nor purple. And these lines draw a stark, even black, conclusion: that the "kingdom" is in "peril," indeed, in "chains," and that the "fated hand" will wake the world, not with a kiss, but with a blow. Burne-Jones was always troubled by an artistic identity that centered upon production for the wealthy, and, as Wildman and Christian note, "uneasy with the fact that easel paintings could be bought and tucked away in private collections."[33] As he expressed it, "I want big things to do and vast spaces, and for common people to see them and say Oh!"[34] Morris's description of the sleeping beauty as "horded love" suggests that the resting place of the paintings is a treasure vault.

Mindful, it seems, of the tale as the form of the "common people," Burne-Jones opens up a populist space in the Buscot Park Saloon, all the while appearing to capitulate to the spirit of private collection. He permits the tale to overrun its frames and spill into the manor house, and thus defaces the frame with a counter-frame, a plain, unvarnished tale, the writing on the wall.[35] Burne-Jones clearly needed Morris's poems to complete this effect, and in this sense poetry is prevented from becoming a sleeping form; because the paintings generated this poetry, the verse does, however, labor in the service of the paintings—possibly a necessary reversal for Burne-Jones, after thirty years in the studio with the "impressions left by poems."

Burne-Jones's membership in the Folk-Lore Society and attendance at the International Folk-Lore Congress gave him ample evidence of folklore's movement into a discipline and into the social sciences. He would have heard Andrew Lang, Joseph Jacobs, and Alfred Nutt stress the universality of folklore, and insist upon the fairy tale as the "oral literature," first of the "savage" and then of the "common" people. After the Folk-Lore Congress in particular (which was almost certainly held between his sale of the paintings and his redesign of the Saloon), he may have come away with a clearer sense of the fairy tale, not as timeless or eternal, but as a vigorous, changing form. And it might have occurred to him that with the sale of his paintings to Buscot Park, he had been given the opportunity to reinsert the fairy tale into the Saloon, the *salon,* where, in another form, another frame, it could make subversive commentary, just as its paper and ink predecessors had done in centuries gone by. Of course, the nature of that drawing room had changed over a hundred years. Women were becoming folklorists in much greater numbers, and beginning to conduct their own studies of the fairy tale.[36] And, as Burne-Jones registered with a mixture of apprehension and reluctant admiration, Margaret's generation brought about the rise of the New Woman, with her refusal to be bound (by corsets or mores), with her own very definite notions of arousal, and with her challenges to established ideals of both progress and beauty.

The play between "form" and "frame" is important to both narrative poetry and narrative painting, and the history of play between the words themselves is instructive. *Frame* is originally from Old Norse *freme:* to advance, move forward. It means the formulation or arrangement of words; it signifies a definite form or shape; it means to create an orderly or regular procedure; it describes an animal, and especially human, body. *Form* is from Latin *forma:* shape. It means "that which makes matter determinate"; more specifically (or less metaphysically), it defines the shape or arrangement of parts, the visible aspect of a thing; it means to give a specified form, to mold or fashion into a certain shape; it means to body forth; it means to frame in the mind, to conceive an idea, to imagine. In terms of verbs, then, both form and frame mean to give a definite shape, to make into a regular, orderly figure (and indeed, *frame* and *form* each employ the other word in its verb definitions). In terms of nouns, though, the frame is the shaping, ordering force, while the form is the thing subjected to that force. The form lies within the frame's regulating boundaries.

Because framing implies advancement and progression, *to frame* is not merely to create, but to narrate. The term "frame-tale" (or "-narrative" or "-story") did not come into literary use until the early twentieth century. Nevertheless, "Eve of St. Agnes," "The Day Dream," and the *Briar Rose* series are all frame-narratives: a form (of literature, a fairy tale) within an (authoritative) frame. Burne-Jones's resistance to concluding the "Sleeping Beauty" plot notwithstanding, his preoccupation with series and versions indicates his abiding interest in advancing, progressing, framing. The overwhelming question for Burne-Jones, as for Keats and Tennyson before him, is what meaning of frame pertains here? What frame shall be empowered to *freme:* drive forward, advance? Shall it be the painterly body that shapes the paintings, the ordered, material world that encircles the paintings, or the arrangement of words, the poems past and present, that make up this particular frame? Temporally speaking, linear time seems to belong to the framer. Indeed, in Julia Kristeva's view, narration is the mode through which linear time is articulated.

But there is another, rarer definition of "frame" that throws any easy opposition or hierarchy between form and frame into profound doubt. In horological terms, *frame* is "the outwork of a clock or watch, consisting of the plates and pillars." In other words, the frame is that which contains a clock, the great symbol of inexorable temporal progress; it is not the clock itself, but merely the receptacle of it. Time is marked within the frame. In this definition, the thing inside the frame—the *form* inside the frame—is the thing that advances, shapes, determines, regulates. Frame: an arrangement of words, the clock's home, the human body. This is the convergence that Gerard Manley Hopkins surely understood in "To His Watch":

> Mortal my mate, bearing my rock-a-heart
> Warm beat with cold beat company, shall I
> Earlier or you fail at our force, and lie
> The ruins of, rifled, once a world of art?
> The telling time our task is; time's some part,
> Not all, but we were *framed* to fail and die—
> One spell and well that one. (emphasis added)

Artists both tell and are told, frame and are framed, spell and are spelled. And that Hopkins attached this knowledge, however obliquely, to "Sleeping Beauty" demonstrates that he, like Keats, Tennyson, and Burne-Jones, understood that there was no easy framing: no certain power or authority over form. It is, in every case, the fairy tale that progresses, not the frame that houses it.

Gendering the form "female" attempts to stave off similarities between framer and form. But in the very act of evoking this fairy tale, this princess, this body that is penetrated and claimed, artists insert themselves into a tradition that moves promiscuously in and out of temporal and generic frames. In this way their own oeuvres, their own (artistic) bodies are violated. This notion returns us to Jennifer Schacker's discovery of Mother Bunch's figurative potency in England as the disseminator of "densely symbolic fluids that threaten (or promise) to obfuscate boundaries, that intoxicate, impregnate, and nourish, that defy efforts to contain them." The very process of circulating fairy tales, then, both within and between an artist's oeuvres, gives rise to vexations of gender and genre. There is anxiety of influence at work to be sure; but in Harold Bloom's terms, anxiety of influence necessitates that there is an author to be made anxious by. Therefore, there is also, and more fundamentally, an anxiety of no influence, of the perceived power of the narrative beyond any creator. With splinters of the fairy tale working into Victorian discourse, indeed, shaping our tropes of conception to this day, it was currency authors aimed for, currency they feared—that each author was, after all, "telling again . . . some tale," not like modern gentlemen, but like old wives. After periods of slumber, the tale gets "pored upon" by young men, penetrated, awakened, brought to circulation. This pattern enacts simultaneously a movement to contain and a temporal rupture: the tale courses through the temporal artery, but it bursts that frame and circulates in other heads, in other times, providing other artists with its use for material acquisition. To resurrect the tale is to spell the previous artist, relieve him of duty, but ultimately, to be spelled by the tale that, every hundred years, will rise, and learn the world, and sleep again.

PART 3

Produce

CHAPTER 9

Fairy Footsteps and Goblin Economies

If a literate Victorian picked up a newspaper, took a volume out of her library, walked into a child's nursery, or purchased a penny dreadful from a book cart, she could find a fairy in any or every one of these disparate forms. They were everywhere, sometimes depicted as sweet maidens in butterfly wings and tutus, at other times as wise and benevolent protectors. But the collected fairy legends so current in this period presented a far darker view of fairies: here, they were creatures depicted as quixotic at best, and at worst, murderous. Nevertheless, because fairies could bestow both wealth and useful aid, a constant, uneasy, trafficking between the human and fairy worlds characterizes the fairy legend, and this theme was carried to Victorian literary representations of the fairy folk. I will show that fairies were not drawn into an industrial economy and corrupted: that would suggest the existence of a pure, ideal fairy in a remote past that never existed. Rather, materiality and mercantilism was part of the fairy legend from the beginning.

Before the English Renaissance, supernatural accounts were most often compiled in demonologies, cautionary texts, and persecution manuals for exterminating sorcery. Gervase of Tilbury's *Otia Imperialia* (1214), Heinrich Kramer and Jacob Sprenger's *Malleus Maleficarum* (1486), Reginald

Scot's *Discoverie of Witchcraft* (1584), and Thomas Nash's *Terrors of the Night* (1594) exemplify early literature in which fairies are associated with terror and evil doings. Diane Purkiss, examining accounts of witchcraft trials, concludes that when men and women were tortured and interrogated for sorcery they produced, not confessions of satanic worship, but versions of the common fairy legends that circulated among rural Britain.[1] Moreover, as Maureen Duffy reveals, because the interrogator is the mediating voice in these confessions, authorial terminology moves freely between "devils," "witches," "spirits," and "fairies."[2] These terms were interchangeable to interrogators, and all reducible to satanic forces.

As humanism, scientific discovery, and dawning nationalist sentiment began to free literature from the hold of the church in the Middle Ages, fabulous accounts of impious dealings slowly gave way to collections of "natural histories." These works focused on the material and customary aspects of lore. In them, fairies were shifting from something to be rooted out and destroyed into a valued part of English history. A very different kind of fairy appeared in the romance and hero narrative, beginning with troubadour culture in twelfth-century France and Italy, and passing into manuscript form through the likes of Marie de France, Thomas Chestre, and the Pearl poet. Though emerging contemporaneously with the demonology and persecution manual, the fairies of romance were, by contrast, regal and alluring, if also powerful and dangerous. Forming their own monarchy on the borders of human kingdoms, fairies of romance served as allies and participants in the political and sexual lives of heroes, potent equals in love and war.

Fairies have a long association with transaction, not only in the content of the stories about them, but through the mode in which those stories were disseminated. Spenser's overt ploy to gain the favor of the queen and so retire from his minor government posts in Ireland resulted, of course, in *The Faerie Queene*, an allegory of Elizabeth and her realm scantily disguised as fairy subjects.[3] Shakespeare, too, demonstrated that fairies were a lucrative dramatic subject, reiterating the idea that fairy spirits are the stuff dreams (and livelihoods) are made on. In *Poems and Fancies* (1653), Margaret Cavendish contemplated the commercial relationship between fairies and the poetic imagination:

> Who knowes, but in the Braine may dwel
> Little small Fairies; who can tell?
> And by their severall actions they may make
> Those formes and figures, we for fancy take.

And when we sleep, those Visions, dreames we call,
By their industry may be raised all;
And all the objects which through senses get,
Within the Braine they may in order set.
And some pack up as Merchants do each thing
Which out sometimes may to the memory bring.[4]

In this analogy, fairies that live in the brain activate the "fancy" or imagination. These fairies are responsible for converting dreams into ordered images. Like merchants, they labor to "pack up" the brain's wares, and sell them to the memory. Cavendish implies that the memory can then convert these images into poems. In other words, the fairies of fancy translate ideas into printable, and thus vendible, goods.

By the mid-nineteenth century there was a major literary industry in collections of antiquarian lore, which included both fairy legends and fairy tales. English antiquarian societies[5] unearthed and reprinted medieval and renaissance miscellanies, and produced edited volumes of county and parish historical records. Perceiving that the works interested the general public, these armchair scholars began to produce new collections. Especially popular among these were John Brand's *Observations on the Popular Antiquities of Great Britain* (1777); Thomas Crofton Croker's *Legends and Traditions of the South of Ireland* (1825) and Thomas Keightley's *Fairy Mythology* (1828), both illustrated jointly by W. H. Brooke and Daniel Maclise; Joseph Ritson's *Fairy Tales* (1831); Anna Eliza Bray's *Traditions, Legends and Sketches of Devonshire on the Borders of the Tamar and Tavy* (1838) and *A Peep at the Pixies* (1854), illustrated by Hablot K. Browne ("Phiz"); and Jeremiah Curtin's *Tales of the Fairies and of the Ghost World, Collected from Oral Tradition in South-West Munster* (1895).[6] The fairy legend was an important feature of these volumes.

The term *fairy* entered English use around the thirteenth century, probably through the French *fee*, replacing the Anglo-Saxon terms *dueorh* (later "dwarf") and *aelf* (later "elf"). Like fairies, *dueorh* and *aelfes* were generally smaller than human stature, but could change shape, appearing as tiny and grotesque, or as beautiful and bewitching, hominids.[7] Fairy legend collectors noted the similarity between Anglo-Saxon belief in the *dueorh* and certain aspects of nineteenth-century fairy belief. Bray was convinced that the entire fairy tradition stemmed from an older belief, shared by the Anglo Saxons, but possibly originating "in the northern nations."[8] These ancestors, she said, "believed in a certain race of little devils, that were neither absolutely spirits nor men, called Duergar or dwarfs; and to whose supernatural skill they attributed sundry petty acts of good or evil that far exceeded the power of men."[9] She adds, this "race of genii" was known as "Duergi or *pigmies,*" and wonders, "may not this have given origin to the word pixies?"[10] Bray's hypothesis (that is, that belief in a "race" of magic dwarfs transformed into fairy legends) was shared by scholars like Ritson and Keightley. Whether or not fairies "evolved" in this way is not the issue here. More important is that fairies become one basis for an evolutionary theory of British (and more specifically English) philology, culture, and nation, and secondly that this investigation was tremendously marketable to English readers. As I have argued, these collections were successful in part because they played upon the reading public's sharpened awareness of England's fast-changing physical and economic boundaries. However, these books themselves were integral to that economic change: so popular that they enjoyed multiple editions, they were lucrative for their writers and illustrators, and ensured the importance of the fairy in literary and visual representation for the rest of the century.

The plots of these fairy legends are insistently material, depicting a constant commerce between human and fairy worlds; magic salve in exchange for a drink of water, a magic bottle in exchange for a cow, magic healing powers in exchange for transport across a river, fairy lovers for human lovers. People stumble across fairy markets, or into underground empires, or onto hoards of glittering fairy wealth. Ritson tells a story of a poor man given healing powers by a "fair woman in fine clothes" who lives in an underground hall.[11] Lancashire fairy lore relates that a ploughman at his labor is petitioned by a pretty lady to mend a broken spade; she rewards him generously, then vanishes into the earth.[12] In this same volume, a mother filling her jug at a spring called "Fairies' Well" is "mildly accosted by a handsome man," who presents her with salve for her infant's eyes.[13]

Fairy–human exchange very often begins with mutual observation. As with the Lancashire story, fairy legends often focus upon eyes; whether characters look with repulsion or acquisitiveness, these humans and fairies watch each other watching. In one of Croker's Irish legends, a man meets a fairy as he takes his cow to market; he observes that the fairy's "eyes never were quiet, but looking at everything, and although they were red, they made Mick feel quite cold when he looked at them.[14] Bray finds a story in which a human midwife is fetched by an ill-favored man. His house appears as any other country dwelling, until she is asked to salve the new baby with ointment. When she accidentally rubs her eye with the balm, the birthing chamber is transformed: "The new-made mother appeared as a beautiful lady attired in white . . . the babe . . . appeared much prettier than before, but still maintained the elfish cast of the eye."[15] In Bray's *A Peep at the Pixies*, a pixie girl is revealed only by her stare; hers is a face "with blue cunning eyes, but very sparkling and pretty . . . for all the world like a little old child, neither one thing nor the other."[16] Like collections of fairy legends, the fairy painting and illustration of the nineteenth century offered a veritable feast for the eyes: whether representing Shakespeare's regal retinue, the gauzy Victorian fairy child, or the erotic grotesqueries of hallucination, painters Henry Fuseli, Joseph Noel Paton, John Anster Fitzgerald, and Richard Dadd stressed visual glut: the materiality of sheer number. Duffy has noted the "sly, cool" stare that these fairy men and women level at the viewer[17]; the gaze suggests visually what the motif of exchange renders in narrative: the recognition of mutual desire, for labor, for wealth, or for the body.

Fairy legends also produced the nightmare side of fairy exchange. Fairies who petition the services of a professional, such as a midwife, nurse, or doctor, may neglect to give these people back. In Curtin's Irish legend of "The Fairies of Rahonain and Elizabeth Shea," Elizabeth is rudely snatched to nurse a fairy babe, and is replaced at home by a corpse. As Croker indicates, service in the fairy realm usually lasts seven years, provided that the human does not eat or drink fairy fare (an act that invariably leads either to death or to permanent residence with the fairies).[18] Ritson tells of a man who stumbles across a fairy feast: though attracted by the sight of "a great number of little people, sitting round a table, and eating and drinking in a very jovial manner," he marvels to see several of his townfolk. One of these men, in the act of serving food, "forbad him, whatever he did to taste anything he saw before him; for if you do, added he, you will be as I am, and return no more to your family."[19] Consumption of fairyland produce lands abductees in eternal limbo.

Fairies may seduce, entrap, or snatch outright nubile persons of both sexes: fairies are evidently not especially fertile, and often require human surrogates.[20] Such fairy brides and grooms may return months or even years afterward, but altered—vague, strange, no longer able to take part in human concerns.[21] In fact, trafficking in any manner with fairies may result in similar symptoms. Such people are said to be "elf-struck"; some suffer blinding or laming, while others simply pine away.[22]

Fairies in market settings pose an especial danger. In the Lancashire fairy legend, the woman presented with fairy ointment for her infant's weak eyes is told that the salve is "a specific remedy" for the baby:

> [L]ove for her child made her somewhat mistrustful; so she first applied the ointment to one of her own eyes. Shortly afterwards, she saw her

benefactor at Preston, stealing corn from the mouths of the sacks open for sale, and, much to his amazement, accosted him. On his inquiry how she could recognise him, since he was invisible to all else around, she told him how she had used his ointment, and pointed to the powerful eye; when he immediately struck it out.[23]

In *Pandemonium* (1684), Richard Bovet describes an unlucky man who infiltrates a fairy market in England, and becomes elf-struck. The rider:

> saw just before him, on the side of the hill, a great company of people, that seemed to him like country folks, assembled, as at a fair; there were all sorts of Commodities to his appearance as at our ordinary fairs . . . it being near the road he was to take, he resolved to ride in amongst them, and see what they were; accordingly, he put on his horse that way. . . . He found himself in pain, and so hasted home; where being arrived, a lameness seized him all on one side. . . .[24]

Violent treatment from fairies at market is particularly self-reflexive: the legend's physical setting mirrors the dangerous exchange depicted in every fairy legend. Fairy "commodities" are not for human consumption. In visual imagery (indeed, often the very same painting that depicts the fetishized fairy object) fairies symbolized the horrors of surfeit, the nightmare of addiction. John Anster Fitzgerald's *The Artist's Dream* (1857) divides attention between the lovely fairy woman posing for her portrait and the animalistic fairies bearing the laudanum that prompts the dream. *The Nightmare* (1857–58) portrays a woman, also presumably in the throes of an opium fix. Here, too, grotesque fairies bear a chalice to the sleeper, who lies contorted, her red sash falling across the bed like a bleeding wound.[25]

Our modern idea that there are good fairies and wicked fairies depends upon a Victorian difference between the words *fairy* and *goblin*—moral and physiognomic distinctions that did not exist in legend. According to the *OED*, the noun "fairy" means "one of a class of supernatural beings . . . supposed to possess magical powers and to have great influence for good or evil over the affairs of man." This definition has existed since 1393. But the attributive form, "resembling a fairy, fairy-like; delicate, finely formed or woven," became common only after 1838.[26] In other words, "fairy" is a sentimentalized attributive that came into existence only in the Victorian period. According to European fairy legends, the goblin[27] is simply a type of fairy that serves in human homes, cleaning house, milking cows, and so forth, in exchange for room and board. As these fairy legends reveal, whether a fairy lives in your home or you stumble across his, the "fair folk" can turn on you—all fairy commerce is a dangerous exchange. In legends, fairies are expert grifters: the same fairy can appear as a beautiful, full-sized man or woman, or as a grotesque and atavistic miniature.

Victorians pulled "fairy" and "goblin" into opposing signifiers: the "fairy" associated with benevolent powers, the "goblin" characterized as ungoverned and voracious. Fairies, Victorians decided, live in richly arrayed splendor, while goblins simply hoard. So although a goblin was a kind of fairy, it became important for the uncomfortably brutal aspects of the fairy to be displaced onto the goblin, for the fairy to become more like a human—an English human—and for the goblin to become a more other Other.

Ultimately, though, despite attempts to uproot and transplant that which was dreadful to a Victorian self-portrait, Victorians could not shake the goblin's close association with humanity and the concerns of domestic production. Certainly, the fairy had "survived" into the Victorian period, but I shall contend that fairies, with their ties to commerce and transaction, in part informed this mercantile society, having produced some of its most abiding metaphors.

CHAPTER 10

The Great Exhibition
Fairy Palace, Goblin Market

Ever resistant to taming, the fairy legend burst into the critical and popular reception of the Great Exhibition of 1851. It is appropriate that the fairy, already made to labor in the service of middle-class literary wealth, was also employed in the periodicals, bluebooks, and chapbooks surrounding this monument to middle-class endeavor. Beginning with Thomas Richards's seminal discussion of the Great Exhibition in his *Commodity Culture of Victorian England*,[1] the Exhibition has become a text in the Victorian canon, and a vital discursive space for Victorian self-assessment. For instance, Louise Purbrick's Foucaultian reading describes the Exhibition as a site of class surveillance and containment.[2] Joseph Childers and Laura Kriegel center upon the imperial project of the Exhibition in fact and in fancy.[3] Both Eileen Gillooly and Steve Edwards examine the physical space of the exhibit halls and the epistemological space of the exhibition catalog, and demonstrate that figurative language enabled a conflation of exhibits, visitors, and nations.[4] Richard Pearson has investigated the subtle critique leveled at the Great Exhibition, and the Crystal Palace more specifically, in *Punch* and other illustrated media.[5] This chapter joins these categories of inquiry into the Exhibition.

There was something about the Great Exhibition that led its creators and earliest chroniclers to render the building and its contents fancifully. Richards argues that the Exhibition became for its commissioners, and later for its paying public, a "semiotic laboratory,"[6] a space to work through representations of labor, value, and commodity. Edwards accounts for the Exhibition's imaginative construction with Franco Moretti's theory of figurative language in the nineteenth-century novel, which holds that "troping" increases when the narrative "encounters national borders."[7] A critic like Pearson would be more likely to understand this figurative play to open space for resistance and critique, an interpretation grounded in Bakhtin's theory of the carnivalesque; Gillooly works formally, understanding such devices as analogy, personification, and antithesis to create their own form of taxonomic discipline (and punishment). It seems that there was room enough in the Exhibition for figuration to work and to play, to subvert and to contain. However we choose to explain it, critical consensus indicates that the Great Exhibition of 1851 was a material, but not necessarily a realist, project.

Surprisingly, then, little attention has been paid to the Crystal Palace's other nickname, one just as ubiquitous to discourse of the Great Exhibition before, during, and after its run. The hall was also called the "Fairy Palace," and it is an important, and hitherto overlooked, image of the Great Exhibition. The fairy legend so familiar in mid-century England—steeped, as we have seen, in spectacle, industry, and merchandise—resonated profoundly with the exhibition organizers' rhetorical aims. Indeed, the fantastic proved a tool for self-assessment every bit as keen as more overtly politicized exhibition rhetoric. The larger purpose of this section is to trouble the common idea that the fairy opposes the Victorian commercial world, to argue rather that the language of material realism is in part supplied by this fantastic figure. Plaudits for the Exhibition employed a cleansed image of the fairy—regal, industrious, exotic, and erotic—to stand for the noble qualities of England that the palace embodied; criticism of the Exhibition hinted at goblin desires lurking within England's boundaries.

Fairies were said to have shaped, not only the construction of the palace, but also the assembly of its exhibits. Reverend William Whewell imagined the hall to have been conjured by the Exhibition's "good fairy" commissioners.[8] Inventor Sir Henry Bessemer described the hall emerging over Hyde Park carriages and crowds, "glittering like a fairy palace."[9] Eliza Brightwen, naturalist and wife of banker George Brightwen, recalled in her memoirs "rumors of a fairy palace of glass springing up in Hyde Park."[10]

Punch made a facetious plea to the hall's architect, Joseph Paxton, to transform the Houses of Parliament into glass (rendering the MPs' actions transparent). In this essay *Punch* calls the Exhibition "a fairy Palace of Glass."[11] Thomas Macaulay wrote of the hall as "a most gorgeous sight; vast; graceful; beyond the dreams of the Arabian romances."[12] In her private journal, Queen Victoria described her first view of the hall: "the sun shining in through the Transept gave a fairy-like appearance," and "we went up into the Gallery, and the sight of it . . . had quite the effect of fairyland."[13] Once the Exhibition had opened, she noted and admired "the fairy like effect of the different objects that fill [the palace]."[14] As in Margaret Cavendish's poem, where the imagination is rendered as merchant fairies that convert industry into ideas with commercial value, the fairy metaphor helps Victorians describe the industry that erected the Crystal Palace.

For Victoria herself, "fairy" means both the commodity and the industry that created it. Her similes reflect England's desire for the produce of that industry: the "different objects" become the wealth of fairyland, the same mercantile allure that drives humans to bargain with fairies. Here fairy objects inhabit a fairy palace, both of which signify superhuman industry. Small wonder that the Exhibition evoked those industrious creatures who built a vast *sub rosa* empire, when Britain was doing much the same above ground. That Victoria's subjects linked the fairy to marketplace economics is further underscored in a December 1852 pantomime. Earlier in the year, the Crystal Palace moved from Hyde Park to Sydenham, and the pantomime evoked this change in its transformation scene. The "abode of antiquity" gives way to "the New Crystal Palace and Gardens at Sydenham," which is populated by the fairies Art, Science, Progress, Invention, Wealth, Health, Industry, and Plenty. A boy imp announces, "Behold my treasures here, there's naught forbid in 'em / And all will be revealed though now *it's hid in 'em*" [i.e., "it's Sydenham"].[15] The pantomime reflects the Great Exhibition of 1851, while simultaneously signaling the Crystal Palace's rebirth as a pleasure grounds. The fairies represent the cultural function of the Great Exhibition as well as the splendor and wealth of the hall and exhibits; the thinly veiled sexual innuendo of fairy girls as available "treasures" to "be revealed" fuses the scopophilic pleasure of the palace with that of the fairies. Indeed, Victoria and her subjects may have been drawn to the fairy simile by memories of the last fairy queen, who ushered in an era of spectacle and prosperity. In these examples, fairies are not confined to signifying a national past: instead, they work both progressively and nostalgically, representing the new Britannia metal as much as the mettle of Old Britannia.

Of course, no item in the Exhibition was for sale as such; like Purbrick, I understand the contents of the Crystal Palace in Marx's terms of the commodity fetish, "objects with representational rather than useful properties," and "consumption . . . as a process of looking at representations rather than buying actual objects."[16] Indeed, some of the palace's foreign exhibits were "arranged as a native bazaar," to the delight of Queen Victoria.[17] Perhaps what so pleased the queen was the symbolism of the foreign market brought home, the prospect of foreign goods increasingly produced for England. It was the same draw, the same desire that made the queen exclaim in delight over the "fairy like effect . . . of the objects" in the palace. In other words, the monied classes were meant go to the Exhibition, and return home with an appetite for all sorts of things newly available for purchase. Consumption through looking and longing, a feast for the eyes, internalizing that which was not formerly in reach all become metaphors for both empire and expanding industrial skill. Fairies are situated in this mix of mimetic desire, the fairy's powerful draw reflected as it is through the gaze. Eileen Gillooly's analysis of Exhibition taxonomy shows how these objects were made to wear literal faces: "Foreign objects—in some cases limited to just a handful of objects—came in consequence to represent their nations synecdochically. . . . This apprehension of displayed objects as synecdoches exacerbated the common tendency not only to characterize nations by their putative attributes (that is, to stereotype them), but to personify them as well."[18] Pointing to such examples as "small-eyed China" and "half-civilized Russia, with a . . . bearskin on her shoulders,"[19] Gillooly demonstrates how figurative language simultaneously exoticized and personified the objects in the national exhibitions. One has only to recall the many stories of the fairy markets perched on England's borders to draw the connection to the fairy's simultaneous exoticism and familiarity: we stare at the fairies, and in the "fairy palace" they stare back with the face of industry and of commodity.

But it is important to remember that fairies in market settings punish those caught looking, striking scopophilic eyes blind, and laming the eager tread among fairy produce. Critics of the Exhibition took full measure of the dangers of enchanted trafficking, making the fairy stand in for the surfeit of commodity culture. For instance, in an 1850 *Household Words* article describing plans for the exhibit hall, Charles Dickens reports the plan "that [the hall] should be all made of glass, as we might find in an *Arabian Nights* tale." But Dickens criticizes the proposal for producing, not "the most excellently useful and economic structure for the purpose required, but the most perfect exhibition of the artist's especial taste, 'regardless of expense.'"[20] The palace-building geniis here imply impractical extravagance. In May of 1851, Dickens called the palace a "tremendous pile of transparency" and added, "I find I am 'used up' by the Exhibition. I don't say there is nothing in it: there's too much. . . . I have a natural horror of sights, and the fusion of so many sights in one, has not decreased it."[21]

In illustrated literature, ambivalence about the Great Exhibition's phantasmagoria is registered as a surfeit of spectacle. One such example is George Cruikshank's engraving for Henry Mayhew's serial novel *1851, or the Adventures of Mr. and Mrs. Sandboys and Family*, titled "The Dispersion of the Works of All Nations from the Great Exhibition of 1851."[22] This final illustration disrupts the comic subject matter of the book with the effect of overwhelming consumption (fig. 7). Here the glittering hoard of exhibits becomes an animate horde of commerce—canons sprouting legs, tiger-skin rugs taking wing—magically pouring out of the fairy palace and, presumably, invading the middle-class home.

This ambivalence recurs in *Punch*'s anonymous poem "The Cinderella of 1851."[23] Two workhouse girls find a volume of fairy lore in their schoolroom and, rather than join the other "little bodies, sore and sinking, / That scarce hold up on bench and stool," they pore over the "book of mystery, awe and pleasure" that "charms even pauper childhood's leisure." Reading of Cinderella's transformation by the fairy godmother, "Their little heads and hearts are working, / And wond'ring if fairy godmothers now / In chimney corners may be lurking." They are discovered, beaten for shirking their lessons, and sent to bed, where "the fairy-ridden pair" dream, "for the Fays are busy there. . . . Scatter Fancy's treasures, hoarded / In the workhouse, sad and sordid, / With a liberal hand afforded— / Wealth of dreamland, rich and rare!" The next morning they are taken to the Crystal Palace, where they exclaim:

> Oh yes! I know we are not dreaming;—
> The book we yesterday read is true:
> 'Tis Fairy-land, so bright and beaming;
> The fairy god-mother of the story;
> Because we are friendless, and sad, and sorry,
> Has changed the workhouse into a glory,
> For pauper children like me and you.[24]

A palace created "for pauper children like me and you" echoes the contemporary view that the Crystal Palace offered to the poor the healthful benefits of visual stimuli. The effect of the palace is identical to that of the fairy tale:

Figure 7. George Cruikshank, "The Dispersion of the Works of all Nations from the Great Exhibition of 1851" in Henry Mayhew, *1851, or the Adventures of Mr. and Mrs. Sandboys and Family* (London: David Bogue, 1851)

when children's "heads and hearts are working," the result is healthier, more engaged, more productive members of the working class. However, we can also detect the critical undertone so common to *Punch* features. "The Cinderella of 1851" is not a girl—it is the palace itself, and there is no abiding transformation offered to these children. The palace will dissolve into the workhouse again, and the prince who visited the fairy palace every day would never come to rescue them. The girls claim to be satisfied, but the illustration by John Tenniel shows paupers gazing about them with troubled, joyless faces (fig. 8). That these orphans are out of place is emphasized by the foregrounded trinity of middle-class father, mother, and child staring at the girls rather than at the Crystal Fountain towering beside them. According to the aims of the organizing committee, the palace was meant to unify the classes through shared scopophilia, but the gaze in this drawing instead registers exclusion from middle-class wealth. Mimetic desire is not functioning in the way the Royal Commission intended. Whether the poet meant to praise or condemn the hall as a "fairy palace" for the poor, the image implies that no fairy godmother can alter the lot of these little drudges.

"The Cinderella of 1851" portrays an English fairyland, even if a troubled one. More overt satire of the Exhibition hinted at goblin economies lurking within England's boundaries, and implied that the fairy palace might contain a regressive, foreign mercantile at its center.[25] Critics Carole Silver and Diane Purkiss have demonstrated that literary and visual representations of fairies were overtly associated with racial physiognomy and evolutionary theory. With the discovery of tribal peoples in Africa and South America, the fairy story began to merge with the pseudo-science of cultural relativism. Fitzgerald's painting *The Fairy's Lake* (exhibited 1866) features an atavistic, clawed, and topknotted fairy on the verge of impaling a white, winged creature in the back as she dabbles innocently in the water. In a detail of Paton's *Reconciliation of Oberon and Titania* (1847), a border of white-skinned, blonde fairies chase, caress, and woo each other, while a group of fairies with racially caricatured faces (Moorish, Asiatic, and Spanish?) and animalistic bodies occupies the center. While the white fairies are courting, the fairies in the middle are engaged in business: paying the tribute of a slug to a fairy with knife and fork at the ready. Such paintings show the relationship between fairies and foreign stranger-danger coming to bear in the middle of the nineteenth century.

Exhibition commentary upon goblin economies can be found in one of *Punch*'s fictitious letters; titled "The Exhibition Plague" (1850) it purports to be written by a woman who frets about foreign incursion: "I am

Figure 8. John Tenniel, detail, illustration for [Anonymous,] "The Cinderella of 1851," *Punch* 21 (1851): 132

told . . . that the Exhibition . . . will bring another Great Plague of London . . . all along of the millions of foreigners that, like herrings in a barrel, will begin to wedge up London . . . the Plague on one hand . . . and the famine on the other—for how are these millions to be boarded?"[26] Richard Doyle's mock-illumination of the drop-capital G, which opens the letter with the salutation "Good Mr. Punch," features a goblin gnawing a bone (fig. 9). Doyle means for the goblin to symbolize the gnawing fear of foreign gnawing. Because the goblin—the fairy that inhabits human homes—was too close to the newly mercantile English self for comfort, making the goblin into a foreign Other was a comforting displacement. As Pearson argues, it is difficult to fix a single way of interpreting literature about the Exhibition. Much of *Punch*'s commentary was meant to satirize public fears rather than perpetuate them, but, as Pearson says, "the voice of *Punch* remains ambivalent: simultaneously reveling in the diversity produced, and maintaining the English monocle" (184).

THE EXHIBITION PLAGUE.

OOD MR. PUNCH,—I am a wife, and the mother of, at present, five healthy children; and write without my husband's knowledge, who—except that he will have his own way, which was never meant for men, whatever they may say to the contrary—is as good a creature (for a man) as ever broke bread. I write, I say, about this show that they're going to put under a glass case in Hyde Park. I am told—and I believe it— that the Exhibition, as they call it, will bring another Great Plague of London. I hear that in the *Union Jack*,

Figure 9. Richard Doyle, illustration for [Anonymous,] "The Exhibition Plague," *Punch* 19 (1850): 191

Doyle perpetuates this simultaneity in his independent work; one such example is a shilling book titled "An overland journey to the Great Exhibition, showing a few extra articles and visitors."[27] The work is more precisely one long illustration folded accordion-fashion to form a book. When unfolded to its full extent, the long strip presents a procession of several troupes of tiny people, each of a different nation, each nation carrying an item several times larger than its bearers toward the Exhibition. The first foldout depicts representatives of each of these caricatured nations, at the head of which procession John Bull marches, leading the way to the Crystal Palace in the distance (fig. 10). Some of the figures, like the Scot, have benevolent profiles (Doyle was Scottish), but others—the Russians, Italians, and the Irish bringing up the rear—sport sinister smiles or knit brows; the Arabian figure pins the viewer's eye with a knowing, uncomfortably complicit look behind John Bull's broad back. Doyle's title itself riffs on Victorian travelogues, the titles of which often began "An Overland Journey to . . . ." As with the *Punch* illustrations, it is unclear how Doyle means for this book to be read. The book's other pages, each dedicated to a country and its identifying symbols, are as ambiguous as the first. Some of the "visitors" seem harmless if somewhat ludicrous, like the Swiss bearing a giant beer stein or the tiny Italian opera singers carrying a violin. In other pages, the overland journey appears more sinister, as with

Figure 10. Richard Doyle, detail of *An overland journey to the Great Exhibition*, showing a few extra articles and visitors (London: Chapman and Hall, 1851)

the tiny Americans leading tiny bound slaves, and wielding a huge cat o' nine tails, or the French hefting a liberty tree hung with the Phrygian cap, coq Galois, and imperial eagle, along with other reminders of both the revolution and the Napoleonic wars. All in all, it seems that Doyle, however facetiously, imagines the Exhibition causing a reverse colonization, in which he asks readers to wonder just what England was inviting into its borders.

Importantly, Doyle's "guests" in "Overland Journey" mimic the characteristic fairy processions he drew elsewhere. Indeed, the picture-book is a striking precursor to Doyle's *Fairy Tree,* painted in 1870.[28] Here, too, Doyle associates fairy Otherness and racial difference. These fairies are turbaned, wear loincloths, or sport Asian queues. All fairies orient to the white king seated in the middle of the tree. These racialized fairies sitting on the branches of a tree indicate that, in the wake of Darwin's publications, the fairy Other converged with theories of evolution and racial lineage. Especially provocative is the detail of the painting in which a procession of fairies bears trays of produce to the occidental king (fig. 11). Their fare is as varied as their caricatured physiognomies—a pear, a pipe, cigars, liquor, a pineapple, a plate of citrus. As with much of the comic drawing and illustration of the day, it is difficult to know to what extent Doyle parodies others' xenophobia, and to what extent he offers a genuine warning. Did Doyle intend to attribute goblin cunning to the face of commerce, or did he mean to poke fun at an unreasonable fear of free trade? In any event, as with the "fairy-like" objects of the Great Exhibition, these gifts represent the "fruits" of imperial trade and conquest, and here, too, commerce leers with goblin face.

Richard Menke notes that by the mid-nineteenth century, "British scientists and horticulturalists were attempting as never before to cultivate an enormous variety of foreign plants . . . in the gardens and greenhouses of Britain."[29] The Crystal Palace represented, not the birth of the greenhouse, but perhaps its coming of age. I will conclude this section by reflecting on an additional figuration for the Great Exhibition that played upon Paxton's use of the newly fashionable conservatory as his architectural model. Such works imagined the hall not merely in the style of a greenhouse, but as a veritable greenhouse for commercial "produce." *Punch* noted that "the Crystal Palace, doubtless, would make a magnificent orangery,"[30] and advocated that the hall be transformed into a winter garden after the Exhibition closed. Mindful of the Exhibition's aim to educate Britain's classes in their proper places in the market economy, F. W. N. Bayley (at this time the *Illustrated London News* editor, but here in his role as a children's verse writer)

Figure 11. Richard Doyle, detail of *The Fairy Tree* (1870). Watercolor with sepia ink and gouache on paper. Cotsen Children's Library, Department of Rare Books and Special Collections, Princeton University Library

called the Exhibition "A sort of greenhouse in the mind / Transparent to the searching eye / And very crystal to the sky. . . . "[31] Prince Albert characterized the palace as celebrating both peace and intellectual innovation, a space "that should graft the olive on the laurel."[32] The clever metaphor not only "grafts" England to Greek rootstock, but also transplants two Mediterranean cultivars exotic to England save, of course, through hothouse techniques.

Exotic produce that could now be cultivated in England came to stand—like fairies—for England's industrial ingenuity and its imperial hunger. Conservatories had been a novelty for the aristocracy alone prior to 1851, but the Exhibition left in its aftermath a fad for greenhouse construction and exotic cultivation among the wealthy middle classes, too. One horticultural expert noted:

> When we consider the success which attended the covering in of the large space of ground occupied by the Exhibition building of 1851, there can be little doubt that a new era has commenced in the construction of large glass houses for horticultural purposes. . . . I would therefore direct the attention of gardeners and their employers to a more extensive cultivation of exotic fruits . . . looking at the variety of exotic fruits that have come under my notice both at home and abroad, I feel

persuaded that their culture can be carried much farther than it ever yet has been . . . adding to the dessert a variety of handsome and delicious fruits, which are now only known by reputation, or procured with difficulty from foreign countries.[33]

In this *Journal of the Royal Horticultural Society* article, P. Wallace suggests a natural progression from "Exhibition building" to "glass houses" to "exotic fruit." That he takes the association for granted identifies the Crystal Palace as an impetus to the growing and consuming of foreign fruit. The author goes on to enthusiastically analyze the flavor, scent, and flesh of limes, lemons, loquats, guavas, longans, alligator pears, custard apples, pomegranates, and four kinds of orange. The Exhibition left behind an abiding fascination with things to eat, and particularly with fruit.

While fruit was not literally cultivated within the walls of the palace, the Exhibition nevertheless housed a garden of fruit. Fruit took a central role in the foreign displays, which were organized by nation, and not regulated by the four-tier taxonomy Britain gave to its own exhibits. Foreign produce represented a substantial percentage—in many cases the majority—of the exhibits from other nations. Madeira, for instance, offered 119 items for display, ninety-six of which were fruit and other comestibles sent by plantation owners.[34] Britain's differentiation between itself and the rest of the world in its organization of the exhibits is crucial here. Compared to Britain's organizing system, which encouraged contemplation of the industrial *process,* foreign nations became, in Gillooly's words "characterized by their putative *attributes.*" The abundance of edible produce in the colonial exhibits opened a rhetorical space for visitors to decide not merely that those countries were fruitful, but that they were fruit. Just as the fairy became both the commodity and its industry, the import represented its nation, and these imports were edible. The very idea of exotic fruit stood for the seemingly limitless possibilities of both free trade and colonial expansion, and visitors were invited to imagine a consumable empire.

In the British section of the display, fruit fell under the heading "Raw Materials, Substances Used as Food," and was located in a small section of the upstairs galleries. That England downplayed agriculture in favor of industrial technology is unsurprising. But, significantly, one sign greeting guests in the manufactures portion of the British section of the hall announced: "Commercial Produce." In signaling the shift from agrarian to industrial economy, the organizers supplanted the actual fruit of English soil with the metaphorical fruit of industry. While exhibitors from the colonies may have wanted to characterize these nations as fertile grounds, bursting with raw resources, the Exhibition of the Industry of Nations billed its home exhibits as the fruits of labor. "Produce" historically has meant both "the result of action or effort; product, fruit" and in its verb form, "to exhibit."[35] In the context of an emerging consumer society, born equally of free trade and industrial wealth, the commissioners needed for the products of skilled and unskilled labor, domestic and foreign toil alike to be perceived as fruits to be enjoyed in the world for a price. Within the boundaries of Exhibition iconography, then, longing for a pixie or a peach symbolizes a complex desire for fantastic luxury.

Prince Albert envisioned the great greenhouse as metonymic of science, a space where humans take almost supernatural dominion over nature:

> So man is approaching a more complete fulfillment of that great and sacred mission which he has to perform in this world. His reason being created after the image of God, he has to use it to discover the laws by which the Almighty governs his creation, and, by making these laws his standard of action, to conquer nature to his use, himself a divine instrument. . . . Science discovers these laws of power, motion, and transformation: industry applies them to the raw matter, which the earth yields in abundance, but which becomes valuable only by knowledge. Gentlemen—the Exhibition of 1851 is to give us a true test and a living picture of the point of development at which the whole of mankind has arrived in this great task.[36]

The greenhouse, like scientific inquiry itself, makes "raw matter . . . valuable" by controlling it, and thus brings humans nearer to understanding the master plan. Distinct from agriculture, the success of which depends upon the vagaries of the land, this projection of the garden, this other, "other Eden" was conceived entirely on human terms: man has "conquer(ed) nature to his use." Albert and the commissioners saw in the Great Glass House England's independence from seasonal rituals and exigencies. This is a bold revision of the Fall, the other narrative in which humans presumed to approach godly knowledge by meddling with fruit, to disastrous results. In the garden of industry, the fruit of knowledge may be enjoyed: hitherto forbidden by seasonal variation or by harsh tariffs, it was now within easy reach.

Despite the triumph with which the Great Exhibition announced British ascendancy to the world market, there was ample evidence of Britain's lurking discomfort with its own hunger for luxury. The *Times* denounced Paxton's design as "a monster greenhouse."[37] Augustus Pugin called the structure a "glass monster." Edward Reynolds, noting how the working classes were ignored in the closing ceremony, called the hall "The Monster Bubble."[38] Delicacies in the fairy palace become all-consuming in the glass monster. A William Morris wallpaper design, first issued in 1866, played upon this very idea. The design mingles the branches of several kinds of fruit that could not possibly grow naturally together: lemons, oranges, peaches, pomegranates (fig. 12). Like Doyle's fruit bearers in *The Fairy Tree*, Morris's tapestry offers a magical view of several kinds of fruit in one place and time: "all ripe together / In summer weather."[39] Because his textile and decorative arts designs deliberately shunned the techniques of the Industrial Revolution so proudly displayed at the Exhibition, Morris may have been playing upon the heterogeneous "produce" of the Crystal Palace. In the same way that the fairy's voracity mirrors the desiring self, commercial produce in the fairy palace blurs the distinction between self and other, home and away. One cannot help but reflect on forbidden fairy feasts: consuming food in fairyland prevents you from returning home.

All in all, then, the Crystal Palace was, in figurative terms, a conservatory for both exotic fruit and fairies. Another text that houses fruits and fairies, the text I have purposely delayed introducing, is Christina Rossetti's "Goblin Market." Rossetti's fairy glen contains foreign bodies, the same enchanted space imagined in Victoria's "glass bazaar." Rossetti's themes in that poem—fairies, forced fruit, consumption, contamination—all appeared first in images of the fairy palace, which for some concealed a goblin market taking place within.

Figure 12. William Morris, *Fruit* (1866). Wallpaper, block-printed in distemper colors by Jeffrey & Co for Morris, Marshall, Faulkner & Co. Victoria and Albert Museum, London

CHAPTER 11

Rossetti's Homeopathy

This chapter resonates between Rossetti's "Goblin Market" and the print media surrounding the Great Exhibition, and numbers "Goblin Market" among the critiques of the Crystal Palace. As such, the poem also reflects upon mid-century literary production and publication. Fairies in the Great Exhibition labor in the service of mass production, both in the Exhibition itself and in the illustrated literature turned out to describe it. As Catherine Gallagher has argued, Victorian women "did not need to find a female metaphor for authorship; they needed to avoid or transform the one that was already there."[1] And this, Gallagher concludes, is "not the metaphor of the writer as father, but the metaphor of author as whore.... According to the father metaphor, the author generates real things in the world through language; according to the whore metaphor, language proliferates itself in a process of exchange through the author."[2] "Goblin Market" prevents the fairy story from being identified with alienated labor. Rossetti seeks to reinstate the fairy tale as the artisan produce of female storytelling, by writing a poem mindful of antecedents, both poetic and folkloric.

Critics minimize the fairy tale's influence upon Rossetti, subordinating it to a brief acknowledgment of juvenile tastes en route to treating her more sober literary attachments. But the adult Rossetti siblings owned and enjoyed Perrault's *Contes du Temps Passé,* The Grimms' *Kinder- und Hausmärchen,*[3] and an edition of the *Arabian Nights* tales. Rossetti was also connected to two fairy legend collectors; Thomas Keightley was a friend of Rossetti's father, and Rossetti read his *Fairy Mythology* during a family visit to Keightley's home. There she would have discovered legends cautioning against the wares of fairy merchants, in which death is the penalty for eating fairy food.[4] Anna Eliza Bray was a cousin of the Rossettis, and the family read her *Tamar and Tavy* with interest, as well as her volume for children, *A Peep at the Pixies,*[5] both of which recount fairy abductions, transformations, and other dangerous transactions. While teaching in the family school on Arlington Street (1851–1852), Christina Rossetti returned to these books as lesson material for her young charges, and became enchanted herself once again. The style of her short story "Nick" (1857) derived from her rekindled interest in fairy tales. During this time, she encountered the fairy tale works of George Cruikshank and Archibald MacLaren, and applauded their explicit moral agendas. For some time after the publication of "Nick," Rossetti's letters (through tantalizing hints at "Little Red Riding Hood" and "Bluebeard") indicate that she contemplated her own collection of tales. However, she seems to have abandoned this project in favor of "Goblin Market."

There is no evidence that Rossetti visited the Great Exhibition. There are, in fact, relatively few extant letters from Rossetti at all during the run of the Exhibition. She was living at Arlington Street in Camden when the Crystal Palace opened, and she remained there until the beginning of July, when she departed for a two-month visit to her aunt at Longleat. Thus, despite her absence during the busiest months of the Exhibition (itself perhaps significant), she could have attended in the spring or early autumn. Her resolute silence upon the project may, in fact, indicate her reception of it: her letters to brother William and closest friend Amelia Heimann were filled with the concrete details of her days, and one would suppose that a trip to the palace—or even general London news of the Exhibition— would merit report. This uncertainty notwithstanding, it would have been impossible for Rossetti to remain impervious to the news of the Exhibition splashed across the London media during its run. An avid reader of *Punch,*[6] she would have perceived the periodical's probing, slippery commentary upon the Hyde Park spectacle, and would have noted its development of the two figurative bodies—the fairy and the greenhouse—that I have outlined.

Rossetti originally called the poem "A Peep at the Goblins" in homage to her cousin Bray's *A Peep at the Pixies,* and while the title (thankfully) changed, what the title signals—looking and exhibiting—remained. The poem centers upon the alluring vision of creatures and foods outside the sisters' homely ken, the desires provoked through the gaze, and the dangers attendant upon visual as well as oral consumption. Laura's "fall" is initiated, not by eating forbidden fruit, but by seeing it. It is Laura herself who states "we must not look at goblin men, / We must not buy their fruits" (42–43), and thus pairs looking and buying as transgressions of equal danger. Yet she immediately pops up to see them, and is lost: "Look, Lizzie, Look Lizzie, / Down the glen tramp little men . . . / How fair the vine must grow whose grapes are so luscious" (54–61). The goblins themselves equate visual and palatal pleasures at the end of their seductive shopping list: "Sweet to tongue and sound to eye / Come buy, come buy" (30–31). To look, in other words, is to consume. Following those critics who see the Exhibition as the crystallization of the department store, and its exhibits as commodities consumed visually, I would argue that Laura's desire for the fruit is synonymous with the hunger promoted by the Great Exhibition. The goblins' forced fruits hold the same exotic draw as the Crystal Palace's cultivated exhibits.

The superhuman powers that erected and furnished the "fairy palace" also ripened the fruit of the goblin market. What the goblins call their "orchard fruit" is actually the produce of many different countries. In fact, their elaboration of the peddled fruit reads like P. Wallace's analysis of exotic cultivation in the *Royal Horticultural Journal*. Of the twenty-nine kinds of fruit mentioned in the poem, lemons, oranges, melons, pineapples, apricots, pomegranates, dates, cranberries, and citrons are fruits foreign to England. Apples, pears, bilberries, blackberries, gooseberries, mulberries, grapes, and plums grow in England, but are fall fruits.[7] The impossibility of these fruits being "all ripe together in summer weather" (15) points to the industrial harvest coming to bear in the middle of the century. Both Richard Menke and Mary Wilson Carpenter note that the exotic fruits of "Goblin Market," while enticing precisely because they are beyond the mundane, were rapidly becoming part of the well-to-do English table.[8] Thus the assertion that "men sell not such in any town" (101) is ironic: at the time of the poem's composition, men were attempting to sell just such in every town. These are the fruits of a greenhouse and import culture—the same phenomenon driving the figurative power of the greenhouse in the Great Exhibition.

Like Bray's description of pixies or Croker's portrayal of changelings, Rossetti's goblins are a hybrid of man and animal. One is "cat-faced," another "rat-paced," one moves "like a wombat," another is "parrot-voiced." Though Laura hears "a voice like voice of doves / Cooing all together" (77–

78), when Lizzie crosses the goblins, they are "no longer wagging, purring / But visibly demurring, / Grunting and snarling / . . . Lashing their tails" (391–98). And, just as foreign and domestic produce is intermingled in the goblin market, the goblin merchants themselves mimic a diverse collection of creatures, some exotic (the South African ratel, the South American parrot, the Australian wombat), some garden-variety English (cat, rat, snail, and fish).[9] The merchants, then, like their fruit, represent a "strange mixture" of English self and alien Other. The Victorian definition of fairies is precisely that: a creature that slides between domestic and foreign—that which is strange to and yet lies at the very heart of England.[10]

To Rossetti, what is "goblin" is not merely commercial produce, but the domestic consumerism that feeds upon it. Maidens and merchants meet in the "haunted glen" (552), a no man's land to which both girls and goblins are foreign bodies: the homebody in the marketplace, the exotic bazaar in England. Like a visitor to the Great Exhibition, Laura goes out to the market, samples visually and orally, and brings home her longing. As with other figurative examples of the consumer's stare, where the gaze symbolizes the transaction, Laura's plight turns upon a dangerous mutuality of "gobblin'": Laura eats the fruit and the fruit eats (away at) Laura, causing her to pine as one who has been elf-struck. In their metaphorical registers, both "Goblin Market" and critiques of the Great Exhibition conflate foreign merchants and their wares; but these works also, and simultaneously, conflate foreign and domestic merchants. Any market economy, then, is "goblin" by virtue of its high-stakes exchange. Therefore, while Doyle's precise intentions in his "Overland Journey" remain inscrutable, for instance, one can read the cartoon retrospectively through Rossetti's poem. It is mercantile design that gives the uncanny men a common purpose, and a common appearance despite distinguishing racial signifiers. Likewise, in adding a miniature goblin market to his "Fairy Tree," Doyle possibly reflects upon Rossetti's earlier work. These goblins stand for the corruptive influence of a global market economy. In fact, goblin referred not merely to mercantile wares, nor to English hunger for them, but to the English money to buy them too: until at least 1925, "goblin" was slang for a sovereign.[11] In his illustration for the poem, Dante Gabriel Rossetti drew the goblins as animals with human hands. This is not what Rossetti herself describes in the poem, but it is nonetheless a powerful image: the only human part of the goblins is that which can exchange money and goods; the brain and body are bestial.

The machines on display in the Crystal Palace mechanized labor formerly conducted in the home, and thus represented the displacement of female activity and production. Rossetti's merchant men reflect many kinds of legendary little folk—goblins, but also pixies, fairies, and so forth. Yet she never calls her creatures "fairies," because she needs goblins—the fairy that inhabits houses—to stand for the infiltration of commercial greed into the middle-class home. Laura is no innocent victim of a sinister, commercial fairy world filled with dangerous exchange and bad bargains. Anyone participating in this market becomes consumed, but it is a self-consumption, an eating away at the healthy, active, serviceable part of the self through vain longing. These two industries, the regional/domestic and the centralized/mechanized, appear in "Goblin Market" as a battle between natural and contrived production.[12] Once Laura realizes that she cannot have more goblin fruit, she ceases housework:

> She no more swept the house
> Tended fowls or cows
> Fetched honey, kneaded cakes of wheat
> Brought water from the brook:
> But sat down listless in the chimney-nook
> And would not eat. (293–98)

Goblin fruit is decadent and sterile, and Laura is what she eats. Like the beguiled consumers of fairy legends who eat fairy food and are trapped forevermore in fairyland, Laura, by abandoning her domestic economy, is unable to return home after eating the goblin fruit. (How will you keep her down on the farm after she's seen Faerie?) The goblin of legend conducts housework in exchange for room and board, but once invited into the home frequently wreaks havoc there. As in the Fairy Palace, Rossetti's goblins stand in for the alienation of labor in every sense, and the uncomfortable recognition in the self of that which must be called goblin, Other. The most *heimlich* fairy is made *unheimlich*.

Several critics have argued that Rossetti saw any woman's participation in England's economy as limited to the exchange value of her own body.[13] In this interpretation, when Laura attempts to enter the economic market as a buyer, she is betrayed by her own desire; she goes to consume, and instead is herself consumed. The "iterated jingle" (233) of the market, "Come buy," is paired with the secret language of the market. The goblins, conspiratorially "[l]eering at each other / Brother with queer brother / Signaling each other / Brother with sly brother" (93–96) indicate a masculine market from which Laura is fundamentally excluded; though she may understand the injunction to "come buy," she lacks the market skills necessary to keep from being put on the block herself. Laura's transaction with the goblins therefore metaphorizes either prostitution or seduced and fallen womanhood. Such readings are compelling: after all, Laura, lacking other capital, barters with her body. And as many have noted, her decline bears all the literary markers of fallen womanhood: premature aging ("Her hair grew thin and gray" [277]), haggard wasting ("She dwindled, as the fair full moon doth turn / To swift decay and burn / Her fire away" [278–80]), and uncontrollable bursts of emotion (she "sat up in a passionate yearning, / And gnashed her teeth for baulked desire, and wept / As if her heart would break" [267–69]). However, many such interpretations tend to conclude that feminine production and consumption in Rossetti's terms is necessarily—and fatally—inscribed upon the body.[14] These critics understand the poem as an injunction to leave business to men, and see in Lizzie and Laura's return to the home the silence of defeat.

But Rossetti herself did not believe that women's lives fit into the binary of passive, decorative dependence in the home or illicit economic interaction in the streets. In "Goblin Market," Rossetti's rural maidens cannot afford to buy in more ways than one. Wanting what you cannot have leads not just to "baulked desire" (267) but to blood poisoning (555). In "The Cinderella of 1851," the pauper girls imaginatively connect the Crystal Palace and the fairy tale, and though the Exhibition cannot supply their basic needs, being "fairy-ridden" means their "little heads and hearts are working." In Rossetti's poem, the fairy-ridden pauper is another matter entirely: far from being restorative, Laura's beguiled longing is deadly, and Rossetti rejects the notion that mimetic desire nourishes the healthy heart of England. Instead, Lizzie's and Laura's snug domestic economy, where labor is functional and fulfilling, presents a "working model" for middle-class women as well: these "warbling" (213) farm girls, however sentimentalized, nevertheless epitomize women who are gainfully employed. Together Laura and Lizzie allegorize England itself, a feminine nation of workers—a nation of feminine labor. Reversing the Exhibition organizers' agenda to teach middle-class commerce and consumption to the nation, Rossetti has her agrarian maidens teaching home economy to the middle classes. Critics who read "Goblin Market" as an indictment of feminine hunger for knowledge do not account for Lizzie, who formerly fled the market with "a dimpled finger in each ear" (67–68), but once she has a job to do, "for the first time in her life beg[ins] to listen and to look" (327–28). By teaching herself how to hear the language of the market, when to answer back and when to keep her mouth closed, she is able to take the goblin fruit home and to save her silver penny. In "Goblin Market," Rossetti displaces the locus of speech and knowledge from the industrial into the domestic space, which she figures as a political and poetical space as well.

Christina Rossetti was active in the Oxford Movement, and especially interested in the Anglican sisterhoods that emerged out of it (the first appearing in 1845 and established in greater number and force in London over the rest of the century).[15] Though her sister Maria joined All Saints' Anglican convent in 1872, Rossetti herself did not attempt to enter cloistered life. Instead, she appears to have valued these London convents for the work opportunities that they both generated and attracted to themselves. For instance, in the Crimean war, Catholic and Anglican churches alike were recruited for nursing volunteers, and in 1854 Rossetti and several of her friends and family members applied to join Florence Nightingale's nursing team. Rossetti, at age twenty-four, was deemed too young. Undaunted, she turned to volunteer opportunities within the convent system itself. Situated throughout London, the Anglican convents were each chartered for a different kind of ministry: shelters for battered women, hospice care for elderly women, schools for poor girls, and penitentiaries for prostitutes and sexually abused women and girls. These homes, cohabited by sisters and "rescued" women, were assisted by a task force of lay volunteers. While the physical and spiritual ministering in which these women engaged might appear to conform to rather than transgress Victorian gender-normative activities, the sisterhoods' many critics nevertheless considered these homes to be dangerously radical. The convents presented opportunities for women to work in the fields of nursing, teaching, social work, and community organization. They insisted on a woman's right to meaningful labor that removed her from a marriage market still dominated by unions arranged for wealth rather than affection. Finally, they upset women's accepted role as keepers of men's homes by legitimating spaces in which women cared for women. As is well known, Rossetti herself worked at the St. Mary Magdalene house on Highgate Hill from 1858 through the 1860s as a volunteer. Thus, during the composition of "Goblin Market," Rossetti's literary production was bound up in her associations with the Anglican sisterhood, and intimately tied to ideals of women's work.

Dante Gabriel Rossetti asked Ruskin to read and evaluate some of Rossetti's poetry from this period of composition. In his now apocryphal letter of response, Ruskin deemed the poems to be highly irregular:

> I sate [sic] up till late last night reading poems. They are full of beauty and power. But no publisher—I am deeply grieved to know this—would take

them, so full are they of quaintnesses and offences . . . your sister should exercise herself in the severest commonplace of meter until she can write as the public like. Then if she puts in her observation and passion all will become precious. But she must have the Form first.[16]

Ruskin was right about Rossetti's "offenses"—not in the formal sense that he means, but in her attack upon monoliths of Victorian literary convention. While "Goblin Market" draws upon the putative physical markers of fallen womanhood, it refuses to recapitulate the supposedly inevitable tragic end for women who succumb to appetite. Though Laura pines and dwindles, Rossetti permits her restoration to perfect health; she is not merely penitent, but "innocent" once more, awaking "as from a dream" (537–38). The poem also denies any ontological difference between women. To be sure, one sister eats the fruit, and the other does not. It would be easy enough to read this as a simple allegory of sexual and/or commercial fall: give in like Laura and you are in jeopardy body and soul. Resist like Lizzie and you may redeem others. However, the names "Lizzie" and "Laura" are so similar as to be confusing; indeed, it may be this similarity that leads many scholars to overlook the fact that Laura, not Lizzie, first cautions against looking and buying. This small but important moment denies Lizzie any prim or censorious moral high ground; she is simply faster, the first to "thrust a dimpled finger in each ear, / Shut eyes and [run]" (67–68) before the goblin spell engulfs her. Laura is not bad, just unlucky. Likewise, once Laura returns home after eating the fruit, Rossetti shows the sisters curling up to sleep together in identical purity:

> Golden head by golden head,
> Like two pigeons in one nest
> Folded in each other's wings,
> They lay down in their curtain'd bed:
> Like two blossoms on one stem,
> Like two flakes of new-fall'n snow,
> Like two wands of ivory
> Tipp'd with gold for awful kings . . .
> Cheek to cheek and breast to breast
> Lock'd together in one nest. (184–98)

Though coming *after* Laura's supposed "fall," this scene, replete with its white and golden imagery, imagines the sisters mingling without difference and without taint. If, as many critics argue, Rossetti was writing "Goblin

Market" to read at St. Magdalene's, the sisters' similitive proximity may represent the physical proximity of nuns and inmates living together at Highgate. The cohabitation drew fire from convent opponents, since it contradicted the common Victorian ideology that sexually experienced women were irreparably stained, and should be forever removed from contact with the "pure" members of their sex. Rossetti imagines a "nest" where women are not differentiated "warden" from "penitent," but rather where both bear the designation "sister."

I do not, however, mean to condense "Goblin Market" into a historical riddle the answer to which resides in Highgate Penitentiary. Instead, I would argue that Rossetti's work at the Magdalene house brought into focus associations between authorship and prostitution that had existed at least since classical Greece. Gallagher posits that, just as Aristotle "speaks of the written word as an arbitrary and conventional sign multiplying unnaturally in the mere process of exchange,"[17] in the nineteenth century as in classical Greece, "prostitution . . . is linked to writing through their joint inhabitation of the realm of exchange."[18] In fact, Gallagher determines, the entire "sphere of exchange as opposed to production is traditionally associated with women."[19] I think that Rossetti approached the task of "Goblin Market" in order to both acknowledge this conventional equation, and to overturn it. If, as Purbrick contends, the Great Exhibition was an event in which objects had "representational rather than useful properties," and consumption was "a process of looking at representations rather than buying actual objects," then its emphasis on circulation rather than production is implicit. To return to Gillooly's argument, commentators during the Exhibition personified nations in the feminine gender,[20] reinforcing associations between commodity and prostitution by rendering the Exhibition as the possession of feminized exotica. Rossetti, by contrast, inverts this gendering of circulation, supplanting the metaphor of feminine prostitution with the metaphor of masculine goblin vendors. In Victorian literary discourse, "one detects a growing hostility toward groups that seem to represent a realm of exchange divorced from production: for example, traders in general, but especially costermongers."[21] In creating her own fairy costermongers, Rossetti displaces the ills of circulation away from female authors and into the patriarchal realm of industrial commerce. In a rape-like scene they force fruit upon Lizzie, much as the Exhibition's critics felt that the "forced fruit" of the Great Glasshouse was spectacularly thrust upon England.

Again, while I think that "Goblin Market" comments retrospectively upon the Great Exhibition, I do not want to suggest that it stands as a simple allegory for the Exhibition. Rather, "Goblin Market" is about mid-century literary circulation; whether or not Rossetti attended the Great Exhibition, we know that she read *Punch, Household Words,* and other periodicals that minutely canvassed the Exhibition and London culture as a whole. Like critics Catherine Maxwell and Elizabeth Helsinger, I see the import of Lizzie turning the market to her own account, enabling herself and her sister to become powerful storytellers by the end of the poem. Unlike either of these two critics, though, I think Rossetti's attention in this poem is tuned to popular literature, and perhaps particularly print media. Gallagher suggests that mass-produced popular literature, in the form of both serial publication and periodical literature, was perceived to be alienated from its production.[22] Print media—magazines, journals and illustrated newspapers—may have been especially prone to this assessment. With nearly 200 new periodicals created between 1830 and 1900,[23] their contributions often anonymous and passed through an editorial mangle to produce a unified voice, the periodical movement may have seemed like the quintessential embodiment of alienated labor, what Menke calls "fruits without roots."[24] It would not be accurate to claim that popular publication rejected the influence of literary precursors: *Punch,* for instance, the quintessential mid-century periodical, demonstrated that any parodic form must be hyperaware of its antecedents. However, to any observer of the periodical movement, it must have seemed that an entire genre had sprung fully formed into the mid-century. Print media was a famously, and sometimes infamously, interdisciplinary genre: poetry, fiction, and engravings often cohabitated with political, sociological and economic treatises. It was a genre that played deliberately on the boundaries of "high" and popular culture; literary magazines and journals sold to the same subscribers that bought gentlemen's magazines, illustrated periodicals, chapbooks, blue-books, and "penny dreadfuls." Production, like consumption, was eclectic: for instance, Bradbury and Evans, *Macmillan*'s publisher, also published *Punch,* the *Daily News,* and works by Dickens. While other scholars have treated Rossetti's literary influences, none have cited periodical literature's effects on "Goblin Market"; I will conclude by suggesting that the poem engages not only with the Great Exhibition, but with the print media that responded to the event, and that was sprouting, flourishing, and coming to bear during the decade of the 1850s.

Victorian response to the form in which Rossetti launched her writerly career was mixed. Many rejoiced that print media in all of its forms exemplified the democratization of reading. Costing between four pence and two and a half shillings,[25] the periodicals in which Rossetti published, and which she herself read avidly, were accessible to a massive popular readership at mid-century; Rossetti appears to be fully attuned to the play between items working-class England cannot afford (that is, luxury objects in the Crystal Palace) and items it can afford (that is, popular publications that interpret such monolithic structures). In this sense, editorial uniformity apparently sacrifices authorial individuality in order to offer forth cultural critique at affordable prices. To others, perhaps especially contributors, print media's very democratization raised concerns; to Thomas Hughes, in an article for Macmillan's titled "Anonymous Journalism," unsigned periodical writing was dangerously populist; not merely unnamed, but potentially "lowering" of character: "The notion that he is to put aside his own individuality, that he is to 'reflect' the opinions of a journal, or, indeed, that he is to 'reflect' anything, is about as mischievous a one as a man can have in his head when he sits down to write; and it this which lowers the character of so much of our public writing."[26] To be a nameless writer is to be too much like the public itself, perhaps. And though Rossetti published poems in periodicals (both anonymously and signed) between 1858 and 1861, "Goblin Market" appears to have been deliberately withheld from print media publication, and instead reserved for the title work of her first book, published under her own name. The creation and dissemination of "Goblin Market," then, seems to coincide with Rossetti's reflections on what (popular) publication meant for her as a woman writer.

Rossetti's earliest involvement with media publication turned upon issues of authority. Rossetti contributed to all four issues of her brothers' quarterly, *The Germ,* as the only female submitter. In the first issue, all authors published anonymously; in the other issues she wrote under Ellen Alleyn, the name selected for her by Dante Gabriel. Once *The Germ* dissolved, Rossetti published briefly in an all-women's magazine, the aristocratic *Bouquet from Marylebone Gardens,* in which contributors took on flower pseudonyms (Rossetti was "Calta," that is, "marigold" in Italian).[27] *Macmillan's Magazine,* in which Rossetti first published in 1861, ushered in a trend toward authorial signature in the second half of the nineteenth century. (Charles Dickens notably persisted in his authors' anonymity in *Household Words* and *All the Year Round* after that convention had waned.)

Alexis Easley has demonstrated that the broader movement away from anonymous publication coincided with the rise of Rossetti's poetic fame. This began with Rossetti's named publication in *Macmillan's,* but blossomed fully with the publication of *Goblin Market and Other Poems* as an independent volume with Alexander Macmillan.[28] Easley argues that Rossetti, making her figurative and literal "name" in the print media, illustrates the larger complexities of female publication in the mid-Victorian period. While Rossetti chose to pursue signed publication, she remained ambivalent about "making a name" for herself; both because Victorian England expected of its female writers a performative "fear of self-display," and because Rossetti wished for her writing "to be appreciated on its own terms rather than as the production of a sentimentalized female author, Rossetti had good reason to be protective of how her gendered identity and poetry were received and represented."[29] Easley concludes that this is why Rossetti, though she eventually signed her publications, nevertheless strove to retain a sense of "indeterminacy in her work."[30] It is also why both her poetry and her fiction sustain a generic and formal hybridity, in which Rossetti casts herself "as the active editor of her own miscellaneous text,"[31] rather than as the creative force behind it.

Easley's arguments are persuasive; but I also think that this same "indeterminacy," this namelessness that allied male and female writers with the voice of the people, was more vexing for Rossetti than Easley allows, and this has everything to do with popular literature's implicit connections to folklore, and with folklore's class and gender inscriptions. Certainly Rossetti was very well aware of those conventions I have traced that split the feminized anonymous folkloric voice from the masculine authorial/editorial eye and hand. As I have suggested, fairies were intimately connected to the popular literature movement, and particularly to those illustrated periodicals and occasional books that self-avowedly treated modern life in London. Rossetti could hardly help but recognize how often fairies in print media were the subject of ribald humor. From F. W. N. Bayley's fairy tale subjects in his "Comic Nursery Tales" series (published between 1842 and 1850), to Charles Dickens's "Gaslight Fairies" in *Household Words* (1855), to articles in *The Day's Doings* (1871) and its successor *Here and There* (1872),[32] and in *Punch* across this entire span of time, popular literatures often drew upon the highly sexualized fairy girls of the pantomime and burlesque theaters when presenting the figure of the fairy to their readerships. I address each of these examples in their various print media in chapters thirteen and fourteen; but I introduce them here to indicate the ways in which popular literature connected the fairy with the prostitutive character of the theater actress. To withhold "Goblin Market" from periodical publication in favor of book publication, then, may have had to do with its fairy subject, and with Rossetti's need to be taken seriously, to be sure that she was identified, not with the anonymous folkloric subject, but as the authorial agent. Like other artists, Christina Rossetti may have been working through the proper place, the proper form and genre for the fairy. I would argue that

"Goblin Market" is both profoundly indebted to print media, and resists the most iconic Victorian periodicals in ways both overt and subtle.

Of course, periodical editors themselves often disagreed bitterly about how journalistic humor ought to be conducted. For instance, M. H. Spielman has claimed that under Mark Lemon (conductor from 1846 to 1870), *Punch* lost the keen edge of radical satire that it had with Douglas Jerrold (1841–46) to the broad comedy of lampoon. About *Punch* in Lemon's hands ("Lemon Punch," as the editor of the *Illustrated Times* quipped),[33] Jerrold himself remarked: "I am convinced that the world will get tired (at least I hope so) of this eternal guffaw at all things. After all, life has something serious in it. It cannot be a comic history of humanity.[34] Rossetti may have decided to craft a response to "the eternal guffaw," for while "Goblin Market" is undoubtedly indebted to Doyle's and Tenniel's goblinish illustration of *Punch*, like its heroine it resists "hissing" and "mocking" (402). And while Dickens's *Household Words* criticized the Crystal Palace in ways that resonated with Rossetti's own critique, she might have wanted to resist other ideas that had become as "familiar in their mouths as household words." The magazine's title had certainly become a bitter taste to Dickens, who was compelled to change the name to *All the Year Round* in 1859, after a year of wretchedly public separation proceedings and court battles—all the more wretched since the publicity was of his own making. During this year many a reader—friends as well as critics—cited the uncomfortable irony in Dickens's retention of a title that suggested his domestic authority. Rossetti composed "Goblin Market" during Dickens's *annus horribilis*, and thus it may be that her description of the goblin fruit as "honey to the throat but poison in the blood" also describes the familiar taste of *Household Words*. Moreover, *Household Words*'s Shakespearean homage emphasizes popular literature as male lineage; if Rossetti sought to attack the literary convention of the fallen woman, *Household Words* would have presented an imposing storehouse of this trope. *Hard Times* was serialized there in 1854, and "Goblin Market" almost certainly echoes its ending, but with a significant change. While a peep at the future shows Sissy Jupe and Louisa Bounderby, "grown learned in childish lore,"[35] caring for Sissy's children in a kind of sisterly bliss, and though Louisa is freed from marriage by her husband's death, Dickens prevents Louisa herself from remarrying. She is guilty, not of adultery, but of considering it, and, taking the will for the deed, Dickens places her with his other fallen characters, beyond the pale of matrimony and motherhood, announcing firmly, "such a thing was never to be."[36] Rossetti, in giving Lizzie and Laura "children of their own"

(545), and investing both alike with powerful household words, imagines a different tale of sisterhood in the face of industry.

She imagines it in poetic form, but as verse shot through with the popular literature of the fairy legend. Though Rossetti's fairy sources come from male as well as female editors, in "Goblin Market" as well as in her later fairy fiction *Speaking Likenesses,* the ordering and telling of tales is a decidedly female occupation. "Men sell not such in any town," Rossetti parenthesizes (101) and then repeats (556) at the end of the poem, and while in its first iteration this phrase appears to modify the goblin fruit, in its second it modifies the tale Laura tells the assembled "little ones." Men sell (and tell) not such, but women might. A jingle, "the affected repetition of the same sound or of a similar series of sounds, as in alliteration, rime, or assonance; any arrangement of words intended to have a pleasing or striking sound without regard to the sense; a catching array of words, whether in prose or verse," is a word supposed to be "chiefly contemptuous," and in the goblins' mouths the "iterated jingle" (233) of "come buy" is indeed a "catching" and "striking" repetition of "sugar-baited words" (234).[37] In Rossetti's hands, however, the principals of rhyme are turned to another account, to bring home an investigation, not of lives bound up in tender, but of "lives bound up in tender lives" (547). Of course, *Goblin Market and Other Poems* had tendered Rossetti more currency than she had ever before received. Rossetti's letters to Alexander Macmillan and the magazine's editor, David Masson, demonstrate her ambivalence with this very currency—that is, with both wages and fame. She repeatedly refers to the volume as her "little book," and once, her "minute book"[38] (the book was indeed small, about 7" × 5", but it was 200 pages long). The letters waver between disavowal of her worth, and diligence to be paid her due, and contain such ambiguous phrases as this to Alexander Macmillan: "you may think whether I am not happy to attain fame (!) and guineas by means of the Magazine."[39] The syntactically obscure "you may think whether I am not happy" and the parenthetical register of alarm suggests the urgency with which Rossetti charges herself as a woman on the market to enter into print with a "jingle" that is simultaneously feminine, artisanal, and of clear use value.

As I have noted, Ruskin recommended that Rossetti "exercise herself in the severest commonplace of meter," faulting her for a supposed ignorance of prosody. He went on to complain to Dante Gabriel, "Irregular measure (introduced to my great regret in its chief willfulness by Coleridge) is the calamity of modern poetry." However, as Yopie Prins demonstrates, Ruskin appears to ignore what nineteenth-century metrical theory made clear: that meter "is neither an imitation of voice nor a script for voice but a formal mediation that makes 'voice' a function of writing."[40] And with this in mind, what unsettled Ruskin was not Rossetti's lack of formal discipline, but rather her refusal to conform to a single prosodic pattern within a poem. Nigel Fabb and Morris Halle define Ruskin's "irregular measure" as "meters . . . characterized by lines which have the same numbers of feet but vary greatly in their numbers of syllables."[41] George Saintsbury, early-twentieth-century critic of Victorian poetry, thinks of "irregular measure" more generally as the "infinite variety" of Rossetti's metrical practice as a whole.[42] Too, Saintsbury defines Rossetti's meter as of a kind wherein "various scansions of the same line and piece express themselves."[43] Like Saintsbury, Prins understands Rossetti's metrical proliferation as deliberate multivocalism:

> Her wide metrical range is evident in "Goblin Market" . . . as it produces various discriminations of value that correspond thematically to the logic of the marketplace. In this way the poem meditates on the production of insatiable desires, not only in its content but also through its very form. The wide range of lyrics in Christina Rossetti's *Goblin Market & Other Poems* can thus be understood . . . as a poet's response to current ideas about prosody.[44]

If "Goblin Market" responds to prosodic convention, then how to represent oral literature in writing is most certainly part of that response. The goblins tout their fruit as "sweet to tongue and *sound to eye*" (my emphasis): the ways in which translation—from mouth, to ear, to eye, and from fruit to words—is everywhere signaled in this poem. If a fairy is an unsettling combination of parts, then this is veritably a fairy poem—a goblin poem—with fragments of poetic form, poetic meter, print media, and fairy tales in uneasy dialogic relations. Like *Punch, Household Words,* and many other examples of print media, this is a hybrid form.

The difference is that Rossetti sees these multiple genres as radically mediated by the female authorial body. Lizzie transforms fruit from the economy of exchange into that of pure use.[45] Because "goblin pulp and goblin dew" (470) become Lizzie's "juices" (468), which have salvational powers, many critics have noted the resonance of this portion of the poem with the mystery of the Eucharist. But whereas Marylu Hill reads this episode as a discourse upon transubstantiation itself,[46] I see this scene as a series of embedded metaphors, in which Lizzie's redemptive fruit juices suggest transubstantiation, but where transubstantiation itself figuratively restructures the economic and gender politics of the literary market. Like Lizzie,

Rossetti does not refuse the influence of popular literature, but she does modify it into more beneficial pulp, creating not a goblin market but a market for goblins. The poem incorporates both poetic and folkloric influence, yet offers something other than the prostitutive reproduction of signs. Rossetti's metaphor is of neither author as father nor author as whore, but rather of author as conductor of an oral feminine power into the literary market.

In spite of divergent and often embattled readings, most critics agree that Rossetti's poem is an *antidote, or anti-dotum,* that which is "given against."[47] In other words, whether the goblin market represents capitalist commerce, the marriage market, the phallogocentric literary market, or some combination thereof, we tend to emphasize the portions of the poem that renounce, overturn, and shut down. Rossetti herself describes the juices Laura takes from Lizzie as "the fiery antidote" (559). However, because she delivers a dose of the same substance that caused Laura's illness, what Lizzie administers is more accurately homeopathy. And Rossetti is likely to have known this, since from 1851 onward her family was good friends with the family of John Epps, a homeopathic physician.[48] This "system of medical practice, founded by Hahnemann of Leipzig about 1796, according to which diseases are treated by the administration (usually in very small doses) of drugs which would produce in a healthy person symptoms closely resembling those of the disease treated,"[49] arrived in England in 1832, when Dr. Harvey Quinn opened a homeopathic practice in London. In 1850 the first London Homeopathic Hospital was opened in Golden Square. In 1859, the year of the poem's composition, the hospital moved to Great Ormond Street, Camden,[50] not far from Rossetti's home, at that time in Albany Road. Rossetti may well have had this new neighbor, this unorthodox practice, in mind as she wrote the conclusion of the title work of her first published volume. Rossetti proposed to introduce into the body politic, not strange fruit, but "like suffering." The goblins are not foreign bodies, but uncomfortably familiar, sickeningly Heimlich, *omeos*. The poison is the cure here; the market enters the home, but the home also infiltrates the market. Goblins become—not harmless, never that—but useful, productive. Rossetti, with deliberation and care, markets a homeopathic product; to counteract an entire fairy palace, she delivers a deceptively little thing, a minute book, a jingle, to work its way into the market and cure its ills. With "Goblin Market," Rossetti turns the commercial produce of the fairy palace to good account.

PART 4

Paraphrase

CHAPTER 12

Little Red Riding Hood Arrives in London

The Latin phrase *"Lupus in fabula"* ("the wolf in the tale") means the same as the English proverb "speak of the devil,"[1] and the connection is suggestive: the very idea of this tale conjures forth images of wolves lurking on forest paths. In colloquial French, as Yvonne Verdier and Catherine Orenstein point out, *"elle a vu le lupe"* ("she has seen the wolf") has long signified a girl or woman who has lost her virginity—a clear legacy of the "Little Red Riding Hood" tale.[2] Like the devil, then (or a seducer with a devilish grin), the wolf is a corrupt and corruptive character. But the wolf is also a useful figure, popping up alongside of girls and teaching them lessons in self-sufficiency, restraint, chastity or mortality, as the case demands.

This section demonstrates how "Little Red Riding Hood," with its themes of pursuit, shameful knowledge, and violent ends, offered Victorians a fairy tale figure in which to dress the story of endangered virtue. As it moved into London's urban center, it became a tale about predations upon poor girls in a market economy. The narrative pleasures of threatened girlhood cannot be overestimated; "Little Red Riding Hood" proved eminently adaptable to the lucrative plot of the seduced and ruined girl. Adaptors perceived the tale itself as a vendible thing, and Little Red Riding Hood (the devoured heroine) often stood metonymically for "Little Red Riding Hood" (the appropriated tale). The fairy tale was ingested into the popular theater, the popular press, and the novel, and unites these forms in uncomfortable but productive ways. In *Our Mutual Friend*, Dickens suggests that "Little Red Riding Hood" has paraphrastic force, that it is "[a] rewording of something written or spoken by someone else, esp[ecially] with the aim of making the sense clearer," and "a free rendering of a passage." But long before Dickens's late, great novel, London authors had endued this tale with the power to paraphrase, to "(represent) a subject so as to convey its essential reality."[3] In this part I investigate the ways in which the "Little Red Riding Hood" tale moved *para phrase* (*para,* "alongside of, by, past, and beyond" and *phrase,* "an expression" or "way of speaking"); in other words, I am interested in the several ways in which the tale paralleled discourses of urban poverty.

How did Little Red Riding Hood, a child of the woodlands, arrive in London? Possible antecedents of "Little Red Riding Hood" (circulating throughout Europe as early as the ninth century, but most prevalent in the late medieval and early modern periods) were oral and printed accounts of werewolves living among and preying upon their neighbors—especially their young, female neighbors. "Werewolf trial" narratives, which treated dangerous masculinity and endangered rural maidens, may have influenced the story cycle we now call "Little Red Riding Hood."[4] Scholars of the tale argue that "The Story of Grandmother," a print version collected in France in 1885, is one such descendant of the werewolf narrative, and as such is a nineteenth-century record of a much older version of the tale—perhaps as old as the sixteenth century.[5]

In this version, the heroine (identified only as "the little girl," and without cloak or cap), when sent to her grandmother's house with bread and milk, meets a *bzou* or werewolf. He discovers her destination, precedes her there, kills and eats the grandmother, and stores her remains in the pantry. When the girl arrives, the *bzou* (now dressed as grandmother) directs her to "take some of the meat . . . and a bottle of wine on the shelf."[6] Once the girl cannibalizes her grandmother, the *bzou* instructs her to undress (throwing her clothes piece by piece in the fire as she does so) and lie beside him in bed.

"Oh Grandmother, those big shoulders that you have!"
"All the better to carry kindling from the woods, my child!"
"Oh Grandmother, those big ears that you have!"
"All the better to hear with, my child!"

"Oh Grandmother, that big mouth you have!"
"All the better to eat you with, my child!"
"Oh Grandmother, I need to go outside to relieve myself."
"Do it in the bed, my child!"
"No Grandmother, I want to go outside."
"All right, but don't stay long."[7]

He ties a rope to her ankle; she slips her shackle and by means of this trick, the hitherto gullible girl turns the tables and escapes naked through the woods, evading pursuit.[8]

"The Story of Grandmother" and similar versions were probably not available in print prior to the twentieth century. The versions most available and familiar to an English audience were those of Perrault and Grimm, and these overwrote the more subversive version of the tale. In "The Story of Grandmother" a girl learns to defend herself against a rapacious male antagonist: useful advice for girls near the age of consent. The bawdy, graphic humor of the plot merely underscores its cautionary tale: be alert and self-reliant, learn to tell the difference between men and wolves, wolves and grandmothers, blood and wine. The heroine of "The Grandmother's Tale" is not the passively eaten grandmother, but the granddaughter who can use (and thus keep) her head. The girl's feigned request to defecate deflects the werewolf's animal magnetism, and though he commands her to "do it in bed" she declines to heed the call of the wild. The girl's brush with wolfish desires seasons but does not sully her.

Charles Perrault's 1697 "*Le Petit Chaperon Rouge*" suggests a very different moral to the story. Here, the grandmother makes the girl a little red hat, which suits her so well that she is called "*Petit Chaperon Rouge*." Her mother sends her with a cake and a pot of butter to visit her sick grandmother, and on the way she meets "*compere le loup*" in the woods.[9] "The poor child, not knowing that it was dangerous to stop and listen to a wolf," tells him where grandmother lives. While she stops to gather nuts and flowers, the wolf eats grandmother, and dresses in her clothes. The girl arrives at the house, and is told to climb into bed. In this version, with the final exchange ("My grandmother, what big teeth you have!" "They're for eating you"[10]), the wolf "thro[ws] himself upon *Petit Chaperon Rouge*"[11] and devours her, ending the tale.

Perrault's addition of the *chaperon*[12] and the heroine's demise are the most characteristic elements of this version, and the two features are intimately connected. A small, ornamental headdress of velvet or satin, the *chaperon* is an unlikely *coiffure* for a cottager.[13] The girl's pride of appearance may seem innocent enough, but is not the less perilous for that. Perrault's moral reveals that ignorance of danger is no excuse:

> As one can see by this, children,
> especially pretty young girls
> well bred and refined
> would not do well to listen to just anyone,
> in which case it would be no strange thing
> if a wolf should eat them.
> I say wolf, because all wolves
> are not of the same sort:
> some of them are quite charming,
> not loud or rough at all,
> cajoling sweet-talkers who
> follow young ladies
> right into their homes, right to their *ruelles*.[14]

Though the antagonist is no longer a werewolf, Perrault's moral equates wolves with seductive men. Being devoured becomes the inevitable conclusion to both the girl's dalliance with a *roué* and her dressing above her station. And because by 1697 the color red symbolized both vanity and sexual tarnishing,[15] the girl's red cloak is a mantle of shame for both social and corporal transgressions.

In "*Rotkäppchen*" (1812) the Grimms present the cap as a symbol of dangerous indulgence and childish vanity: "It was her grandmother who loved her the most. She could never give her enough. One time she made her a present, a small red velvet cap, and since it was so becoming, the girl wanted to wear only this."[16] Both grandmother and girl are eaten, as in the Perrault version, but the Grimms' political agenda made rebirth a more fitting conclusion for the tale. The Grimms added a hunter to their story, who slits open the sleeping wolf's stomach, freeing *Rotkäppchen* and her grandmother. *Rotkäppchen* ruefully concludes, "never again in your life will you stray by yourself in the woods when your mother has forbidden it."[17] The Grimms claimed that their ending more closely resembled the conventional structure of oral tales.[18] But it also served their nationalist project; just as the hunter brings wolves and females under control, a unified Germany would mete out justice and/or redemption to those who strayed from the path. Young girls who were either impressively self-sufficient or irretrievably doomed did not fit this model—and so they were eliminated in favor of the dependent, chastened child.

In each of these three seminal versions, the heroine's age is difficult to determine. She is called everything from *"petite fille"* and *"mon enfant"* (little girl, my child) to *"Mädchen"* (maiden—any unmarried girl), to *"jeune fille"* (young girl), to *"demoiselle"* (young lady). The erotic exchange between wolf and girl in each version indicates that no matter how little, the girl is on the verge of womanhood. In the nineteenth century, this seeming paradox was bound up in discourses of childhood, class, and work. Carolyn Steedman acknowledges her difficulty with approaching issues of childhood and labor: "Sometimes it seemed to me that what I was really describing was [not childhood, but] *littleness* itself, and the complex register of affect that has been invested in the word 'little.'"[19] Steedman suggests that the visceral quality of smallness, regardless of actual age, is an important determinant in the range of affect and arousal surrounding the child; in other words, the maiden, young girl, *enfant* was so interesting to Victorians because she could represent a wide range of ages from near babyhood to adolescence. She could be, like Little Red Riding Hood, simultaneously little and denied littleness.

As Steedman argues, the Romantic movement in literature, psychological and cognitive studies, and scientific developments (such as cell theory) combined to make "the child-figure a central vehicle for expressing ideas about the self and its history . . . [moreover,] the complex understanding that there was such a thing as childhood focused new forms of attention on actually living and real children."[20] Little Red Riding Hood is equally "an old word for new meanings,"[21] an iconic name and costume that could represent an endangered body. It therefore makes sense that the story of a girl beset by wolves, when taken up by artists steeped in London news, might take on the hue of current events.

Catherine Robson's *Men in Wonderland* details how the Victorian obsession with loss and its attachment to an imagined past in part inspired the cult of the little girl. The Victorian gentleman imagined a feminized childhood for himself, one forever lost in the adult, masculine sphere of the marketplace. Robson foregrounds unresolved anxieties of "the glaring disparity between the construct of idealized girlhood and the depiction of girlhood as a lived experience for the working class."[22] She demonstrates that the central image of the exploited girl child in the 1840s was a midlands miner or collier, but after the 1885 publication of William Stead's exposé *Maiden Tribute of Modern Babylon,* it was a London prostitute. If the girl's body was a laboring body, a defiled body, or merely a hungry body, it could not simultaneously be inscribed with an innocent middle-class past. Similarly, I argue that Victorian appropriations of "Little Red

Riding Hood" describe an urban working-class girlhood that was tacitly ungirlish. Nearly all Victorian incarnations of "Little Red Riding Hood" that I examined were written by authors living in London; taken together, these texts remake Little Red Riding Hood into a girl of the London streets. As such, she signifies childhood's end in "the mart of the world,"[23] but simultaneously registers the subtle ways that the fairy tale resists standing for an unsullied English childhood.

In 1729 Robert Samber translated into English Perrault's "*Le Petit Chaperon Rouge,*" and in 1823, Edgar Taylor translated the Grimms' "*Rotkäppchen*"; after this, the tale (both redemptive and fatal conclusions) was ubiquitous to English storybooks. It was Samber who first called the red garment a "riding hood" (instead of a cap) and his new term specified the class commentary latent in the tale. The girls and women who wore riding hoods were the daughters, not of rustics, but of the monied classes who rode for pleasure. English adaptors perceived the irony of a *riding* hood bestowed upon a cottager obliged by economic circumstances to *walk* alone to grandmother's. In these versions, it is the hood—a garment above the girl's station—that captures the wolf's attention. Authors adopt the narrative to show the way in which pure things become defiled in the city, and yet, paradoxically, to these authors Little Red Riding Hood is a girl always already lost—doomed before she sets foot in the metropolis. How did Little Red Riding Hood arrive in London? Like other country girls journeying to London, she arrived on foot, with a bundle under her arm, and headed for the theater district.

CHAPTER 13

Little Red Riding Hood's Progress

his chapter explores the relationship between working-class childhood and fairy theatricals through the tale of "Little Red Riding Hood" (a favorite theatrical subject, and one that generated numerous pantomimes, burlesques, and extravaganzas in the nineteenth century). I demonstrate that this tale, which moves between dressing up (that is, trying on other identities) and dressing "up" (that is, masquerading in garments of a higher class) offered productive narrative connections between childhood, theater, and commerce. This is, after all, a tale in which a maiden's sartorial vanities and transgressions bring her to the attention of a predator, who lures her into bed and into destruction. It is a story that turns upon the consequences of artifice and disguise, and this made it an especially suggestive topic for the Victorian theater.

A letter by Charles Dodgson to Evelyn Hatch (a former "child-friend," but at this time an adult) suggests that "Little Red Riding Hood" and theatrical performance were inextricably, if unconsciously, linked in the Victorian mind:

> I should like to know, for curiosity, who that sweet-looking girl was, aged 12, with a red cap . . . ? I fear I must be content with her *name* only: the

social gulf between us is probably too wide for it to be wise for us to make friends. Some of my actress-friends are of *rather* a lower status than myself. But below a certain line, it is hardly wise to let a girl have a "gentleman" friend—even one of 62![1]

Dodgson had long been interested in actresses, and more abstractly in costuming, and his "child-friends" had been trying on identities for his camera for years by that time. The red cap in the letter is only a coincidence; nevertheless, the sight of "that sweet-looking girl" seems to have triggered for Dodgson connections between forbidden class contact, young actresses, and "Little Red Riding Hood"—connections that permeated the culture more broadly.

Dodgson was one of many literary and visual artists of the nineteenth century who understood the stakes of "trying on" and "dressing up" in the "Little Red Riding Hood" tale. His now infamously theatrical photograph, "Agnes Grace Weld as Little Red Riding Hood" (1857), was produced in the wake of the fairy tale pantomimes, extravaganzas, and burlesques so integral to the Victorian theater. Even the title of this photo presents the costumed subject as if commemorating a dramatic performance. Nevertheless, like most of Dodgson's sitters, Agnes was a middle-class child, and her social status separated her from theater actresses. His letter to Evelyn Hatch reflects Victorians' preoccupation with the theater and the social and sexual status of actresses—whatever their ages. Dodgson didn't take costumed pictures of girls he deemed to be "below a certain line" because what was for a middle-class child a game of imaginative play was for a working-class child a livelihood. His photograph was developed in a culture divided between those who played dress-up and those who *worked* dress-up. J. Jeffrey Franklin has said that "play functioned as a lynch-pin concept . . . by which Victorian society represented itself to itself,"[2] and that this notion of play permits Victorian texts to "stage within their pages discursive contests between figures representing their own realist form and figures representing other cultural forms."[3] Franklin's theory is helpful in understanding how conventions of the popular theater projected "Little Red Riding Hood" as a Victorian narrative of fallen girlhood.

Little Red Riding Hood Takes to the Stage

Popular theater forms were conceived in a carnivalesque spirit of resistance to authoritative restrictions. The popular theater describes those forms arising from the licensing restrictions of 1737 to 1843, which disbursed patents to perform comedy and tragedy only to the Royal theaters.[4] The unlicensed theaters navigated these restrictions by inventing forms that relied on visual and musical conventions, rather than spoken dialog. Theatrical forms like the melodrama, historical spectacles, animal dramas, nautical dramas, pantomime, burlettas, burlesques, extravaganzas, and revues all arose from the popular theater as adaptations to the requirements of the burletta license.[5] The fairy tale was a subject first for the pantomime, burlesque, and extravaganza, and it is upon these three forms that I shall focus.[6] The subjects of these theatricals were "primarily urban, social and terrestrial,"[7] mixing fantasy with topical content, often parodying the licensed theaters, and taking the pulse of theatrical issues and, more broadly, the social discourse that affected theatrical culture.

But well before 1843, the major theaters had discovered the lucrative success of the pantomime and extravaganza, and had incorporated them into their regular programming. Pantomime and other theatricals became mainstream, spectacular forms in the licensed as well as minor theaters. Therefore, it is difficult to distinguish popular theatricals as rigidly differentiated from the licensed theater itself. And far from receding after 1843, popular theater forms proliferated across London, in minor and Royal theaters alike. While the pantomime predates the burlesque and extravaganza, and undoubtedly influenced those forms, the later pantomime is inflected with burlesque and spectacular motifs and sequences. As Jane Moody notes, "the language of theatrical nomenclature, especially on minor playbills, is often vague, indistinct, and gloriously arbitrary" displaying a cross-pollination of forms, such as "melo-dramatic burletta," "operatic melodrama," and "serio-comic pantomime."[8] It is commonly held that the first English pantomime was Thomas Dibden's "Harlequin and Mother Goose; or, the Golden Egg" (1806).[9] But this pantomime was produced at Covent Garden, a licensed theater, and this fact troubles the very definitions of "popular" and "elite." There were permeable boundaries between the minor and patent theaters, then, and the popular theater itself was "marked by a wholesale proliferation and confusion of genres and forms."[10] This, argues Lance Bertelson, is because English popular culture was so deeply intermeshed with an emergent middle class "as to make drawing of distinct lines of aesthetic or material demarcation virtually impossible."[11]

It was precisely this viral quality that produced an ambivalent response in even the most ardent theatergoers. To be sure, elite critics "execrated pantomimes as vulgar spectacles signaling the decline of the English stage."[12] And, as John O'Brien observes, "Pantomime's enormous popularity . . . not just with the lower classes but with fashionable theatergoers as well, scandalized and infuriated many observers, who saw it as the regrettable sign that performance genres that had originated in the fairgrounds had now found a permanent place in the patent theaters."[13] Here pantomime is figured as the thing of the streets brought into the respectable home. Londoners were perhaps especially offended by the light the popular theater shone on the drama itself, on theater culture as a whole, and on the relationship between performance and beholder. Victorian criticism mused "about works and performances that seem to have no higher purpose than sensual gratification. . . . And that anxiety frequently derives from a considerable concern about the effects of such entertainments on the audience, which since the eighteenth century has frequently been figured as a faceless, unpredictable, and ungovernable mass."[14] In Tracy C. Davis's words, "Drama of the Victorian period is rife with experimentation about dramatic ambiguity, the trustworthiness of representation, and the respective roles of artists and spectators in making and assenting to the mimetic contract."[15]

The pantomime, burlesque, extravaganza, and other highly visual and auditory forms of popular drama underscored, as O'Brien says, a "fear that the theater's materiality—its use of costumes, scenery and the bodies of performers . . . compromised its claim to be a site whose rules were those of the . . . written word."[16] The materiality of the fairy tale, its sensuality, its similar disruption of the written word, gave it a prominent place in the theater. While most critics have held that the golden age of pantomime and other popular theater forms ended with the relaxation of licensing in 1843, scholars like Jennifer Schacker and Davis have recently argued that the 1840s–1880s are interesting precisely because they were the most prolific years for fairy tale pantomimes. Davis suggests that stories of fairies are especially useful for dramatic adaptation, since "[o]nstage, a symbolic world is created in which the phantasmic is a necessary condition of making narrative."[17] In Schacker's opinion, fairy tales are especially equipped, "to explore . . . the vagaries of sexual, political, and material desires" in the English theaters,[18] a process "in which performers and audience alike were engaged."[19]

The commercial viability and prosperity of the fairy tale theatrical turned in part upon the "fairy actress" herself. However, critics like Davis, Carolyn Steedman, Jane Moody, and Deborah Vlock have argued, in various ways, that the carnivalesque liberties of the theater did not extend to its actresses. Victorian theatrical conventions—"the neighborhoods of playhouses, costuming, and customary gestural language"[20]—served to perpetuate the social stigma of actresses. And the fairy tale theatrical in particular illuminates a society that flocked to the theater, yet deemed that genre and the working women who gave it flesh to be prostitutive.

Working-class women and girls were the staple of the theatrical work force, albeit as temporary laborers; historical records indicate that no more than two-thirds of those women who called themselves actresses (including dancers) had regular work—and regular by no means meant permanent. Theatricals that featured women (burlesque, extravaganza, ballet, and pantomime) either hired a dance troupe for a short season (eight months), or only employed at Christmas time.[21] Even with these restrictions, acting was an attractive career for women in the working classes. The theater provided better quality of life than the notoriously exhausting skilled work of seamstressing or millinery, offered greater independence than jobs in service, paid more generously than costermongery,[22] was safer and less openly degrading than prostitution. While there would have been a difference in the size of the role and thus of the salary between the fairy ensemble and the speaking roles in a pantomime, even the starring roles of fairy tale heroines would have been played by young, unmarried, and relatively unknown actresses. But actresses in popular theaters went on to fame just often enough for the promise of betterment to seem real and attainable. There was for working-class women, therefore, a relationship between dressing up in the theater and dressing "up" in society outside it: a trying on of higher class that could, if one were enterprising, result in acceptance into a more fashionable social circle, or even in a marriage match with a member of a higher social order. No matter that this class elevation was achieved by a miniscule percentage of actresses; the narrative was sufficiently potent to make acting a romantic ideal for the working class, and for the anti-theatricalists, according to Vlock, "the ultimate, deceitful mobility."[23]

To be sure, the theater often commented obliquely upon the class status of its own labor force, and reflected upon the relationship between the actress's social position and the costumes she wore. Women and girls were required for bit parts in pantomime and burlesque because nearly every such theatrical featured a fairy transformation scene. In casting the "corps de ballet" for the fairy scenes, managers preferred girls to boys because they could be paid less and they could be dressed in titillating costumes. The fairies wore low-cut bodices, short skirts, and high-laced boots, a costume that changed little throughout the nineteenth century.[24] This ensemble cast was dressed identically, with girls of eight and women of eighteen in the same costume.[25] One dance-hall song cheerfully reduces the pantomime girl to her essential signifiers: "Oh the fairies! Whoa the fairies! Nothing but splendor / And feminine gender."²⁶ The song captures the intersection between spectacle and sexuality often associated with the theater; too, it erases the youth of the working-class girl, leaving only the erotically charged outline of the fairy form.

Like the body of the fairy actress, the space of the fairy theatrical was surveyed and mapped as an erotic landscape. In an *All the Year Round* article, the author recalls that "The impression left had been of something so exquisitely unearthly, so paradisal, that I never could look back to it without an uneasy feeling reaching nearly to pain."²⁷ In *The World Behind the Scenes* (1881) Percy Fitzgerald describes the fairy transformation in similarly orgasmic terms:

> First, the gauzes' lift slowly one behind the other—perhaps the most pleasing of all scenic effects—giving glimpses of 'the Realms of Bliss,' seen beyond in tantalizing fashion. Then is revealed a kind of half-glorified country, clouds and banks, evidently concealing much. . . . Now we hear the faint tinkle—signal to those aloft on bridges to open more glories . . . fairies rising slowly here and there . . . femmes suspendues seems to float in the air . . . while finally, perhaps, at the back of all, the most glorious paradise of all will open, revealing the pure empyrean itself, and some fair spirit aloft in a cloud among the stars, the apex of all.²⁸

Here transformation is rendered satirically; while Fitzgerald's depiction is all unfolding and upward movement, it is couched in the language of sexual receptivity. In place of social and fiscal mobility, women's stagework earned their comparison to the corporal mobility of the street walker.

The prostitute and the actress, as Catherine Gallagher says, were in the public imagination "alternatives with such similar structures that their very alternativeness calls attention to their interchangeability."²⁹ The actress, like the prostitute, substitutes domestic production for a (seemingly) "exhilaratingly dangerous love affair with a multitude."³⁰ In the public mind, pleasure and self-serving independence marked the career paths of both actress and prostitute. And most obviously of all, like the prostitute, the actress received money in exchange for a certain form of leisure entertainment. Partial employment itself proved damaging to the actress' moral credibility. Henry Mayhew's investigations suggested that poor young women and girls only seasonally employed (in any capacity) turned to illicit means to keep themselves year round: this reportage most likely fed the public rumor that actresses engaged in prostitution to supplement their incomes in the off-season. In Mayhew's terms these are the "hidden occupations": women, in other words, had one livelihood that acted as a cloak for another, illicit one. Davis has demonstrated that Mayhew's allegations were unsubstantiated, but by the 1860s, public opinion nonetheless held it as a sovereign truth. After the passage of the 1843 deregulatory act, which increased the hire of children, titillated and scandalized attention was turned to the theater as a training ground for a future in prostitution, and middle-class critics fretted over the young actress's "terrible knowingness," her "thirst for admiration," and her "consciousness of being watched."[31]

This issue was addressed and redressed in many fairy tale theatricals, but, as I shall argue, particularly "Little Red Riding Hood." The first Little Red Riding Hood theatrical was probably J. R. Planché's 1818 pantomime *Rodolph the Wolf; or, Columbine Red Riding Hood*, and the tale soon became a favorite subject for pantomimes, burlesques, and extravaganzas. These theatrical plots imaginatively synched the narrative trajectory of Little Red Riding Hood with the actresses playing her: they feature a heroine hard at work to preserve her maidenhood and negotiate her class position. Though these Riding Hoods are called "child" and "girl," a young woman played the part; moreover, the scripts' sexual banter serves both to advertise Red Riding Hood's delectability and to punish her for it.

The conventional plots of pantomime and burlesque prove especially useful for exploring the Victorian social applications of "Little Red Riding Hood." In most theatrical adaptations, Little Red Riding Hood is pursued, not by a wolf, but by a wolfish aristocrat or gentleman. For example, the character is "Count Rodolph, Surnamed Wolf" in J. R. Planché's "Comic Melo-Dramatic Pantomime," *Rodolph the Wolf; or, Columbine Red Riding Hood* (1818, for the New Olympic Theater in the Strand); in J. V. Bridgeman and H. Sutherland Edwards's pantomime *Little Red Riding Hood: or, Harlequin and the Wolf in Granny's Clothing* (1859 for Covent Garden), he is a baron who can transform into a wolf with a magic elixir;[32] and "Baron Reginald de Wolf" appears in Leicester Buckingham's "Burlesque Extravaganza," *Little Red Riding Hood and the Fairies of the Rose, Shamrock, and Thistle* (1861, for the Royal Lyceum Theater).[33]

The plots often revolve around competition between the aristocrat and a rustic lover for the attentions of Red Riding Hood, the nobleman plotting to gain the girl through marriage, seduction, or outright snatching. Planché's Count Rodolph vows to abduct the maid, here called "Rosine," from her swain "Alidor," saying "Yes, insulting fair one, I will revenge the slights I have suffered for thee—thine hour is come—beware of the wolf" (7). Buckingham's "Baron Reginald de Wolf has planned / A wicked scheme to gain by force her hand" (7). Bridgman and Edwards's Baron observes Red Riding Hood dancing at a village May fair, and attempts to purchase her:

> Little Red Riding Hood! (*examines her.*) How very charming!
> Don't be afraid, dear, am I so alarming? . . .
> Give me your hand, and though it's scarce worth proffering,
> Accept this purse, simply as friendship's offering.
> You will not? Then the fact no more I'll hide;
> I love you, and I'll have you for my bride.
>   [*Seizes her.*] (19)

In all cases, when Red Riding Hood rejects the aristocrat, he lays in wait at the girl's grandmother's house, where the threat of rape becomes explicit. Planché plays the scene in the manner of a drawing-room assault:

> ROSINE: Dear me grandmother, your voice is altered again—
> RODOLPH: 'Tis with the pleasure I feel in seeing you my love.—(*still more fervently*)
> ROSINE: (*alarmed*) Gracious, how your eyes glare, you frighten me!
> RODOLPH: (*throwing off his disguise*) Read in them my adoration of you, lovely Rosine.
> ROSINE: (*screams*) I am betray'd! (13)

Bridgeman and Edwards's Baron states, "I'll teach young ladies to be rude to me. / The young Red Riding Hood will soon be here, / I feel that I could eat her—little dear" (20). Buckingham burlesques the questioning exchange, with his Red Riding Hood character, called "Blondinette," not eyeing, but kissing, whiskers:

> Blond. What's that tickled me so?
> Some mouths are round—some straight—but, granny dear,
> Yours is elliptical, it would appear!
> A big mustache! a man!—with fear I tremble. (29)

If, as O'Brien and Davis argue, these theatricals turned the footlights upon the watching audience, perhaps these plots acknowledge the familiar narrative of well-heeled gentlemen pursuing stage actresses with gifts, money, and wolf-whistles.

Little Red Riding Hood's dramatic trials also play with the relationship between actresses and their costumes. In Planché's plot, Rosine is doomed to wander the earth with Alidor, she transformed into Columbine and he into Harlequin, until she has proven that she can keep her red cloak on at all times.³⁴ As in most harlequinade portions of a pantomime, the two travel to London. But unlike other pantomimes, in which the London traversal goes unexplained, Planché treats their arrival as a kind of immigration into the city, with Rosine/Columbine Red Riding Hood expressing a wish to see "London . . . the mart of the world" (16). It is when they reach a "masquerade warehouse" that Rosine/Columbine Red Riding Hood falls prey to urban temptation. When a ball gown magically appears, she removes her cloak to put it on. Count Rodolph snatches her up and takes her to his subterranean castle, from which she must be rescued by Alidor. In Planché's play, Red Riding Hood experiences two moments of bodily peril, one in grandmother's cottage, the other on the streets of London, as the direct result of succumbing to the finery of the masquerade. Planché's conclusion renders the sexual moral overtly: "Maidens, who would unmolested / Pass thro' life's bewildering wood, / Mark the truth that's here attested, / Prudence is the Riding Hood" (23). In Buckingham's burlesque, a troupe of fairies give Blondinette a magic flower, directing her to "pluck a bud" each time her virtue is in danger from the Baron de Wolf, which will transport her out of harm's way.³⁵ Each time she does so, she reappears disguised in the clothing of "a sailor, "a Scotchman," and "an Irish lad." The costuming here alternates between the feminine dress that inflames the Baron, and the breeches parts that excite the male audience. All in all, then, Little Red Riding Hood theatricals commonly explore the excitement and risk of costumed performance.

Ultimately, the dramatic action prevents Red Riding Hood's union with a gentleman, and returns her to her rustic lover and home; simultaneously, though, it places her again and again in eroticized physical danger, and touts her to audiences as a tender morsel. The *Dramatis Personae* from Buckingham's *Little Red Riding Hood and the Fairies* renders the relationship between wolf and audience explicit:

> BLONDINETTE: (known as Little Red Riding Hood—a pretty little dear, a nice little duck, and a good little soul—happily combining all the best qualities of fish, flesh, and fowl, dressed in a variety of styles, but always flavoured with her own piquant sauce, and first rate capers . . . . (1)

Lydia Thompson, the twenty-three-year old cast as Blondinette, was famous—and just a bit infamous—as a London danseuse. Born Eliza Hodges Thompson, she began her career as a dancer and pantomime child, and by fifteen was dancing in solo roles in both the minor and licensed theaters. The Blondinette role followed a four-year dancing tour on the continent. In London, she was known professionally for her breeches roles and personally for her breech of contract suit against an unnamed party. Buckingham's burlesque was produced before her stint in America with her second husband's burlesque revue "The British Blondes" (where she was arrested and fined for horsewhipping a man who insulted her), but *Little Red Riding Hood and the Fairies* depended upon Thompson's already scandalous fame.[36] Like the drama itself, the program offers up the actress to the audience as three-course meal with accompaniments. Play theorist Matthew Kaiser reflects on our tendency as readers to "measure play against its supposed antitheses: work, seriousness, suffering" and asks us to imagine by contrast, "what if nothing was intrinsically external to the concept of play . . . ?" (107). His theory helps us to understand these theatricals as a form at play with the work of their actresses, with the suffering of the fairy tale heroine. The consumable fairy girl is synecdoche for the commercial theater. Once more, instead of producing a narrative space outside of progressive modernity, fairy tales contribute to the language and images of urban England.

If the popular theater was a fixture of London's landscape, the red cloak was a moving target in it. The pantomime way of seeing Little Red Riding Hood, in her endless cycles of vanity, infraction and punishment, played out every Christmas for decades, and the themes of deception, disguise, mimesis, and usurped place bound together the tale, the theater, and the city.

Little Red Riding Hood Takes to the Streets

Sexually charged performance also permeated the neighborhood around the theaters. An 1872 issue of the gentleman's magazine *Here and There* reports:

> Recently in the Strand a tall, dashing brunette, with the unmistakable air which belongs to all members of the theatrical profession, was hurrying along encumbered in no slight degree by a somewhat bulky bundle . . . the lady slipped and fell, and with her the bundle, which bursting open from the shock, scattered its contents around . . . it . . . contained a number of theatrical odds and ends . . . amongst them, prominently figuring, a pair of jeweled wings such as the spectacular cherub wears.[37]

This passage amalgamates sexual, geographical, and fairy images. The author makes the actress into public property, the exhibition of her fairy garb likened to an involuntary striptease performed on the street. The working-class girl on her way somewhere purposeful with a parcel, the wolfish attention to her bundle and to her emblematic clothing: the author probably does not mean to signify the "Little Red Riding Hood" plot, but nevertheless creates a coincidence between the perception of the fairy actress and the representation of the hounded fairy girl.

The fairy actress spilling into the streets of London was no uncommon image. Actresses' engagement in economic transaction served to disrupt any nostalgic mingling of girlhood and fairyland, as Dickens indicates in a *Household Words* article, "Gaslight Fairies." Walking in the theater district, he overhears a producer place an order for "five and thirty more Fairies, and let them be good ones. I saw them next day. They ranged from an anxious woman of ten, learned in the prices of victual and fuel, up to a conceited young lady five times that age." Despite the disparity in age and figure, however, Dickens discerns an essential sameness in these fairies:

> they have been sliding out of the clouds for some years, like barrels of beer delivering at a public house . . . and you resign yourself to what must infallibly take place when you see them armed with garlands. You know all you have to expect from them by moonlight. . . . You are acquainted with all these peculiarities of the gaslight fairies, and you know by heart everything that they will do with their arms and legs, and when they will do it.[38]

Dickens parodies the disjuncture between production and exchange. These fairies do not produce anything new: their performance is simply an automated replication of *A Midsummer Night's Dream*. Nevertheless, the show does have a "producer," and he buys and sells fairies in bulk. Their performance is tainted by their imbrication in exchange, delivered from the flies, as they are, like beer to a public house. Creating fairy theatricals for commercial success demanded that the theater produce a number of working-class girls and women, and transform them into identical fairies: Dickens reveals this act as the commercial replication of fairy commodities. Artistic ubiquity hints at sexual gratuity as well. Knowing what to "expect" from these young women "by moonlight" is bound up in knowing what "they will do with their arms and legs." Here Dickens's fairies are as public and urban a commodity as beer.

The fairy is again associated with laboring women in John Weylland's account of the London City Mission. He describes the scavengers of dust heaps in this way:

> The women who are called, and delight in the name of "Fairies," stand in long rows upon these heaps, sifting, from early morning to late at night.... Things of value are constantly found in the sifting, such as silver spoons, rings, money, and even cheques and bank notes. The homes of the "Fairies" are decorated with strange "findings" in the way of ornaments. Pieces of dinner and tea services, some of great beauty and even crested, are to be seen in their filthy rooms.[39]

Weylland's "dust fairies" evidently parody the fairy's treasure horde. These women's connection to metropolitan commerce and industry coincides with the other accounts of working-class "fairies" I have provided here. All three passages merge fairy performances with the publicity and defilement of the London streets. Each tableau is rendered as grotesquerie, but what remains unclear in this nexus of fairy, theater, labor, and street, is just what is pollutant and what is polluted. To the anonymous *Here and There* author, the actress's fall litters the city sidewalk with her clothing; for Dickens, the nineteenth-century fairy seems to cheapen the noble drama of Shakespeare; though the dust heap sifter's job is ostensibly to cleanse and sort, the missionary's eye sharply delineates the filth of her home from the glitter of her hoard. These examples serve to remind us that the fairy tale has always been associated with filthy lucre.

Scholars of the Victorian theater often read London as a performative space, and London life as having "a curious theatrical quality."[40] The theater and other forms of London commerce were interpenetrated in many ways. The popular theater owed its shape and content to forms like the street fairs, where strolling singers, actors, tumblers, and dancers worked the peripheries of the theater districts, as well as the pop-up Penny Gaffs that roved London, eluding the law. One might say that the very streets of London were brought inside the theater walls in the harlequinade business of the pantomime. The theater also drew another form of street commerce in the form of prostitutes who served gentlemen in attendance, and whose presence was winked at since it plumped ticket sales. At the same time, audiences were made mindful of the London streets by the very journey, as Moody notes, "whether on foot going across the fields to Sadler's Wells . . . across the river in a Thames wherry, or by rattling along the streets in a carriage or omnibus,"[41] which served to emphasize the physical and thematic proximities between city and theater. Theaters in London were located in a zone particularly given to the intermingling of classes and professions in a way that troubled social critics. The fashionable shopping districts—Mayfair, Piccadilly, Bond, and Regent Streets, the Haymarket, and parts of the Strand—lay in fairly close proximity to the theater district—Trafalgar and Leicester Squares, Soho and Covent Garden. Actors, therefore, lived or at least transacted business in the neighborhoods in which they performed. Central London prostitution was concentrated by day in Bond, Oxford, and Regents Streets, and by night in the theater districts and the Strand. As Davis notes, "the work places of actresses and prostitutes were . . . close in fact and fancy."[42]

Because of its connections to the street, theater performance was bound up in middle-class anxieties about London labor. In Henry Mayhew's complex taxonomy of London labor, performance connected the costermonger, the strolling musician and actor, and the prostitute: according to him, all of these trades utilized vocal allure and performativity, a certain amount of artifice in the crying of one's wares:

> Such are, in the metropolis more particularly, the pickpockets—the beggars—the prostitutes—the street sellers—the street performers. . . . In each of these classes—according as they partake more or less of the purely vagabond, doing nothing whatsoever for their living, but preying upon the earnings of the more industrious portions of the community . . . there is a greater development of the animal than of the intellectual or moral nature of man. . . . "[43]

An actor and a costermonger, an actress and a prostitute—Mayhew's blurring of these trades allowed middle-class readers to imagine that these professions all sold something unsavory or ill-gotten. To authors like Mayhew in particular, the value of these trades was degraded because they embodied circulation, not production, of goods. In Mayhew's model, actors and prostitutes converge, not merely metaphorically, but in fact—as simply two types of street seller.

Carolyn Steedman finds that children in particular troubled the differences between street sellers and street performers. She notes "a continuum between children whose existence on the street merged with entertainment, theatrical children, and children represented on the stage."[44] When authors like Mayhew represent girl children in this setting, the selling of their meager wares—their importuning and being importuned, their various performances providing a thin cover for begging—always suggest "other sorts of selling."⁴⁵ In the center of London, a working-class woman or girl out on the streets of its most populated district could be an actress, a prostitute, or a purveyor of more material goods, but these respective trades seemed to the middle and upper classes to be tacitly equivalent.

F. W. N. Bayley's bizarre little verse book *Little Red Riding Hood* (1846) will serve to demonstrate how thoroughly the "Little Red Riding Hood" theatrical had permeated Victorian culture by mid-century.⁴⁶ Bayley, the first editor of the *Illustrated London News,* mimicked the popular drama in his verse form by compounding strings of puns and other wordplay. Bayley's "Little Red Riding Hood" was ostensibly published as children's entertainment, but is characterized by the risqué double entendre and topical subject matter that also defined the popular theater. The book's location jokes and cosmopolitan quips, like the pantomime, would have registered with adult consumers in London. His "Little Red Riding Hood" begins with an idealized pastoral heroine, but transports her into an urban mis-en-scène. In its very entanglements with performance, Bayley's verse exemplifies the cultural ambivalence toward the fairy actress, and indicates the extent to which the "Little Red Riding Hood" tale allowed Victorian London to imagine itself as a devourer of working-class girls.

Bayley draws Little Red Riding Hood into the city as if she were entering the throng of Covent Garden for the first time. Here he contrasts his titular heroine with a child street performer:

> Had you seen her you then would have loved her by half, O,
>   And admired her far
> More than the serene self-possessed little Sappho,
> Who sang night and day at the Lowther Bazaar:
>   A smart little creature,
>   In form and in feature,
> With notes of an actress and not of a child.
> Now my beauty's carols—were wood notes, and wild—
> She ne'er thought of gain at their end or beginning,
>   But Sappho "keeps varbling bekase she is *Vinning.*" (original emphasis)

Bayley refers to Louisa Vinning, the "Infant Sappho." Born in Devon in 1837, she was discovered singing at the age of three, and hired to sing at Adelaide Gallery north of the Strand. She was a media darling: popular songs were written for and about her. However, Charles Montague's circus memoir, *Recollections of an Equestrian Manager,* reveals that he hired twenty-three-year-old Vinning to sing for him in 1860, at that time near destitution as the result of "a heartless lover, disgrace, distress."[47] Replacing "w" with "v" to indicate the Cockney accent, Bayley uses this real child performer's name to emblematize those mercenary girls who warble for winnings. Her location is equally suggestive; Vinning performed at the Royal Adelaide Gallery of Practical Science (Blending Instruction with Amusement). This scientific museum was located at the northern end of the Lowther Bazaar, a covered shopping arcade stretching between Covent Garden and the Strand.[48] In 1843 the Bazaar consisted mostly of elegant toyshops.[49] While Louisa Vinning's singing engagement was with the museum, and predicated upon her exhibition in the scientific community as a prodigy, Bayley associates her rather with the mercantile allure of the shops; Sappho's songs are the calculated modulations of a working girl.[50]

Sappho's location between Covent Garden and the Strand, where she sings "night and day," evokes London's theater district as well. In Bayley's verse the Greek poetess is burlesqued by the low art of the girl street performer, who sings "with notes of an actress and not of a child." The lines of demarcation between "actress" and "child" are both performance and monetary gain. But it is surely ironic for Bayley to protest a connection between Little Red Riding Hood and actresses that was already institutional. And while he initially distinguishes "the creature" Sappho from "the beauty" Red Riding Hood, as the poem progresses, Bayley alters his heroine from a child of nature into a child of the London working class. Indeed, the mention of Sappho signals this shift, as if Little Red Riding Hood had come into transformative and soiling contact with the performer. Perhaps Bayley means to allegorically describe the literary history in which the fairy tale is drawn into London performance culture. Though Bayley indicts Sappho for her meretricious use of herself, his Little Red Riding Hood, "though she ne'er thought of gain" and "sings to the woodbirds and not to the throng," also solicits monetary transaction:

> She was, then, most prime,
> For a child of her time;
> You'd have spared her a tanner,
> For mildness of manner;
> Then, her sweet thankful smile would have finished your job,
> And no doubt, in your joy, you'd have spared her a bob!

Henry Mayhew also referred to "the pleasures of making a little girl smile"[51] in exchange for a coin. Evidently a maiden's grateful response was considered money well spent. But giving a girl money, whether for "prime" looks or "prime" performance, reproduces the transaction involved in both acting and prostitution. And Little Red Riding Hood, like Sappho, is out and about in suggestive ways in the poem:

> she never made bold,
> Without leave, to depart
> From home,—so when absent—this proves beyond doubt—
> That her mother must always have—*known she was out*. (original emphasis)

"Out" in the social sense refers to the marriageable age for the middle- and upper-class girl—her entrance to entertainments and engagements in the adult world. But to go "out" in mean streets parlance is to earn a working wage in service or in labor.[52] A girl who "goes out" in the city, with or without her mother's knowledge, was always supposed to be in danger of ruin. Bayley does not permit any genteel meaning of "out":

> Her neighbours
> (Were *they* boors?)
> Subscribed to procure her a little red hood;
> A hood that while going out walking she'd wear,
> (And not indoors abiding)
> To shelter her shoulders and bind down her hair
> By land or by meadow, in hay or in clover,
> Which accounts for their calling her Little Red *Riding*
> Hood—all the world over!
> She was a lively little pet,
> So full of playfulness and honour,
> That though she couldn't earn one yet,
> They put a lively-hood upon her. (original emphases)

Bayley puns upon the impending "lively-hood "of a girl who will be compelled to travel on foot. Not a doting grandmother but rather her "boorish" neighbors "subscribe to procure" a livelihood for the girl, one that is ultimately a scarlet mantle. This passage echoes those critics who fretted over the dangers of environmental influence to young city dwellers.

Little Red Riding Hood's mother knows she is "out" and, like Mayhew's distressed seamstresses and strawberry sellers, this mother is an urban laborer whose work points to prostitutive gain:

> Her favorite place of pleasure was her oven,—
> Her noblest virtue was her way of heating it;—

The sphere—for she, too, had her sphere—she'd move in,
She made quite flagrant with her way of sweeting it.

Mrs. Hood's very "sphere" is sexualized through the innuendo of her "oven"; her talent for heating and spicing things up reflects the vexed position of all working-class women viewed through the middle-class cult of domesticity. The London puns come thicker and faster here than anywhere else in the poem: when she puts a peel in the oven to take her cakes out, Bayley inserts a sixty-five-line comic aside, asserting that were she to put other sorts of peels into the oven—among them Robert Peel, his "peelers" the Metropolitan Police, Mark Lemon (*Punch*'s main "appeal"), and Dan O'Connell, the "re-pealer" of anti-Catholic legislation—she would be "tried, condemned, and hung / . . . The blackest Jezebel that ever swung!" It might be overdetermined to associate this section with the increasing fear during the "Hungry Forties" of working-class riots, but it does serve to situate Little Red Riding Hood unequivocally in a London mis-en-scène.

Bayley's version of the fairy tale mimics the oft-imagined downfall of girls at work in the streets. The girl's mother sends her off to grandmother's "ground-floor" apartment:

By . . . the dark green water whose rivulets flow
Where no pretty sunbeams glisten or glow
    But you'll not be afraid
    For an innocent maid
Has little to tremble at whether or no.

The river that flows through a place without sunlight evokes the pollution that Dickens would later link with the Thames banks in *Our Mutual Friend*; the river docks were a site of sexual as well as maritime commerce. Indeed, the girl's encounter with the wolf is construed in the conventional language of a poor girl's seduction; "fate would not exempt her / From his unhappy list / There came to her a tempter / Whom she could not resist." The hints of sexual predation resemble those in "Little Red Riding Hood" theatricals, but his heroine is lured into a death that is more like ravishment: "The Wolf, who surveyed her, began with a kiss / And the short conversation that followed, was this: "Oh! come to bed Red Riding Hood, / Oh! come to bed with me!"; when she complies, "he [gives] her a bite and a crunch and a roll."

Bayley contrasts those popular theatricals in which Little Red Riding Hood can be made respectable by following Perrault's chosen ending: here the girl ends life as a fallen urban figure. Neither Little Red Riding Hood (the character) nor "Little Red Riding Hood" (the tale she inhabits) can be returned to a rural idyll. This conclusion normalizes the allure, but also the demise, of all the Sapphos of London, both girl and her fall too common to be a source of dismay. It also suggests that innocence is impossible for the fairy tale genre when its reproduction and transmission are sources of revenue. As in the "Little Red Riding Hood" theatricals, Bayley remains alert to the ways in which his own book and its readers consume the fairy tale girl. The speaker casts a speculative eye up and down her body, from her "ringlets wild" to her "blithesome heels and hips." It comes to rest more than once on the actions of the "sweetest mouth that ever smiled," opened to issue song or to receive "sweetmeats . . . which she . . . suck[s] with a vast deal of pleasure." Bayley, like other literary artists who traded upon the fairy tale, has an oral fixation—the desire to play with, to devour, to absorb the (supposedly peasant) vigor of this form, and to transform it into literary wealth.

CHAPTER 14

Little Red Riding Hood and Other Waterside Characters

In the introduction to this book, I described "A Christmas Tree," a *Household Words* article dedicated to the simultaneous delights and horrors of memory. Writing in December of 1850, Charles Dickens recollects the early influences upon his imagination, in the form of toys, tales, books, pantomime characters, and historical figures. Halfway through this essay written halfway through his career (one might say, at the very heart of Dickens), lie the remains of a boyhood passion for a fairy tale child: "She was my first love. I felt that if I could have married Little Red Riding Hood, I should have known perfect bliss. But, it was not to be; and there was nothing for it but to look out the Wolf in the Noah's Ark there, and put him late in the procession on the table, as a monster who was to be degraded."[1] The reminiscence portrays Little Red Riding Hood as a lost object of desire. Dickens the boy is cheated of his love by the "monster" that devours her. More particularly, Dickens's first stirrings of romantic love shift into a sexual competition between boy and wolf, in which the boy loses and the girl is lost. What ought to have been a pure, childish union becomes a narrative of fallen womanhood. Yet though Dickens characterizes his passion for Riding Hood as "not to be," this putting aside of childish, but possibly not innocent, desire and possession is only temporary. Importantly, though little Charles Dickens "degrades" the wolf as a "monster," he does not exclude him from the ark, but only defers his entrance. The wolf has his uses: the death of Red Riding Hood is both dreadful and instructive for the boy who would become a writer. Notably, the wolf in Dickens's childhood is associated with engulfing waters from the first. The devoured girl is here linked, however obliquely, to the drowned woman, and points to Dickens's running narrative of fallen women and their drowning, real or imagined, in the river Thames.

I began the book by showing how Dickens's first novel both longs for and fails to achieve sole authorship, and I pointed to Dickens's awareness that "perfect novelty" means the interleaving of fairy tales and other matter into his fiction. Dickens may attempt to spin an evolutionary narrative in which miscellany becomes novelty, but he ultimately concedes to a dependence upon the fairy tale to build the novel. His permission for tales to "well up" in *Pickwick Papers* reads like a prospectus for his oeuvre as a whole. Dickens's novels delivered more and more extended treatments of specific folk narratives: fairies in the *Old Curiosity Shop,* "Sleeping Beauty" in *Bleak House,* "Cinderella" in *Great Expectations,* and "Little Red Riding Hood" in *Our Mutual Friend.* Indeed, Dickens's long meditation upon the fairy tale came to a crisis in *Our Mutual Friend;* to conclude this book, therefore, I turn to this last complete novel in order to demonstrate how a single fairy tale influenced Dickens's novel writing in ways hitherto unacknowledged.

Here I rearticulate the fragments of "Little Red Riding Hood" scattered through *Our Mutual Friend,* and insert them into the critical conversation about Dickens's working-class master-plots. Crucial economic readings cite the various devouring forces in the novel; yet no discussion locates among these forces the threads of "Little Red Riding Hood" that wind through the text. To do so is to realize that Dickens's portrayal of Red Riding Hood is effected through the ravening Rogue Riderhood, himself swallowed in the end by the river Thames. As with so many other rearticulations in the novel, then, assembling the folk tale produces, not a whole and easily readable narrative, but a derangement of the now familiar story of a maiden's pursuit by a monster. These fragmented and redistributed elements generate a reading of the tale in which the wolf and girl become alike. If we look closely at Dickens's toying with the ark, it might occur to us that the wolf in the "procession" should have a female companion. Dickens does not invoke the Biblical mating of "two of every sort . . . after their kind,"[2] and the implication is that it is Red Riding Hood herself who has become amalgamated with the wolf, an unholy matrimony to contrast Dickens's imagined "perfect bliss." Dickens's conflation of his lost ideal with wolfish consumption makes sense within the Victorian literary construct of fallen womanhood I have been tracing, in which the woman is always depicted as that great paradox, a creature who has succumbed to appetite—her seducer's and her own—who, having consumed, is herself consumed. These brief moments in *Household Words*, the whisper of a love that abides, and yet is not to be, together with the ark, that great metonymic signifier of the Flood and its simultaneous destruction and restoration of life, anticipate Dickens's speculation upon nostalgia and the literary value of folklore in his last novel. When Dickens says his love of Little Red Riding Hood "was not to be," he mourns the loss of folklore, remembered as the hallowed source of imagination. Paradoxically, however, Dickens knows that his own market value depends upon maintaining the currency of these related themes—the ruined maiden, the nostalgic burial of folklore. In *Our Mutual Friend*, the author recognizes that to decry the commercial value of girls is itself commercially valuable, and that to mourn the death of Riding Hood is to eternally resurrect her body.

As with the other authors in part 4, Dickens situates the fairy tale's commercial value within the mushrooming urban center. Robert Alter has coined the phrase "experiential realism" to describe "the novel as a searching response to the felt new reality of the European city."[3] In London, "the overabundance of sensory stimuli . . . was compounded . . . by a feeling of being dwarfed by the cityscape and sometimes menaced by the material products of compacted urban existence."[4] Julian Wolfreys argues that, in the early part of Victoria's reign, London began to be "perceived as a modern city. London of the nineteenth century assumed a central importance to the world and in the minds not only of its inhabitants but of people everywhere. . . . Certainly, London becomes more than merely real."[5] For Wolfreys, London was not simply a setting for early to mid-century fiction, but an integral part of the narrative itself, as important, and as imagined, as character or plot. A modern city, it yet had something about it that begged the figural. According to Wolfreys, because London altered and expanded at an alarming rate, literary artists found control by imposing upon it "secrets and dark corners," and, in the face of constant change, an identity "out of time suggesting the eternal."[6] Robert Alter acknowledges that "many readers have noticed a fairy-tale perspective in Dickens's writing by virtue of which monsters, ogres, and other supernatural creatures suddenly manifest themselves, usually through the agency of figurative language, in the most mundane contemporary settings."[7] In *Dickens on the Romantic Side of Familiar Things*, Robert Newsom has adduced that the author "imposes upon the reader a kind of unsettled and unsettling double perspective which requires us to see things as *at once* 'romantic' and 'familiar'" (original emphasis).[8] Real and unreal plots merge in Dickens's London in order to draw upon but also confront and disrupt nostalgia's play between past and present.[9]

As "Gaslight Fairies" demonstrates, Dickens thought fairy theatricals were integral to this double vision of London. Like London itself, William Axton has noted, the "pantomime as Dickens knew it was a curious amalgam of fantasy, realism, topicality, anachronism, grotesquerie, burlesque, spectacle, music, verse, dance, and a serious story . . . if there is one feature of the drama known to Dickens . . . it is this grotesque mixture of the real and the fantastic."[10] If Dickens's London is a deconstructed space, his now legendary response to it as "the attraction of repulsion"[11] is equally vexed. Dickens moved in the peripheries of the theatrical circles I have described, and while he took an ardent interest in the popular theater, his was an enthusiasm always modulated by a sense of himself and his works as uncomfortably part and parcel of performing London. Dickens dated his own preoccupation with the stage from "the period when I believed the Clown was a being born into the world with infinite pockets"[12]; this quote reminds us that in "Nurse's Tales" the Uncommercial Traveler admits to a morbid fear of his own pockets, and what might come out of them. It would seem that the disruptive, amalgamative nature of the theater was seminal to Dickens's development as a writer. As Edwin Eigner has noted about the harlequinade portion of the pantomime: "Man's plight is often created by the transformation, misbehavior, and relentless hostility of objects and mechanical devices: things are not what they seem to be, or rather they are, but then they change frighteningly into something else. Nothing can be relied on. . . . As is usual in extreme forms of comic theater, a terrible seriousness underlies the jollity and 'animal spirit' of pantomime."[13] Dickens also comments upon the slipperiness of the pantomime world in "A Christmas Tree," of the time of year "when Everything is capable, with the greatest ease, of being changed into Anything; and 'Nothing is, but thinking makes it so.'"[14] In the arboreal evolution of "A Christmas Tree," the pantomime sits on the branches above the fairy tale, suggesting both the fairy tale as source for other forms of literature, and also the generic proximity between tale and popular theatrical. Part of the goal in this chapter, then, is to demonstrate Dickens's ongoing struggle with both the fairy tale and the fairy tale theatrical as tributary forces to his novel making.

As I have suggested, Little Red Riding Hood is located among the harshest realities of Dickens's unreal (or more than merely real) city. When she enters the urban scene, she is made into an emblem of literary artists' ideas about labor and lost innocence in London. Dickens's correspondence with a German author demonstrates his familiarity with the tale as a part of the folkloric tradition, but also shows that, as with Bayley, the destruction of Little Red Riding Hood was a necessary component of the story for Dickens, and apparently from his earliest memory: "Little Red Cap under the name of Little Red Riding Hood is a very old English story—a hundred years old at the least, I should say. But the cutting open of the Wolf by the Hunter, and the restoration of Little Red Cap to life, which is no part of the English story, seems familiar to me, as if I had read it before."[15] His letter makes clear that, while he was aware of the Germans' happier ending, Dickens imagined Little Red Riding Hood to be a girl always already lost. To Dickens, the recovery of this girl is "no part of the English story"; however, there were plenty of British adaptations of the story that did spare the girl. Dickens therefore chooses to remember only the version by Charles Perrault, the first in which the girl is devoured. But while he undoubtedly makes his own recollection of the tale into the national standard, Dickens does not merely shape the story to suit his novel; rather, the story shapes Dickens, or at least, shapes the way Dickens imagines devoured girls in London. As with the other texts I have explored, Dickens's use of "Little Red Riding Hood" describes an urban working-class girlhood that was implicitly ungirlish.

Dickens's lost "first love" exemplifies his master-plot of fallen girls and their smooth, plausible seducers. Dickens created a long series of predatory pairings: Nancy and Sykes (who is more feral than his dog), Alice and Carker (who is all teeth), Little Em'ly and Steerforth. David Copperfield's boyhood passion for his social inferior Little Em'ly is especially reminiscent of the love that was "not to be." David describes a childhood moment in which Em'ly foreshadows her own sexual future by a headlong dash toward the ocean: "There has been a time since when I have wondered whether, if the life before her could have been revealed to me at a glance . . . and if her preservation could have depended on a motion of my hand, I ought to have held it up to save her."[16] Martha, the fallen woman who shadows Little Em'ly throughout the novel, has a similarly watery interlude by the Thames, where she stands "as if she were a part of the refuse it had cast out, and left to corruption and decay" before David snatches her from a suicidal plunge:

> "I know it's like me!" she exclaimed. "I know that I belong to it. I know that it's the natural company of such as I am! It comes from country places, where there was once no harm in it—and it creeps through the dismal

streets, defiled and miserable.... I can't keep away from it.... It's the only thing in all the world that I am fit for, or that's fit for me."[17]

As Catherine Robson has noted, "The river, and more specifically the River Thames, is always the place of the prostitute's suicide, or at the least, her suicidal thoughts.... Dickens repeatedly presents us with images of the desperate harlot either on the brink of, or immersed within, the swirling waters which represent her muddied moral turbulence and will secure her release from a hated world."[18] In Dickens's mind, if not in the Victorian imagination at large, a drowned woman is a fallen woman. In these scenes, Dickens suggests that country lasses transplanted to the city become morally pestilential, ruinous to themselves and others. But the scenes show something else: David the writer standing contemplatively beside girls poised for drowning. Whether or not these endangered girls' "preservation . . . depended on a motion of (David's) hand," they certainly depended on a motion of Dickens's hand. Undeniably, in terms of Dickens's book sales, the Nells and Nancies, Alices and Em'lies were more valuable when they "were not to be"—that is, when pursued, defiled, decried, or beaten into the ground. If the author is indicted in the market that swallows up maidens, the wolf, the author, and those devouring waters flow together. Nevertheless, these girls were sacrifices that Dickens offered up uneasily. As early as 1850, Dickens entertains the possibility of writing a new ending for the lovely, doomed, working-class girlhood that had hitherto marked his oeuvre.

For all the many glancing references at Dickens's ruined "first love" throughout his novels, it is not until *Our Mutual Friend* that he dilated at length upon "Little Red Riding Hood."[19] I argue that the tale serves as a retrospection of poverty and girlhood in the Victorian imagination, but most particularly in Dickens's own work. Early in the novel, Bella complains that the Wilfer's money is endlessly snatched by "the Monster who swallows up so much" when the family "want—Everything."[20] Bella figures the capitalist market as a devouring agent, cannibalizing its own society with bold rapine. Is this the same degraded "monster" that devoured Dickens's darling? A wolfish avidity dogs most characters in *Our Mutual Friend,* and this image of swallowing becomes a driving figurative force in the novel. Gail Turley Houston argues that, after 1859, "the themes of orality, predation, and the translation of human flesh into economic gain—all metaphoric cannibalism—dominate Dickens's fiction."[21] Importantly, metaphoric cannibalism in the respectable classes has analogs among working-class characters in the novel.

Catherine Gallagher theorizes that *Our Mutual Friend* marks an authorial trend wherein the physical condition of the working class metaphorizes the spiritual condition of the nation.[22] For Dickens, working-class hunger and the working-class body, in Gallagher's terms "the theater of struggling food,"[23] symbolize marketplace economics. Dickens's "attraction of repulsion" often centers on the utter physicality of survival, both as a harsh reality in itself and in its potential to represent society's relationship to a market economy. Gallagher underscores a common middle-class concern: "the fear that society is in danger of reducing human value to its most primitive biological needs."[24] For authors like Henry Mayhew this fear was centered upon the appetite: "Everything is sacrificed . . . in the struggle to live—aye! And to live *merely*. Mind, heart, soul, all are absorbed in the belly. The rudest form of animal life, physiologists tell us, is simply a locomotive stomach. Verily, it would appear as if our social state had a tendency to make the highest animal sink into the lowest" (original emphasis).[25] Like Mayhew, Dickens often compares avidity to animalism. In *Our Mutual Friend,* Little Red Riding Hood stands in both for the working appetite, and for those tailed by nightmarish greed—the "locomotive stomach" unleashed upon the city. Together, of course, with many other figural counterparts, she prowls through Dickens's scenes of hunger in the novel.

Ultimately, we find not one, but two devouring forces in *Our Mutual Friend,* two "monsters that swallow up so much." Gallagher has divided the novel according to the Ruskinian principals of wealth and "illth"; in doing so, she reads Dickens's narrative as a sanitizing process, a movement from wet to dry: from the Thames, the site of pollution, the organic garbage of corpses, to the inorganic garbage of the dust heaps, which can then be transformed from the trash of commerce into "true golden gold," like Bella (752). Thus John Harmon progresses from the river and the appearance of death, to "suspended animation"[26] through the guise of Rokesmith, to life and wealth through the inheritance of the dust heaps. For Gallagher, then, since "the novel arranges its inquiry into the nature of wealth around the disposal of human remains,"[27] the river is the primary source of illth, and "[t]he heroism and horror of dragging bodies out of the water"[28] is underscored; to Gallagher, the dust world is the place of transformations, the river the place of tragedy. Gallagher's work has vitally shaped the way we understand the river in *Our Mutual Friend;* yet I would argue that, to Dickens, the river is not merely an illthy sewer, but also a powerfully corrective force.

The Thames winds through Dickens's oeuvre, binding it on either end, advancing and resolving plots, transporting certain characters, eliminating others. It therefore has both a narrative role and considerable authoritative powers. If the cannibalism of the market is entirely evil in Dickens's literary construct, the destructive force of the river has its uses, acting as a "valuable" agent of death in the same sense as the wolf of Dickens's "Little Red Riding Hood." The language that surrounds the river attempts to resolve those very anxieties about the working girl and her appetite, and the authoritative powers of the Thames alter the course of the devoured girl plot Dickens himself set in motion. Whereas in 1847, the "restoration" of the girl was "no part of the English story," by 1865, it becomes clear that her salvation was, as he suggests, "familiar," lurking somewhere in his memory all along. In *Our Mutual Friend,* the Riding Hood of Dickens's youth is replaced by a nightmarish incarnation of herself in the grotesque body of a criminal. Rogue Riderhood is fed to the Thames so that Red Riding Hood may be pulled from its belly, restored and whole.

Riderhood is a self-proclaimed "waterside character" (152), and his link to Riding Hood is indivisible from his association with the river. The Riderhood subplot gleefully invokes the fairy tale girl. Lawyer Mortimer Lightwood first voices the kinship, offhandedly remarking upon "little Rogue Riderhood—I am tempted into the paraphrase by remembering the charming wolf who would have rendered society a great service if he had devoured Mr. Riderhood's father and mother in their infancy" (405). And it is not only Riderhood's surname that reminds Lightwood of the hooded heroine. Lightwood first meets Riderhood when he appears at the lawyer's door, bearing not a basket of goodies but false witness. And like his namesake, Riderhood, too, wears a hat: "[The lights] showed the visitor to be an ill-looking visitor with a squinting leer, who, as he spoke, fumbled at an old sodden fur cap, formless and mangey, that looked like a furry animal, dog or cat, puppy or kitten, drowned and decaying" (151). This horrid cap resurfaces throughout the novel, identifying Riderhood as the riding hood does the folk heroine. His other emblematic garb is a red neckerchief, which he dons to trap Bradley Headstone. If Little Red's riding hood is a mantle of vanity, a wolf lure, a signal of her eventual bloody devouring, Rogue Riderhood's red scarf similarly encircles his neck, pointing (like the drowned hat) to his demise. The police inspector, pulling up Gaffer Hexam's towline on the river (in which Hexam's body is tangled), also appears to comment upon the homophonic qualities of Riderhood's name: "'I mean to have it, and the boat too,' said Mr. Inspector, playing the line. . . . 'Take care,' said Riderhood. 'You'll disfigure. Or pull asunder, perhaps.' 'I am not going to do either, not even to your Grandmother,' said Mr. Inspector" (174). In one sense, then, "Little Rogue Riderhood" is an inside joke for everyone but Riderhood himself; both Michael Kotzin and Cynthia DeMarcus argue that it is an ironic name for a man characterized by wolfishness, whose greatest talent is lying in wait for victims.[29] Like the fairy tale villain, he attempts to appear in the guise of an "honest man": the wolf in Alfred David's clothing. More than once he asks his dupes, "where are you going?" echoing the wolf's obligatory salutation to Red Riding Hood.

But Rogue Riderhood is more than Dickensian catachresis. For Riderhood *is* swallowed in the end, and society *is* rendered a great service. What is more, the Thames performs this "service" regularly throughout the novel. I do not suggest that Riderhood equals Riding Hood, or that the Thames equals the "charming wolf" in any kind of mathematically precise fashion. Rather, I mean that when Dickens takes his characters alongside the water, he evokes not only the story, but our remembrance of the story. In this way, Riderhood is, as Lightwood says, a "paraphrase": "[a] rewording of something written or spoken by someone else, esp[ecially] with the aim of making the sense clearer; a free rendering of a passage."[30] Fairy tale representation paradoxically serves to clarify Dickens's realism. Riding Hood moves *para phrase*—"alongside of, by, past, and beyond" an "expression," a "way of speaking."[31] She is, like the London surrounding her, "more than merely real"; she is a way of speaking about working-class labor, hunger, and desire.

Rogue Riderhood epitomizes guilty, shameful work. He embodies the perceived rapacity of the working classes, to warn of what the London poor can become when kept needy and ignorant. But Riderhood also serves as a scapegoat for other forms of work, other kinds of desire, so that other waterside characters may be stainless, may err and be redeemed, or, more poignantly, may stand silently without name. An audacious, edacious villain, he represents a guilt that is not named in the novel, but that is touched often with an uneasy hand. Hints of this guilt surface in the "found drowned" posters in the Hexam cottage, many of which advertise the deaths of young women: "This one was the young woman in gray boots, and her linen marked with a cross. Look and see if she warn't. . . . This is them two young sisters wot tied themselves together with a handkecher. . . . They pretty well papers the room, you see, but I know 'em all" (31). The particular shame of the young woman and sisters remains obscure; however, as in *David Copperfield* (as well as *Oliver Twist*, *Bleak House*, and the *Uncommercial Traveler*), the riverside of *Our Mutual Friend* is haunted by the shades of desperate women. Even working-class women who escape sexual disgrace, Dickens suggests, are beset by the degradation of poverty and the terrors of the workhouse. Betty Higden pauses outside London to contemplate the summons of the Thames: "from the bridge you may see the young river, dimpled like a young child, playfully gliding away among the trees, unpolluted by the defilements that wait for it on its course, and as yet out of hearing of the deep summons of the sea . . . she heard the tender river whispering to many like herself, 'Come to me, come to me! When the cruel shame and terror you have so long fled from, most beset you, come to me! I am the Relieving Officer appointed by eternal ordinance to do my work'" (497). The passage echoes Martha's haunted self-assessment at the Millbank riverside. The river has the narrative power to simultaneously signify a country child on its way toward "defilements" in the city and Death the Receiver to those same defiled children. The Thames thus endlessly repeats (among other stories) the story of Little Red Riding Hood "gliding . . . among the trees" and wolf who swallows her at her journey's end. Betty's determination to drown herself and Johnny reflects the horror of postindustrial London's poor laws, and reveals the unsheathed claws of capitalist society, when death in the "tender river" is preferable to life in the alms house: "No! Never for me, nor for the child, while there's water enough in England to cover us" (324).[32] "Little Rogue Riderhood," the waterside character eventually "found drowned," is both the iteration of what becomes of Little Red Riding Hood in the city, and the sacrificial rogue for impoverished womanhood, behind whom stand the specters of other waterside characters—the woman in the gray boots, the sisters bound together with a handkerchief. These women, and not Bella, are the true victims of "the monster who swallows up so much when we want—Everything." Dickens can have a great deal of mercy upon the nameless fallen with the aid of a whipping boy/girl.

In Rogue Riderhood's grotesque body, then, Red Riding Hood becomes an amalgam of wolf and girl[33]; in its climactic moment, the "Little Red Riding Hood" tale blurs the same boundaries: the wolf's ultimate rejoinder, "The better to eat you with," seeks to erase the girl's escalating statements of difference ("what big ___ you have") by absorbing the girl into himself. In a novel that takes every opportunity to dissolve categories, the collapsing distinction between wolves and girls becomes another facet of *Our Mutual Friend*'s insistence upon mutuality. If Riderhood paraphrases devoured girlhood and devouring manhood, he performs the entire folk tale, a "free rendering of a passage" indeed.

Of course, Riderhood is not the only male imbrued with shades of Red Riding Hood. As DeMarcus has noted, the river claims a variety of waterside characters: Jesse Hexam, Bradley Headstone, Eugene Wrayburn, and, I would add, John Harmon. Not coincidentally, all "Little Red Riding Hood" references take place by the river: as with Riderhood, whenever a character becomes too devouring, he is swallowed by the river in its bed. And this pattern is part of Dickens's overall treatment of gender as well as class. Like Gallagher, Gail Turley Houston believes that working-class hunger stands as an analog to middle-class commercial desire; she examines the "oscillations between suppression of appetite and voracious desire in Dickens' [sic] male alter egos," contending that "this struggle is so intense that it must be acted out in a series of carnivalesque characters or sequences."[34] However, there is no fixed integrity between these class distinctions in *Our Mutual Friend*. Instead, the effect of violent contact in the novel is, as Mary Poovey points out, "to locate difference inside of man, hence to imperil . . . the integrity of male identity itself."[35] In Poovey's model, "when one man can be taken for another . . . then a man can be taken down with another like himself. . . . The contradiction—the other is like me, the other is different—is essential to the economic and representational systems that *Our Mutual Friend* simultaneously participates in and resists."[36] And, just as Poovey "imperils" class boundaries, Gallagher troubles gender binaries. She argues that, because women in the novel are self-evidently items of exchange, naturally prone to and resistant toward commodification, "men are knocked out, drowned, dried out, stored up, and finally reanimated . . . so that women need not undergo any such alienation. The state of suspended animation is thus exclusively masculine in *Our Mutual Friend* because it is so naturally feminine."[37] To extrapolate upon these economic readings, then: Dickens attaches elements of the fairy tale girl to multiple male characters across the class spectrum, creating seemingly endless waves of guilty men transformed into headstones for fallen women. In doing so, he seeks to displace the grotesqueries of labor and physicality onto criminalized masculinity.

When Wrayburn, Lightwood, Riderhood, and the inspector set out in search of Gaffer Hexam, we are offered an especially haunting fragment of the tale:

> Very little life was to be seen on either bank . . . and the staring black and white letters upon wharves and warehouses "looked," said Eugene to Mortimer, "like inscriptions over the graves of dead businesses."
>
> As they glided slowly on, keeping under the shore and sneaking in and out among the shipping by back alleys of water, in a pilfering way that seemed to be their boatman's normal manner of progression, all the objects among which they crept were so huge in contrast with their wretched boat, as to threaten to crush it. . . . Not a figure-head but had

the menacing look of bursting forward to run them down. Not a sluice gate, or a painted scale upon a post or wall, showing the depth of water, but seemed to hint, like the dreadfully facetious Wolf in Grandmamma's cottage, "That's to drown *you* in, my dears!" (173)

It is a warning, not only to Riderhood, but to Eugene Wrayburn, and to Gaffer Hexam, too, already drowned and tangled in his own line. The passage points to the "luck" tied to Hexam's boat. His is a "dead business" in more ways than one: bodies are his capital, and he has paid for this unsavory work with his own, as the stain on his boat foretold. Like Riderhood, Hexam is a working-class metaphor for societal greed: the grotesque iteration of the grasping avarice that gnaws at the Lammles, Wegg, the Podsnaps, and Bella Wilfer. And yet, Hexam's death associates him, not with the devouring wolf, but with the devoured Little Red Riding Hood—an ignorant (but not innocent) victim of circumstances. Dickens's river scenes constantly symbolize the shame of other kinds of work: always associated with the defiled and rotting commercial piers she frequented, the prostitute who plunged into the river was the very embodiment of dead business. How appropriate that Eugene's vague, nameless sense of guilt and self-association with criminality eddies around this chapter, with his intentions to seduce Lizzie already taking shape in his mind. That's to drown *you* in, my dears.

Indeed, "the inscriptions over the graves of dead businesses" foretell the wreck of many wolfish business arrangements in the novel. Schoolmaster Bradley Headstone has a "manner that would be better described as one of lying in wait. . . . Yet there was enough of what was animal . . . still visible in him" (218). And indeed, Headstone lies in wait for Lizzie like the wolf at the crossroads: "The best-looking among us will not look very well, lurking at a corner, and Bradley came out of that disadvantage very poorly indeed" (386). Later, Headstone even costumes himself to look like Riderhood, and thus, since they drown together, foreshadows the "dead business" their illicit partnership will become. Headstone's spontaneous, gushing nosebleeds also clothe him in red—another link to Riding Hood as a sign of ungovernable passion. In this way, Hexam and Headstone, both "pardners" at some point with Riderhood, perhaps represent those soiled by his contact; contaminated by the dark work at which he labors, they become echoes of his more overt paraphrase of Red Riding Hood. It is fitting that when Headstone and Riderhood are found at the bottom of the river, Headstone lies atop Riderhood (781), the pair not only evoking marital union, but embodying the commercial signage at the city docks—a Headstone over the grave of dead businesses.

The drownings of Riderhood, Hexam, and Headstone replay Perrault's ending, in which the heroine remains entombed in the wolf's belly. It is, notably, with middle-class men that Dickens can begin to imagine making "the restoration of Red Cap" into "part of the English story." Eugene Wrayburn is another strange mixture of wolf and Red Riding Hood. Like Riderhood, he turns up on thresholds: "A man's figure paused on the pavement at the outer door. 'Mr. Eugene Wrayburn, ain't it?' said Miss Wren. . . . 'You may come in, if you're good.' 'I am not good,' said Eugene, 'but I'll come in'" (234). Like Headstone, he lurks on street corners for Lizzie: "another figure loitering discontentedly by, and looking up the street and down it, and all about, started and exclaimed, 'Lizzie! why, where have you been?'" (398) His pursuit of Lizzie is lupine in its intensity (even he calls himself "a bad idle dog" [234]). Yet at his own most wolfish moment, when he plans to seduce and ruin Lizzie, he is attacked by Headstone and cast into the river. Baptism is only the most obvious metaphor here; when Lizzie pulls him out again, he is delivered from the Thames to the same effect as the Grimms' Red Cap is pulled from the belly of the wolf—he emerges, sadder, wiser, and undoubtedly domesticated.

Even the ultimately triumphant heir John Harmon paraphrases "Little Red Riding Hood," and thus it seems that, through characters' repeated derangement from man to wolf to swallowed girl, Dickens muzzles male appetite of every kind, in every class category. During his long soliloquy, Harmon admits that he, like Bella, was lured by the Harmon fortune, noting that he was "attracted" back to England "by the accounts of [his] fine inheritance" and that he was "mistrustful that [he] was already growing avaricious" (360). At precisely this pass, he is tricked into the complex identity theft that leaves him lying drugged in a room by the riverside. He hears the sound of his double, Radfoot, being murdered in his place: "I heard a noise of blows, and thought it was a woodcutter cutting down a tree. I could not have said that my name was John Harmon—I could not have thought it—I didn't know it—but when I heard the blows, I thought of the woodcutter and his axe, and had some dead idea that I was lying in a forest" (363). It is a strange analogy, unless we are on the watch for "Little Red Riding Hood." As many have noted, the scene, so brimful of violence and apparent death, is actually the first sign of life in the Harmon money, the veritable turning of his fortune. Yet, far more subtly, the passage also points toward the avenging woodsman in the Grimm version, on his way to deliver Red Riding Hood from the wolf's belly. For Harmon, the sound of the woodcutter signals redemption, a second chance at living without greed. Like Wrayburn, he must be submerged to be restored.

As with Riderhood, these men in one way and another carry the variant endings of "Little Red Riding Hood" in their bodies. DeMarcus recognizes that Dickens "seized on the tale as a metaphor for the modern world," but explains this argument with the generalization that "each individual, like Little Red Riding Hood, is a potential victim and faces Wolves [sic] at every turn, including the abstract figure of Death."[38] I have attempted to deepen this statement by taking account of the class and gender implications of Dickens's "paraphrase." Following Poovey, I have suggested that the men in the novel who bear elements of both wolf and Red Riding Hood become, concomitantly, metaphors for rapacity, and for the effects of that rapacity upon society. The Red Riding Hoods who are punished in the novel are indeed men: defiled, desiring, and difficult to distinguish from wolves. However, Gallagher also contends that "all of the commodity corpses, the discarded and suspended bodies in *Our Mutual Friend* are male"[39]; we have seen the posters for the women found drowned, and we know that this is simply not true: and yet, ghostly as those drowned women are, it is an understandable omission. Wolfreys's argument that London inhabits novels as much as novels inhabit London is useful here in seeing the river as an integrated part of the city. As in the texts Wolfreys analyzes, in *Our Mutual Friend* "London as both discourse and place of the imaginary flows . . . through the various narratives in question, barely containable, even as those narratives flow through the city."[40]

Wolfreys does not invoke the Thames specifically, but its "flow" is everywhere implied. Dickens sees the river not merely as synecdoche of defiled and defiling London; instead, the river, too, is a paraphrase, running alongside of, but also beneath and beyond the narrative. It contains many other stories, the leaves of which may be fished out to line pockets. In other words, the women that paper the room of the Hexam house are the same women that paper this and all of Dickens's novels: the stories of dead working-class women, from whom Dickens gleaned a living.

Bodies have been Dickens's capital too. The drenched and devoured men in the novel effectively serve to drown out the sound of other voices in the Thames, to cloak the shame of other waterside characters. In the case of Hexam, Headstone, Wrayburn, and Harmon, the effect is to surround them with the language, the rhetorical force of the tale, to imprint on them ghostly afterimages of Little Red Riding Hood. Riderhood cast in the river makes the impact—the other, repeated instances ripple out from his iconic center. Dickens tells the story, then tells it again, and again, and again, causing different men to step up and take the brutal b/eating for Red Riding Hood: rich man, poor man, beggar man, thief. These men are in one way or another forced to dress in the victim's costume, to take a turn as gaslight fairies. Those who have gained by watching, or who have whistled as others worked, become the object of intense scrutiny. As Poovey demonstrates, people are repeatedly both "taken in" and "taken for" in the novel.[41] When we understand this, it is less surprising that a man might be taken for—that is, *taken in place of*—a ruined girl.

Like the pantomime transformation in the popular theater, Riderhood—a character both comically and seriously transformed—draws a reader's attention to the performance of the novel.[42] When Riderhood confronts Headstone with the knowledge that the schoolmaster has attempted murder while costumed as Riderhood himself, he does so before an audience of Headstone's schoolchildren, whom he draws into a choric performance:

> "Wot's the diwisions of water, my lambs? Wot sorts of water is there on the land?"
>
> Shrill chorus: "Seas, rivers, lakes, and ponds."
>
> "Seas, rivers, lakes, and ponds," said Riderhood. "They've got all the lot, Master! Blowed if I shouldn't have left out lakes, never having clapped eyes upon one, to my knowledge. Seas, rivers, lakes, and ponds. Wot is it, lambs, as they ketches in seas, rivers, lakes, and ponds?"
>
> Shrill chorus (with some contempt for the ease of the question): "Fish!"
>
> "Good a-gin!' said Riderhood. "But wot else is it, my lambs, as they sometimes ketches in rivers?" Chorus at a loss. One shrill voice: "Weed!"
>
> "Good agin!" cried Riderhood. "But it ain't weed neither. You'll never guess, my dears. Wot is it, besides fish, as they sometimes ketches in rivers? Well! I'll tell you. It's suits o' clothes."
>
> Bradley's face changed.
>
> "Leastways, lambs," said Riderhood, observing him out of the corners of his eyes, "that's wot I my own self sometimes ketches in rivers. For strike me blind, my lambs, if I didn't ketch in a river the wery bundle under my arm!"
>
> The class looked at the master, as if appealing from the irregular entrapment of this mode of examination. The master looked at the examiner, as if he would have torn him to pieces.
>
> "I ask your pardon, learned governor," said Riderhood, smearing his sleeve across his mouth as he laughed with a relish, "tain't fair to the lambs, I know. It wos a bit of fun of mine. But upon my soul I drawed this here

bundle out of a river! It's a Bargeman's suit of clothes. You see, it had been sunk there by the man as wore it, and I got it up."

"How do you know it was sunk by the man who wore it?" asked Bradley.

"Cause I see him do it," said Riderhood.

They looked at each other. Bradley, slowly withdrawing his eyes, turned his face to the black board and slowly wiped his name out. (774)

In this scene, performance disrupts lecture. The grotesque takes over the respectable stage. Audiences are drawn into performing. Transformations are drawn to the surface and deconstructed. The oral literally obliterates the written word. Underlying this struggle is Dickens's sense of his own performativity and that of his novels, his reliance upon and fear of audience involvement. Emily Allen traces the media representation of Dickens not only as an author and businessman but also as a showman, as "characterized by quick production, tied to limitless reproduction, and as undermining 'real' literary value."[43] Dickens was aware of and hypersensitive to this portrayal of his work, and his self-reflexivity is part of what Renata Miller calls a widespread, uneasy sense among Victorian novelists that drama is "less susceptible to corruption by commercialism than the novel is," and that the literary "artist, despite—or perhaps because of—her self-fashioning, is at the mercy of her audience."[44] Through Riderhood's death, then, Dickens deflects the novel's oral fixations back onto fairy tale and pantomimic subjects, and buries those subjects in the waters of the Thames.

For among the throng of waterside characters and unnamed drowned in *Our Mutual Friend,* Lizzie is the endangered girl who is spared, the final incarnation of the Alices and Em'lies and Marthas of Dickens's imagination, and the love who *is* to be. Dickens sought to displace Riding Hood (her dangerous knowledge, her problematic class status, her performativity) onto other laboring figures, in order for Lizzie to go unscathed.

Importantly, there are no other female Red Riding Hood analogues in *Our Mutual Friend.* Though Bella decries the "Monster who swallows up so much," she herself is not in sexual jeopardy. Mercenary Sophronia Lammle is not bested by her husband, though he has "pervadingly too much nose of a coarse wrong shape, and his nose in his mind and his manners; too much smile to be real; too much frown to be false; too many large teeth to be visible at once without suggesting a bite" (407). Canny, unsentimental and unsentimentalized, Pleasant Riderhood from the outset declines "to be regarded in that boney light" (90). Dickens equips these characters—self-avowedly part of the market economy—with enough worldliness to deflect the devouring forces of the novel. He carefully sets Lizzie apart to be compared with the endangered fairy tale heroine. Ultimately, though, Dickens's authorial energy goes into rescuing Lizzie from association with Little Red Riding Hood—and Little Red Riding Hood's fate.

Jenny Wren articulates the menacing likeness between Lizzie and Red Riding Hood when she imagines Lizzie and Riah in mortal opposition: "You are not the godmother at all!" said she. "You are the Wolf in the forest, the wicked Wolf! And if ever my dear Lizzie is sold and betrayed, I shall know who sold and betrayed her!" (562). And Lizzie is, tellingly, "a deep, rich piece of color" in Eugene's prying eyes (166). Dickens's tiny laboring heroines—Amy Dorrit, Charley Necket, The Marchioness, Jenny Wren herself—offer a panoply of characters whose troubling, incipient womanhood is swept away by looking younger, smaller, weirder than their age warrants. The warping of childish innocence and beauty by premature care and labor is evident in Jenny's twisted frame, the battle to survive plainly inscribed on her body. Unlike these abnormally small women, Lizzie is physically strong, almost mannishly so when she deadlifts Eugene after his attack. Lizzie, in other words, is not little; her luxuriant body suggests that she does not deny physical appetite. Then too, in contrast to her working-class exterior, there is a refinement about Lizzie that emphasizes her femininity, even as her labor undermines it. She, like the ill-fated Little Em'ly, was "born to be a lady."[45] Lizzie is not theatrical in the sense that, for instance, the Lammles are, but she is dressed "up"; her accent, devoid of the working-class intonation of her father or even her more educated brother, clothes her in borrowed class, and makes her a target for seduction. Her employment—first as seamstress, then factory girl—represents two of the most notorious jobs in nineteenth-century reportage, perhaps equal to acting for their perceived incompatibility with virginity.[46]

However unwillingly, Lizzie is herself a waterside character in this novel, steeped—if not drowned—in Thames commerce, as her father reminds her: "As if it wasn't your living! As if it wasn't meat and drink to you! . . . How can you be so thankless to your best friend, Lizzie?" (15). She shrinks from the river, from the bodies found there, from the posters of the drowned women on the walls, all of which have a special horror for her as a beautiful working girl. Lizzie fears sharing the fate of the woman in gray boots. Hers is the terror of the metaphoric fall that brings young working-class bodies to the literal plunge into the Thames. Dickens encourages this indelible tie from the outset: "Allied to the bottom of the river rather than the surface, by reason of the slime and ooze by which it was covered, and its sodden state, the boat *and the two figures in it* obviously were doing something that they often did and seeking what they often sought" (13, emphasis added). Like Martha's conflation with Thames ooze, this introduction to Lizzie places her on Dickens's list of threatened suicides.

Dickens demonstrates his uneasy navigation between the fairy tale and the novel when he attempts to sacrifice one kind of Little Red Riding Hood tale—the defiled, prostituted heroine, the commercial, grasping wolf—so that Lizzie might live unsullied within his pages. Dickens constructs a series of sacrifices so that no one can tempt Lizzie into a paraphrase of Little Red Riding Hood. Her father's death, Headstone and Riderhood's death, Wrayburn's attack—all variations on the "Little Red Riding Hood" theme, and all evidence that the river does indeed prove to be Lizzie's "best friend," neatly removing the threat to her virtue at convenient moments. Of the many authorial voices and hands that operate in the novel—those of John Harmon, Jenny Wren, Silas Wegg, even Lizzie herself—the Thames is surely the most powerful of all.[47] The river follows the preservational motion of Dickens's hand: a tender wolf, a charming wolf, a mutual friend, washing away the "monsters" for the endangered girl.

Though Jenny, usually preternaturally sharp at suturing together social scraps into meaning, mistakes the villain (Riah is possibly the least wolfish character in the novel), she correctly identifies Lizzie as a consumable woman—by characters in the novel, but perhaps also by producers and purchasers *of* the novel. DeMarcus notes the relationship between imagination and value for Dickens, citing Jenny Wren as one who "makes dolls' bonnets, turning scraps into something valuable through art and imagination," and allies Jenny's function to Dickens as narrator: "In classing people according to fairy-tale types, Jenny reveals a self-reflexive Dickens, since such categorizing is the author's *modus operandi* in his fiction."[48] However, DeMarcus concludes that Dickens's (and Jenny's) "solution" to "brutish humanity" lies in "using fairy tales to interpret life."[49] As I have shown, Dickens—like many other Victorians—understood fairy tales themselves to be brutish, and recognized the fairy tale for the complex and multilayered form it was. They are not a "precious old escape" from "the world that is too much with us," but powerfully current, a powerful current, a powerful currency. To read the value of imagination as psychic value only is to miss Dickens's subtle understanding of the relationship between nostalgia and commercial success.

And here I return to the idea that Dickens's doomed "first love" is a metaphor for the fairy tale devoured by encroaching modernity. These fragments of Little Red Riding Hood stand in context with the many examples of protoliteracy and prereading that occur in *Our Mutual Friend*, and the very fact that we do *read* the fairy tale embedded in Dickens's novels is a vital part of his market success. Through the Charlie and Lizzie Hexam plot of *Our Mutual Friend*, Dickens acts out his own vexed authorial relationship to oral literature. Lizzie is one of the few characters to harbor a nostalgic connection to her childhood. Bella's early recollections are of beating her father with a bonnet; Pleasant's "own unfortunate experience" was of being "shoved and banged out of everyone's way until [she] should grow big enough to shove and bang" (346). But Lizzie's musings over the fireplace take her back to a time of unconditional love from her little brother, Charlie. Like many of her Dickensian sisters—girls like Nell, Amy, and Biddy—Lizzie remains faithful to a vanished past. Charlie, by contrast, refuses to recognize that Lizzie both raised him (in the absence of a mother) and raised him up (by funding his schooling). Vladimir Propp's words resonate here once more: "folklore is the prehistory of literature . . . literature soon abandons the mother that reared it."

Motivated by self-aggrandizement, Charlie schemes to educate Lizzie so that her illiteracy will not embarrass him, and finally casts her aside when she refuses to follow his marriage plot (to his schoolmaster, Headstone). As if speaking back to her author, as if resisting being turned from a resilient oral form into a degraded literate one, Lizzie constantly evades other's mercenary uses for her—seduction plots, marriage plots, and offers of unpleasant labor. In other words, a working-class girl resists the authoritative machinations of an upstart boy who cannot recognize that he has betrayed his "first love" for social elevation. Charlie Hexam—his name is one of many plays upon the author's own[50]—may represent Dickens's mature reflection upon his uses of enchantment, his apprehension of the dangers inherent in lightly using and discarding childhood attachments.

Because Lizzie ultimately marries Wrayburn, she is subsumed into a Victorian middle-class identity. Dickens attempts to make Little Red Riding Hood *Heimlich:* removed from the fantastic, dark corners of the woods, the river, the city itself, and placed in the bright realism of the middle-class home, where, in her book jacket, she earned a living wage for him. Nevertheless, while Dickens worked to sever Lizzie's ties to pantomime Riding Hood, connections to performance in the novel remained. Dickens was perpetually concerned that his novels were like both the fairy tale and the fairy tale actress: infinitely reproducible and transmittable. In *Our Mutual Friend,* the fractured figure of Little Red Riding Hood serves to dredge up associations between oral performance and novel production, between market spectacle and domestic privacy. Dickens does not forget that in the Victorian era, Little Red Riding Hood had come to sing "with notes of an actress and not of a child;" his use of this tale in *Our Mutual Friend* works as a meditation upon his own "lively-hood."

CONCLUSION

Andrew Lang, Collaboration, and Fairy Tale Methodologies

When Thomas Hardy died in 1928, it was without having forgiven Andrew Lang for his various reviews of *Tess of the D'Urbervilles;* in *The Daily News,* Lang accused Hardy of "Tessimism."[1] In *The New Review,* he exclaimed, "If there be a God, who can seriously think of Him as a malicious fiend?"[2] If Hardy had cause for hurt feelings, though, so had Lang; his invective against *Tess* may have been especially sharp in remembrance of another literary text of Hardy's, "Tryst at an Ancient Earthworks," discussed in the beginning of part 1. That story caricatures and critiques the mode of scholarship and media production practiced by Lang and his circle. If Lang was familiar with Hardy's unflattering depiction of antiquarian and/or folklore collectors, he might be forgiven for revenging himself upon Hardy's "Tessimism."

This book began with a fictional account of "trysting" between a literary artist and a collector in order to exemplify both the interpenetrated nature of Victorian cultural production, and the ambivalence with which authors regarded such entanglements. The chapters in part 1 established that fiction writers introduced the antiquarian/folklore collector as a figure that embodied their anxieties about the abiding power of tales (including fairy tales) to shape the course of authored fiction. Far from being resolved by the end of the century, the conflict had simply shifted into one over discipline and method. The real-life feud between Hardy and Lang is one example of the much larger conversation about book production, and about writing itself, taking place in the 1880s and 90s. This book closes by offering Lang as an example of an alternate model to the cult of the solo literary genius that occupied so much of the Victorian literary landscape. This alternate model was defined by collaboration and coterie production, and troubles the rigidities of discipline and genre.

Andrew Lang was, as Nathan K. Hensley notes, a "central node whose shaping influence extended into every corner of the cultural marketplace and across any number of what are now separate disciplines."[3] A student of Classics at Oxford, he was one of the founders of the Folklore Society, and active in anthropological research. He was an important journalist and literary critic of the day, as indicated by his column "At the Sign of the Ship," which ran in *Longman's Magazine* from 1885–1905. He was a champion of popular literature, having mentored Robert Louis Stevenson and collaborated with H. Rider Haggard. But while Lang's entire oeuvre is important, I am most interested in his work on the fairy tale. For me, Lang is one practitioner of a kind of discourse generated in the wake of the Victorian fairy tale surge—that is, the widespread incorporation of fairy tales into other Victorian literary and cultural forms. Because his career throws into relief the extent to which all authorship is a collective endeavor, Lang enables us to consider the extent to which the fairy tale had invaded the production of literature, occupying its methods of production and consumption. Lang's treatment of the fairy tale places him at the end of a century-long conversation about the nature of originality. This conclusion considers how Lang's position at the center of multiple, linked networks is intimately related to his play with the fairy tale, arguably the most "networked" of forms. Lang's own interdisciplinarity can help us to understand the hybridizing work of the fairy tale: namely how its language, figures, structure, methods of production, and multiple authors reappear in other forms of cultural production. Certainly, the fairy tale allowed Lang to allegorize contemporary discourse about literary production, discussions like the copyright debates, the plagiarism debates, and the ongoing conversation about whether social science writing was or was not a kind of creative work.

Given his investment in nearly every kind of literary and social science venture at the turn of the century, Lang might be surprised to know that he remains best known today for his collections of fairy tales. His extended introductions to Margaret Hunt's edition of Grimm's *Household*

Tales (1884), Perrault's *Popular Tales* (1888), Marian Roalfe Cox's comparative study of Cinderella (1893), and Robert Kirk's *The Secret Commonwealth of Elves, Fauns and Fairies* (1893) are still cited by contemporary folklorists and anthropologists as the groundbreaking work validating fairy tale study as a serious academic discipline. But it was his "Colored Fairy Books," written between 1889 and 1910 that captured popular attention. Capitalizing on the British fascination with the fairy tale, these twelve books were styled and marketed for children. However, in spite of their frankly commercial nature and self-consciously modest presentation, they are more important to late-century culture than even Lang himself deemed them to be. The Color Fairy Books include contributions from a small team of amateur and professional folklorists (including Lang's wife Leonora), as well as Lang's translations of tales already in print. At the same time, all are retold in Lang's own literary style. The books exemplify coterie production, a trysting of genres and authors.

As I have shown in this book, tales, with their viral and invasive qualities, with their tendency to spill into virtually every genre of Victorian literary and visual art, offer both an example of and metaphor for the networking of Victorian disciplines, and even call into question our contemporary notion of "disciplinarity" itself. The founding of the Folklore Society in 1878, in which Lang was instrumental, suggests the extent to which folklore study came of age in tandem with the fiction and poetry of the Victorian period—the multiplot novels of Eliot and Dickens, the narrative poetry of Tennyson, Browning, and Rossetti—which have been the subjects of my investigation. As these chapters have shown, like literary artists, folklorists were fascinated with historical retrospection, with linking stories together in an integrated, contiguous chain. And like folklorists, literary artists claimed and reminted tales and legends for their own artistic and remunerative purposes.

Even so, the authors most responsible for these intergeneric networks continued to express ambivalence—that "strange mixture of obscure dread and intense desire"—toward folkloric narrative through the end of the century. The concept of the "wild and childish" fairy tale was so widespread that even the most eager compilers and adaptors tended to diminish the genre's import. Ironically, though Lang was instrumental in codifying and legitimating fairy tale study (and thus ensuring fairy tale currency in the age of science and academic discipline), he belonged to a group of scholars that displaced tales into a "savage" past. As with other Victorian thinkers, Lang's relationship to what he called "savagery" was complicated. He began his career by attacking Friedrich Max Müller's theories in his 1873 essay

"Mythology and Fairy Tales." Lang furthered Edward Tylor's anthropological theory of folklore in the 1870s and 1880s, sharing Tylor's belief in "survivals": that is, in the idea that fragmented remains of ancient cultures persist into the present. (This theory presumed that "savage" cultures are dead rather than living traditions; only their fragments survive.) Unlike Tylor, Lang did not believe that tales were decayed myths, but rather thought they retained their own generic form across the ages, each story transmitted from the "Original tale (probably of savage origin)" to the "Popular tale of peasants" to the "Modern literary version ([of] Perrault, etc.)."[4] As Lang put it in his introduction to *Perrault's Popular Tales* (1888), "in their rustic weeds, they wandered out of the cabins of the charcoal burners, out of the farmers' cottages, and after many adventures, reached that enchanted castle of Versailles."[5] Lang suggested that the "irrational and 'infantile' character" of tales and legends "is derived from their origin, if not actually among children, at least among childlike peoples, who have not arrived at 'raison,' that is, at the scientific and modern conception of the world and of the nature of man."[6] In this way, Lang's work appears to fulfill Walter Scott's early-century request for a study "on the . . . transmission of popular tales from age to age," which he hoped would explain why "such fictions, however wild and childish," continue to "possess such charms for the populace."[7] Lang constructs his historical explanation of fairy tales' power using an evolutionary rhetoric that began long before Darwin's *Origin of Species*. Like his contemporary, James George Frazer, who, as Supritha Rajan notes, averred that "magic is the next of kin to science" but is its "bastard sister,"[8] Lang defined the fantastic narrative as debased, sexualized, and essentially female; he claimed, for instance, that fairy tales were first told by "naked savage women to naked savage children."[9] Here we see, as in the literary works that this book treats, Lang's conflation of material and narrative bodies. Like many nineteenth-century authors, Lang characterized folk narrative as a developmental stage that the civilized west had essentially traversed.

In the prefaces to his fairy books, Lang repeatedly asseverates that he was "the Editor, and not the author of the Fairy Tales, just as the distinguished man of science is the Editor, not the Author of Nature"; that "nobody really wrote most of the stories" because "they are older than reading and writing"; that in fact "the thing is impossible. Nobody can write a new fairy tale; you can only mix up and dress up the old, old stories"; and that the "authors who try are very tiresome."[10] The job of "learned men," Lang explains is to "[collect] and [print] the country people's stories, and these we have translated, for the amusement of children. Their tastes remain like the tastes of their naked ancestors, thousands of years ago."[11] But in the very same prefaces, Lang reveals a hand not merely curatorial, but creative. He explains, for example, that the stories have been "adapted to the needs of British children by various hands, the Editor doing little beyond guarding the interests of propriety, and toning down to mild reproofs the tortures inflicted on wicked stepmothers, and other naughty creatures" (*Crimson Fairy*, v). Elsewhere, he credits his wife with authoring certain tales outright: "Mrs. Lang . . . does not give them exactly as they are told by all sorts of outlandish natives, but makes them up in the hope white people will like them, skipping the pieces which they will not like."[12]

The prefaces are directed, not at child readers, but at the adult purchasers of the books; Lang uses this forum to remind the reader that the books were best-selling items on the Christmas market, and that they presented the commercial face of his scholarly endeavors in the emerging field of folklore.

> "What cases are you engaged in at present?" "Are you stopping many teeth just now?" "What people have you converted lately?" Do ladies put these questions to the men—lawyers, dentists, clergymen, and so forth—who happen to sit next them at dinner parties?
>
> I do not know whether ladies thus indicate their interest in the occupations of their casual neighbours at the hospitable board. But if they do not know me, or do not know me well, they generally ask "Are you writing anything now?" (as if they should ask a painter "Are you painting anything now?" or a lawyer "Have you any cases at present?"). Sometimes they are more definite and inquire "What are you writing now?" as if I must be writing something—which, indeed, is the case, though I dislike being reminded of it. It is an awkward question, because the fair being does not care a bawbee what I am writing; nor would she be much enlightened if I replied "Madam, I am engaged on a treatise intended to prove that Normal is prior to Conceptional Totemism"—though that answer would be as true in fact as obscure in significance. . . . One nymph who, like the rest, could not keep off the horrid topic of my occupation, said "You never write anything but fairy books, do you?" (*Lilac Fairy*, v–vi)

Here Lang emphasizes that authorship is essentially a profession like the law, the church, or the dentist, but recognizes that academic writing is not worth "a bawbee" (a Scottish coin worth 3 pennies) to the general public; if one goal of his prefaces, then, is "advertising [his] own fairy books (which are not 'out of print'; if your bookseller says so, the truth is not in him)"

(*Lilac Fairy*, vii), another is demonstrating that his sanitized alterations (and those of the rest of his team) make the books a sound investment:

> I take this opportunity of recommending these fairy books—poor things, but my own—to parents and guardians who may never have heard of them. They are rich in romantic adventure, and the Princes always marry the right Princesses and live happy ever afterwards; while the wicked witches, stepmothers, tutors and governesses are never cruelly punished, but retire to the country on ample pensions. (*Lilac Fairy*, vi)

It is fascinating to observe Lang claim the Colored Fairy books as "my own" in the same preface in which he insists "*I do not write the stories out of my own head*" (*Lilac Fairy*, vii original emphasis). The fundamental modernity of the fairy tale, then, exposes Lang's insistence that fairy tales are "savage" as a prevarication, albeit one of the most interesting (and commercially successful) kind.

Lang's involvement in the "plagiarism debates" of the late century exemplifies his complicated relationship to collection. In his essay for the *Contemporary Review*, "Literary Plagiarism" (1887), Lang considers what it means to make, to trade, and to collect, offering an analysis that challenges the rhetorical primacy of both intellectual property and literary genius:

> The success or failure lies not in the materials, but in the making...and no dullard can make anything, even if he steals all his materials. On the other hand, genius, or even considerable talent, can make a great deal, if he chooses, even out of stolen material—if any of the material of literature can be properly said to be stolen, and is not rather the possession of whoever likes to pick it up.[13]

As Letitia Henville argues,[14] Lang emphasizes in this passage the physical nature of ideas. In using the word "material" four times in two sentences, for instance, Lang describes literature not as subjects (that is, topics), but as *objects* that can be picked up and possessed anew.

Though an author like Dickens was undoubtedly more conservative with regard to intellectual property than is the "open-access" Lang of the "Plagiarism" essay, it is important to note that for both Lang and Dickens "old tales and legends" are "traditions peculiarly adapted" for appropriation because they are perceived to be both authorless and genreless. They belong to no one and are thus available to anyone.[15]

This is especially interesting given what Lang leaves out of his prefaces. His own dedication to collaborative production mimics the fairy tale salons run by the French *conteuses* of the seventeenth century: authors like Madame d'Aulnoy, Madame de Beaumont, Madame de Murat, Mademoiselle L'H'éritier, and Mademoiselle Bernard, who together formed a network in which they both retailored and created afresh fairy tales for a hungry literary market. Lang makes no mention of the vigorous coterie print culture whose products he repackages, and while he does credit d'Aulnoy, he describes her as Perrault's "imitator . . . a wandering lady of more wit than reputation."[16] While in the earliest Colored Fairy Books, Lang carefully credits the contributors and translators of the stories—a whole host of young, or at least unmarried, women—by the end of the series he has abandoned this practice, preferring instead to condense these women writers into a single, iconic laborer with Biblical pedigree: "My part has been that of Adam, according to Mark Twain, in the Garden of Eden. Eve worked, Adam superintended. I also superintend. I find out where the stories are, and advise, and, in short, superintend" (*Lilac Fairy*, vii). Though Lang is willing to present himself as the firm editorial hand over a body of narrative pulled from the savage margins for the pleasure of a civilization predicated on literacy, he was more reluctant to own his debt to a literary fairy tale tradition that was explicitly female. However, if we consider that the rise to ubiquity of the fairy tale was what helped spur the late-century plagiarism debate, and that the fairy tale in fact gestated Lang's very methods of authorial production, then Lang's characterization of both tales and their transmission as uncivilized and infantile becomes ironic. Lang was happy to cast himself, with a self-reflexive wink, as an uncivilized and infantile producer. But the more accurate characterization of fairy tale transmission would acknowledge its highly literate, intellectual collaboration and sophisticated, market-savvy book production—all skills that Lang himself, however he pretended naiveté, also exhibited. The fairy tale has its roots, not in savagery, but in modernity.

Then too, Walter Benjamin's typology in *The Arcades Project*, analyzed in chapter 1, helps expose the idiosyncrasy of Lang's position—at least from our modern point of view of authorship. For by Lang's very self-definition, he was simultaneously editor, compiler, superintendent, translator, and adaptor, yet also guardian and owner of the material in the Colored Fairy Books. Lang's language in the Fairy Book prefaces makes him both an author and a collector in Benjamin's terms. This tension in Lang's prefaces—is the book or is it not literature, is it or is it not the product of coterie production, is it or is it not Lang's "own"?—signals the larger and more widespread tensions over what constitutes authorship in a for-profit media environment. It is, needless to say, a conflict that continues in various forms to this day. Lang, however reluctantly, follows in the footsteps of the French *conteuses,* of Mother Bunch, of Coleridge's, Brontë's, and Dickens's nurses, of Samuel Weller, of all of those purveyors of disruptive fairy tale matter.

ALL IN ALL, *Spellbound* reveals that the fairy tale—and with it its language, figuration, and means of circulation—was so deeply imbedded in nineteenth-century literature that it passed beyond simple allegory, beyond any one author, beyond any one social issue. In the texts I have presented, the fairy tales speaks with the voices of England's critics, enchants its castles, hoards its treasure, walks its paths, blows its houses down.

NOTES

Notes to Introduction

1. Walter Scott, *The Lady of the Lake,* ed. William J. Rolfe (Boston: J. R. Osgood, 1883), Penn State Electronic Classics Series Publication, accessed July 23, 2008, http://www2.hn.psu.edu/faculty/jmanis/w-scott/lady-lake.pdf, note to Canto Fourth, line 345, p. 188.

2. Carolyn Steedman, *Strange Dislocations: Childhood and the Idea of Human Interiority.* (London: Virago, 1995), 16.

3. Anna Eliza Bray, *The Borders of the Tamar and the Tavy* (London: W. Kent and Co., 1879; originally published as *Traditions, Legends, Superstitions, and Sketches of Devonshire on the Borders of the Tamar and the Tavy* [London: J. Murray, 1838]), 2.

4. Thomas Keightley, *The Fairy Mythology: Illustrative of the Romance and Superstition of Various Countries* (1828; London: Wildwood House Ltd, 1981), 281.

5. Geoffrey Chaucer, "The Wife of Bath's Tale," in *The Riverside Chaucer,* ed. Larry D. Benson, 3rd ed. (Boston: Houghton Mifflin, 1987), lines 864–72.

6. Charlotte Brontë, *Jane Eyre* (London: Penguin, 1996), 139.

7. Benedict Anderson, *Imagined Communities: Reflections on the Origin and Spread of Nationalism* (London: Verso, 1991).

8. Samuel Taylor Coleridge, *On the Constitution of the Church and State* (1830; London: Dent, 1972), 34.

9. Jennfer Schacker, *National Dreams: The Remaking of Fairy Tales in Nineteenth-Century England* (Philadelphia: University of Pennsylvania Press, 2003).

10. John Harland and T. T. Wilkinson, *Lancashire Folk-Lore: Illustrative of the Superstitious Beliefs and Practices, Local Customs and Usages of the People of the County Palatine* (London: Frederick Warne and Co., 1867), 2.

11. Robert Patten, "Who Tolls Nell's Knell?" Lecture delivered at the University of California Dickens Project, July 28, 2003.

12. William Wordsworth, *The Fourteen-Book Prelude*, ed. W. J. B. Owen, (1850; Ithaca, NY: Cornell University Press, 1985), V: lines 175–79.

13. Charles Dickens, "A Christmas Tree," in *Christmas Books and Reprinted Pieces* (New York: John Lovell, 1879), 825–40; originally published in *Household Words*, December 1850.

14. Dickens, *The Old Curiosity Shop* (London: Penguin, 2000), 20, 536, 556.

15. Vladimir J. Propp, *Theory and History of Folklore* (Minneapolis: University of Minnesota Press, 1984), 14.

16. Samuel Taylor Coleridge, *Letters of Samuel Taylor Coleridge*, vol. 1, ed. Ernest Hartley Coleridge (Boston: Houghton, Mifflin and Company, 1895), 12.

17. Charles Dickens, "Nurses Stories," in *The Uncommercial Traveller* (London: Chapman and Hall, 1895), 89.

18. Una Taylor, "Burne-Jones, His Ethics, and Art," *Edinburgh Review* 189 (April 1899), 34.

19. See, for example, Mikhail Bakhtin's notion of the "valorized temporal category." "Epic and Novel: Toward a Methodology for the Study of the Novel," in *The Dialogic Imagination*, ed. Michael Holquist (Austin: University of Texas Press, 1981), 15.

20. George Eliot, *Middlemarch* (London: Bantam, 1992), 19.

21. Christina Rossetti, "Goblin Market," in *Christina Rossetti: The Complete Poems* (London: Penguin, 2001), line 233.

22. Dickens, *Our Mutual Friend* (London: Penguin, 1997), 405.

23. Catherine Gallagher, "George Eliot and *Daniel Deronda:* The Prostitute and the Jewish Question" in *Sex, Politics and Science in the Nineteenth-Century Novel,* ed. Ruth Bernard Yeazell (Baltimore: The Johns Hopkins University Press, 1986), 40.

24. According to the American Folklore Society website's most current definition ("folklore," Amercian Folklore Society official website, accessed Sept 9, 2013, http://www.afsnet.org/?page=WhatIsFolklore.) In Jan Brunvand's textbook definition, folklore comprises the unrecorded traditions of a people; it includes both the form and content of these traditions and their style or technique of communication from person to person. Folklore is the traditional, unofficial, non-institutional part of culture. It encompasses all knowledge, understandings, values, attitudes, assumptions, feelings, and beliefs transmitted in traditional forms by word of mouth or by customary examples (Jan Harold Brunvand, *The Study of American Folklore: An Introduction*, 2nd ed. [New York: W.W. Norton, 1978], 5).

25. However, as Holly Tucker points out, in recent years, studies of legends have moved away from "considerations of whether such narratives are *true* or actually *believed* to focus on the way in which truth claims themselves are constructed and received." *Pregnant Fictions: Childbirth and the Fairy Tale in Early Modern France* (Detroit: Wayne State University Press, 2003), 5–6.

26. As evidenced by Vladimir Propp's formalist study of the thirty-one functions of the fairy tale (*Morphology of the Folktale*, ed. Louis A. Wagner and trans. Lawrence Scott, American Folklore Society Publications, 2nd ed., [Austin: University of Texas Press, 1968]). See also Brunvand, *The Study of American Folklore;* Gary Alan Fine, *Manufacturing Tales: Sex and Money in Contemporary Legends* (Knoxville: University of Tennessee Press, 1992); and Linda Degh, "What Is the Legend After All?" *Contemporary Legend* 1 (1991): 11–38.

27. Richard Dorson, *The British Folklorists: A History* (Chicago: University of Chicago Press, 1968).

28. Including Aantii Aarne and Stith Thompson, *The Types of the Folktale,* 2nd revision, Folklore Fellows Communication No. 184 (Helsinki: Academia Scientiarum Fennica, 1973);

Alan Dundes, *Folklore Matters* (Knoxville: University of Tennessee Press, 1989); Sigmund Freud and D. E. Oppenheim, *Dreams in Folklore*, trans. A. M. O. Richards (New York: International Universities Press, 1958); and Jack Zipes, *Fairy Tales and the Art of Subversion: The Classical Genre for Children and the Process of Civilization* (London: Heinemann, 1983); *The Brothers Grimm: From Enchanted Forests to Modern Worlds* (London: Routledge, 1988); *The Trials and Tribulations of Little Red Riding Hood* (New York: Routledge, 1993).

29. Aarne and Thompson Types 300–749 of *The Types of the Folktale*, commonly known as the "AT Tale Type Index."

30. Many critics, however, add the tales from the *Arabian Nights* tradition.

31. See Ruth Bottigheimer, *Grimm's Bad Girls and Bold Boys: The Moral and Social Vision of the Tales* (New Haven, CT: Yale University Press, 1987); Elizabeth Harries, *Twice Upon a Time: Women Writers and the History of the Fairy Tale* (Princeton, NJ: Princeton University Press, 2001).

32. Andrew Lang, *The Violet Fairy Book* (London: Longmans, Green and Co., 1901), vii.

33. *Pasquil's Jests and Mother Bunch's Merriments* is the oldest print record of the Mother Bunch character; it is a seventeenth-century collection of jokes and tales, in which Mother Bunch features as brewer, tapstress, and storyteller. Jennifer Schacker, "Generic Transformation and the Body of Mother Bunch," paper presented at Metamorphoses: An International Colloquium on Narrative and Folklore, University of Utah, October 2008, 10.

34. In this I follow Jennifer Schacker in *National Dreams*, as well as Carole G. Silver in *Strange and Secret Peoples*, who treat collections of both fairy tales and fairy legends.

35. Nancy and Melvin Palmer, "English Editions of French Contes des Fees Attributed to Mme D'Aulnoy," *Studies in Bibliography* 27 (1974), 228.

36. See, for example, Diane Purkiss, *Troublesome Things: A History of Fairies and Fairy Stories* (London: Allen Lane, The Penguin Press, 2000).

37. John Brand, *Observations on the Popular Antiquities of Great Britain*, 3 vols, ed. Henry Ellis (1777; London: Bell and Daldy, 1873); Thomas Crofton Croker, *Legends and Traditions of the South of Ireland* (1825; Cork: The Collins Press, 1998); Thomas Keightley, *Fairy Mythology: Illustrative of the Romance and Superstition of Various Countries* (1828; London: Wildwood House Ltd, 1981); Joseph Ritson, *Fairy Tales* (London: Thomas Davison, 1831); Anna Eliza Bray, *Traditions, Legends, Superstitions and Sketches of Devonshire on the Borders of the Tamar and Tavy* (London: J. Murray, 1838); Bray, *A Peep at the Pixies* (London: Grant and Griffith, 1854); Jeremiah Curtin, *Tales of the Fairies and of the Ghost World, Collected from Oral Tradition in South-West Munster* (Boston: Little, Brown, & Company, 1895).

38. See, for example, Harries, *Twice Upon a Time;* Susan Stewart, *Crimes of Writing: Problems in the Containment of Representation* (Oxford: Oxford University Press, 1991); and Katie Trumpener, *Bardic Nationalism: The Romantic Novel and the British Empire* (Princeton: Princeton University Press, 1997).

39. Schacker, "Generic Transformation," 1.

40. Ibid., 2.

41. Bruno Bettelheim, *The Uses of Enchantment: The Meaning and Importance of Fairy Tales* (Knopf, New York, 1976); Alan Dundes, *Little Red Riding Hood: A Casebook* (Madison: The University of Wisconsin Press, 1989); Maria Tatar, *Off with Their Heads! Fairy Tales and the Culture of Childhood* (Princeton, NJ: Princeton University Press, 1992).

42. Nicola Bown, *Fairies in Nineteenth-Century Art and Literature* (Cambridge: Cambridge University Press, 2001); U. C. Knoepflmacher, *Ventures Into Fairyland: Victorians, Fairy Tales and Femininity* (Chicago: University of Chicago Press, 2000); Michael Kotzin,

Dickens and the Fairy Tale (Bowling Green, OH: Bowling Green University Popular Press, 1972); Diane Purkiss, *Troublesome Things;* Schacker, *National Dreams;* Carole G. Silver, *Strange and Secret Peoples;* Harry Stone, *Dickens and the Invisible World: Fairy Tales, Fantasy, and Novel-Making* (Bloomington: Indiana University Press, 1979); and Caroline Sumpter, *The Victorian Press and the Fairy Tale* (Basingstoke: Palgrave Macmillan, 2008).

43. See also Elaine Ostry, *Social Dreaming: Dickens and the Fairy Tale* (London: Routledge, 2002).

Notes to Chapter 1

1. Thomas Hardy, "Tryst at an Ancient Earthworks," in *A Changed Man and Other Tales* (New York and London: Harper and Brothers, 1913), 171–83. The story was first published as "Ancient Earthworks and What Two Enthusiastic Scientists Found Therein" in *The Detroit Post*, and in 1893 as "Ancient Earthworks in Casterbridge" in the *English Illustrated Magazine*. All subsequent references appear parenthetically in the text.

2. Walter Benjamin, *The Arcades Project* (Harvard: Belknap, 2002). All subsequent references appear parenthetically in the text.

3. Dorson, 2.

4. Qtd. in Dorson, 2.

5. John Brand, *Observations on the Popular Antiquities of Great Britain*, ed. Henry Ellis (London: Bell and Daldy, 1873), xiii.

6. James G. Paradis, "The Natural Historian as Antiquary of the World: Hugh Miller and the Rise of Literary Natural History," in *Hugh Miller and the Controversies of Victorian Science*, ed. Michael Shortland (Oxford: Clarendon Press, 1996), 125.

6. Ibid., 127.

7. Ibid.

8. Ibid.

9. Philippa Levine, *The Amateur and the Professional: Antiquarians, Historians and Archaeologists in Victorian England, 1838–1886* (Cambridge: Cambridge University Press, 1986), 13.

10. Paradis, 130.

11. Gilbert White, *The Natural History and Antiquities of Selbourne* (London: George Routledge and Sons, 1891), viii.

12. Thomas Bewick, *History of British Birds* (Newcastle: Beilby and Bewick, 1797; Newcastle: Walker, 1804).

13. Hugh Miller, *First Impressions of England and Its People* (New York: Robert Carter and Brothers, 1882), 35.

14. Mary Ellen Bellanca, "Recollecting Nature: George Eliot's 'Ilfracombe Journal' and Victorian Women's Natural History Writing," *Modern Language Studies* 27:3/4 (1997), 29.

15. Bewick, 282.

16. Paradis, 143.

17. Bray, *Tamar and Tavy*, xii.

18. Dorson, 81.

19. Ibid., 2.

20. Levine, 4.

21. Rosemary Levy Zumwalt, *American Folklore Scholarship: A Dialogue of Dissent* (Bloomington: Indiana University Press, 1988), 2.

22. Dorson, 162.

23. Lang, in Marian Roalfe Cox, *Cinderella: Three Hundred and Forty-five Variants of Cinderella, Catskin, and Cap O'Rushes* (London: David Nutt for the Folk-Lore Society, 1893), xiv.

24. Dorson, 191.

25. Thomas Bewick, *Select Fables* (Newcastle: Saint, 1776) and *The Fables of Aesop* (Newcastle: Walker, 1818); John Bewick, *Fabliaux* (London: W. Bulmer, 1796).

26. Schacker, *National Dreams*, 10.

27. "novel, *n.*," *Oxford English Dictionary Online* (Oxford: Oxford University Press), accessed June 1, 2009, http://dictionary.oed.com.

28. Levine, 16.

29. Alexander Pope, *The Dunciad* (London: Lawton Gilliver, 1727), Book III, 150–52; 181–86.

30. Robert Burns, "On the Late Captain Grosse's Peregrinations," in *The Works of Robert Burns,* ed. William Scott Douglass (1793; Edinburgh: William Patterson, 1877), 233–36 (poem is not published with line numbers).

31. Schacker, *National Dreams*, 2.

Notes to Chapter 2

1. See, for example, John Butt and Kathleen Tillotson, *Dickens at Work* (London: Methuen. 1957); Mary Colwell, "Organization in *Pickwick Papers*," *Dickens Studies* 3 (1967): 90–110; N. N. Feltes, "The Moment of Pickwick, or the Production of a Commodity Text," *Literature and History: A Journal for the Humanities* 10 (1984): 203–17; John Lucas, "*The Pickwick Papers*," in *The Melancholy Man: A Study of Dickens's Novels* (London: Methuen, 1970), 1–20; Steven Marcus, "The Blest Dawn," in *Dickens from Pickwick to Dombey* (New York: Basic Books, 1965), 13–53; J. Hillis Miller, "Sam Weller's Valentine," in *Literature in the Marketplace: Nineteenth-Century British Publishing and Reading Practices,* ed. John O. Jordan and Robert L. Patten (Cambridge: Cambridge University Press, 1995), 93–122.

2. Charles Dickens, *The Pickwick Papers* (London: Penguin, 1999), 15–16. All subsequent references appear parenthetically in the text.

3. See Peter Wilson for his study "The Corpus of Jinglese: A Syntactic Profile of and Idiolectal 'System of Stenography'," *Critical Survey* 16:3 (2004): 78–93.

4. *Pickwick Papers,* 778 n.1.

5. Dickens, *Our Mutual Friend* (London: Penguin, 1997), 472.

6. Dickens, "Frauds on the Fairies," *Household Words* (1 October 1853): 100.

7. Robert Patten, *George Cruikshank's Life, Times, and Art*, vol. 1 (New Brunswick: Rutgers University Press, 1992), 336.

8. Philip Cox, *Reading Adaptations: Novels and Verse Narratives on the Stage, 1790–1840* (Manchester: Manchester University Press, 2000), 21.

9. Dickens, *Nicholas Nickleby* (London, Penguin: 2003), 598.

10. Robert Alter, *Imagined Cities: Urban Experience and the Language of the Novel* (New Haven, CT: Yale University Press, 2005), 47.

11. Ibid., 48.

12. A notable exception is Silver, who situates Dickens's use of the fairy tale in the larger context of a Victorian fascination with physiognomy.

13. *Our Mutual Friend,* 429.

14. Dickens, "Nurse's Stories," in *The Uncommercial Traveler* (London, Chapman and Hall, 1868), 89. All subsequent references appear parenthetically in the text.

15. See Shuli Barzuli: "The Bluebeard Barometer: Charles Dickens and Captain Murderer," *Victorian Literature and Culture* 32:2 (2004): 505–24 for the importance of the "Bluebeard" tale to Dickens.

16. See, for example: John Bowen, *Other Dickens: Pickwick to Chuzzlewit* (Oxford: Oxford University Press, 2000) and "Pickwick and the Postal Principle," *Imprimatur* (University of Luton) 1:2 (1996): 180–85; Michael Cotsell, "*The Pickwick Papers* and Travel: A Critical Diversion," *Dickens Quarterly* 3 (1986): 5–17; Richard Lansdown, "*The Pickwick Papers*: Something Nobler than a Novel?" *Critical Review* 31 (1991): 75–91; Sally Ledger, *Dickens and the Popular Radical Imagination* (Cambridge: Cambridge University Press, 2007); and Alex Woloch, *The One vs. The Many: Minor Characters and the Space of the Protagonist in the Novel* (Princeton, NJ: Princeton University Press, 2003).

17. While Patten himself uses the term "interpolation" in "The Art of Pickwick's Interpolated Tales," *ELH* 34:3 (September 1967): 349–66, his most recent lecture for the Dickens Project, "Pickwick Redivivus" (July 2007), suggested an amendment to "intercalation."

18. Meredith McGill, unpublished lecture for the Dickens Project, July 2007.

19. Ledger, 49–54.

20. In *The One vs. the Many*, Woloch is more concerned with the character of Jingle and his oral powers; these observations on Sam Weller were made in Woloch's 2007 unpublished lecture for the Dickens Project, "Partial Representation in *The Pickwick Papers*" (July 2007).

21. Miller, "Sam Weller's Valentine," 105.

22. George B. Bryan and Wolfgang Mieder, "'As Sam Weller Said, when Finding Himself on the Stage': Wellerisms in Dramatizations of Charles Dickens' Pickwick Papers," *Proverbium: Yearbook of International Proverb Scholarship* 11 (1994): 57.

23. Dickens, *The Old Curiosity Shop* (London: Penguin, 2000), 556.

Notes to Chapter 3

1. Charlotte Brontë, *Jane Eyre* (London: Penguin, 1996), 14. All subsequent references appear parenthetically in the text.

2. Susan B. Taylor, "Image and Text in *Jane Eyre*'s Avian Vignettes and Bewick's *History of British Birds*," *Victorian Newsletter* 101 (Spring, 2002): 2.

3. Charlotte Brontë, *The Letters of Charlotte Brontë: With a Selection of Letters by Family and Friends,* vol. 1, ed. Margaret Smith (Oxford: Oxford University Press, 2002), 131.

4. Qtd. in Levine, 12.

5. Andrew Lang, *The Violet Fairy Book* (London: Longmans, Green and Co., 1901), vii.

6. Barbara Gates, "Introduction: Why Victorian Natural History?" *Victorian Literature and Culture* 35 (2007): 540.

7. See also Levine, 9; Bellanca, 25.

8. Robyn R. Warhol, "Double Gender, Double Genre in *Jane Eyre* and *Villette*," *SEL: Studies in English Literature* 36:4 (1996): 857–75.

9. Carla Kaplan, "Girl Talk: *Jane Eyre* and the Romance of Women's Narration," *NOVEL: A Forum on Fiction* 30:1 (Autumn 1996): 7.

10. Ibid., 8.

11. James Buzard, *Disorienting Fiction: The Autoethnographic Work of Nineteenth-Century British Novels* (Princeton, NJ: Princeton University Press, 2005), 197.

12. Ibid., 198.
13. Ibid., 202.
14. Ibid., 205.
15. Warhol, 867.
16. Ibid.
17. See, for example, Micael M. Clarke, "Brontë's *Jane Eyre* and the Grimms' 'Cinderella,'" *SEL* 40:4 (Autumn, 2000): 695-710; Maria Tatar, *Secrets Beyond the Door: The Story of Bluebeard and His Wives* (Princeton: Princeton University Press, 2006).
18. See Introduction.
19. Interestingly, Jane's "full and free forgiveness" (269) proves more viscerally intolerable to Mrs. Reed than Jane's verbal abuse.
20. "cabinet, *n.*," *Oxford English Dictionary Online*.
21. Emily Brontë, *Wuthering Heights* (London: Penguin, 1995), 19.
22. Ibid., 20.
23. Ibid.

Notes to Chapter 4

1. George Eliot, *Middlemarch* (London: Bantam, 1992), 19. All subsequent references appear parenthetically in the text.
2. Gillian Beer, *Darwin's Plots: Evolutionary Narrative in Darwin, George Eliot, and Nineteenth-Century Fiction* (Cambridge: Cambridge University Press, 2000).
3. Kathleen McCormack, "George Eliot and the Pharmakon: Dangerous Drugs for the Condition of England." *Victorians Institute Journal* 14 (1986): 35–51.
4. David Carroll, "*Middlemarch* and the Externality of Fact," in *This Particular Web: Essays on Midddlemarch,* ed. Ian Adam (Toronto: University of Toronto Press, 1975), 73–90.
5. Sophia Andres, "The Unhistoric in History: George Eliot's Challenge to Victorian Historiography." *Clio* 26:1 (1996): 79–96.
6. John Clark Pratt and Victor A. Neufelt, eds., *George Eliot's* Middlemarch *Notebooks: A Transcription* (Berkeley: University of California Press, 1979), xxvi, xxv.
7. Ibid., 6.
8. Rosemary Ashton, *George Eliot: A Life* (London: Penguin, 1996), 297.
9. In Brian Swann, "Middlemarch and Myth," *Nineteenth-Century Fiction* 28:2 (September 1973): 212.
10. Sally Shuttleworth, "*Middlemarch:* An Experiment in Time," in *George Eliot and Nineteenth-Century Science: The Make-Believe of a Beginning* (Cambridge: Cambridge University Press, 1984), 142–74 and "Sexuality and Knowledge in *Middlemarch,*" *Nineteenth-Century Contexts* 19 (1996): 425–41.
11. Michael Carignan, "Fiction as History or History as Fiction? George Eliot, Haydon White, and Nineteenth-Century Historicism" *Clio* 29:4 (2000): 395–415.
12. Jessie Givner, "Industrial History, Pre-industrial Literature: George Eliot's *Middlemarch.*" *ELH* 69 (2002): 223–44.
13. U. C. Knoepflmacher, "Fusing Fact and Myth: the New Reality of *Middlemarch,*" in *This Particular Web: Essays on* Midddlemarch, ed. Ian Adam Toronto: University of Toronto Press, 1975), 43–71.
14. Penny Boulmelha, "George Eliot and the End of Realism," in *Women Reading Women's Writing,* ed. Sue Roe (New York: St. Martin's Press, 1987), 13–35.

15. Gillian Beer, "Myth and the Single Consciousness: *Middlemarch* and 'The Lifted Veil'," in *This Particular Web: Essays on* Middlemarch, ed. Ian Adam (Toronto: University of Toronto Press, 1975), 96.

16. Dominick La Capra, "In Quest of Casaubon: George Eliot's *Middlemarch*," in *History, Politics and the Novel* (Ithaca, NY: Cornell University Press, 1987), 56–82.

17. Henry James, "George Eliot's Life," *The Atlantic Monthly* 55:331 (May 1885): 675.

18. Ashton, 325.

19. Neil Hertz, "Recognizing Casaubon," in *The End of the Line: Essays on Psychoanalysis and the Sublime* (New York: Columbia University Press, 1985), 76.

20. Ibid., 78.

21. Ibid., 79.

22. Beer, "Myth and the Single Consciousness," 97.

23. Ashton, 166; Middlemarch *Notebooks*, 179.

24. Daniel Tyler, "Dorothea and the 'Key to All Mythologies'," *The George Eliot Review* 33 (2002): 27–32.

25. Carol Senf, "The Vampire in *Middlemarch* and George Eliot's Quest for Historical Reality." *New Orleans Review* 14:1 (1987): 87–97.

26. Virginia Hyde, "George Eliot's Arthuriad: Heroes and Ideology in *Middlemarch*," *Papers on Language and Literature* 24:44 (1988): 404–11.

27. Jacob Grimm and Wilhelm Grimm, "Rumpelstiltskin" ("*Rumpelstilzchen*") In *German Fairy Tales* (*Kinder- und Hausmärchen*), ed. Helmut Brackert and Volkmar Sander, trans. Margaret Hunt (New York: Continuum, 1985), 140–43.

28. Hertz, 80.

Notes to Chapter 5

1. Thomas Carlyle, *Past and Present*, in *The Norton Anthology of English Literature*, vol. 2, 7th ed., ed. M. H. Abrams et al., (New York: Norton, 2000), 1117.

2. Ibid., 1118.

3. John Ruskin, *The Stones of Venice. Volume the Second: The Sea Stories* (London: Smith, Elder and Co., 1853), 181.

4. George Eliot, "Looking Backward," in *Impressions of Theophrastus Such* (Edinburgh and London: William Blackwood and Sons, 1879), Project Gutenburg, accessed June 7, 2008, http://www.gutenberg.org/files/10762/10762-h/10762-h.htm.

5. Gerard Manley Hopkins, "To His Watch," in *The Poems of Gerard Manley Hopkins*, 4th ed., ed. W. H. Garner and N. H. MacKenzie (Oxford: Oxford University Press, 1970).

6. "temporal, *adj.*," *Oxford English Dictionary Online*.

7. Mikhail Bakhtin, *The Dialogic Imagination*, ed. Michael Holquist (Austin: University of Texas Press, 1981).

8. According to Jack Zipes: "'Sleeping Beauty' ('Briar Rose') appears in the Catalan *Frayer de Joy e Sor de Placer* (fourteenth century), as 'Troylus and Zellandine' in the French *Perceforest* (sixteenth century), as 'Sole, Luna, e Talia' in *Il Pentamerone* (1634–36) by Giambattista Basile, as 'La Belle au Bois Dormant' in *Histoires ou contes du temps passé* (1697) by Charles Perrault, and as 'Dornröschen' in *Kinder- und Hausmärchen* (1812–15) by Jacob and Wilhelm Grimm." The Catalan version would not have been available to English readers. *Perceforest* was first printed in French in 1528, and Italian in 1558, but few copies existed, and

these would not have been widely available in England. Jack Zipes, ed., *Oxford Companion to Fairy Tales* (Oxford: Oxford University Press, 2000), 467.

9. To this list of possible sources other scholars have tentatively added "The Ninth Captain's Tale" from the *Arabian Nights* tradition, in which a girl is cast into a swoon from a chip of flax under her fingernail. In 1704–1717 Antoine Galland produced the first translation in French, and before he had even completed the task, parts of the work appeared in English translation. However, almost every edition included a different collection of the tales; translations passed through so many editions and so many authorial changes that it is nearly impossible to verify whether Basile took his plot from this tale, or whether the chip of flax episode was added to "The Ninth Captain's Tale" after Basile's version. And while nearly every literate Victorian read the *Arabian Nights Tales,* is it impossible to know precisely who read which versions of the *Tales,* as authors never identify the tales by their compilers.

10. Giambattista Basile, "Sun, Moon, and Talia" ("*Sole, Luna e Talia*"), In *The Pentamerone (Il Pentamerone),* trans. Richard Burton (London: Spring Books, n.d.), 374.

11. Charles Perrault, "The Sleeping Beauty in the Wood" ("*La Belle au Bois Dormant*"), in *The Fairy Tales of Charles Perrault* (*Histoires ou contes du temps passé*), trans. A. E. Johnson (New York: Dover, 1969), 3–21.

12. Jacob Grimm and Wilhelm Grimm, "Little Briar Rose" ("*Dornröschen*") in *German Fairy Tales* (*Kinder- und Hausmärchen*), ed. Helmut Brackert and Volkmar Sander, trans. Margaret Hunt (New York: Continuum, 1985), 118–21.

Notes to Chapter 6

1. John Keats, "Eve of St. Agnes," in *The Complete Poems of John Keats,* ed. Jack Stillinger (Cambridge, MA: Harvard University Press, 1982), st. XVI, line 136. All subsequent references appear parenthetically in the text.

2. For example, see Andrew J. Bennett, "'Hazardous Magic': Vision and Inscription in 'The Eve of St. Agnes'," *Keats-Shelley Journal* 41 (1992): 100–121.

3. *Keats House and Museum Historical and Descriptive Guide*. Hampstead: n.p., n.d.

4. He may, for instance, have read them in schoolmaster Rev. John Clarke's library; or he may have had them from the fantastically inclined Isabella Jones, the friend (and perhaps also lover) who loaned him books and sparked the idea for both "The Eve of St. Agnes" and "The Eve of St. Mark."

5. Hyder Edward Rollins, ed., *The Letters of John Keats: Volume II, 1814–1821* (Cambridge, MA: Harvard University Press, 1958), 157. Keats definitely read and enjoyed Boccaccio's bawdy *Decamerone,* from which he derived the subject for "Isabella." Basile is Boccaccio's literary disciple; the courtly setting of his framing device, and some of the stories it contains, are drawn from Boccaccio. Most scholarship mentions the two works in the same sentence.

6. "The Eve of St. Agnes" was composed at the Dilke home in Chichester, and Charles Dilke's sister's home in Bedhampton; Andrew Motion notes that the extensive libraries of both homes furnished Keats with sources for the poem; *Keats* (London: Faber and Faber, 1997), 38–45.

7. Keats, "The Eve of St. Agnes," in *Romanticism: An Anthology,* ed. Duncan Wu (Oxford: Blackwell, 1994), 1049.

8. *Letters,* 163.

9. From the ancient Greek πορφυρο- "purple." "Porphyro-, *comb. form*," *Oxford English Dictionary Online*. See also Marcia Gilbreath, "The Etymology of Porphyro's Name in 'The Eve of St. Agnes'," *Keats-Shelley Journal* 37 (1988): 20–25.

10. See, for example, Mary Arseneau "Madeline, Mermaids and Medusas in 'The Eve of St. Agnes'," *Papers on Language and Literature* 33 (1997): 227–43; John Kerrigan, "Keats and Lucrece," *Shakespeare Survey* 41 (1988): 103–118; Marjorie Levinson, *Keats's Life of Allegory: The Origins of a Style* (Oxford: Basil Blackwell, 1988); Jack Stillinger, "The Hoodwinking of Madeline: Scepticism in 'The Eve of St. Agnes'," in *The Hoodwinking of Madeline and Other Essays on Keats's Poems* (Chicago: University of Illinois Press, 1971), 67–93; James Twitchell, *The Living Dead: A Study of the Vampire in Romantic Literature* (Durham, NC: Duke University Press, 1981); Earl Wasserman, *The Finer Tone: Keats's Major Poems* (Baltimore: Johns Hopkins University Press, 1953); Daniel P. Watkins, *Keats's Poetry and the Politics of the Imagination* (Rutherford, NJ: Farleigh Dickenson University Press 1981).

11. *Letters*, 163.

12. Wu (ed.), 1041.

13. Judith Arcana, "St. Agnes' Source," *Journal of Ritual Studies* 2 (1987): 43–57; Sheila Delany, ed., *A Legend of Holy Women: A Translation of Osbern Bokenham's* Legends of Holy Women (Notre Dame, IN: University of Notre Dame Press, 1992); Leslie A. Donovan, *Women's Saints' Lives in Old English Prose* (Suffolk: Boydell and Brewer, 1999).

14. Tereus cuts out Philomel's tongue to prevent her from naming her attacker; Lavinia is victim to the same punishment; Philomel reveals Tereus by sewing it into a piece of needlework; Lavinia reveals her attackers by pointing to the story of Philomel in a book; later she assists to kill them and bake them in a pie, as Procne does to avenge her sister Philomel. Philomel is ultimately turned into a nightingale.

15. Beverly Fields, "Keats and the Tongueless Nightingale: Some Unheard Melodies in 'The Eve of St. Agnes'," *Wordsworth Circle* 14 (1983): 246–50.

16. Gilbreath provides further evidence that Keats meant for Porphyro's actions to be read ominously by pointing out that Banier's 1739 *Mythology and Fables of the Ancients, Explained from History*, a book Keats owned, contains not only the rape of Philomel, but also tells of a Porphyrion, a giant, who was struck down by Zeus when he tried to rape Hera.

17. Keats, "Ode to a Nightingale," in *Complete Poems*, lines 11–13. All subsequent references appear parenthetically in the text.

18. Keats, "Sonnet to Sleep" in *Complete Poems*, line 1. All subsequent references appear parenthetically in the text.

19. Keats, "Sleep and Poetry," in *Complete Poems*, 37–47; "Fall of Hyperion," in *Complete Poems*, lines 9–12. All subsequent references appear parenthetically in the text.

20. In George Ford, *Keats and the Victorians: A Study of His Influence and Rise to Fame, 1821–1895* (London: Arcehon, 1962), 18.

21. Alfred Tennyson, "Rosalind," in *The Poems of Tennyson in three volumes*, ed. Christopher Ricks (Essex, UK: Longman, 1987), vol. 1, 471–78, lines 49–51. James Hood, *Divining Desire: Tennyson and the Poetics of Transcendence* (Aldershot: Ashgate, 2000).

22. Tennyson, "Lilian," in *Poems of Tennyson*, vol. 1, 200–201; lines 27–30.

23. Tennyson, "The Day Dream," in *Poems of Tennyson*, vol. 2, lines 48–59, *The Sleeping Beauty*, lines 9–16. "The Day Dream" is divided into nine sections. Each section is titled ("Prologue," "The Sleeping Palace," "The Arrival," "The Sleeping Beauty," "The Revival," "The Departure," "The Moral," "*L'Envoi*," and "Epilogue"). In *Poems of Tennyson*, the lines are not numbered consecutively, but rather begin anew with each new section. Because the section titled *The Sleeping Beauty* remained unchanged between its independent publication

in 1830 and its publication as part of "The Day Dream" in 1842, Ricks does not print "The Sleeping Beauty" fragment separately from the longer work. All subsequent references appear parenthetically in the text.

Notes to Chapter 7

1. John R. Reed, though stating that all of Tennyson's framing devices allow him "to suggest the vitality of the past for the present," stresses "but it is important to note that the vitality of the past inheres in its events being significant enough to transcend time." "Epic/ Morte D'Arthur" is "significant enough"; "The Day Dream" by contrast "uses the same device for a more frivolous subject." "Tennyson's Magic Casements," *Victorian Poetry* 30:3–4 (1992): 215.
2. Hood, 31–32.
3. "reflex, *n.*," *Oxford English Dictionary Online*.
4. Tennyson, "The Epic," in *The Poems of Tennyson in three volumes*, vol. 2, ed. Christopher Ricks (Essex, UK: Longman, 1987), 1–19, lines 37–38. All subsequent references appear parenthetically in the text.
5. Clinton Machann, "Tennyson's King Arthur and the Violence of Manliness," *Victorian Poetry* 38:2 (2000): 205.
6. John Hughes, "'Hang There Like Fruit, My Soul': Tennyson's Feminine Imaginings," *Victorian Poetry* 45:2 (2007): 98.
7. Hallam Tennyson, *Alfred, Lord Tennyson: A Memoir by His Son* (London and New York: Macmillan, 1897), vol. 2, 287.
8. Linda Shires, "Patriarchy, Dead Men, and *Idylls of the King*," *Victorian Poetry* 30 (1992): 403.
9. Recent criticism has deftly traced the way in which scientists and literary artists mutually informed each other through "metaphoric, or analogical, thinking as a powerful tool for imagining the natural world." Barri Gold, "The Consolation of Physics: Tennyson's Thermodynamic Solution," *PMLA* 117:3 (May 2002): 456. Beginning with the work of Gillian Beers, scholars like Harold Fulweiler, Gold, Michael Tomko, and Virginia Zimmerman have argued that metaphor, allegory, and, more broadly, narrative itself is fundamental to scientific writing, and thus erodes the boundaries between material realism and fantastic representation.
10. Kirstie Blair, *Victorian Poetry and the Culture of the Heart* (Oxford: Clarendon Press, 2006), 2.
11. Ibid., 80.
12. James Paget, in the Croonian lecture to the Royal Society, proposed a similarly metonymic relationship between the rhythm of the individual heart and the "time-keeping" function of all natural processes. See also ibid., 89, for reference to Paget.
13. According to the Encyclopaedia Britannica of 1911, Wilkinson was a homeopathic physician and Swedenborgian philosopher who was friends with Carlyle and Tennyson. *Encyclopaedia Britannica*, 11th ed. (New York: Encyclopaedia Britannica Inc., 1911), vol. 28, 647.
14. James John Garth Wilkinson, *The Human Body and Its Connexion with Man: Illustrated By the Principal Organs* (London: Chapman and Hall, 1851), 183. All subsequent references appear in the text.
15. Julia Kristeva, "Women's Time." *Signs* 7:1 (1981): 13–35.

16. See, for example, Peter Burke, "Reflections on the Cultural History of Time," *Viator* 35 (2004): 617–26; Elizabeth Campbell, *Fortune's Wheel: Dickens and the Iconography of Women's Time* (Athens: Ohio University Press, 2003); Steven Dillon, "Watches, Dials and Clocks: Victorian Illustrations of Time," in *The Victorian Illustrated Book*, ed. Richard Maxwell (Charlottesville: University Press of Virginia, 2002), 52–90; N. N. Feltes, "To Saunter, To Hurry: Dickens, Time, and Industrial Capitalism," *Victorian Studies* 20 (1977): 245–67; Patricia Murphy, *Time Is of the Essence: Temporality, Gender, and the New Woman* (Albany: State University of New York Press, 2001).

17. Especially Jerome Buckley, *The Triumph of Time: A Study of the Victorian Concepts of Time, History, Progress and Decadence* (Cambridge, MA: Harvard University Press, 1966).

18. That is, geological and, even more unimaginably, astronomical or universal time.

19. Blair, 81.

20. Whereas medical practice today interprets the heart from the position of the observer, and thus determines that the right aorta and ventricle process arterial blood and the left aorta and ventricle process venous blood, Wilkinson interprets the heart from the position of the heart's owner, and thus inverts the model.

21. And lest this convergence should seem implausible, it is useful to remember that Tennyson's line from "Locksley Hall," "Here about the beach I wander'd, nourishing a youth sublime / With the fairy tales of science, and the long result of Time" (lines 11–12) prompted the popular adoption of the phrase "the fairy tales of science" for decades afterwards: becoming, among other things, the title of a bestselling science book for children by John Cargill Brough (*The Fairy Tales of Science: A Book for Youth* [London: Griffith and Farran, 1858]), which framed various scientific theories (energy, volcanism, the fossil record, matter, physiology, etc.) through the narrative structure of the fairy tale. Tennyson, "Locksley Hall." In *The Poems of Tennyson in three volumes*, vol. 2, ed. Christopher Ricks (Essex, UK: Longman, 1987), 120–30.

22. Certainly the earliest versions of "Sleeping Beauty," with which I began this essay, imagine a reproductive awakening for the princess. See also fairy tale scholars Holly Tucker (*Pregnant Fictions: Childbirth and the Fairy Tale in Early Modern France* [Detroit: Wayne State University Press, 2003]) and Ruth B. Bottigheimer ("Fertility Control and the Birth of the Modern European Fairy-Tale Heroine," *Marvels and Tales* 14:1 [2000]: 64–79), who have discovered that at least since the Early Modern period, fairy tales have been used to explore the relationship between female reproduction and literary authorship.

23. Indeed, the Victorian "Sleeping Beauty" was so successful in joining temporal and physiological tropes that, as both Emily Martin ("The Egg and the Sperm: How Science Has Constructed a Romance Based on Stereotypical Male-Female Roles." *Signs* 16:3 [1991]: 485–501) and Londa Schiebinger have pointed out, the narrative is still very much in use in modern biology textbooks: "In these sagas of conception, the spermatic hero actively pursues the egg, surviving the hostile environment of the vagina and defeating his many rivals. The large and placid egg, like Sleeping Beauty, drifts unconsciously along the fallopian tube, until awakened by a valiant sperm" (Londa Schiebinger, *Has Feminism Changed Science?* [Cambridge, MA: Harvard University Press, 1999], 145).

24. Kristeva, 17.

25. Ibid.

26. Gallagher, "George Eliot and *Daniel Deronda*," 125.

27. Or what Kristeva calls "matrix space": that is, "extrasubjective," "cosmic time," or "monumental temporality," which "has so little to do with linear time (which passes) that the very word 'temporality' hardly fits" (16).

28. "spell, *n. and v.*," *Oxford English Dictionary Online*. In the sixteenth century "spell" from German *spellen* to split, cleave also becomes "a splinter, chip, or fragment." It is interesting to remember that in early versions of "Sleeping Beauty" it is not an irritated fairy or a finger prick to an enchanted spindle that drops the princess into sleep, but a splinter (chip, fragment) of flax under her nail. In these versions, too, then, it is a spell that fells her.

29. "Scott, Sir Walter," *Oxford Companion to British Literature*, 6th ed., ed. Margaret Drabble (Oxford, Oxford University Press, 2000), 655.

30. That is, "wayward," with its history bound (via Shakespeare) to the word "weird," and "mood," with connections to both verb tense and rhythmic patterns. "wayward, *adj.*," *Oxford English Dictionary Online*.

31. Jago Morrison, "Narration and Unease in Ian McEwan's Later Fiction." *Critique* 42:3 (2001): 261.

32. In addition to Hughes, Machann, and Shires, see also James Eli Adams, "Women Red in Tooth and Claw: Nature and the Feminine in Tennyson and Darwin," *Victorian Studies* 33:1 (1989): 7–27; Margaret Linley, "Sexuality and Nationality in Tennyson's *Idylls of the King*," *Victorian Poetry* 30 (1992): 365–86; Lynne B. O'Brien, "Male Heroism: Tennyson's Divided View," *Victorian Poetry* 32:2 (1994): 171–82; William Weaver, "Identifying Men at Ida's University: Education, Gender, and Male/Male Identification in Tennyson's *The Princess*," *Nineteenth-Century Contexts* 23 (2001): 121–48.

33. For the purposes of this section, I have treated male-authored revisions of "Sleeping Beauty." This is not to imply, however, that female literary artists did not respond to the tale. Indeed, Christina Rossetti's called the poem titled "The Prince's Progress," her "reverse of the Sleeping Beauty," presumably because the prince is delayed by worldly pleasures, and the princess dies of ennui before he can reach her; but she concludes, "except in fairy land such reverses must often occur; yet I don't think it argues a sound or grateful spirit to dwell on them as predominantly as I have done." (Antony H. Harrison, ed., *The Letters of Christina Rossetti* [Charlottesville: The University Press of Virginia, 1997], vol. 1, letter 199, Tuesday, ? [*sic*] Oct. 1863, 184). Anne Thackeray Ritchie's "The Sleeping Beauty in the Wood" (1868) offers another such "reverse" (in *Five Old Friends and a Young Prince* [London: Smith and Elder, 1868], 1–26). In both verse and prose narratives, the princess is not sleeping but bored to a stupor by the trappings of Victorian leisure. Importantly, Rossetti wrote "Prince's Progress" in response to, and in defiance of, her brother Dante Gabriel's pressure for her to write an epic (Jan Marsh, *Christina Rossetti: A Writer's Life* [London: Penguin, 1994], 324). Though she joked to him in her usual self-effacing manner that she doubted whether "the latent epic should "by huge upthrust" come to the surface some day" (329), "Prince's Progress" marks Rossetti's critical response to the epic project broadly, and to the Tennysonian epic specifically. By treating "Sleeping Beauty" herself, Rossetti appears to comment upon Tennyson's rejection of the princess (and *The Princess*) in favor of the epic hero.

34. "epic, *n.*," *Oxford English Dictionary Online*.

35. Georg Wilhelm Friedrich Hegel, *Hegel's Aesthetics: Lectures on Fine Art*, vol. 2. Edited and translated by T. M. Knox (Oxford: Oxford University Press, 1998), 1047. See also Peter Middleton, "Lyric Temporality," *Shark* 3 (2001): 14–15.

36. However, given the reception of Tennyson's Arthur (Henry Crabbe Robinson called him "unfit to be an epic-hero," Henry James called him "a prig," and T. S. Eliot complained that Tennyson had created "suitable reading for a girl's school" [Machann, 199]), this may have been a more difficult task than anticipated. As Linda Shires contends: "In spite of the lengthy time period involved in composition and arrangement, both the general movement of the finished poem and the complicated order of the published parts indicate Tennyson's

abiding concern with a fragile and disempowered masculinity" ("Patriarchy," 408). I wonder, though, whether it is not *in spite* of his habitual length of composition time but *in this very fact* that Tennyson's concerns reside.

Notes to Chapter 8

1. Helen Groth, *Victorian Photography and Literary Nostalgia* (Oxford: Oxford University Press, 2003).
2. For example, Hunt's "The Lady of Shalott," completed in 1905.
3. Anonymous, "The Legend of Briar Root," *Punch* 98 (1890): 209.
4. According to Chris Brooks, in a private communication, November 2001.
5. Kristen Powell, "Edward Burne-Jones and the Legend of Briar Rose," *Journal of Pre-Raphaelite Studies* 6:2 (1986): 21.
6. Penelope Fitzgerald, *Edward Burne-Jones: A Biography* (London: Michael Joseph, 1975), 225
7. Ibid.
8. Robert de la Sizeraine, "In Memoriam," *The Magazine of Art* 21 (1898): 516.
9. Ibid.
10. Una Taylor, "Burne-Jones, His Ethics, and Art," *Edinburgh Review* 189 (April 1899): 34.
11. The Faringdon Trustees, *The Faringdon Collection*, (Hampshire, England: BAS Printers Limited, 1998), 57; Stephen Wildman and John Christian, *Edward Burne-Jones: Victorian Artist-Dreamer* (New York: Metropolitan Museum of Art, 1998), 160.
12. Lady Georgiana Burne-Jones, *Memorials of Edward Burne-Jones* (London: Macmillan, 1904), vol. 1, 151.
13. In *Memorials,* Georgiana Burne-Jones characterized his fairy tale work in this way: "a welcome outlet for his abounding humor, and in this form the stories took at his hands as quaint a shape as they wear in the pages of the Brothers Grimm of blessed memory" (249).
14. Reproduced in Powell, 28.
15. This first series is held in the Museo de Arte, Ponce, Puerto Rico.
16. *Faringdon Collection,* 56–57.
17. Stephen Wildman and John Christian, *Edward Burne-Jones: Victorian Artist-Dreamer* (New York: Metropolitan Museum of Art, 1998), 161–62.
18. After the sale of the final *Briar Rose* series to Henderson, Burne-Jones returned to the group he had abandoned in 1885. These he sold individually through Agnew's; *The Garden Court* is in Bristol City Art Gallery, *The Council Chamber* is in the Delaware Art Museum, and *The Rose Bower* is at Dublin's Municipal Museum of Modern Art. There is some dispute about whether a fourth painting, *The Briar Wood* ever existed. See Powell, 22, and *Faringdon Collection,* 57.
19. According to Wildman and Christian: "Great care was taken to ensure that the paintings were seen not only by "cultivated people" in the metropolis . . . they were exhibited in Liverpool, and the following year they were shown at Whitechapel, where the enterprising warden of Toynbee Hall, Canon Samuel Barnett, with the active co-operation of Burne-Jones, Watts, Holman Hunt, and other public-spirited artists, organized regular exhibitions as a source of enlightenment in the poverty-stricken East End" (315).
20. These were evidently exhibited with the paintings in London, for *Punch* parodies

them in its cartoon version (e.g., "The fateful odor fumes and goes / About the angle of the Nose.").

21. It is also tempting to wonder whether Burne-Jones designed nine scenes in subtle tribute to the nine sections of Tennyson's "Day Dream."

22. Powell, 19.

23. Mary Lago, ed., *Edward Burne-Jones Talking: His conversations 1895–8 preserved by his studio assistant Thomas Rooke* (London: John Murray, 1982), 74.

24. Ibid.

25. Wildman and Christian, 192–93.

26. Christopher Wood, *The Pre-Raphaelites* (London: Seven Dials, 2000), 128.

27. Ibid., 119.

28. M. H. Spielman, "In Memoriam," *The Magazine of Art* 21 (1898): 524.

29. See, for example, Lago, 80.

30. Elizabeth Campbell, *Fortune's Wheel: Dickens and the Iconography of Women's Time* (Athens: Ohio University Press, 2003); Patricia Murphy, *Time Is of the Essence: Temporality, Gender, and the New Woman* (Albany: State University of New York Press, 2001). Murphy specifically attributes these temporal anxieties to the pervasiveness of the New Woman, while Campbell focuses upon the trope of the wheel of fortune in Dickens's late fiction, as a "symbol for man's fate in the hands of a more powerful feminine principle" (xx) and a "bitter" reflection that "the era of men's [linear] time is over" (xxi). Campbell links Dickens's manipulation of the trope with Burne-Jones's exploration of the subject in his *Wheel of Fortune* (1875–83). Interestingly, while Murphy's and Campbell's theses are quite similar, Murphy locates fears of a female temporal shift at the turn of the century, while Campbell cites it as the terminus of Dickens's career, a response building to a climax only in 1865. Considering that I have already demonstrated that this imaginative struggle over temporal modes existed a good deal earlier than either Campbell or Murphy allow, this very lack of periodic consensus confirms Burke's argument that temporal relativism has long been "a medium for expressing social differences," not only gendered, and not only in the last decades of the nineteenth century.

31. Groth, 2.

32. William Sharp's volume of Severn's memoirs was published in 1892, and a copy of the sketch was included there; however, Burne-Jones and Sharp were friends, and Burne-Jones may have had access to the sketch of Keats prior to its publication.

33. Wildman and Christian, 16.

34. Ibid.

35. It is interesting to note that Gavin, 3rd Lord Faringdon, a noted socialist, donated the estate and grounds to the National Trust, thus giving the public access to the Faringdon collection of art.

36. See, for example, Marian Roalfe Cox's study, *Cinderella: Three Hundred and Forty-five Variants of Cinderella, Catskin, and Cap O'Rushes* (London: David Nutt for the Folk-Lore Society, 1893).

Notes to Chapter 9

1. Diane Purkiss, *Troublesome Things: A History of Fairies and Fairy Stories* (London: Allen Lane, The Penguin Press, 2000).

2. Maureen Duffy, *The Erotic World of Faery* (London: Hodder and Stoughton, 1972), 24.

3. See, for example, ibid.,125–71.

4. Ibid., 175.

5. The Camden Society and the Percy Society were two of the largest and most prolific of these groups. They predated London's Folklore Society and its regional chapters, and died out when the Folklore Society was established in 1878.

6. John Brand, *Observations on the Popular Antiquities of Great Britain,* 3 vols, ed. Henry Ellis (1777; London: Bell and Daldy, 1873); Thomas Crofton Croker, *Legends and Traditions of the South of Ireland* (1825; Cork: The Collins Press, 1998); Thomas Keightley, *Fairy Mythology: Illustrative of the Romance and Superstition of Various Countries* (1828; London: Wildwood House Ltd, 1981); Joseph Ritson, *Fairy Tales* (London: Thomas Davison, 1831); Anna Eliza Bray, *Traditions, Legends, Superstitions and Sketches of Devonshire on the Borders of the Tamar and Tavy* (London: J. Murray, 1838); Bray, *A Peep at the Pixies* (London: Grant and Griffith, 1854); Jeremiah Curtin, *Tales of the Fairies and of the Ghost World, Collected from Oral Tradition in South-West Munster* (Boston: Little, Brown, & Company, 1895).

7. Duffy, 34–36.

8. Bray, *Tamar and Tavy,* 172.

9. Ibid., 170.

10. Ibid., 172.

11. Ritson, 134–36.

12. John Harland and T. T. Wilkinson, *Lancashire Folk-Lore: Illustrative of the Superstitious Beliefs and Practices, Local Customs and Usages of the People of the County Palatine* (London: Frederick Warne and Co., 1867), 113.

13. Ibid.

14. Croker, 88–89.

15. Bray, *Tamar and Tavy,* 186.

16. Bray, *Peep at the Pixies,* 58–59.

17. Duffy, 297.

18. See also Ritson, 33; Curtin, 26.

19. Ritson, 140. Keightley believed this legend to have originated in print with Gervase of Tilbury.

20. See Ritson, 27; Curtin, 62; Croker, 204.

21. See Purkiss, 110–13.

22. See Curtin, 66, 158.

23. Harland and Wilkinson, 113.

24. Purkiss, 133.

25. Jane Martineau, ed., *Victorian Fairy Painting* (London: Royal Academy of Arts, 1997), 114–17.

26. "fairy, *n.* and *attr.,*" *Oxford English Dictionary Online.*

27. French *gobelin,* Welsh *kobold;* Croker, 162; Keightley, 281.

Notes to Chapter 10

1. Thomas Richards, *The Commodity Culture of Victorian England: Advertising and Spectacle 1851–1914* (Stanford, CA: Stanford University Press, 1990).

2. Louise Purbrick, "Introduction," in *The Great Exhibition of 1851: New Interdisciplinary Essays,* ed. Louise Purbrick (Manchester: Manchester University Press, 2001), 1–25.

3. Joseph W. Childers, "Peering Back: Colonials and Exhibitions," in *Victorian Prism: Refractions of the Crystal Palace*, ed. James Buzard, Joseph W. Childers, and Eileen Gillooly (Charlottesville: University of Virginia Press, 2007), 203–15; Lara Kriegel, "Narrating the Subcontinent in 1851: India at the Crystal Palace," in Purbrick (ed.), 146–78.

4. Eileen Gillooly, "Rhetorical Remedies for Taxonomic Troubles" in Buzard, Childers, and Gillooly (eds.), 23–39; Steve Edwards, "The Accumulation of Knowledge, or William Whewell's Eye," in Purbrick (ed.), 26–52.

5. Richard Pearson, "Thackeray and Punch at the Great Exhibition: Authority and Ambivalence Verbal and Visual Caricatures," in Purbrick (ed.), 179–205.

6. Richards, 3.

7. Edwards, 38

8. Ibid., 47.

9. Henry Bessemer, *Sir Henry Bessemer, F. R. S.: An Autobiography* (London: Offices of Engineering, 1905), accessed August 7, 2013, http://www.lucidcafe.com/library/96jan/bessemer.html.

10. Eliza Brightwen. *Memoir of the Crystal Palace*, accessed August 7, 2013, http://freepages.genealogy.rootsweb.ancestry.com/~thegrove/exhibition.html.

11. Anonymous, "Glass Houses of Parliament," *Punch: or the London Charivari*, vol. 19 (1849): 81.

12. Kenneth Spencer Research Library, University of Kansas, exhibit on The Great Exhibition, accessed August 7, 2013, http://liblamp.vm.ku.edu/spencer/exhibits/greatexhibition/contents.htm.

13. C. H. Gibbs-Smith (ed.) and the Victoria and Albert Museum, *The Great Exhibition of 1851: A Commemorative Album* (London: Her Majesty's Stationary Office, 1964), 15 (February 18, 1851).

14. Ibid., 16 (April 29, 1851).

15. Quoted in Lionel Lambourne, "Fairies on the Stage," in *Victorian Fairy Painting*, ed. Jane Martineau (London: Royal Academy of Arts, 1997), 51–52.

16. Purbrick, 15.

17. Gibbs-Smith (ed.), 18 (May 7, 1851).

18. Gillooly, 27.

19. Ibid., 27–28.

20. Charles Dickens, "The Wonders of 1851," *Household Words* (December 28, 1850): 390.

21. Gibbs-Smith (ed.), 26.

22. Henry Mayhew, *1851, or the Adventures of Mr. and Mrs. Sandboys and Family* (London: David Bogue, 1851).

23. Anonymous, "The Cinderella of 1851," *Punch* 21 (1851): 132–33.

24. Ibid., 133.

25. In Great Exhibition literature, the racist perception of foreigners perched with savage appetite on England's borders is analogous to the famished goblin that inhabits the English home, destroying domestic peace with voracious, alien presence. Thomas Onwhyn's 1851 illustrated book, *Mr. and Mrs. Brown's Visit to London to See the Great Exhibition of All Nations: How they were astonished at its wonders, inconvenienced by its crowds, and frightened out of their wits by the Foreigners*, is a particularly racist example of this cultural tension (London: Ackerman, n.d.). One illustration depicts the Browns' encounter in the refreshment court of "a party from the Cannibal Islands, who "after eying little Johnny (Brown) in a mysterious manner, offer a price for him." Topknotted and simian, the "Cannibal Islanders" closely resemble Fitzgerald's murderous fairy. The foreigners' intent to have an En-

glish boy for lunch underscores the economic anxiety that English consumers could instead somehow be consumed by foreign trade. While the proposed exchange inhabits the foreground, ingestion occupies the background. Several stereotyped figures consume English food—an Asian munches an Exhibition wafer, a turbaned Muslim quaffs ale. A sign over the heads of the Browns reads "Bird's Nest Soup," another advertises "Soup a la Hottentot/ Train Oil in his perfection." Bewildering syntax: presumably a train oil broth, but "in *his* perfection" suggests a soup made of, and not by, "Hottentots." While in the real Exhibition, one could purchase only an unappetizing assortment of sandwiches, ices, and biscuits (See Gibbs-Smith [ed.], 26–32; *Punch* vol. 20, 21 [1850, 1851]), which, however stale, were nevertheless decidedly English, in Onwhyn's illustration there can be no comforting homogenization of food. The fear here is that "foreignness" might consume "Englishness," but also that English visitors might accidentally imbibe some transformative foreign fare. Like trafficking with fairies, hunger in the Exhibition brings danger upon the body. In the central tableau, the eyes of the English are locked with the eyes of the cannibals; the stare describes the same relationship between looking and consuming as that of the fairy gaze in fairy legend.

26. Anonymous, "The Exhibition Plague," *Punch* 19 (1849): 191.

27. Richard Doyle, *An overland journey to the Great Exhibition, showing a few extra articles and visitors* (London: Chapman and Hall, 1851).

28. Fairy painting would not become a proper genre until after the Great Exhibition; I would argue that it was in part the figurative playing ground of the fairy palace that enabled this form to come into being.

29. Richard Menke, "The Political Economy of Fruit," in *The Culture of Christina Rossetti*, ed. Mary Arsenau et al. (Athens: Ohio University Press, 1999), 113.

30. Anonymous, "Orangeism in the Crystal Palace!" *Punch* 21 (1851): 15.

31. F. W. N. Bayley, *The Exhibition* (London: Darton & Co., 1851), 20.

32. Anonymous, *Punch* 21 (1851): 5.

33. P. Wallace, "On the Cultivation of Exotic Fruits," *Journal of the Royal Horticultural Society* 8 (1853): 47.

34. *Official Catalogue of the Great Exhibition of the Works of Industry of All Nations, 1851* (London: Spicer, 1851), 1319.

35. "produce, n. and v.," *Oxford English Dictionary Online*.

36. March 21, 1850, Printed Report of Grand Banquet to HRH Prince Albert at Mansion House, London in Honor of the Exhibition of 1851, John Scott Russell Papers, Volume II, RSA, in John Davis, *The Great Exhibition* (Stroud, U.K.: Sutton Publishing, 1999), 67–68.

37. Jeffrey Auerbach, *The Great Exhibition of 1851: A Nation on Display* (New Haven, CT: Yale University Press, 1999), 50.

38. Qtd. in Peter Gurney, "An Appropriated Space: The Great Exhibition, The Crystal Palace, and the Working Class," in Louise Purbrick (ed.), 123.

39. Christina Rossetti, "Goblin Market," *Christina Rossetti: The Complete Poems* (London: Penguin, 2001), 5–20, 15–16. Further citations appear parenthetically in the text.

Notes to Chapter 11

1. Catherine Gallagher, "George Eliot and *Daniel Deronda:* The Prostitute and the Jewish Question" in *Sex, Politics and Science in the Nineteenth-Century Novel*, ed. Ruth Bernard Yeazell (Baltimore: The Johns Hopkins University Press, 1986), 40.

2. Ibid., 41.

3. The Rossetti children read the both of the Grimms' works, the *Märchen* and *Deutsche Sagen* with a family friend, Dr. Adolf Heimann. Jan Marsh, *Christina Rossetti: A Writer's Life* (London: Penguin, 1994), 229.

4. Ibid., 230. See also Ritson, 140

5. Marsh, 230.

6. Antony H. Harrison, ed., *The Letters of Christina Rossetti: vol. 1, 1843–1873* (Charlottesville: The University Press of Virginia, 1997), 18, 22.

7. Grapes, quinces, figs, peaches, and plums are grown out of doors in England with difficulty, and the best quality of these fruits are greenhoused.

8. Menke, 113; Mary Wilson Carpenter, "'Eat Me, Drink Me, Love Me": The Consumable Female Body in Christina Rossetti's *Goblin Market*," *Victorian Poetry* 29:4 (1991): 427.

9. See also Menke, 116.

10. As with transmogrifying fairies of legend, these goblins use their animal shapes to coax as well as frighten. The creatures are like legendary fairies too, in their violence toward Lizzie:

> They trod and hustled her,
> Elbowed and jostled her,
> Clawed with their nails
> Barking, mewing, hissing, mocking,
> Tore her gown and soiled her stocking,
> Twitched her hair out by the roots . . .
> . . . cuffed and caught her,
> Coaxed and fought her,
> Bullied and besought her,
> Scratched her, pinched her black as ink,
> Kicked and knocked her,
> Mauled and mocked her . . . (398–404, 424–29)

Carole G. Silver suggests that artistic depictions of fairy violence to animals "substituted this visual convention for the more forbidden one of fairy cruelty to mortals, displacing evil onto more culturally approved forms" (*Strange and Secret Peoples: Fairies and Victorian Consciousness* [Oxford: Oxford University Press, 1999], 159). Here Rossetti insists upon fairy brutality to humans, reminding us of legends in which fairies strike at humans through physical violence, rape, or murder. As Silver points out (128), Rossetti's goblin violence is the more disturbing for being simultaneously bestial and human: they hiss, growl, bark, mew, and maul, but also elbow, kick, pinch, pull hair, and rip clothing.

11. "goblin²," *Oxford English Dictionary Online*.

12. Lizzie and Laura's work, "neat like bees, as sweet and busy," characterizes the maidens' self-sufficiency prior to Laura's fall. Like bees, they are efficient home economists in this closed system (see also Holt, 53). The beehives on display in the Crystal Palace struck visitors as "exceedingly curious little palaces of industry" (John Tallis, qtd. in Auerbach, 96). Ever self-reflexive, organizers apparently had seized an opportunity to co-opt the symbolism of natural industry into the mechanized production of the Crystal Palace. Today we might say all sorts of things about drones, hive mentality, and mindless devotion to monarchic structure. For Victorians, though, bees symbolized natural labor in their "busy" engagement.

Rossetti might well have found the beehives a woefully misplaced metaphor in the Crystal Palace, where "industry" represented entirely alienated labor.

13. Among these are Holt; Elizabeth Campbell, "Of Mothers and Merchants: Female Economics in Christina Rossetti's 'Goblin Market,'" *Victorian Studies* 33 (1990): 393–410; Elizabeth Helsinger, "Consumer Power and the Utopia of Desire: Christina Rossetti's 'Goblin Market'" *ELH* 58 (1991): 903–33; Sandra Gilbert and Susan Gubar, "The Aesthetics of Renunciation," in *The Madwoman in the Attic: The Woman Writer and the Nineteenth-Century Literary Imagination*, 2nd ed. (New Haven, CT: Yale University Press, 2000), 539–80; Catherine Maxwell, "Tasting the 'Fruit Forbidden': Gender, Intertextuality, and Christina Rossetti's 'Goblin Market,'" in *The Culture of Christina Rossetti: Female Poetics and Victorian Contexts*, ed. Mary Arsenau et al. (Athens: Ohio University Press, 1999), 75–104.

14. See Harrison, especially "Christina Rossetti: Renunciation as Intervention," in *Victorian Poets and the Politics of Culture: Discourse and Ideology* (Charlottesville, VA: The University Press of Virginia, 1998), 125–64; Maxwell, and Menke are notable exceptions.

15. Susan Mumm, *Stolen Daughters, Virgin Mothers: Anglican Sisterhoods in Victorian Britain* (New York: Continuum, 1999), 3.

16. William Michael Rossetti, ed., *Ruskin: Rossetti: Preraphaelitism: Papers, 1854–1862* (New York: Dodd, Mead and Co.; London: George Allen, 1899), 258–59.

17. Gallagher, "George Eliot and *Daniel Deronda*," 40.

18. Ibid., 41.

19. Ibid.

20. Gillooly, 27.

21. Gallagher, "George Eliot and *Daniel Deronda*," 43.

22. Ibid., 126.

23. John S. North, ed., *The Waterloo Directory of English Newspapers and Periodicals: 1800–1900*, accessed August 9, 2013, http://www.victorianperiodicals.com/series2/default.asp.

24. Menke, 113.

25. Hilary Green, Stephanie Fraser, Judith Johnston, *Gender and the Victorian Periodical* (Cambridge: Cambridge University Press, 2003), 212–23.

26. Thomas Hughes, "Anonymous Journalism," *Macmillan's Magazine* 5 (1861): 160. Also qtd. in Alexis Easley, *First Person Anonymous: Women Writers and Victorian Print Media, 1830–70* (Aldershot: Ashgate, 2004), 168.

27. Marsh, 132; Easley, 166.

28. *Macmillan's* emphasized authorship with bylines as a marketing tool: because Macmillan published books by his periodical writers, named authorship would boost later book sales (Easley, 168).

29. Ibid., 157.

30. Ibid., 170.

31. Ibid., 164.

32. *The Days' Doings: An Illustrated and Amusing Record of Passing Events*, published 1870–72, and continued as *Here and There*, was a mildly pornographic gentleman's magazine.

33. F. W. N. Bayley, *Little Red Riding Hood* (London: Orr, 1846).

34. M. H. Spielman, *The History of Punch* (London: Cassell and Co., 1895), 17.

35. Dickens, *Hard Times* (London: Penguin, 2003), 287

36. Ibid.

37. "jingle, *n. and v.*," *Oxford English Dictionary Online*. Possibly also resonating with the clinking sound of coins (jingle is Australian slang for money), and with "jingo": (usually *hey* or *high jingo!*), a conjuror's call for the appearance of something.

38. Christina Rossetti to Alexander Macmillan, December 2, 1861 in *Letters,* letter 146, 152.

39. Christina Rossetti to Alexander Macmillan, April 8, 1861, in ibid., letter 137, 146.

40. Yopie Prins, "Victorian Meter," in *The Cambridge Companion to Victorian Poetry,* ed. Joseph Bristow (Cambridge: Cambridge University Press, 2000), 90.

41. Nigel Fabb and Morris Halle, "Metrical Complexity in Christina Rossetti's Verse," *College Literature* 32:2 (2006): 101.

42. George Saintsbury, *A History of English Prosody from the 12th Century to the Present Day: Vol. III, Blake to Swinburne* (London: Macmillan, 1910), 359.

43. Ibid., 475. Also qtd. in Prins, 108.

44. Prins, 108.

45. See also Menke, 128.

46. Marylu Hill, "'Eat Me, Drink Me, Love Me': Eucharist and the Erotic Body in Christina Rossetti's 'Goblin Market,'" *Victorian Poetry* 43:4 (Winter 2005): 455–72; McGann, Jerome J. "Christina Rossetti's Poems: A New Edition and a Revaluation," *Victorian Studies: A Journal of the Humanities, Arts and Sciences* 23 (1980): 237–54.

47. See, for example, Jerome McGann and Catherine Maxwell.

48. Marsh, 128.

49. "homœopathy," *Oxford English Dictionary Online.*

50. Peter Morrell and Sylvain Cazalet, "The History of the London Homoeopathic Hospital," Royal London Homeopathic Hospital, accessed August 9, 2013, http://www.homeoint.org/morrell/londonhh/index.htm.

Notes to Chapter 12

1. Catherine Orenstein, *Little Red Riding Hood Uncloaked: Sex, Morality, and the Evolution of a Fairy Tale* (New York: Basic Books, 2002), 93.

2. Ibid., 28; Yvonne Verdier, "Little Red Riding Hood in Oral Tradition," *Marvels and Tales* 11:1–2 (1997): 113.

3. "paraphrase, *n.,*" *Oxford English Dictionary Online.*

4. See, for example, Orenstein; Verdier; Alan Dundes, *Little Red Riding Hood: A Casebook* (Madison: University of Wisconsin Press, 1989); Jack Zipes, *The Trials and Tribulations of Little Red Riding Hood* (New York: Routledge, 1993).

5. Paul Delarue's 1951, 1953, and 1956 studies assembled both contemporary oral versions and print versions from the nineteenth century. In Delarue's compilation of tales, the antagonist is not a wolf but a werewolf (*loup-garou,* or in dialect, *bzou*). Verdier's further analysis of Delarue's data demonstrates that these nineteenth-century versions of "Little Red Riding Hood" were concentrated in locations where werewolf trial narratives were most abundant in the sixteenth and seventeenth centuries. Verdier, 102; see also Zipes, *Trials and Tribulations,* 20; Dundes, 15–17.

6. Dundes, 15.

7. Ibid., 16.

8. Some fairy tale scholars—among them Dundes, Orenstein, and Zipes—reflecting upon this and other, similar versions of the tale collected by folklorists in the nineteenth century, believe its textual evidence to indicate that it originated in the sixteenth or seventeenth century, generated by the all-female seamstress collectives common in those regions of France at that time. As Zipes has told me, "There is no clear historical evidence that these

tales were circulating then, nor is there evidence of their origins" (personal communication, July 2008). It is, therefore, impossible to know whether the sewing society origin is true, or whether the 1885 version is simply its own instantiation—oral or literary. However, these folklorists have argued that this version's motifs (eating grandmother, feigning the need to defecate to escape, and a comparatively agential female heroine) make the tale stylistically more similar to other late medieval and early modern fairy tales, and less likely to be a text that entered the oral tradition after Perrault. The fact that the antagonist is a werewolf rather than wolf, and that these tales existed where werewolf trials were common two hundred years before, may also suggest an older origin to this story. Despite the concurrence of these well-respected folklorists, it seems to me to be impossible to date this version of the story with any precision earlier than the nineteenth century. We are merely left with a plausible and tempting suggestion that it might be so.

9. Charles Perrault, "*Le Petit Chaperon Rouge,*" in *Perrault's Popular Tales,* ed. Andrew Lang (Oxford: Clarendon, 1888), 20.

10. Ibid., 22.

11. Ibid.

12. Jan M. Ziolkowski has argued against this, citing a Latin verse text for schoolboys by Egbert of Liege, *Fecunda Ratis* (1022) as evidence of a much earlier presence of the red garment in the tale. In one of the verses, "*De Puella a Lupellis Serruta*" ("Concerning a Girl Saved from Wolf Cubs"), a man gives his goddaughter a woven red wool tunic for a baptismal gift. A wolf attacks her and takes her to its lair, where it leaves her to be eaten by its cubs. The girl is protected (through her baptism, apparently, of which the tunic is a symbol), and the cubs nuzzle her instead of devouring her (Jan M. Ziolkowski, "A Fairy Tale From Before Fairy Tales: Egbert of Liege's 'De Puella a Lupellis Seruata' and the Medieval Background of 'Little Red Riding Hood,'" *Speculum* 67 (1992): 559; Verdier, 119). Delarue and Dundes both feel that the presence of a red tunic and a wolf in the same story is not significant enough to make this an early version of "Little Red Riding Hood," as the plot arcs are too distinct to be considered even variants of each other. Indeed, "De Puella" is not a tale at all, but rather Egbert's rendition of a local legend (the first line of the verse states that the story is "quite true"). Nevertheless, the brief story demonstrates that the themes of "Little Red Riding Hood"—dangers to innocent girls who wander alone, and humanity triumphing over wolfishness—had long been part of European oral narrative.

13. Morna Daniels, "Little Red Riding-Hood," *Electronic British Library Journal,* Article 5 (2006): 1. http://www.bl.uk/eblj/2006articles/pdf/article5.pdf.

14. Perrault, "*Le Petit Chaperon Rouge,*" 22; translation in Orenstein, 38.

15. Zipes, *Trials and Tribulations,* 26.

16. Ibid., 135.

17. Ibid., 137.

18. Dundes, 3.

19. Carolyn Steedman, *Strange Dislocations: Childhood and the Idea of Human Interiority, 1780–1930* (London: Virago, 1995), 9.

20. Ibid., 5.

21. Ibid., 16.

22. Catherine Robson, *Men in Wonderland: The Lost Girlhood of the Victorian Gentleman* (Princeton, NJ: Princeton University Press, 2001), 14.

23. J. R. Planché, *Rodolph the Wolf; or, Columbine Red Riding-Hood* (London: John Lowndes, 1818), 16. All subsequent references appear parenthetically in the text.

Notes to Chapter 13

1. In Carol Mavor, *Pleasures Taken: Performances of Sexuality and Loss in Victorian Photographs* (Durham, NC: Duke University Press, 1995), 38.
2. J. Jeffrey Franklin, *Serious Play: The Cultural Form of the Nineteenth-Century Realist Novel* (Philadelphia: University of Pennsylvania Press, 1999), 4.
3. Ibid., 6.
4. For complete studies on the popular theater, see Lance Bertelsen, "Popular Entertainment and Instruction, Literary and Dramatic: Chapbooks, Advice Books, Almanacs, Ballads, Farces, Pantomimes, Prints and Shows" in *The Cambridge History of English Literature, 1660–1780*, ed. John Richetti (Cambridge: Cambridge University Press, 2005), 61–86; Tracy C. Davis, *Actresses as Working Women: Their Social Identity in Victorian Culture* (London: Routledge, 1991) and "Do You Believe in Fairies?: The Hiss of Dramatic License" *Theater Journal* 57:1 (March 2005): 57–81; Marilyn Gaull "Pantomime as Satire: Mocking a Broken Charm" in *The Satiric Eye: Forms of Satire in the Romantic Period*, ed. Stephen E. Jones (New York: Palgrave, 2003), 207–24; Jane Moody, *Illegitimate Theater in London, 1770–1840* (Cambridge: Cambridge University Press, 2000); Deborah Vlock, *Dickens, Novel Reading, and the Victorian Popular Theater* (Cambridge: Cambridge University Press, 1998). For studies of the pantomime, see William Axton, *Circle of Fire: Dickens' Vision and Style and the Popular Victorian Theater* (Lexington: University Press of Kentucky, 1966); Edwin Eigner, *The Dickens Pantomime* (Berkeley: University of California Press, 1988); David Mayer, *Harlequin in His Element: The English Pantomime, 1806–1836* (Cambridge, MA: Harvard University Press, 1969); John O'Brien, *Harlequin Britain: Pantomime and Entertainment, 1690–1760* (Baltimore: The Johns Hopkins University Press, 2004).
5. Gaull, 209.
6. The studies of Axton, Eigner, Mayer, O'Brien, and Vlock richly detail the conventions of the popular theater forms. Briefly, however, the pantomime is the oldest of these forms, entering the English tradition in the eighteenth century. It is characterized by an opening portion, "which gave the show its title, and drew its subject from the adaptation of a fairy tale or legend, fragment of classical mythology, or a well-known literary classic" (Mayer, 3). In the early decades of pantomime, the plot was highly conventional, and almost always featured the thwarting of two lovers by a father, guardian, or duenna of the girl, who had plans for a financially advantageous match for her to an older, richer suitor. The action is interrupted by a benevolent agent, usually a fairy, who intercedes, and causes the transformation of the characters into the roles of *commedia dell'arte*: the hero becomes Harlequin, the heroine Columbine, the father or duenna Pantaloon, and the rich lover Clown or, alternatively, Dandy Lover. The fairy gives Harlequin a magic bat or "slapstick," and sends the characters off on a journey, in which Pantaloon and Clown (or Lover) chase Harlequin and Columbine through contemporary scenes of London. Harlequin uses the slapstick to transform objects which thwart pursuit. The lovers' guard invariably drops, and the pursuers swoop in to kidnap Columbine. The fairy intercedes again to redirect Harlequin, and the business ends happily in a fairy bower, or on a dais or mountain, or other apotheosic location. The burlesque and the extravaganza developed after and in light of the pantomime; they combine many of the conventions of pantomime with the features of the music hall. Like the pantomime, both forms used folk or classical stories, but were less codified in plot conventions. All forms relied on parody of various kinds, but according to Planché's definition, "extravaganza stressed a 'whimsical treatment of a poetical subject,' as distinct from 'the

broad caricature of a tragedy or serious opera which was correctly described as burlesque.' Like burlesque in its use of traditional stories, extravaganza rather played on the charm of the tale itself than in the gross travesty or grotesque incongruity as in burlesque" (Axton, 23). Many argue that the burlesque is the form that originated the practice of cross-dressed characters, and that this influenced pantomime's adoption of the cross-dressed "principal boy" and "dame" roles in the latter half of the nineteenth century.

7. Gaull, 208.
8. Moody, 80.
9. See O'Brien, *Harlequin Britain*, 231; Mayer, 3.
10. Axton, 17.
11. Bertlesen, 63.
12. Ibid., 81.
13. O'Brien, *Harlequin Britain*, xvii.
14. Ibid., xiii.
15. Davis, "Do You Believe in Fairies?" 58.
16. O'Brien, *Harlequin Britain*, xiii.
17. Davis, *Actresses*, 60.
18. Jennifer Schacker, "Unruly Tales: Ideology, Anxiety, and the Regulation of Genre," *Journal of American Folklore* 120(478) (2007): 395.
19. Ibid., 393.
20. Davis, *Actresses*, 6.
21. Ibid., 34–35.
22. See, for example, Steedman, 135.
23. Vlock, 62.
24. Davis, *Actresses*, 108.
25. Steedman, 142.
26. Lionel Lambourne, "Fairies on the Stage," in *Victorian Fairy Painting*, ed. Jane Martineau (London: Royal Academy of Arts, 1997), 47.
27. Anonymous, "Harlequin Fairy Morgana," *All the Year Round* 12 (1864): 42.
28. Percy Fitzgerald, *The World Behind the Scenes* (London: Chatto and Windus, 1881), 89.
29. Gallagher, "George Eliot and *Daniel Deronda*," 54.
30. Ibid., 55.
31. Steedman, 136.
32. J. V. Bridgeman and H. Sutherland Edwards, *Little Red Riding Hood: or, Harlequin and the Wolf in Granny's Clothing* (London: printed and sold in Royal English Opera theater, Covent Garden 1859). All subsequent references appear parenthetically in the text.
33. Leicester Buckingham, *Little Red Riding Hood and the Fairies of the Rose, Shamrock, and Thistle* (London: Thomas Hales Lacy, 1861). All subsequent references appear parenthetically in the text.
34. Planche's is the only text I have found that makes the cloak into a symbol of chastity and inviolability rather than sexual taint.
35. While one might think that "pluck a bud" is sexual slang similar to "deflower," the *OED* cites no such meaning for the phrase. Instead, the closest definition is to "pluck a rose," a slang term particularly assigned to women's defecation. This idiom, otherwise inexplicably located in this script, may provide an additional clue that "The Story of Grandmother" had reached England.

36. Thompson's biography is explored in Kurt Ganzl, *Lydia Thompson, the Queen of Burlesque* (New York and London: Routledge, 2002).

37. Davis, *Actresses*, 137.

38. Charles Dickens, "Gaslight Fairies," *Household Words* 11 (Feb. 10, 1855), 25-28; 27.

39. John Weylland, *These Fifty Years, Being the Jubilee Volume of the London City Mission* (London: Partridge, 1884), 141.

40. Gaull, 211.

41. Moody, 165.

42. Davis, *Actresses*, 81.

43. Henry Mayhew, *London Labor and the London Poor*, vol. 1, The London Street Folk (London: Griffin, Bohn, and Co., 1861), 2–3.

44. Steedman, 129.

45. Ibid., 118.

46. The work was one of several publications that he presented under the series title "Little Folk's Laughing Library"; these works were cheaply published, featuring the same type of pen and ink illustrations, same diminutive size and pasteboard binding as a chapbook, blue book, or "penny dreadful." He published other verse rewritings of fairy tales in the series, like "Bluebeard," as well as offensive *blason populaire* like "The Remarkable Nigger," and "Paddy's Complaint." The sales of "Little Red Riding Hood" were satisfactory enough that it was later collected and reprinted with other of Bayley's fairy tale verse.

47. Charles Montague, *Recollections of an Equestrian Manager* (London: W&R Chambers, 1881), 22.

48. Cited in VictorianLondon.org, accessed August 11, 2013, http://www.victorianlondon.org/entertainment/adelaidegallery.htm.

49. Ben Weinreb and Christopher Hibbert, eds., *The London Encyclopedia* (London: Macmillan, 1984), 486.

50. Lowther Bazaar was named for the Chief Commissioner for Parks and Forests in 1830 when improvements to the Strand were made, and the covered arcade was erected (ibid). Placing Sappho in front of this particular arcade, then, perhaps parodies "Sappho" as a grotesquerie of the Wordsworthian child, signaling the London performing girl's remove from nature in the middle-class imagination.

51. Steadman, 120.

52. The *OED* suggests a simultaneous origin to both of these definitions of "out," c. 1782.

Notes to Chapter 14

1. Dickens, "A Christmas Tree," in *Christmas Books and Reprinted Pieces* (New York: John Lovell, 1879), 829 (originally published in *Household Words* [December 1850]). See also Michael Kotzin, *Dickens and the Fairy Tale* (Bowling Green, OH: Bowling Green University Popular Press, 1972), 44; Cynthia DeMarcus, "Wolves Within and Without: Dickens's Transformation of 'Little Red Riding Hood' in *Our Mutual Friend*," *Dickens Quarterly* 7:1 (March 1995): 11–12.

2. Gen. 6:19–20 King James.

3. Alter, xi.

4. Ibid., 46.

5. Julian Wolfreys, *Writing London: The Trace of the Urban Text from Blake to Dickens* (London: Macmillan, 1998), 5.
6. Ibid., 22.
7. Alter, 47. As I have also pointed out, Alter dismisses the importance of this "fairy tale perspective."
8. Robert Newsom, *Dickens on the Romantic Side of Familiar Things:* Bleak House *and the Novel Tradition* (New York: Columbia University Press, 1977), 7.
9. See also Maria Bachman and Don Richard Cox, eds., *Reality's Dark Light: The Sensational Wilkie Collins* (Knoxville: University of Tennessee Press, 2003); Robert Polhemus and Roger Henkle, eds., *Critical Reconstructions: The Relationship of Fiction and Life* (Stanford, CA: Stanford University Press, 1994).
10. Axton, 20–23.
11. Rick Allen has demonstrated that the phrase was coined not by Dickens, but by Irish author John Fisher Murray. He notes that in Murray's writing, the phrase originally conveyed, not "the strange allure of physically unsavory aspects of the city," but rather a different urban paradox: the lonely crowd. "John Fisher Murray, Dickens, and 'The Attraction of Repulsion'," *Dickens Quarterly* 16, 3 (September 1999): 139–59; 140. For Dickens, however, the sense remained one of visceral reaction to the urban space.
12. Eigner, 4.
13. Ibid., 9.
14. Dickens, "A Christmas Tree," 832.
15. Dickens, *Letters,* vol. 5, 52 (April 3, 1847), in DeMarcus, 12; Kotzin, 35.
16. Dickens, *David Copperfield* (London: Penguin, 1995), 43.
17. Ibid., 555.
18. Catherine Robson, "Down Ditches, on Doorsteps, in Rivers: *Oliver Twist*'s Journey to Respectability," *Dickens Studies Annual* 29 (2000): 75.
19. See Kotzin, 105.
20. Dickens, *Our Mutual Friend* (London: Penguin, 1997), 50. All subsequent references appear parenthetically in the text. There is no acknowledged authoritative modern text for *Our Mutual Friend,* but Oxford World's Classics and Penguin offer the most recent editions, 1998 and 1997 respectively, both of which are published from Dickens's first, two-volume edition of 1865. I have chosen the Penguin edition as being more widely available.
21. Gail Turley Houston, *Consuming Fictions: Gender, Class and Hunger in Dickens's Novels* (Carbondale: Southern Illinois University Press, 1994), 163. Notably, Dickens's high-society scenes are staged during opulent dinners at the Veneerings, where the guests' endless gorging upon fine provisions is itself a thin veneer: it is in this setting that the wealthy middle classes tear into others' business with as much savagery as rapacity.
22. Gallagher, "The Bio-Economics of *Our Mutual Friend,*" in *Fragments for a History of the Human Body,* vol. 3, ed. Michael Feher et al. (New York: Zone, 1989), 345–65.
23. Gallagher, "Malthus and Mayhew," 101.
24. Ibid., 104.
25. Ibid.
26. Gallagher, "Bio-Economics," 361.
27. Ibid., 360.
28. Ibid.
29. Kotzin, 60; DeMarcus, 13.

30. "paraphrase, *n.*," *Oxford English Dictionary Online*.

31. "para, *prefix*" and "phrase, *n.*," ibid.

32. In drawing our attention to the toy Noah's Ark the Boffins buy for Johnny, Dickens points to another lost innocence: "they would have hurt and tired him, but for an amazing circumstance which laid hold of his attention. This was no less than the appearance on his own little platform in pairs of All Creation on its way into his own particular ark" (326). There is a striking return here of Charles Dickens's "own particular ark" and with it, the premature death of another child. Notably neither Betty nor Johnny die by drowning, but the associations between wolfish devouring and engulfing waters here are too insistent to ignore, with Betty Higden laid in a grave within sight of the Thames (507), and with little Johnny exiting the world as another John Harmon looks soberly down upon him, remembering, no doubt, another virtual drowning.

33. I am grateful to David Simpson for pointing out to me that Riderhood's cap is, after all, a *fur* cap; Riderhood thus "dresses up" as Little Red Cap and the wolf simultaneously in physical as well as metaphysical terms.

34. Houston, 155.

35. Mary Poovey, "Reading History in Literature: Speculation and Virtue in *Our Mutual Friend*," in *Historical Criticism and the Challenge of Theory*, ed. Janet Levarie Smarr (Urbana: University of Illinois Press, 1993), 67.

36. Ibid., 69.

37. Gallagher, "Bio-Economics," 364.

38. DeMarcus, 13–14.

39. Gallagher, "Bio-Economics," 362.

40. Wolfreys, 18.

41. See also Audrey Jaffe, "Our Mutual Friend: On Taking the Reader by Surprise," in *Vanishing Points: Dickens, Narrative, and the Subject of Omniscience* (Berkeley: University of California Press, 1991).

42. Rogue Riderhood is a figure that burlesques the fairy tale Little Red Riding Hood— and perhaps even burlesques the theatrical Little Red Riding Hood. For if Rogue Riderhood is made to perform both Wolf and Red Riding Hood, then following the stock characters of middle- and late-Victorian pantomime, Riderhood is the "skin part" (the animal character) and the "principal boy" (a girl dressed in breeches) simultaneously. And if this is so, then Dickens means for this grotesque body to deny the pleasures of the consumptive gaze at the theatrical girl.

43. Emily Allen, *Theater Figures: The Production of the Nineteenth-Century British Novel* (Columbus: Ohio State University Press, 2003), 28.

44. Renata Miller, "Child Killers and the Competition Between Late Victorian Theater and the Novel," *Modern Language Quarterly* 66:2 (June 2005): 217, 216.

45. *David Copperfield*, 313.

46. See, for example, Poovey, 60.

47. See also Jaffe; Carol MacKay, "Narrating Self-Creation: John Harmon's Soliloquy in *Our Mutual Friend*," The Dickens Project, University of California, Santa Cruz, "*Our Mutual Friend*: The Scholarly Pages," accessed August 11, 2013, http://omf.ucsc.edu/scholarship/article-archive/narrating-self-creation.html.

48. DeMarcus, 14, 15.

49. Ibid., 14.

50. Other such characters are Pickwick in *Pickwick Papers* (see Part 1, 54), Dick Swiveller in *The Old Curiosity Shop*, Master Charlie Bates in *Oliver Twist*, and Charlie Neckett in *Bleak House*.

Notes to Conclusion

1. Quoted in Michael Millgate, *Thomas Hardy: A Biography Revisited* (Oxford: Oxford Univ. Press, 2004): 295.
2. Andrew Lang, review in *The New Review* (February 1892): 248.
3. Nathan Hensley, "What is a Network? (And Who is Andrew Lang?)," *Romantics and Victorians on the Net*, special issue, "The Andrew Lang Effect: Network, Discipline, Method" (forthcoming).
4. Marian Roalfe Cox, *Cinderella: Three Hundred and Forty-five Variants of Cinderella, Catskin, and Cap O'Rushes* (London: David Nutt for the Folk-Lore Society, 1893), xiii.
5. Andrew Lang, ed. *Perrault's Popular Tales* (Oxford: Clarendon, 1888), xvii.
6. Lang, "Tales," *Encyclopaedia Britannica*, 11th ed. (New York: Encyclopaedia Britannica Inc., 1911), 370.
7. See Introduction.
8. James George Frazer, *The Golden Bough: A Study in Magic and Religion*, vol. 1 (London: Macmillan, 1900), 62; see also Supritha Rajan, "Networked Magic: Lang and the Science of Self-Interest," *Romantics and Victorians on the Net*, special issue, "The Andrew Lang Effect: Network, Discipline, Method" (forthcoming).
9. Lang, *The Crimson Fairy Book* (London: Longmans, 1903), v. All subsequent references appear parenthetically in the text.
10. Lang, *The Lilac Fairy Book* (London: Longmans, 1910), vii–viii. All subsequent references appear parenthetically in the text.
11. Lang, *The Violet Fairy Book* (London: Longmans, Green and Co., 1901), vii. All subsequent references appear parenthetically in the text.
12. Lang, *The Brown Fairy Book* (London: Longmans, 1904), viii.
13. Andrew Lang, "Literary Plagiarism," *Contemporary Review* 51 (1887): 833.
14. Letitia Henville, "Lang's 'Literary Plagiarism': Reification, Immaterial Things, and the Literary Market," *Romantics and Victorians on the Net*, special issue, "The Andrew Lang Effect: Network, Discipline, Method" (forthcoming).
15. See Chapter 2.
16. Lang, *The Olive Fairy Book* (London: Longmans, 1907); vi.

BIBLIOGRAPHY

Primary Sources

Anonymous. "The Cinderella of 1851." *Punch* 21 (1851): 132–33.
———. "The Exhibition Plague." *Punch* 19 (1849): 191.
———. "Glass Houses of Parliament." *Punch: or the London Charivari* 19 (1849): 81.
———. "Harlequin Fairy Morgana." *All the Year Round* 12 (1864): 40–48.
———. "The Legend of Briar Root." *Punch* 98 (1890): 209.
———. "Louisa Vinning." *Mirror of Literature, Amusement and Instruction* 28 (November 13, 1841): 307–8.
———. "Mr. F. W. N. Bayley" [Obituary]. *Gentleman's Magazine* 39 (March 1853): 324.
———. n.t. *Punch* 21 (1851): 5.
———. "Orangeism in the Crystal Palace!" *Punch* 21 (1851): 15.
———. "A Remarkable Instance of Musical Powers in a Child." *American Phrenological Journal and Miscellany* 3 (1841): 204–7.
Basile, Giambattista. "Sun, Moon, and Talia" ("*Sole, Luna e Talia*"). In *The Pentamerone* (*Il Pentamerone*), trans. Richard Burton, 372–76. London: Spring Books, n.d.
Bayley, F. W. N. *The Exhibition*. London: Darton & Co., 1851.
———. *Little Red Riding Hood*. London: Orr, 1846.
Bessemer, Sir Henry. *Sir Henry Bessemer, F. R. S.: An Autobiography*. London: Offices of Engineering, 1905.
Bewick, John. *Fabliaux*. London: W. Bulmer, 1796.
Bewick, Thomas. *The Fables of Aesop*. Newcastle: Walker, 1818.
———. *History of British Birds*. Newcastle: Beilby and Bewick, 1797; Newcastle: Walker, 1804.
———. *Select Fables*. Newcastle: Saint, 1776.
Brand, John. *Observations on the Popular Antiquities of Great Britain*. 1777. Edited by Henry Ellis. 3 vols. London: Bell and Daldy, 1873.
Bray, Anna Eliza. *The Borders of the Tamar and the Tavy*. London: W. Kent and Co., 1879; originally

published as *Traditions, Legends, Superstitions, and Sketches of Devonshire on the Borders of the Tamar and the Tavy* (London: J. Murray, 1838).

———. *A Peep at the Pixies*. London: Grant and Griffith, 1854.

Bridgeman, J. V., and H. Sutherland Edwards. *Little Red Riding Hood: or, Harlequin and the Wolf in Granny's Clothing*. London: printed and sold in Royal English Opera theater, Covent Garden, 1859.

Brightwen, Eliza. *Memoir of the Crystal Palace*. http://freepages.genealogy.rootsweb.ancestry.com/~thegrove/exhibition.html.

Brontë, Charlotte. *Jane Eyre*. London: Penguin, 1996.

———. *The Letters of Charlotte Brontë: With a Selection of Letters by Family and Friends*, vol. 1. Edited by Margaret Smith. Oxford: Oxford University Press, 2002.

Brontë, Emily. *Wuthering Heights*. London: Penguin, 1995.

Brough, John Cargill. *The Fairy Tales of Science: A Book for Youth*. London: Griffith and Farran, 1858.

Buckingham, Leicester. *Little Red Riding Hood and the Fairies of the Rose, Shamrock, and Thistle*. London: Thomas Hales Lacy, 1861.

Burne-Jones, Lady Georgiana. *Memorials of Edward Burne-Jones*. 2 vols. London: Macmillan, 1904.

Burns, Robert. "On the Late Captain Grosse's Peregrinations." 1793. In *The Works of Robert Burns*, ed. William Scott Douglass, 233–36. Edinburgh: William Patterson, 1877.

Carlyle, Thomas. *Past and Present*. In *The Norton Anthology of English Literature*. 7th ed., vol. 2. ed. M. H. Abrams et al. New York: Norton, 2000.

Chaucer, Geoffrey. "The Wife of Bath's Tale." In *The Riverside Chaucer*. 3rd ed., ed. Larry D. Benson, 3–328. Boston: Houghton Mifflin, 1987.

Coleridge, Samuel Taylor. *Letters of Samuel Taylor Coleridge*. Edited by Ernest Hartley Coleridge. 2 vols. Boston: Houghton, Mifflin and Company, 1895.

———. *On the Constitution of the Church and State*. 1830. London: Dent, 1972.

Cox, Marian Roalfe. *Cinderella: Three Hundred and Forty-five Variants of Cinderella, Catskin, and Cap O'Rushes*. London: David Nutt for the Folk-Lore Society, 1893.

Croker, Thomas Crofton. *Legends and Traditions of the South of Ireland*. 1825. Cork: The Collins Press, 1998.

Curtin, Jeremiah. *Tales of the Fairies and of the Ghost World, Collected from Oral Tradition in South-West Munster*. Boston: Little, Brown, & Company, 1895.

Dickens, Charles. "A Christmas Tree." In *Christmas Books and Reprinted Pieces*, 825–40. New York: John Lovell, 1879; originally published in *Household Words*, December 1850.

———. *David Copperfield*. London: Penguin, 1995.

———. "Frauds on the Fairies." *Household Words* (October 1, 1853): 97–100.

———. "Gaslight Fairies." *Household Words* (February 10, 1855): 26–28.

———. *Hard Times*. London: Penguin, 2003.

———. *Nicholas Nickleby*. London: Penguin, 2003.

———. "Nurse's Stories." In *The Uncommercial Traveller*. London: Chapman and Hall, 1868.

———. *The Old Curiosity Shop*. London: Penguin, 2000.

———. *Our Mutual Friend*. London: Penguin, 1997.

———. *The Pickwick Papers*. London: Penguin, 1999.

———. "The Wonders of 1851." *Household Words* (December 28, 1850): 388–92.

Doyle, Richard. *An overland journey to the Great Exhibition, showing a few extra articles and visitors*. London: Chapman and Hall, 1851.

Eliot, George. "Looking Backward." In *Impressions of Theophrastus Such*. Edinburgh and London: William Blackwood and Sons, 1879.

———. *Middlemarch*. London: Bantam, 1992.

Fitzgerald, Percy. *The World Behind the Scenes*. London: Chatto and Windus, 1881.
Frazer, James George. *The Golden Bough: A Study in Magic and Religion*. 2 vols. London: Macmillan, 1900.
Freud, Sigmund and D. E. Oppenheim. *Dreams in Folklore*. Trans. A. M. O. Richards. New York: International Universities Press, 1958.
Grimm, Jacob, and Wilhelm Grimm. "Little Briar Rose" ("Dornröschen"). In *German Fairy Tales (Kinder- und Hausmärchen)*, ed. Helmut Brackert and Volkmar Sander, trans. Margaret Hunt. New York: Continuum, 1985.
———. "Rumpelstiltskin" ("Rumpelstilzchen"). In *German Fairy Tales (Kinder- und Hausmärchen)*, ed. Helmut Brackert and Volkmar Sander, trans. Margaret Hunt. New York: Continuum, 1985.
Hardy, Thomas. "Tryst at an Ancient Earthworks." In *A Changed Man and Other Tales*, 171–83. New York and London: Harper and Brothers, 1913.
Harland, John, and T. T. Wilkinson. *Lancashire Folk-Lore: Illustrative of the Superstitious Beliefs and Practices, Local Customs and Usages of the People of the County Palatine*. London: Frederick Warne and Co, 1867.
Harrison, Antony H., ed. *The Letters of Christina Rossetti: Vol. 1, 1843–1873*. Charlottesville: The University Press of Virginia, 1997.
Hegel, Georg Wilhelm Friedrich. In *Hegel's Aesthetics: Lectures on Fine Art*, vol. II. Ed. and trans. T. M. Knox. Oxford: Oxford University Press, 1998.
Hopkins, Gerard Manley. "To His Watch." In *The Poems of Gerard Manley Hopkins*. 4th ed., ed. W. H. Garner and N. H. MacKenzie. Oxford: Oxford University Press, 1970.
Hughes, Thomas. "Anonymous Journalism." *Macmillan's Magazine* 5 (1861): 157–68.
Jacobs, Joseph. *Celtic Fairy Tales*. New York: A.L. Burt, 1892.
———. *English Fairy Tales*. London: David Nutt, 1890.
———. *Indian Fairy Tales*. New York: G. P. Putnam's Sons and A. L. Burt; London: David Nutt, 1892.
Keats, John. "Eve of St. Agnes." In *The Complete Poems of John Keats*, ed. Jack Stillinger, 229–39. Cambridge, MA: Harvard University Press, 1982.
———. "Fall of Hyperion." In *The Complete Poems of John Keats*, ed. Jack Stillinger, 361–73. Cambridge, MA: Harvard University Press, 1982.
———. "Ode to a Nightingale." In *The Complete Poems of John Keats*, ed. Jack Stillinger, 279–81. Cambridge, MA: Harvard University Press, 1982.
———. "Sleep and Poetry." In *The Complete Poems of John Keats*, ed. Jack Stillinger, 37–47. Cambridge, MA: Harvard University Press, 1982.
———. "Sonnet to Sleep." In *The Complete Poems of John Keats*, ed. Jack Stillinger, 275. Cambridge, MA: Harvard University Press, 1982.
Keightley, Thomas. *The Fairy Mythology: Illustrative of the Romance and Superstition of Various Countries*. 1828. London: Wildwood House Ltd, 1981.
Lang, Andrew. *The Brown Fairy Book*. London: Longmans, 1904.
———. *The Crimson Fairy Book*. London: Longmans, 1903.
———. *The Lilac Fairy Book*. London: Longmans, 1910.
———. *The Olive Fairy Book*. London: Longmans, 1907.
———. *The Violet Fairy Book*. London: Longmans, 1901.
———. "Literary Plagiarism." *Contemporary Review* 51 (1887): 831–40.
———. Review in *The Daily News* (October 11, 1892).
———. Review in *The New Review* (February 1892).
———. "Tales." In *Encyclopaedia Britannica*. 11th ed., 369–71. New York: Encyclopaedia Britannica Inc., 1911.
———. *The Violet Fairy Book*. London: Longmans, Green and Co., 1901.

Lyell, James C. *Fancy Pigeons*. London: The Bazaar, 1881.
Mayhew, Henry. *1851, or the Adventures of Mr. and Mrs. Sandboys and Family*. London: David Bogue, 1851.
———. *The London Street Folk, Vol. 1: London Labor and the London Poor*. London: Griffin, Bohn, and Co, 1861.
Miller, Hugh. *First Impressions of England and Its People*. New York: Robert Carter and Brothers, 1882.
Montague, Charles. *Recollections of an Equestrian Manager*. London: W. & R. Chambers, 1881.
Official Catalogue of the Great Exhibition of the Works of Industry of All Nations, 1851. London: Spicer, 1851.
Onwhyn, Thomas. *Mr. and Mrs. Brown's Visit to London to See the Great Exhibition of All Nations: How they were astonished at its wonders, inconvenienced by its crowds, and frightened out if their wits by the Foreigners*. London: Ackerman, n.d.
Perrault, Charles. *The Fairy Tales of Charles Perrault (Histoires ou contes du temps passé)*. Trans. A. E. Johnson. New York: Dover, 1969.
———. In *Perrault's Popular Tales*. Ed. Andrew Lang. Oxford: Clarendon, 1888.
Planché, J. R. *Rodolph the Wolf; or, Columbine Red Riding-Hood*. London: John Lowndes, 1818.
Pope, Alexander. *The Dunciad*. Book III. London: Lawton Gilliver, 1727.
Ritchie, Anne Thackeray. "The Sleeping Beauty in the Wood." In *Five Old Friends and a Young Prince*, 1–26. London: Smith and Elder, 1868.
Ritson, Joseph. *Fairy Tales*. London: Thomas Davison, 1831.
Rollins, Hyder Edward, ed. *The Letters of John Keats: Volume II, 1814–1821*. Cambridge, MA: Harvard University Press, 1958.
Rossetti, Christina. "Goblin Market." In *Christina Rossetti: The Complete Poems*, 5–20. London: Penguin, 2001.
———. "The Prince's Progress." In *Christina Rossetti: The Complete Poems*, 89–104. London: Penguin, 2001.
Rossetti, William Michael, ed. *Ruskin: Rossetti: Preraphaelitism Papers 1854–1862*. New York: Dodd, Mead and Co.; London: George Allen, 1899.
Ruskin, John. *The Stones of Venice. Volume the Second: The Sea Stories*. London: Smith, Elder and Co, 1853.
Scott, Walter. *The Lady of the Lake*. Ed. William J. Rolfe. Boston: J.R. Osgood, 1883.
Spielman, M. H. *The History of Punch*. London: Cassell and Co, 1895.
———. "In Memoriam." *Magazine of Art* 21 (1898): 522–24.
Taylor, Una. "Burne-Jones, His Ethics, and Art." *Edinburgh Review* 189 (April 1899).
Tennyson, Alfred. "The Day Dream." In *The Poems of Tennyson in three volumes*. Vol. II, ed. Christopher Ricks, 48–59. Essex, UK: Longman, 1987.
———. "The Epic." In *The Poems of Tennyson in three volumes*. Vol. II, ed. Christopher Ricks, 1–19. Essex, UK: Longman, 1987.
———. *In Memoriam*. New York: Norton, 2003.
———. "Lilian." In *The Poems of Tennyson in three volumes*. Vol. I, ed. Christopher Ricks, 200–201. Essex, UK: Longman, 1987.
———. "Locksley Hall." In *The Poems of Tennyson in three volumes*. Vol. II, ed. Christopher Ricks, 120–30. Essex, UK: Longman, 1987.
———. "Rosalind." In *The Poems of Tennyson in three volumes*. Vol. I, ed. Christopher Ricks, 471–78. Essex, UK: Longman, 1987.
Wallace, P. "On the Cultivation of Exotic Fruits." *Journal of the Royal Horticultural Society* 8 (1853): 47–52.

Weylland, John. *These Fifty Years, Being the Jubilee Volume of the London City Mission.* London: Partridge, 1884.
White, Gilbert. *The Natural History and Antiquities of Selbourne.* London: George Routledge and Sons, 1891.
Wilkinson, James John Garth. *The Human Body and Its Connexion with Man: Illustrated By the Principal Organs.* London: Chapman and Hall, 1851.
Wordsworth, William. *The Fourteen-Book Prelude.* 1850. Ed. W. J. B. Owen. Ithaca, NY: Cornell University Press, 1985.

Secondary Sources

Aarne, Anti, and Stith Thompson. *The Types of the Folktale.* 2nd revision, Folklore Fellows Communication No. 184. Helsinki: Academia Scientiarum Fennica, 1973.
Adams, James Eli. "Women Red in Tooth and Claw: Nature and the Feminine in Tennyson and Darwin." *Victorian Studies* 33:1 (1989): 7–27.
Allen, Emily. *Theater Figures: The Production of the Nineteenth-Century British Novel.* Columbus: Ohio State University Press, 2003.
Allen, Rick. "John Fisher Murray, Dickens, and 'The Attraction of Repulsion'." *Dickens Quarterly* 16:3 (September 1999): 139–59.
Alter, Robert. *Imagined Cities: Urban Experience and the Language of the Novel.* New Haven, CT: Yale University Press, 2005.
Anderson, Benedict. *Imagined Communities: Reflections on the Origin and Spread of Nationalism.* London: Verso, 1991.
Andres, Sophia. "The Unhistoric in History: George Eliot's Challenge to Victorian Historiography." *Clio* 26:1 (1996): 79–96.
Arcana, Judith. "St. Agnes' Source." *Journal of Rural Studies* 2 (1987): 43–57.
Arseneau, Mary. "Madeline, Mermaids and Medusas in 'The Eve of St. Agnes'." *Papers on Language and Literature* 33 (1997): 227–43.
Ashton, Rosemary. *George Eliot: A Life.* London: Penguin, 1996.
Auerbach, Jeffrey. *The Great Exhibition of 1851: A Nation on Display.* New Haven, CT: Yale University Press, 1999.
Axton, William. *Circle of Fire: Dickens' Vision and Style and the Popular Victorian Theater.* Lexington: University Press of Kentucky, 1966.
Bachman, Maria, and Don Richard Cox, eds. *Reality's Dark Light: The Sensational Wilkie Collins.* Knoxville: University of Tennessee Press, 2003.
Bakhtin, Mikhail. "Epic and Novel: Toward a Methodology for the Study of the Novel." In *The Dialogic Imagination*, ed. Michael Holquist, 3–40. Austin: University of Texas Press, 1981.
Barzuli, Shuli. "The Bluebeard Barometer: Charles Dickens and Captain Murderer." *Victorian Literature and Culture* 32:2 (2004): 505–24.
Beer, Gillian. *Darwin's Plots: Evolutionary Narrative in Darwin, George Eliot, and Nineteenth-Century Fiction.* Cambridge: Cambridge University Press, 2000.
———. "Myth and the Single Consciousness: *Middlemarch* and 'The Lifted Veil'." In *This Particular Web: Essays on Middlemarch*, ed. Ian Adam, 91–115. Toronto: University of Toronto Press, 1975.
Bellanca, Mary Ellen. "Recollecting Nature: George Eliot's 'Ilfracombe Journal' and Victorian Women's Natural History Writing." *Modern Language Studies* 27:3/4 (1997): 19–36.
Benjamin, Walter. *The Arcades Project.* Harvard: Belknap, 2002.

Bennett, Andrew J. "'Hazardous Magic': Vision and Inscription in 'The Eve of St. Agnes'." *Keats-Shelley Journal* 41 (1992): 100–121.
Bertelsen, Lance. "Popular Entertainment and Instruction, Literary and Dramatic: Chapbooks, Advice Books, Almanacs, Ballads, Farces, Pantomimes, Prints and Shows." In *The Cambridge History of English Literature, 1660–1780*, ed. John Richetti, 61–86. Cambridge: Cambridge University Press, 2005.
Bettelheim, Bruno. *The Uses of Enchantment: The Meaning and Importance of Fairy Tales*. New York: Knopf, 1976.
Blair, Kirstie. *Victorian Poetry and the Culture of the Heart*. Oxford: Clarendon Press, 2006.
Bottigheimer, Ruth B. "Fertility Control and the Birth of the Modern European Fairy-Tale Heroine." *Marvels and Tales* 14:1 (2000): 64–79.
———. *Grimm's Bad Girls and Bold Boys: The Moral and Social Vision of the Tales*. New Haven, CT: Yale University Press, 1987.
Boulmelha, Penny. "George Eliot and the End of Realism." In *Women Reading Women's Writing*, ed. Sue Roe, 13–35. New York: St. Martin's Press, 1987.
Bowen, John. *Other Dickens: Pickwick to Chuzzlewit*. Oxford: Oxford University Press, 2000.
———. "Pickwick and the Postal Principle." *Imprimatur* 1:2 (1996): 180–85.
Bown, Nicola. *Fairies in Nineteenth-Century Art and Literature*. Cambridge: Cambridge University Press, 2001.
Brown, James D., and Stephen S. Stratton. *British Musical Biography: A Dictionary of Musical Artists, Authors and Composers Born in the British Isles*. Birmingham: S.S. Stratton, 1897.
Brunvand, Jan Harold. *The Study of American Folklore: An Introduction*. 2nd ed. New York: W.W. Norton, 1978.
Bryan, George B., and Wolfgang Mieder. "'As Sam Weller Said, when Finding Himself on the Stage': Wellerisms in Dramatizations of Charles Dickens' Pickwick Papers." *Proverbium: Yearbook of International Proverb Scholarship* 11 (1994): 57–76.
Buckley, Jerome. *The Triumph of Time: A Study of the Victorian Concepts of Time, History, Progress and Decadence*. Cambridge, MA: Harvard University Press, 1966.
Burke, Peter. "Reflections on the Cultural History of Time." *Viator* 35 (2004): 617–26.
Butt, John, and Kathleen Tillotson. *Dickens at Work*. London: Methuen, 1957.
Buzard, James. *Disorienting Fiction: The Autoethnographic Work of Nineteenth-Century British Novels*. Princeton, NJ: Princeton University Press, 2005.
Buzard, James, Joseph W. Childers, and Eileen Gillooly, eds. *Victorian Prism: Refractions of the Crystal Palace*. Charlottesville: University of Virginia Press, 2007.
Campbell, Elizabeth. *Fortune's Wheel: Dickens and the Iconography of Women's Time*. Athens: Ohio University Press, 2003.
———. "Of Mothers and Merchants: Female Economics in Christina Rossetti's 'Goblin Market'." *Victorian Studies* 33 (1990): 393–410.
Carignan, Michael. "Fiction as History or History as Fiction? George Eliot, Haydon White, and Nineteenth-Century Historicism." *Clio* 29:4 (2000): 395–415.
Carpenter, Mary Wilson. "'Eat Me, Drink Me, Love Me': The Consumable Female Body in Christina Rossetti's Goblin Market." *Victorian Poetry* 29:4 (1991): 415–34.
Carroll, David. "*Middlemarch* and the Externality of Fact." In *This Particular Web: Essays on Middlemarch*, ed. Ian Adam, 73–90. Toronto: University of Toronto Press, 1975.
Childers, Joseph W. "Peering Back: Colonials and Exhibitions." In *Victorian Prism: Refractions of the Crystal Palace*, ed. James Buzard, Joseph W. Childers, and Eileen Gillooly. Charlottesville: University of Virginia Press, 2007.
Clarke, Micael M. "Brontë's *Jane Eyre* and the Grimms' 'Cinderella.'" *SEL* 40:4 (Autumn, 2000): 695-710.

Colwell, Mary. "Organization in Pickwick Papers." *Dickens Studies* 3 (1967): 90–110.
Cotsell, Michael. "The Pickwick Papers and Travel: A Critical Diversion." *Dickens Quarterly* 3 (1986): 5–17.
Cox, Philip. *Reading Adaptations: Novels and Verse Narratives on the Stage, 1790–1840*. Manchester: Manchester University Press, 2000.
Daniels, Morna. "Little Red Riding-Hood." *Electronic British Library Journal*, Article 5 (2006): 1–8. http://www.bl.uk/eblj/2006articles/pdf/article5.pdf.
Davis, John. *The Great Exhibition*. Stroud, U.K.: Sutton Publishing, 1999.
Davis, Tracy C. *Actresses as Working Women: Their Social Identity in Victorian Culture*. London: Routledge, 1991.
———. "Do You Believe in Fairies?: The Hiss of Dramatic License." *Theatre Journal* 57:1 (March 2005): 57–81.
———. "What are Fairies For?" In *The Performing Society: Nineteenth-Century Theatre's History*, ed. Tracy C. Davis and Peter Holland, 32–59. New York: Palgrave Macmillan, 2007.
de la Sizeraine, Robert. "In Memoriam." *Magazine of Art* 21 (1898): 515–19.
Degh, Linda. "What Is the Legend After All?" *Contemporary Legend* 1 (1991): 11–38.
Delany, Sheila, ed. *A Legend of Holy Women: A Translation of Osbern Bokenham's Legends of Holy Women*. Notre Dame, IN: University of Notre Dame Press, 1992.
DeMarcus, Cynthia. "Wolves Within and Without: Dickens's Transformation of 'Little Red Riding Hood' in Our Mutual Friend." *Dickens Quarterly* 7:1 (March 1995): 11–17.
Dillon, Steven. "Watches, Dials and Clocks: Victorian Illustrations of Time." In *The Victorian Illustrated Book*, ed. Richard Maxwell, 52–90. Charlottesville: University Press of Virginia, 2002.
Donovan, Leslie A. *Women's Saints' Lives in Old English Prose*. Suffolk: Boydell and Brewer, 1999.
Dorson, Richard. *The British Folklorists: A History*. Chicago: University of Chicago Press, 1968.
Duffy, Maureen. *The Erotic World of Faery*. London: Hodder and Stoughton, 1972.
Dundes, Alan. *Folklore Matters*. Knoxville: University of Tennessee Press, 1989.
———. *Little Red Riding Hood: A Casebook*. Madison: University of Wisconsin Press, 1989.
Easley, Alexis. *First Person Anonymous: Women Writers and Victorian Print Media, 1830–70*. Aldershot: Ashgate, 2004.
Eberhard, Wolfram. "The Story of Grandaunt Tiger." In *Alan Dundes, Little Red Riding Hood: A Case Book*, 21–63. Madison: University of Wisconsin Press, 1989.
Edwards, Steve. "The Accumulation of Knowledge, or William Whewell's Eye." In *The Great Exhibition of 1851: New Interdisciplinary Essays*, ed. Louise Purbrick, 26–52. Manchester: Manchester University Press, 2001.
Eigner, Edwin. *The Dickens Pantomime*. Berkeley: University of California Press, 1988.
Fabb, Nigel, and Morris Halle. "Metrical Complexity in Christina Rossetti's Verse." *College Literature* 32:2 (2006): 91–114.
The Faringdon Trustees. *The Faringdon Collection*. Hampshire, England: BAS Printers Limited, 1998.
Feltes, N. N. "The Moment of Pickwick, or the Production of a Commodity Text." *Literature and History: A Journal for the Humanities* 10 (1984): 203–17.
———. "To Saunter, To Hurry: Dickens, Time, and Industrial Capitalism." *Victorian Studies* 20 (1977): 245–67.
Fields, Beverly. "Keats and the Tongueless Nightingale: Some Unheard Melodies in 'The Eve of St. Agnes'." *Wordsworth Circle* 14 (1983): 246–50.
Fine, Gary Alan. *Manufacturing Tales: Sex and Money in Contemporary Legends*. Knoxville: University of Tennessee Press, 1992.
Fitzgerald, Penelope. *Edward Burne-Jones: A Biography*. London: Michael Joseph, 1975.

Ford, George. *Keats and the Victorians: A Study of His Influence and Rise to Fame, 1821–1895*. London: Arcehon, 1962.
Franklin, J. Jeffrey. *Serious Play: The Cultural Form of the Nineteenth-Century Realist Novel*. Philadelphia: University of Pennsylvania Press, 1999.
Freud, Sigmund, and D. E. Oppenheim. *Dreams in Folklore*. Trans. A. M. O. Richards. New York: International Universities Press, 1958.
Gallagher, Catherine. "The Bio-Economics of *Our Mutual Friend*." In *Fragments for a History of the Human Body*, vol. 3, ed. Michael Feher et al., 345–65. New York: Zone, 1989.
———. "The Body Versus the Social Body in the Works of Thomas Malthus and Henry Mayhew." *Representations* 14 (1986): 83–106.
———. "George Eliot and *Daniel Deronda*: The Prostitute and the Jewish Question." In *Sex, Politics and Science in the Nineteenth-Century Novel*, ed. Ruth Bernard Yeazell, 39–62. Baltimore: The Johns Hopkins University Press, 1986.
Ganzl, Kurt. *Lydia Thompson, the Queen of Burlesque*. New York: Routledge, 2002.
Gates, Barbara. "Introduction: Why Victorian Natural History?" *Victorian Literature and Culture* 35 (2007): 539–49.
Gaull, Marilyn. "Pantomime as Satire: Mocking a Broken Charm." In *The Satiric Eye: Forms of Satire in the Romantic Period*, ed. Stephen E. Jones, 207–24. New York: Palgrave, 2003.
Gibbs-Smith, C. H. (ed.) and the Victoria and Albert Museum. *The Great Exhibition of 1851: A Commemorative Album* (London: Her Majesty's Stationary Office, 1964).
Gilbert, Sandra, and Susan Gubar. *The Madwoman in the Attic: The Woman Writer and the Nineteenth-Century Literary Imagination*. 2nd ed. New Haven, CT: Yale University Press, 2000.
Gilbreath, Marcia. "The Etymology of Porphyro's Name in 'The Eve of St. Agnes'." *Keats-Shelley Journal* 37 (1988): 20–25.
Gillooly, Eileen. "Rhetorical Remedies for Taxonomic Troubles." In *Victorian Prism: Refractions of the Crystal Palace*, ed. James Buzard, Joseph W. Childers, and Eileen Gillooly, 23–39. Charlottesville: University of Virginia Press, 2007.
Givner, Jessie. "Industrial History, Pre-industrial Literature: George Eliot's Middlemarch." *ELH* 69 (2002): 223–44.
Gold, Barri. "The Consolation of Physics: Tennyson's Thermodynamic Solution." *PMLA* 117:3 (May 2002): 449–64.
Green, Hilary, Stephanie Fraser, and Judith Johnston. *Gender and the Victorian Periodical*. Cambridge: Cambridge University Press, 2003.
Groth, Helen. *Victorian Photography and Literary Nostalgia*. Oxford: Oxford University Press, 2003.
Gurney, Peter. "An Appropriated Space: The Great Exhibition, The Crystal Palace, and the Working Class." In *The Great Exhibition of 1851: New Interdisciplinary Essays*, ed. Louise Purbrick, 114–45. Manchester: Manchester University Press, 2001.
Harries, Elizabeth. *Twice Upon a Time: Women Writers and the History of the Fairy Tale*. Princeton, NJ: Princeton University Press, 2001.
Harrison, Antony H. "Christina Rossetti: Renunciation as Intervention." In *Victorian Poets and the Politics of Culture: Discourse and Ideology*, ed. Antony H. Harrison, 125–64. Charlottesville, VA: The University Press of Virginia, 1998.
Helsinger, Elizabeth. "Consumer Power and the Utopia of Desire: Christina Rossetti's 'Goblin Market'." *ELH* 58 (1991): 903–33.
Hensley, Nathan. "What Is a Network? (And Who Is Andrew Lang?)." *Romantics and Victorians on the Net*, special issue, "The Andrew Lang Effect: Network, Discipline, Method" (forthcoming).
Henville, Letitia. "Lang's 'Literary Plagiarism': Reification, Immaterial Things, and the Literary

Market." *Romantics and Victorians on the Net,* special issue, "The Andrew Lang Effect: Network, Discipline, Method (forthcoming).

Hertz, Neil. "Recognizing Casaubon." In *The End of the Line: Essays on Psychoanalysis and the Sublime.* New York: Columbia University Press, 1985.

Hill, Marylu. "'Eat Me, Drink Me, Love Me': Eucharist and the Erotic Body in Christina Rossetti's 'Goblin Market'." *Victorian Poetry* 43:4 (Winter 2005): 455–72.

Holt, Terrence. "Men Sell Not Such in Any Town: Exchange in 'Goblin Market'." *Victorian Poetry* 28:1 (1990): 51–67.

Hood, James. *Divining Desire: Tennyson and the Poetics of Transcendence.* Aldershot: Ashgate, 2000.

Houston, Gail Turley. *Consuming Fictions: Gender, Class and Hunger in Dickens's Novels.* Carbondale: Southern Illinois University Press, 1994.

Hughes, John. "'Hang There Like Fruit, My Soul': Tennyson's Feminine Imaginings." *Victorian Poetry* 45:2 (2007): 95–115.

Hyde, Virginia. "George Eliot's Arthuriad: Heroes and Ideology in Middlemarch." *Papers on Language and Literature* 24:44 (1988): 404–11.

Jaffe, Audrey. "Our Mutual Friend: On Taking the Reader by Surprise." In *Vanishing Points: Dickens, Narrative, and the Subject of Omniscience.* Berkeley: University of California Press, 1991.

James, Henry. "George Eliot's Life." *Atlantic Monthly* 55:331 (May 1885): 668–78.

Kaplan, Carla. "Girl Talk: Jane Eyre and the Romance of Women's Narration." *NOVEL: A Forum on Fiction* 30:1 (Autumn 1996): 5–31.

Keats House and Museum Historical and Descriptive Guide. Hampstead: n.p., n.d.

Kerrigan, John. "Keats and Lucrece." *Shakespeare Survey* 41 (1988): 103–18.

Knopfelmacher, U. C. "Fusing Fact and Myth: the New Reality of *Middlemarch.*" In *This Particular Web: Essays on Middlemarch,* ed. Ian Adam, 43–71. Toronto: University of Toronto Press, 1975.

———. *Ventures Into Fairyland: Victorians, Fairy Tales and Femininity.* Chicago: University of Chicago Press, 2000.

Kotzin, Michael. *Dickens and the Fairy Tale.* Bowling Green, OH: Bowling Green University Popular Press, 1972.

Kriegel, Lara. "Narrating the Subcontinent in 1851: India at the Crystal Palace." In *The Great Exhibition of 1851: New Interdisciplinary Essays,* ed. Louise Purbrick, 146–78. Manchester: Manchester University Press, 2001.

Kristeva, Julia. "Women's Time." *Signs* 7:1 (1981): 13–35.

La Capra, Dominick. "In Quest of Casaubon: George Eliot's *Middlemarch.*" In *History, Politics and the Novel,* 56–82. Ithaca, NY: Cornell University Press, 1987.

Lago, Mary, ed. *Edward Burne-Jones Talking: His conversations 1895–8 preserved by his studio assistant Thomas Rooke.* London: John Murray, 1982.

Lambourne, Lionel. "Fairies on the Stage." In *Victorian Fairy Painting,* ed. Jane Martineau, 43–57. London: Royal Academy of Arts, 1997.

Lansdown, Richard. "The Pickwick Papers: Something Nobler than a Novel?" *Critical Review* 31 (1991): 75–91.

Ledger, Sally. *Dickens and the Popular Radical Imagination.* Cambridge: Cambridge University Press, 2007.

Levine, Philippa. *The Amateur and the Professional: Antiquarians, Historians and Archaeologists in Victorian England, 1838–1886.* Cambridge: Cambridge University Press, 1986.

Levinson, Marjorie. *Keats's Life of Allegory: The Origins of a Style.* Oxford: Basil Blackwell, 1988.

Lewis, Philip. *Seeing Through Mother Goose: Visual Turns in the Writings of Charles Perrault.* Stanford, CA: Stanford University Press, 1996.

Linley, Margaret. "Sexuality and Nationality in Tennyson's Idylls of the King." *Victorian Poetry* 30 (1992): 365–86.

Lipscomb, Susan Bruxvoort. "Introducing Gilbert White: An Exemplary Natural Historian and His Editors." *Victorian Literature and Culture* 35:2 (2007): 551–67.

Lucas, John. "*The Pickwick Papers*." In *The Melancholy Man: A Study of Dickens's Novels*, 1–20. London: Methuen, 1970.

MacKay, Carol. "Narrating Self-Creation: John Harmon's Soliloquy in *Our Mutual Friend*." The Dickens Project, University of California, Santa Cruz, "*Our Mutual Friend*: The Scholarly Pages." http://omf.ucsc.edu/scholarship/article-archive/narrating-self-creation.html.

Machann, Clinton. "Tennyson's King Arthur and the Violence of Manliness." *Victorian Poetry* 38:2 (2000): 199–226.

Marcus, Steven. "The Blest Dawn." In *Dickens from Pickwick to Dombey*, 13–53. New York: Basic Books, 1965.

Marsh, Jan. *Christina Rossetti: A Writer's Life*. London: Penguin, 1994.

Martin, Emily. "The Egg and the Sperm: How Science Has Constructed a Romance Based on Stereotypical Male-Female Roles." *Signs* 16:3 (1991): 485–501.

Martineau, Jane, ed. *Victorian Fairy Painting*. London: Royal Academy of Arts, 1997.

Maxwell, Catherine. "Tasting the 'Fruit Forbidden': Gender, Intertextuality, and Christina Rossetti's 'Goblin Market'." In *The Culture of Christina Rossetti: Female Poetics and Victorian Contexts*, ed. Mary Arsenau et al., 75–104. Athens: Ohio University Press, 1999.

Mavor, Carol. *Pleasures Taken: Performances of Sexuality and Loss in Victorian Photographs*. Durham, NC: Duke University Press, 1995.

Mayer, David. *Harlequin in His Element: The English Pantomime, 1806–1836*. Cambridge, MA: Harvard University Press, 1969.

McCormack, Kathleen. "George Eliot and the Pharmakon: Dangerous Drugs for the Condition of England." *Victorians Institute Journal* 14 (1986): 35–51.

McGann, Jerome J. "Christina Rossetti's Poems: A New Edition and a Revaluation." *Victorian Studies* 23 (1980): 237–54.

McGill, Meredith. Unpublished lecture for the Dickens Project, July 2007.

Meckier, Jerome. *Dickens's Great Expectations: Misnar's Pavilion Versus Cinderella*. Lexington: University Press of Kentucky, 2002.

Menke, Richard. "The Political Economy of Fruit." In *The Culture of Christina Rossetti*, ed. Mary Arsenau et al., 105–36. Athens: Ohio University Press, 1999.

Middleton, Peter. "Lyric Temporality." *Shark* 3 (2001): 10–28.

Miller, J. Hillis. "Sam Weller's Valentine." In *Literature in the Marketplace: Nineteenth-Century British Publishing and Reading Practices*, ed. John O. Jordan and Robert L. Patten, 93–122. Cambridge: Cambridge University Press, 1995.

Miller, Renata. "Child Killers and the Competition Between Late Victorian Theater and the Novel." *Modern Language Quarterly* 66:2 (June 2005): 197–226.

Millgate, Michael. *Thomas Hardy: A Biography Revisited*. Oxford: Oxford University Press, 2004.

Moody, Jane. *Illegitimate Theater in London, 1770–1840*. Cambridge: Cambridge University Press, 2000.

Morrell, Peter, and Sylvain Cazalet. "The History of the London Homoeopathic Hospital." Royal London Homoeopathic Hospital, http://www.homeoint.org/morrell/londonhh/index.htm.

Morrison, Jago. "Narration and Unease in Ian McEwan's Later Fiction." *Critique* 42:3 (2001): 253–68.

Motion, Andrew. *Keats*. London: Faber and Faber, 1997.

Mumm, Susan. *Stolen Daughters, Virgin Mothers: Anglican Sisterhoods in Victorian Britain*. New York: Continuum, 1999.

Murphy, Patricia. *Time Is of the Essence: Temporality, Gender, and the New Woman*. Albany: State University of New York Press, 2001.

Newsom, Robert. *Dickens on the Romantic Side of Familiar Things: Bleak House and the Novel Tradition*. New York: Columbia University Press, 1977.
North, John S., ed. *The Waterloo Directory of English Newspapers and Periodicals: 1800–1900*. http://www.victorianperiodicals.com/series2/default.asp.
O'Brien, John. *Harlequin Britain: Pantomime and Entertainment, 1690–1760*. Baltimore: The Johns Hopkins University Press, 2004.
O'Brien, Lynne B. "Male Heroism: Tennyson's Divided View." *Victorian Poetry* 32:2 (1994): 171–82.
Orenstein, Catherine. *Little Red Riding Hood Uncloaked: Sex, Morality, and the Evolution of a Fairy Tale*. New York: Basic Books, 2002.
Ostry, Elaine. *Social Dreaming: Dickens and the Fairy Tale*. London: Routledge, 2002.
Palmer, Nancy, and Melvin Palmer. "English Editions of French Contes des Fees Attributed to Mme D'Aulnoy." *Studies in Bibliography* 27 (1974): 228–32.
Paradis, James G. "The Natural Historian as Antiquary of the World: Hugh Miller and the Rise of Literary Natural History." In *Hugh Miller and the Controversies of Victorian Science*, ed. Michael Shortland, 122–50. Oxford: Clarendon Press, 1996.
Patten, Robert. "The Art of Pickwick's Interpolated Tales." *ELH* 34:3 (September 1967): 349–66.
———. *George Cruikshank's Life, Times, and Art*. Vol. 1. New Brunswick, NJ: Rutgers University Press, 1992.
———. "Pickwick Redivivus." Lecture delivered at the University of California Dickens Project, July 2007.
———. "Who Tolls Nell's Knell?" Lecture delivered at the University of California Dickens Project, July 28, 2003.
Pearson, Richard. "Thackeray and Punch at the Great Exhibition: Authority and Ambivalence in Verbal and Visual Caricatures." In *The Great Exhibition of 1851: New Interdisciplinary Essays*, ed. Louise Purbrick, 179–205. Manchester: Manchester University Press, 2001.
Polhemus, Robert, and Roger Henkle, eds. *Critical Reconstructions: The Relationship of Fiction and Life*. Stanford, CA: Stanford University Press, 1994.
Poovey, Mary. "Reading History in Literature: Speculation and Virtue in *Our Mutual Friend*." In *Historical Criticism and the Challenge of Theory*, ed. Janet Levarie Smarr, 42–80. Urbana: University of Illinois Press, 1993.
Powell, Kristen. "Edward Burne-Jones and the Legend of Briar Rose." *Journal of Pre-Raphaelite Studies* 6:2 (1986): 15–28.
Pratt, John Clark, and Victor A. Neufelt, eds. *George Eliot's Middlemarch Notebooks: A Transcription*. Berkeley: University of California Press, 1979.
Prins, Yopie. "Victorian Meter." In *The Cambridge Companion to Victorian Poetry*, ed. Joseph Bristow, 89–114. Cambridge: Cambridge University Press, 2000.
———. *Victorian Sappho*. Princeton, NJ: Princeton University Press, 1999.
Propp, Vladimir. *Morphology of the Folktale*. Ed. Louis A. Wagner and trans. Lawrence Scott. American Folklore Society Publications, 2nd ed. Austin: University of Texas Press, 1968).
———. *Theory and History of Folklore*. Minneapolis: University of Minnesota Press, 1984.
Purbrick, Louise, ed. *The Great Exhibition of 1851: New Interdisciplinary Essays*. Manchester: Manchester University Press, 2001.
Purkiss, Diane. *Troublesome Things: A History of Fairies and Fairy Stories*. London: Allen Lane, The Penguin Press, 2000.
Rajan, Supritha. "Networked Magic: Lang and the Science of Self-Interest." *Romantics and Victorians on the Net*, special issue, "The Andrew Lang Effect: Network, Discipline, Method" (forthcoming).
Reed, John R. "Tennyson's Magic Casements." *Victorian Poetry* 30:3–4 (1992): 211–27.

Richards, Thomas. *The Commodity Culture of Victorian England: Advertising and Spectacle 1851–1914*. Stanford, CA: Stanford University Press, 1990.

Robson, Catherine. "Down Ditches, on Doorsteps, in Rivers: Oliver Twist's Journey to Respectability." *Dickens Studies Annual* 29 (2000): 61–81.

———. *Men in Wonderland: The Lost Girlhood of the Victorian Gentleman*. Princeton, NJ: Princeton University Press, 2001.

Saintsbury, George. *A History of English Prosody from the 12th Century to the Present Day: Vol. III, Blake to Swinburne*. London: Macmillan, 1910.

Schacker, Jennifer. "Generic Transformation and the Body of Mother Bunch." Paper presented at Metamorphoses: An International Colloquium on Narrative and Folklore, University of Utah, October 2008.

———. *National Dreams: The Remaking of Fairy Tales in Nineteenth-Century England*. Philadelphia: University of Pennsylvania Press, 2003.

———. "Unruly Tales: Ideology, Anxiety, and the Regulation of Genre." *Journal of American Folklore* 120:478 (2007): 381–400.

Schiebinger, Londa. *Has Feminism Changed Science?* Cambridge, MA: Harvard University Press, 1999.

Senf, Carol. "The Vampire in Middlemarch and George Eliot's Quest for Historical Reality." *New Orleans Review* 14:1 (1987): 87–97.

Shires, Linda. "Patriarchy, Dead Men, and Idylls of the King." *Victorian Poetry* 30 (1992): 401–19.

———. "Rereading Tennyson's Gender Politics." In *Victorian Sages and Cultural Discourse: Renegotiating Gender and Power*, ed. Thais Morgan, 46–65. New Brunswick, NJ: Rutgers University Press, 1990.

Shuttleworth, Sally. "*Middlemarch*: An Experiment in Time." In *George Eliot and Nineteenth-Century Science: The Make-Believe of a Beginning*, 142–74. Cambridge: Cambridge University Press, 1984.

———. "Sexuality and Knowledge in Middlemarch." *Nineteenth-Century Contexts* 19 (1996): 425–41.

Silver, Carole G. *Strange and Secret Peoples: Fairies and Victorian Consciousness*. Oxford: Oxford University Press, 1999.

Steedman, Carolyn. *Strange Dislocations: Childhood and the Idea of Human Interiority, 1780–1930*. London: Virago, 1995.

Stewart, Susan. *Crimes of Writing: Problems in the Containment of Representation*. Oxford: Oxford University Press, 1991.

Stillinger, Jack. "The Hoodwinking of Madeline: Scepticism in 'The Eve of St. Agnes'." In *The Hoodwinking of Madeline and Other Essays on Keats's Poems*, 67–93. Chicago: University of Illinois Press, 1971.

Stone, Harry. *Dickens and the Invisible World: Fairy Tales, Fantasy, and Novel-Making*. Bloomington: Indiana University Press, 1979.

Sumpter, Caroline. *The Victorian Press and the Fairy Tale*. Basingstoke: Palgrave Macmillan, 2008.

Swann, Brian. "Middlemarch and Myth." *Nineteenth-Century Fiction* 28:2 (September 1973): 210–14.

Tatar, Maria. *Off with Their Heads! Fairy Tales and the Culture of Childhood*. Princeton, NJ: Princeton University Press, 1992.

———. *Secrets Beyond the Door: The Story of Bluebeard and His Wives*. Princeton, NJ: Princeton University Press, 2004.

Taylor, Susan B. "Image and Text in *Jane Eyre*'s Avian Vignettes and Bewick's *History of British Birds*." *Victorian Newsletter* 101 (Spring, 2002): 2-12.

Tennyson, Hallam. *Alfred, Lord Tennyson: A Memoir by His Son*. New York: Macmillan, 1897.

Trumpener, Katie. *Bardic Nationalism: The Romantic Novel and the British Empire*. Princeton, NJ: Princeton University Press, 1997.
Tucker, Holly. *Pregnant Fictions: Childbirth and the Fairy Tale in Early Modern France*. Detroit: Wayne State University Press, 2003.
Twitchell, James. *The Living Dead: A Study of the Vampire in Romantic Literature*. Durham, NC: Duke University Press, 1981.
Tyler, Daniel. "Dorothea and the 'Key to All Mythologies'." *George Eliot Review* 33 (2002): 27–32.
Verdier, Yvonne. "Little Red Riding Hood in Oral Tradition." *Marvels and Tales* 11 (1–2) (1997): 101–23.
Vlock, Deborah. *Dickens, Novel Reading, and the Victorian Popular Theater*. Cambridge: Cambridge University Press, 1998.
Warhol, Robyn R. "Double Gender, Double Genre in Jane Eyre and Villette." *SEL: Studies in English Literature* 36:4 (1996): 857–75.
Wasserman, Earl. *The Finer Tone: Keats's Major Poems*. Baltimore: Johns Hopkins University Press, 1953.
Watkins, Daniel P. *Keats's Poetry and the Politics of the Imagination*. Rutherford, NJ: Farleigh Dickenson University Press, 1981.
Weaver, William. "Identifying Men at Ida's University: Education, Gender, and Male/Male Identification in Tennyson's The Princess." *Nineteenth-Century Contexts* 23 (2001): 121–48.
Weinreb, Ben, and Christopher Hibbert, eds. *The London Encyclopaedia*. London: Macmillan, 1984.
Wildman, Stephen, and John Christian. *Edward Burne-Jones: Victorian Artist-Dreamer*. New York: Metropolitan Museum of Art, 1998.
Wilkinson, James John Garth. In *Encyclopaedia Britannica*. 11th ed. New York: Encyclopaedia Britannica Inc, 1911.
Wilson, Peter. "The Corpus of Jinglese: A Syntactic Profile of and Idiolectal 'System of Stenography'" *Critical Survey* 16:3 (2004): 78–93.
Wolfreys, Julian. *Writing London: The Trace of the Urban Text from Blake to Dickens*. London: Macmillan, 1998.
Woloch, Alex. *The One vs. The Many: Minor Characters and the Space of the Protagonist in the Novel*. Princeton, NJ: Princeton University Press, 2003.
———. "Partial Representation in *The Pickwick Papers*." Lecture delivered at the University of California Dickens Project, July 2007.
Wood, Christopher. *The Pre-Raphaelites*. London: Seven Dials, 2000.
Wu, Duncan, ed. *Romanticism: An Anthology*. Oxford: Blackwell, 1994.
Ziolkowski, Jan M. "A Fairy Tale from Before Fairy Tales: Egbert of Liege's 'De Puella a Lupellis Seruata' and the Medieval Background of 'Little Red Riding Hood'." *Speculum* 67 (1992): 549–75.
Zipes, Jack. *The Brothers Grimm: From Enchanted Forests to Modern Worlds*. London: Routledge, 1988.
———. *Fairy Tales and the Art of Subversion: The Classical Genre for Children and the Process of Civilization*. London: Heinemann, 1983.
———. *Oxford Companion to Fairy Tales*. Oxford: Oxford University Press, 2000.
———. *The Trials and Tribulations of Little Red Riding Hood*. New York: Routledge, 1993.
Zumwalt, Rosemary Levy. *American Folklore Scholarship: A Dialogue of Dissent*. Bloomington: Indiana University Press, 1988.

INDEX

actresses: the "fairy actress," 182–85; prostitution linked with, 183, 184–85, 194–95. *See also* theatricals, popular
aelf ("elf"), 133
"Agnes Grace Weld as Little Red Riding Hood" (Dodgson), 180
agrarian–industrial shift, 150–51
Albert, Prince, 149, 151
Allen, Emily, 212
Allen, Rick, 250n11
All the Year Round, 166
Alter, Robert, 44, 199
Anderson, Benedict, 3
Andres, Sophia, 64, 66
"Anonymous Journalism" (Hughes), 164
antidote, Rossetti's "Goblin Market" as, 169
antiquarianism and antiquities: Dickens and, 39–42, 46; Eliot's *Middlemarch* and novelty vs., 64–65, 68; fairy legends and, 133; field of antiquarian studies, 28–30; folklore studies as replacement for, 32; Hardy's antiquarian in "Tryst at an Ancient Earthwork," 23–26; literary discomfort displaced onto, 46; natural history and, 30–31; novelists' mocking of, 36–37; novels vs., 24, 34–37
antiquarian societies, 29, 133, 240n5
The Antiquary (Burns), 36

anxiety of influence, 126–27
appetites. *See* hunger and appetites
appropriation, 16, 43–44
Arabian Nights, 15, 57–58, 65, 233n9
Arcades Project (Benjamin), 26–28, 223
archival method, 17–18
Aristotle, 162
Arthurian legend cycle, 19, 72. *See also* "The Epic" (Tennyson); *Idylls of the King* (Tennyson)
The Artist's Dream (Fitzgerald), 136
Aubrey, John, 29
Auerbach, Nina, 17–18
Aulnoy, Madame d,' 15, 68, 223
authorship: Brontë's *Jane Eyre,* protagonist/speaker vs. narrator/writer in, 53–55, 57–58; collection distinguished from, 35–36; Dickens, originality, and novelty, 43–49; Eliot's *Middlemarch* and, 67–68, 73; fairy tales and female authorship, 14; Lang and, 220–24; periodicals and anonymous vs. signed works, 164–65, 244n28; prostitution, associations with, 162; Rossetti's "Goblin Market" and, 162–67, 168; whore, metaphor of author as, 154. *See also* novels and "novelty"
Axton, William, 200

Bakhtin, Mikhail, 6, 79, 105, 139
Banier, abbé Antoine, 234n16
Barthes, Roland, 67
Basile, Giambattista: Boccaccio and, 233n5; *Il Pentamerone,* 15, 83; "*Sole, Luna e Talia,*" 79–80, 84–85, 87
Bayley, F. W. N., 148, 165, 192–96, 249n46
Beardsley, Aubrey, 121
Beaumont, Madame de, 223
Beer, Gillian, 63, 67, 68
bees and beehives, 243n12
Bellanca, Mary Ellen, 31
"La Belle au Bois Dormant" (Perrault), 80–81, 84–85, 87
Benjamin, Walter, 26–28, 34, 35, 223
Bernard, Mlle. de, 223
Bertelson, Lance, 181
Bessemer, Sir Henry, 139
Bettleheim, Bruno, 17
Bewick, John, 34
Bewick, Thomas, 31, 34, 50–51, 53, 58
bildungsroman, English, 32
Blair, Kirstie, 97, 100
Bleak House (Dickens), 198
Bloom, Harold, 126–27
Boccaccio, Giovanni, 66, 68, 233n5
bodies: in Dickens's *Our Mutual Friend,* 203, 204, 208, 210, 213; fairy tales and the marginally civilized female body, 14; foreign, 152, 157; frames and, 125–26; Great Exhibition and danger to, 242n25; "growing up" and, 2; heart and circulatory-temporal analogies, 97–103; in Hopkins's "To His Watch," 78, 126; metaphorical fall of, in Dickens's *Our Mutual Friend,* 213–14; novels compared to, 68; penetration of, 95, 126
bodies, female: antiquarianism and, 15; author-as-whore metaphor, 154; cabinet in *Jane Eyre* and *Wuthering Heights* and, 59–60; Dickens's tiny laboring heroines, 213; exchange value and, 158–59; exploited girl child figure and, 177; fairy tales transmitted through, 14; fallen woman convention, 166; natural history and, 51; prostitution trope and, 177–78; Rossetti and the female authorial body, 168; Rossetti's "Goblin Market" and, 158–59
bodies, male: in Burne-Jones's *Briar Wood* series, 113; Carlyle on heartbeat, male climax, and civic duty, 101; in Keats's "Eve of St. Agnes," 85, 86–87, 90–91. *See also* masculinity
The Borders of the Tamar and Tavy (Bray), 2, 15, 31–32, 133, 155
Bottigheimer, Ruth, 13, 236n22
Boulmelha, Penny, 67
Bouquet from Marylebone Gardens, 164
Bovet, Richard, 136
Bowler, Henry Alexander, 109
Bown, Nicola, 18
Brand, John, 15, 29, 133
Bray, Anna Liza: *The Borders of the Tamar and Tavy,* 2, 15, 31–32, 133, 155; on fairy origins, 133–34; *A Peep at the Pixies,* 34, 133, 135, 155
"Briar Rose." *See* "Sleeping Beauty"
Briar Rose series (Burne-Jones): *The Briar Wood,* 110, 111–12, 113, 114f, 116f; Buscot Park installation, 111–12, 123–25; *The Council Chamber,* 110, 112, 113, 117f, 118f; exhibition and critical reception of, 108–9, 111–12, 119–21, 123, 238n19; first series, 111, 113, 114f–115f; framing and, 111, 123–27; *The Garden Court,* 110, 112; gender anxiety and, 121–23, 125; models for, 113, 123; Morris quatrains for 3rd series, 111–12, 119, 124; poetry and, 108; *Punch* parody of, 109; reviews of, 5; *The Rose Bower,* 110, 112, 113, 119, 120f; second series, 111, 117f, 238n18; *The Sleeping Beauty,* 115f; *Sleeping Beauty* decorative tiles, 111, 112–13; as study in generic dialogism, 108; Tennyson and, 109, 122, 123; third series (Buscot Park), 111–12, 113, 116f, 118f, 119–22, 120, 120f
Bridgeman, J. V., 185–86
Brightwen, Eliza, 139
Brontë, Charlotte, 37, 51, 52. *See also Jane Eyre*
Brontë, Emily, 59–60
Brooke, W. H., 133
Brough, John Cargill, 236n21

Browne, Hablot K. ("Phiz"), 133
Brunvand, Jan, 12, 226n24
Bryant, Jacob, 66
Buckingham, Leicester, 185, 187–88
burlesque, 181, 185, 247n6
Burne-Jones, Edward: aesthetic movement, relationship to, 121; empire building, opposition to, 119; industrialization, view of, 122; influence of verse on, 109; intertextuality and, 123; masculinity and, 122–23; romance and fairy tale, interest in, 110; self-caricature (1883), 110–11, 122; *Sleeping Beauty* decorative tiles, 111, 112–13. See also *Briar Rose* series
Burne-Jones, Georgiana, 113, 238n13
Burne-Jones, Margaret, 119
Burns, Robert, 36
Burton, Sir Richard, 15
Buzard, James, 53

Le Cabinet des Fées, 58–59
cabinets of curiosities, 58–60
Camden, William, 28–29, 32
Camden Society, 29, 240n5
Campbell, Elizabeth, 121, 239n30
cannibalism in Dickens's *Our Mutual Friend*, 202
Carignan, Michael, 66
Carlyle, Thomas, 77, 93, 98–102
Caroll, Lewis (Charles Dodgson), 179–80
Carpenter, Mary Wilson, 156
Carroll, David, 63–64
Cavendish, Margaret, 132, 140
Celtic borderlands, 2
Chaucer, Geoffrey, 2–3
Chestre, Thomas, 132
Childers, Joseph, 138
Christian, John, 124, 238n19
"A Christmas Tree" (Dickens), 4, 200
"The Cinderella of 1851" (*Punch*), 142–44, 145f, 159
circulation: actors, prostitutes, and, 191; currency and, 127; fairy tales as coins out of circulation, 4, 5; gender and genre vexed by, 126; natural vs. unnatural, 102–3; procreative and infectious metaphors and, 11; Rossetti's "Goblin Market," periodicals, and, 162–66; Tennyson's "Day Dream" and circulatory-temporal analogies, 97–103
Clarke, John, 233n4
classes: Dickens's *Our Mutual Friend* and, 207, 209; "dressing up" and, 179; Great Exhibition and, 138, 144, 148–49; "Little Red Riding Hood" and, 178, 185; theater and, 183, 191–92. See also middle class; working class
Coleridge, Samuel Taylor, 3, 5, 58
collaboration, 218–24
collectors and collection: antiquarian studies, 28–30; Benjamin's *Arcades Project* and, 26–28; cabinets of curiosities in *Jane Eyre* and *Wuthering Heights*, 58–60; creation vs., 26; Dickens and, 41, 47–48; fairy tales and legends, collections of, 33–34, 58–59; folklore studies and, 32–33; Hardy's "Tryst at an Ancient Earthwork," 23–26; Lang and, 223; natural history, 30–32; novelty-antiquity distinction and, 34–37
Color Fairy Books (Lang), 14, 34, 219, 222, 223
commercialization. See markets, commerce, and commercialization
"Comparative Mythology" (Müller), 33
conservatories, 148–52
consumption: Bayley's *Little Red Riding Hood* and, 196; Burne-Jones and, 122; Dickens's *Our Mutual Friend* and, 199; Dickens's *Pickwick Papers* and, 45; fairy exchange and, 135–36; fears of foreignness and, 242n25; Great Exhibition and, 141–42, 150–52, 162; Rossetti's "Goblin Market" and, 156–59; theatricals and, 188. See also hunger and appetites
Contes de Fées (d'Aulnoy), 15
Contes du Temps Passé (Perrault), 15, 83, 155
control, narrative: Brontë's *Jane Eyre* and, 51, 55, 58, 60; Burne-Jones and, 122; collection and, 37; Dickens and, 44; editorial hand in Brontë's *Jane Eyre*, 37. See also authorship
convents, Anglican, 160–62
coterie print culture, 223–24

INDEX

Cox, Marian Roalfe, 32
Croker, Thomas Crofton, 15, 33, 133, 134, 135
Cruikshank, George, 43, 142, 143f, 155
Crystal Palace (Great Exhibition of 1851), 139–40, 148–52
cultural studies of fairy tales, 18
Curtin, Jeremiah, 15, 133, 135

Dadd, Richard, 135
Darwin, Charles, 148, 220
David Copperfield (Dickens), 201–2
Davis, Tracy C., 182, 185, 186, 191
"The Day Dream" (Tennyson): "The Arrival," 96, 101; Burne-Jones and, 109; categorization of, 93; circulatory-temporal metaphor and, 100–102; critical inattention to, 92; "The Departure," 103; development of, 93; "L'Envoi," 96–97, 101; epic, remodeled model, and, 94–95, 100, 103–4, 106–7; "The Epic" compared to, 94; form and, 94, 105, 108; frame and tale in, 105–6, 108; Keats and, 91, 103–4; meter in, 100; "The Moral," 96; "Prologue," 93–94; sections of, 234n16; "The Sleeping Beauty," 91, 93, 103; "The Sleeping Palace," 95, 100, 101
Decamerone (Boccaccio), 66, 233n5
Delarue, Paul, 245n5, 246n12
de la Sizeraine, Robert, 110
DeMarcus, Cynthia, 204–5, 206, 210, 214
"*De Puella a Lupellis Serruta*" ("Concerning a Girl Saved from Wolf Cubs") (Egbert of Liege), 246n12
Deutsche Sagen (Grimm), 15
dialogism, 6, 79, 105, 108
Dibden, Thomas, 181
Dickens, Charles: *Bleak House*, 198; Campbell on wheel of fortune trope in, 239n30; "A Christmas Tree," 4, 200; *David Copperfield*, 201–2; evolutionary model of fairy tales and, 4, 42–43; on fairy tales, 5; fallen women and seducer narratives of, 198, 201–2; "Frauds on the Fairies," 43; "Gaslight Fairies," 165, 189, 200; on Great Exhibition, 141–42; *Great Expectations*, 198; *Hard Times*, 166; *Household Words/All the Year Round*, 166, 199; Little Red Riding Hood as Dickens's lost love, 197–98, 201, 215–16; loss of folklore mourned by, 199; *Nicholas Nickleby*, 43–44, 49; Noah's ark and, 197–99, 251n32; "Nurses's Stories," 44–45, 47–48, 200; *The Old Curiosity Shop*, 4, 49, 198; orality and, 45–49; originality, novelty, and, 43–49; performativity, sense of, 212; periodical and serial publication and, 164–66; *The Pickwick Papers*, 36, 38–42, 45–49, 62; Stone and Kotzin on, 19; telling stories and telling coins and, 4. See also *Our Mutual Friend*
"The Dispersion of the Works of All Nations from the Great Exhibition of 1851" (Cruikshank), 142, 143f
Dodgson, Charles (Lewis Caroll), 179–80
"*Dornröschen*" (Grimm), 81, 83
Dorson, Richard, 12, 28
"The Doubt: Can These Dry Bones Live?" (Bowler), 109
Doyle, Richard: *The Fairy Tree*, 148, 149f, 157; *Fruit*, 152, 153f; illustration for "The Exhibition Plague" (*Punch*), 145, 146f; "Overland Journey," 146–48, 147f, 157
dueorh ("dwarf"), 133
Duffy, Maureen, 132, 135
Dundes, Alan, 17, 245n8, 246n12

Easley, Alexis, 164–65
Edwards, H. Sutherland, 185–86
Edwards, Steve, 138, 139
Egbert of Liege, 246n12
Eigner, Edwin, 200
elf-struck people, 135–36
Eliot, George (Marian Evans), 66–68, 73, 78. See also *Middlemarch*
Eliot, T. S., 237n36
"The Epic" (Tennyson), 94
Epps, John, 169
Evans, Marian (George Eliot), 66–68, 73, 78
"The Eve of St. Agnes" (Keats): Burne-Jones and, 109; frame breaking in, 85–86; influences on, 82–85; Keats's defense of,

86–87; raped and voiceless heroines and, 87–88; sleep and the poetic subject in, 88–91; Tennyson and, 19; title of, 82
evolutionary theory, 144, 148, 220
excavation, 24
exchange, 134–37, 184–85. *See also* markets, commerce, and commercialization
"The Exhibition Plague" (*Punch*), 144–45, 146f
extravaganza, 181, 247n6
eyes in fairy legends, 134–36

Fabb, Nigel, 168
The Faerie Queene (Spenser), 15, 132
fairies and fairy legends: Bray's origin hypothesis, 133–34; in Brontë's *Jane Eyre*, 55–56; dramatic adaptation, appropriateness for, 182; "elf-struck" people, 135–36; exchange between humans and, 134–37; eyes, focus on, 134–36; "fairy," *dueroh* ("dwarf"), and *aelf* ("elf"), 133; fairy processions, 148, 149f; foreignness, racial physiognomy, and, 144, 148–49, 149f; goblins vs. fairies, 136–37, 158; history of English representations of, 131–32; labor and fairies, 139–41, 144, 154; laboring women, association with, 189–90; as legends, 13; in market settings, 135–36; print history of, 15; sexualized fairy girls in popular literature, 165; theater and, 157, 183–84, 189, 200; transaction, association with, 132–33. *See also specific authors and works, such as* "Goblin Market" (Rossetti)
"The Fairies of Rahonain and Elizabeth Shea," 135
fairy market. *See* "Goblin Market" (Rossetti)
The Fairy Mythology (Keightley), 15, 33, 133, 155
fairy paintings, 135, 242n28. See also *Briar Rose* series (Burne-Jones)
The Fairy's Lake (Fitzgerald), 144
fairy tales: book and print media development and, 14–16; classification of, 13; collections of, 33–34; debate over generic definition of, 12–14; dialogic power and, 79; Lang's "savagery" view of,

219–20; origin theories, Victorian, 14; Victorian ambivalence and, 4–6; as "wild and childish" and premodern, 1–4, 18, 219–20. *See also specific authors, works, and topics*
Fairy Tales (Ritson), 33
The Fairy Tales of Science (Brough), 236n21
The Fairy Tree (Doyle), 148, 149f, 157
"The Fall of Hyperion" (Keats), 88–89, 96
Faringdon, Gavin, 3rd Lord, 239n35
Fecunda Ratis (Egbert of Liege), 246n12
female bodies. *See* bodies, female
female labor. *See* labor
feminist theory, 14
Feuerbach, Ludwig, 66
Fields, Beverly, 87
Fiske, John, 66
Fitzgerald, John Anster, 135, 136, 144
Fitzgerald, Percy, 184
folklore: Brundvand's definition of, 226n24; debate over generic definition of, 12–14; English lack of, supposed, 16–17; novelty distinguished from, 34–37; Victorian vs. Romantic uses of, 19. *See also* fairy tales; *specific authors and works*
Folklore Society, 32, 124, 219
folklore studies and fairy tale studies: antiquarianism as precursor to, 28–30; antiquarianism supplanted by, 32; Casaubon as folklorist in Eliot's *Middlemarch*, 61–62; classification in, 11–12; positivism, philology, and, 32–33; review of scholarship, 17–18; Thoms's coining of "folk-lore," 32
foreignness: fruit in Rossetti's "Goblin Market" and, 156; national synecdoches at Great Exhibition, 141; racial/evolutionary themes at Great Exhibition, 144–48, 146f, 147f, 149f, 241n25
form: Burne-Jones's *Briar Rose*, 123–25; "frame" and, 125; Tennyson's "The Day Dream," 94, 105, 108
frame narratives: Burne-Jones's *Briar Rose* series, 125; definitions of, 125–26; Keats's "Eve of St. Agnes" and, 85–86; Tennyson's "The Day Dream," 105–6
framing: Burne-Jones's *Briar Rose* series and, 111, 123–27; "form" and "frame," 125

Franklin, J. Jeffrey, 180
"Frauds on the Fairies" (Dickens), 43
Frazer, James George, 220
Freud, Sigmund, 17
fruit, 150–51, 156
Fruit (Doyle), 152, 153f
Fuseli, Henry, 135

Gallagher, Catherine, 11, 102, 154, 162, 163, 184, 210
Galland, Antoine, 15, 233n9
"Gaslight Fairies" (Dickens), 165, 189, 200
Gates, Barbara, 51–52
gender: Burne-Jones's *Briar Rose* series and, 119–21, 122–23; fairy tales and female cultural production, 103; genre and vexation of, 126; heartbeat, linear temporality, and, 99–102; masculinity in Dickens's *Our Mutual Friend*, 207, 209–10; New Woman, 125, 239n30; Romantic writers and masculine anxiety, 95–96, 106–7; sexualized fairy girls, 165; time and mediation of, 106; "woman's time" theory, 121–22, 239n30. *See also* bodies, female; masculinity; novels and "novelty"
generativity, natural vs. unnatural, 102–3
genre: antiquarians and, 7–8; circulation and, 126; collaboration, coterie production, and, 218, 219; dialogism as disjunctive genres, 105; Dickens's *Nicholas Nickleby* and, 43–44; Dickens's *Pickwick Papers* and, 39, 46; fairy tales as literary genre, 12–14; flux and perturbation of Victorian genres, 6; literary genres bound to the fairy tale, 1–3, 7; periodical as, 163; poetry, photography, and, 123; popular theater and, 181–82; print media, Victorian development of, 14–16; Rossetti's "Goblin Market" and, 165–66, 167–69, 168; Tennyson's "Day Dream" and, 105, 106. *See also* antiquarianism and antiquities; collectors and collection; fairy tales; folklore; natural history; novels and "novelty"
The Germ, 164
Gervase of Tilbury, 131

Gilbreath, Marcia, 234n16
Gillooly, Eileen, 138, 139, 141, 150, 162
Givner, Jessie, 66
"Goblin Market" (Rossetti): as antidote or homeopathy, 169; circulation, authorship, and female publication and, 162–66; on female labor, alienation of, 157–60, 163; fruit in, 156; on goblins, market economy, and consumerism, 156–57; original title of, 155–56; periodical humor conventions and, 165–66; prosodic convention, meter, and generic hybridity of, 167–69; Rossetti's Magdalene House work and, 160–62; Ruskin's assessment of, 160–61, 167–68
goblins: as exchange or money, 157; fairies vs., 136–37; fears of foreignness and, 144–45; in Rossetti's "Goblin Market," 156–57, 243n10; violence of, 243n10
Goldsmith, Oliver, 51
Gomme, George Lawrence, 32
gothic romance tropes, Eliot's *Middlemarch* and, 70
Great Exhibition (1851): beehive displays at, 243n12; categories of inquiry on, 138; criticism and satire of, 141–48, 143f, 145f, 146f, 147f; Crystal Palace as "Fairy Palace," 139–40; Crystal Palace as greenhouse or conservatory, 148–52; foreignness and racist themes in, 144–48, 146f, 147f, 149f, 241n25; industry and commodity in, 140–44; markets and, 140–41, 151–52; pantomime (1852) on, 140; Rossetti and, 155
Great Expectations (Dickens), 198
greenhouses, 148–52
Grimm, Jacob and Wilhelm: appropriation by, 16; *Deutsche Sagen*, 15; "Dornröschen," 81, 83; Eliot's reading of, 66; *Kinder- und Hausmärchen*, 15, 34, 83, 155; *Rotkäppchen*, 176
Grose, Francis, 36
Groth, Helen, 108, 123
"growing up," 2
gypsy figure in Brontë's *Jane Eyre*, 56

Haggard, H. Rider, 218

272 INDEX

Halle, Morris, 168
Hard Times (Dickens), 166
Hardy, Thomas, 23–26, 51, 217–18
"Harlequin and Mother Goose" (Dibden), 181
Harries, Elizabeth, 13, 16
Hatch, Evelyn, 179
Hearne, Thomas, 36
heart and circulatory-temporal analogies, 97–103
Hegel, Georg Wilhelm Friedrich, 106
Heimann, Amelia, 155
Helsinger, Elizabeth, 163
Henderson, Alexander, 111
Hensley, Nathan K., 218
Henville, Letitia, 222
Hertz, Neil, 67–68, 73
Hill, Marylu, 168
Histoires ou Contes du Temps Passé (Perrault), 15
historical and archival method, 17–18
History of British Birds (Bewick), 50–51, 58
homeopathy, 169
Hood, James, 91
Hopkins, George Manley, 78, 126
Household Words, 166
Houston, Gail Turley, 202, 207
"How Lisa Loved the King" (Eliot), 66
Hughes, Arthur, 109
Hughes, John, 95–96
Hughes, Thomas, 164
The Human Body and Its Connexion With Man (Wilkinson), 98–102
humor, conventions of, 165–66
hunger and appetites: in Dickens's *Our Mutual Friend*, 203, 204, 209–10, 213; exotic produce and imperial hungers, 149; fallen woman figure and, 199; Great Exhibition and, 141, 241n25; of Laura and of goblins in Rossetti's "Goblin Market," 156, 157, 161. *See also* consumption
Hunt, William Holman, 109
Hyde, Virginia, 72

Idylls of the King (Tennyson), 109
industry: agrarian economy, shift from, 150–51; bees as symbol of, 243n12; fairy metaphor and, 140; Great Exhibition of 1851 and, 140–41; Rossetti's "Goblin Market" and, 158–59. *See also* produce and production
infection metaphor, 11, 38, 48, 81, 121
In Memoriam (Tennyson), 97, 109
"intercalation," 46, 47, 49
International Folk-Lore Congress, 124
"Isabella" (Keats), 233n5

Jacobs, Joseph, 32, 34
James, Henry, 119, 237n36
Jane Eyre (Brontë): Bewick's *Birds of Britain* in, 50–51; cabinets in, 58–60; controlling, editorial hand in, 36–37; Currer Bell pseudonym in, 37, 52–53; fairy exile in, 3; fantastical references in, 55–58, 60; mirroring in, 5, 55–57; protagonist/speaker vs. narrator/writer in, 53–55, 57–58
Jerrold, Douglas, 166
jingles, 167, 244n37
Jones, Isabella, 233n4

Kaiser, Matthew, 187
Kaplan, Carla, 53
Keats, John: access to versions of "Sleeping Beauty," 83–84; art and, 108–9; Burne-Jones's *Briar Rose* series and, 123; "The Fall of Hyperion," 88–89, 96; interest in fairy tales, 19; "Isabella," 233n5; "Ode to a Nightingale," 88; Severn deathbed sketch of, 123; "Sleep and Poetry," 88, 103; "Sonnet to Sleep," 88; Tennyson's "The Day Dream" and, 103–4. *See also* "The Eve of St. Agnes"
Keightley, Thomas, 2, 15, 33, 133, 134, 155
Kinder- und Hausmärchen (Grimm), 15, 34, 83, 155
Knoepflmacher, U. C., 18, 67
Kotzin, Michael, 18, 19, 204–5
Kramer, Heinrich, 131
Kriegel, Laura, 138
Kristeva, Julia, 99, 102, 106, 126, 236n27

labor: actresses linked with prostitution, 183, 184–85, 194–95; of antiquary vs. natural history, 32; bees as symbol of natural labor, 243n12; childhood and, 177–78; of creation and compilation, 26; Dickens's *Jane Eyre* and, 54–55; in Dickens's *Our Mutual Friend*, 207, 212–13; fairies and, 139–41, 144, 154; the "fairy actress," 182–85; Great Exhibition and, 139, 151, 154; in Hardy's "Tryst," 23, 27; Rossetti's "Goblin Market" and alienation of, 157–60, 163; "spell" and, 104; Tennyson's "Day Dream" and, 94–95; theater and middle-class anxieties about, 191–92; Weylland's "dust fairies" and, 190. *See also* authorship; working class

Lane, Edward, 15

Lang, Andrew: on authorship, 220–24; Color Fairy Books, 14, 34, 219, 222, 223; feminization of narration by, 51; folklore studies and, 32; Hardy, feud with, 217–18; influence of, 218; "Literary Plagiarism," 222; "savagery" view of fairy tales, 219–20; on solar mythology, 33

Ledger, Sally, 47

legends, 11–12, 13, 33–34, 226n25

Legends and Traditions of the South of Ireland (Croker), 15, 33, 133, 134

Leland, John, 28

Lemon, Mark, 166

Lesley, J. P., 32

Levine, Philippa, 30, 36

Lewes, George Henry, 66, 69

L'H'éritier, Mlle. de, 223

"Literary Plagiarism" (Lang), 222

Little Red Riding Hood (Bayley), 192–96

"Little Red Riding Hood": age of the character, indeterminacy of, 177; Bayley's *Little Red Riding Hood*, 192–96; Bridge and Edwards's *Little Red Riding Hood; or, Harlequin and the Wolf in Granny's Clothing*, 185–86; Buckingham's *Little Red Riding Hood and the Fairies*, 185, 187–88; childhood, class, and work discourses and, 177–78; in Dickens's *Our Mutual Friend*, 174; Grimm's *Rotkäppchen*, 176; paraphrastic force of, 174; Planché's *Rodolph the Wolf; or, Columbine Red Riding Hood*, 185–87; red cap or cloak in, 175–76; sewing society origin theory, 245n8; "The Story of Grandmother" (French), 174–75, 248n35; theatrical performance and, 179–80, 185–88; translations into English, 178; werewolf trial narratives as antecedents to, 174; wolf symbolism in, 173. *See also Our Mutual Friend* (Dickens) and "Little Red Riding Hood"

Little Red Riding Hood and the Fairies (Buckingham), 185, 187–88

Little Red Riding Hood; or, Harlequin and the Wolf in Granny's Clothing (Bridge and Edwards), 185–86

"Locksley Hall" (Tennyson), 236n21

London: Little Red Riding Hood's move into, 173–74; as modern city and also figural, 199–200; River Thames in Dickens, 195, 201–16; streets of, linked to theater, 188–92. *See also* Great Exhibition (1851)

London City Mission, 190

Lord, Percival, 97

Lowther Bazaar, Lond, 193, 249n50

Macaulay, Thomas, 93, 140

Machann, Clinton, 95

MacLaren, Archibald, 155

Maclise, Daniel, 133

Macmillan, Alexander, 164, 167

Macmillan's Magazine, 164, 244n28

Magdalene House, Highgate Hill, London, 160–62

Maiden Tribute of Modern Babylon (Stead), 177

Malleus Maleficarum (Sprenger), 131

"Mariana" (Millais), 108–9

Marie de France, 132

markets, commerce, and commercialization: as cannibalism in Dickens's *Our Mutual Friend*, 202; commodity fetish, 141; in Dickens's *Pickwick Papers*, 40–41; fairies in market settings, 135–36; fairy commodities, Dickens on, 189; fairy tale collections and, 33–34; "graves of dead businesses" in Dickens's *Our Mutual Friend*, 208; nostalgia, commercial use of, 123; theater and prostitution as street commerce, 190–91; unnatural generativity of money, 102–3; working class hun-

ger as, in Dickens's *Our Mutual Friend* and, 207. *See also* "Goblin Market" (Rossetti); Great Exhibition (1851)
Martin, Emily, 236n23
Marx, Karl, 141
masculinity: Burne-Jones and, 122–23; in Dickens's *Our Mutual Friend,* 207, 209–10; Romantic writers and anxiety over, 95–96, 106–7; Tennyson and, 95–96, 106–7, 237n36. *See also* gender
Mason, David, 167
matrix space, 236n27
"mattering" of folk tales, Dickens and, 45
Maxwell, Catherine, 163
Mayhew, Henry, 142, 184–85, 191, 193, 203
McCabe, Colin, 67
McCormack, Kathleen, 63
McGill, Meredith, 46
men: in Dickens's *Our Mutual Friend,* 206, 207–8, 210–11; in Keats's "Nightingale," 88; "Little Red Riding Hood" and, 175, 176, 187; natural history and, 52; Rossetti's "Goblin Market" and, 157–58, 159, 167; Shakespearean homage in Dickens's *Household Words* and, 166; Tennyson's "Day Dream," author as male in, 103. *See also* bodies, male; masculinity
Men in Wonderland (Robson), 177
Menke, Richard, 148, 156
Mercury, 26
meter in Rossetti's "Goblin Market," 167–68
middle class: antiquarianism and, 29; appetite and, 203, 207; Carlyle on, 100; Dickens's *Our Mutual Friend* and, 209, 215; Dodgson's "Agnes Grace Weld as Little Red Riding Hood" and, 180; goblins and, 158; Great Exhibition and, 138, 144, 149–50; located in the fairy tale, 5–6; popular theater and, 181, 185, 191; Rossetti's "Goblin Market" and, 159
Middlemarch (Eliot): authorship anxieties and, 67–68; Dickens's *Pickwick Papers* compared to, 62; Dorothea as novel in, 64–65; fairy tale matter in, 68–70, 71–73; folk matter vs. realism in, 66–67; notebooks for, 66; oppositions in, 61–66; wills, legacy, and imaginative dependency in, 70–71

A Midsummer Night's Dream (Shakespeare), 189
Millais, John Everett, 108–9
Miller, Hugh, 31
Miller, J. Hillis, 47
Miller, Renata, 212
mimetic desire and the Great Exhibition, 141, 144
Minstrelsy of the Scottish Border (Burns), 104
mirroring in Brontë's *Jane Eyre,* 5, 55–57
miscellanies, Dickens's *Pickwick Papers* and, 40–42. *See also* collectors and collection
modernity, fairy tales as remains in, 2–4
Montague, Charles, 192
Moody, Jane, 181, 182, 190
Moretti, Franco, 139
Morris, Jane, 113
Morris, William, 111–12, 124, 152
Morrison, Jago, 106
Mother Bunch, 11, 14, 126, 227n33
Mother Goose, 14
Mr. and Mrs. Brown's Visit to London (Onwhyn), 241n25
Müller, Friedrich Max, 33, 62, 66, 219–20
Murat, Madame de, 223
Murphy, Patricia, 121, 239n30
myths and mythology, 11, 33, 66–67

narrative folklore, classification of, 11
Nash, Thomas, 132
natural history: Brontë's *Jane Eyre* and, 50–60; cabinets of curiosities, 58–60; collection and, 30–32; demonologies replaced with, 132; fairy and animal lore volumes, 34
Newsom, Robert, 199–200
New Woman, 125, 239n30
Nicholas Nickleby (Dickens), 43–44, 49
"Nick" (Rossetti), 155
Nightingale, Florence, 160
The Nightmare (Fitzgerald), 136
novels and "novelty": antiquarian and folklorist characters in, 36–37; antiquarian mode and folklore vs., 24, 34–37; Brontë's *Jane Eyre* and, 53–54; Dickens and, 43–49; in Eliot's *Middlemarch,* 64–65; novelist, rise of, 34

"Nurses's Stories" (Dickens), 44–45, 47–48, 200
Nussey, Ellen, 51
Nutt, Alfred, 16, 32

O'Brien, John, 181–82, 186
"Ode to a Nightingale" (Keats), 88
The Old Curiosity Shop (Dickens), 4, 49, 198
On Heroes (Carlyle), 93
Onwhyn, Thomas, 241n25
orality: Brontë's *Jane Eyre* and, 57–58; Dickens and, 45–49; Dickens's *Our Mutual Friend* and, 215–16; "spell" and, 104. See also hunger and appetites
Orenstein, Catherine, 173, 245n8
originality. *See* authorship
Our Mutual Friend (Dickens) and "Little Red Riding Hood": appetite and scenes of hunger, 203, 207, 209–10; Betty Higden and poverty, 205–6; cannibalism in, 202; Charlie Hexam, 215; class distinctions, societal greed, and, 207–8; destruction of Red Riding Hood, necessity of, 201; Eugene Wrayburn, 209; evolutionary model of fairy tales and, 42–43; fragments of the tale in the novel, 198; girl and the wolf, amalgamation of, 198–99, 206; Jenny Wren, 213, 214; John Harmon, 209–10; Lizzie Hexam as endangered girl spared, 212–14, 215; London setting and, 199–200; oral performance and novel production and, 215–16; paraphrastic force of Little Red Riding Hood and, 174; Riding Hood as Dickens's lost love, 197–98, 201, 215–16; Rogue Riderhood, 204–7, 210–12, 251n33, 251n42; the Thames, drownings, and waterside characters, 195, 202–16; theatricals and, 200
"Overland Journey" (Doyle), 146–48, 147f, 157
Ovid, 87–88, 234n14

Paget, James, 100, 235n12
"Palace of Art" (Tennyson), 122
Pandemonium (Bovet), 136

pantomime, 140, 181–82, 185, 200, 247n6
Paradis, James, 29–30
Pasquil's Jests and Mother Bunch's Merriments, 227n33
past. *See* temporality and time
Paton, Joseph Noel, 135, 144
Patten, Robert, 4, 45–46, 230n17
Paxton, Joseph, 140, 148, 151
Payne, John, 15
Pearl poet, 132
Pearson, Richard, 138, 139, 145
A Peep at the Pixies (Bray), 34, 133, 135, 155
Il Pentamerone (Basile), *15, 83*
Percy, Thomas, 29
Percy Society, 29, 240n5
periodicals and democratization of reading, 163–65
Perrault, Charles: adaptation by, 16; "*La Belle au Bois Dormant*," 80–81, 84–85, 87; *Contes du Temps Passé*, 15, 83, 155; "*Le Petit Chaperon Rouge*," 175–76, 178
"*Le Petit Chaperon Rouge*" (Perrault), 175–76, 178
philology, 33
Philomel, rape of, 87–88, 234n14
photography, 123, 180
physiology, 97–103
Le Piacevoli Notti (Straparola), 15
The Pickwick Papers (Dickens), 36, 38–42, 45–49, 62
plagiarism debates, 222
Planché, J. R., 185–87, 247n6
Poems and Fancies (Cavendish), 132
Poems Chiefly Lyrical (Tennyson), 93
poetic subjects, 89–91, 96
Poovey, Mary, 207, 210
Pope, Alexander, 36
Popular Antiquities (Brand), 15, 29, 133
positivism in folklore studies, 32–33
poverty, 174, 202, 205–6. *See also* working class
Powell, Kirsten, 119
The Prelude (Wordsworth), 4, 5
Primitive Culture (Tylor), 33
"The Prince's Progress" (Rossetti), 237n33
"The Princess" (Tennyson), 97, 105, 106
Prins, Yopie, 167–68
print media, 14–16, 163–64

produce and production: alienation of female labor in Rossetti's "Goblin Market," 157–60, 163; Crystal palace as greenhouse and, 148–52; fruit, 150–51; periodicals and the democratization of reading, 163–64. *See also* authorship; industry

Propp, Vladimir, 4, 215, 226n26

prosodic convention in Rossetti's "Goblin Market," 167–68

prostitution: actresses and popular theater linked with, 183, 184–85, 190–91, 194–95; exploited girl child figure and, 177

psychoanalytic approach, 17

Pugin, Augustus, 151–52

Punch: *Briar Rose* parody, 109; "The Cinderella of 1851," 142–44, 145f, 159; on the Crystal Palace, 140, 148; "The Exhibition Plague," 144–45, 146f; fairy illustrations, 142, 145, 145f, 146f, 165, 166; under Lemon, 166; periodical movement and, 163

Purbrick, Louise, 138

Purkiss, Diane, 18, 132, 144

Quinn, Harvey, 169

racial physiognomy, 144–48

Rajan, Supritha, 220

rape, 24, 79–80, 87–88. *See also* "Little Red Riding Hood"; "Sleeping Beauty" ("Briar Rose")

realism: Brontë's *Jane Eyre* and, 51, 54, 57; Dickens and, 44, 49, 199, 200, 205; Eliot and, 66–67; Great Exhibition and, 139; metaphor, science, and, 235n9; the novel and, 35

Reconciliation of Oberon and Titania (Paton), 144

"Review of Southey's Colloquies" (Macaulay), 93

Reynolds, Edward, 152

Richard, Thomas, 138, 139

Ricks, Christopher, 103

Ritchie, Anne Thackeray, 237n33

Ritson, Joseph, 33, 134, 135

Robinson, Henry Crabbe, 237n36

Robson, Catherine, 177, 202

Rodolph the Wolf; or, Columbine Red Riding Hood (Planché), 185–87

romance: Eliot's *Middlemarch* and gothic romance tropes, 70; fairies of, 132; natural history imagined as, 51

Romanticism: Burne-Jones and, 121; child figure in, 177; masculine anxiety and, 95–96, 106–7; Victorian rejection of, 96; Victorian vs. Romantic uses of folklore, 19

Romola (Eliot), 67

Rossetti, Christina: ambivalence toward wages and fame, 167; fairy tales, influence of, 154–55; Great Exhibition and, 155; Magdalene House, work at, 160–62; "Nick," 155; "The Prince's Progress," 237n33; *Speaking Likenesses*, 167. *See also* "Goblin Market"

Rossetti, Dante Gabriel, 109, 113, 157, 160, 164, 167

Rossetti, Maria, 160

Rotkäppchen (Grimm), 176

Royal Society, 29

"Rumplestiltskin," 72–73

Ruskin, John, 77–78, 160–61, 167–68

Said, Edward, 29

Saintsbury, George, 168

Samber, Robert, 15, 178

Sartor Resartus (Carlyle), 93, 98–102

Schacker, Jennifer, 3, 11–12, 16–17, 37, 126, 182

Schiebinger, Londa, 236n23

science: analogical thinking, the literary, and, 97, 235n9; fairy tales and, 97; greenhouses and, 151; linear temporality and, 99–100; romance blended with, in natural history, 52; vs. folklore in Eliot's *Middlemarch*, 63–66

Scot, Reginald, 131–32

Scott, Sir Walter, 1–2, 36, 104, 220

Senf, Carol, 72

Severn, Joseph, 123, 239n32

sexual politics, 86–88, 184–85. *See also* prostitution

Seymour, Robert, 38–39
Shakespeare, William, 132, 189
Sharp, William, 239n32
Shires, Linda, 96, 237n36
Shuttleworth, Sally, 66
Silver, Carole, 18, 144, 229n12, 243n10
"Sleep and Poetry" (Keats), 88, 103
"Sleeping Beauty" ("Briar Rose"): Basile's *"Sole, Luna e Talia,"* 79–80, 84–85, 87; earliest versions of, 79, 232n8–233n9, 236n22; fertility control as narrative control, 102; gender of linear time and, 102; Grimms' *"Dornröschen,"* 81, 83; Keats's "The Eve of St. Agnes," 82–91; Perrault's *"La Belle au Bois Dormant,"* 80–81, 84–85, 87; Ritchie's "The Sleeping Beauty in the Wood," 237n33; Rossetti's "The Prince's Progress," 237n33; temporal and physiological tropes and, 97–103, 236n23; Victorian temporality and, 77–78. See also *Briar Rose* series (Burne-Jones); "The Day Dream" (Tennyson)
Smith, Charles Roach, 51
Society of Antiquities, 29
solar mythology, 33
Sole, Luna e Talia (Basile), 79–80, 84–85, 87
"Sonnet to Sleep" (Keats), 88
Southey, Robert, 2, 31–32
Speaking Likenesses (Rossetti), 167
"spell," definitions and origins of term, 104, 237n28
Spenser, Edmund, 15, 132
Spielman, M. H., 121, 166
Sprenger, Jacob, 131
Stead, William, 177
Steedman, Carolyn, 2, 177, 182, 191
Stevenson, Robert Louis, 218
Stewart, Susan, 16
Stone, Harry, 18, 19
Stone of Venice (Ruskin), 77–78
"The Story of Grandmother," 174–75, 248n35
Stowe, Harriet Beecher, 67
Straparola, Giovanni Francesco, 15
Sumpter, Caroline, 18
Swann, Brian, 66

Tatar, Maria, 17
Taylor, Edgar, 15, 34, 178
temporality and time: antiquarian practices, past colonized and aestheticized by, 29–30; Burne-Jones's *Briar Rose* series and, 121–23; fairy tales as remains in modernity, 2–4, 44; frame and, 126; gender mediation and, 106; heart and circulatory analogies and, 97–103; Kristeva's "matrix space" and, 236n27; linear, 99–102, 123, 125–26; meaning of "temporality," 78; past and present in Hardy's "Tryst at an Ancient Earthwork," 25; "Sleeping Beauty" and, 77–78; Tennyson's "The Day Dream" and, 97, 105–6; "woman's time" and fear of female temporal shift, 121–22, 239n30. See also tense
Tenniel, John, 144, 145f
Tennyson, Alfred: art and, 108–9; Burne-Jones's *Briar Rose* series and, 109, 122, 123; epic, remodeled model, and, 94–95, 100, 103–4, 106–7; "The Epic," 94; form, experiments with, 94; *Idylls of the King,* 109; Keats and, 19, 91, 103–4; "Locksley Hall," 236n21; masculine anxiety and, 95–96, 106–7, 237n36; *In Memoriam,* 97, 109; "Palace of Art," 122; *Poems Chiefly Lyrical,* 93; "The Princess," 97, 105, 106; reception of, 237n36; "The Sleeping Beauty," 91. See also "The Day Dream"; "The Eve of St. Agnes"
tense: first person present, in Hardy's "Tryst at an Ancient Earthwork," 25–26; present, in Brontë's *Jane Eyre,* 54–55; Tennyson's "The Day Dream" and shifts in, 105–6
Terry, Ellen, 110
Tess of the D'Urbervilles (Hardy), 217
Thames: in Dickens's *David Copperfield,* 201–2; in Dickens's *Our Mutual Friend,* 195, 202–16
theatricals, popular: Bridge and Edwards's *Little Red Riding Hood; or, Harlequin and the Wolf in Granny's Clothing,* 185–86; Buckingham's *Little Red Riding Hood and the Fairies,* 185, 187–88;

costumes in, 183, 186–87; Dickens and, 200; Dickens's Rogue Riderhood as burlesque of, 251n42; "dressing up" and, 179, 180, 183; the "fairy actress" and, 182–85; fairy tale pantomimes, 182; Franklin's theory of play, 180; licensing and, 180–81; "Little Red Riding Hood" linked to, 179–80; mimicked in Bayley's *Little Red Riding Hood*, 192–96; pantomime, burlesque, and extravaganza, 181–82, 247n6; Planché's *Rodolph the Wolf; or, Columbine Red Riding Hood*, 185–87; prostitution linked with, 183, 184–85, 190–91, 194–95; streets and middle-class anxieties, connection with, 188–92

Theophrastus Such (Eliot), 78
"The Prince's Progress" (Rossetti), 237n33
Thompson, Lydia, 186–87
Thoms, William John, 32, 62
Thousand and One Arabian Nights, 15, 57–58, 65, 233n9
time. *See* temporality and time
Titus Andronicus (Shakespeare), 87–88
"To His Watch" (Hopkins), 78, 126
transaction: association of fairies with, 132–33; exchange, 134–37, 184–85; prostitution and, 194–95; theater and, 193–94. *See also* markets, commerce, and commercialization
Trumpener, Katie, 16
"Tryst at an Ancient Earthwork" (Hardy), 23–26, 51, 217
Tucker, Holly, 226n25, 236n22
Tyler, Daniel, 69
Tylor, Edward, 33, 62, 220

vampire figure in Brontë's *Jane Eyre*, 57
Verdier, Yvonne, 173, 245n5
Verstegen, Richard, 66
Victoria, Queen, 140, 141

Vinning, Louisa, 192–93
violence of goblins, 243n10
Vlock, Deborah, 182

Wallace, P., 150, 156
Warhol, Robyn, 53, 54
Weaver, William, 106
werewolf trial narratives, 174, 245n5
Weylland, John, 190
Whewell, William, 139
White, Gilbert, 30, 31, 51
"The Wife of Bath's Tale" (Chaucer), 2–3
Wilde, Oscar, 121
Wildman, Stephen, 124, 238n19
Wilkinson, James John Garth, 98–102, 235n13, 236n20
wills in Eliot's *Middlemarch*, 70–71
witchcraft trials, 132
Wolfreys, Julian, 199, 210
Woloch, Alex, 47, 230n20
women. *See* actresses; bodies, female; gender
Wood, Christopher, 119–21
Woodhouse, Richard, 84
Wordsworth, William, 4, 5, 43
working class: Bayley's *Little Red Riding Hood* and, 192–93, 195; Dickens's *Our Mutual Friend* and, 202–3, 205–8, 213, 215; Dickens's *Pickwick Papers* and, 45; Dodgson's "Agnes Grace Weld as Little Red Riding Hood" and, 180; girlhood and, 177–78; Great Exhibition and, 144, 152, 164; theatricals and, 183–84; Weylland's "dust fairies," 190
The World Behind the Scenes (Fitzgerald), 184
Wormald, Mark, 41–42
Wuthering Heights (Brontë), 59–60

Zambaco, Maria, 113
Ziolkowski, Jan M., 246n12
Zipes, Jack, 17, 245n8

www.ingramcontent.com/pod-product-compliance
Lightning Source LLC
Chambersburg PA
CBHW020121240426
43673CB00038B/555